WHITE'S
SPORTS
ALMANAC
2008

This edition published in 2007

Copyright © Carlton Books Limited 2007

Carlton Books Limited
20 Mortimer Street
London W1T 3JW

A CIP catalogue record for this book is available from the British Library

ISBN: 978-1-84442-427-6

Editor: Martin Corteel
Project Art Editor: Darren Jordan
Production: Lisa Cook
Assistant Editors: Clare Hubbard and David Ballheimer

Printed in Great Britain

WHITE'S
SPORTS
ALMANAC
2008

Compiled by JOHN WHITE
with a foreword by EAMONN HOLMES

CARLTON
BOOKS

Dedication

This book is dedicated to my father, John McDermott White, who I dearly loved and still miss so very much. My Dad meant everything to me and was the one man who ignited my passion for sport, particularly football and my love of Manchester United. The only sport that I really did not share his passion for was horse racing. My father loved the "Sport of Kings" and was a huge admirer of the legendary jockey Lester Piggott, who he would never bet against in a race. He would also often tell me stories about some of the greatest horses ever to grace the sport including Mill Reef, Nijinsky and his own personal favourite, Arkle.

However, looking back it was my Dad who first got me interested in the Grand National. I will never forget giving him my pocket money, £1, in 1975 to place on Red Rum, who just about everyone you listened to at the time said was a racing certainty to win his third successive Grand National. I sat myself in front of the television, with my bookies' docket safely in my jeans pocket, and watched the entire build-up to the race. I allowed my mind to occasionally wander to think about what I was going to do with the £9 that I was surely going to win (my Dad got me odds of 8/1). I settled for a new football, a few new Subbuteo teams and a new tennis racquet. I couldn't believe it when Red Rum was caught and passed at the Elbow by Tommy Carberry on L'Escargot. I stared at the television in the corner of the room in disbelief as L'Escargot, whose name means "snail" in English, put in a burst of speed over the closing stages of the race to leave my plans in tatters, just like the ripped up docket lying on my Mum's living room floor. I went to my room and felt like crying, I mean £1 to a 12-year-old boy was a lot of money in 1975. All I could think of was that I would not be able to afford to go to the disco in the local church hall that night, never mind buy the Brazilian team for my Subbuteo collection. When my Dad arrived home about an hour after the race he called me downstairs and asked me how I felt, even though the look on my face told him all he wanted to know. I must admit that I felt a lot better when he showed me his beaten docket as he too had bet on Rummy, before giving me my £1 back, which helped cheer me up.

So in closing, I really do hope you enjoy reading this book and that it helps rekindle your own treasured sporting moments, whether they were from this year or from the past. Maybe you are new to sport. I would be as happy as I was when my Dad gave me the £1 back I lost on Red Rum in the 1975 Grand National, if you attributed this book to being the moment you fell in love with sport. And Dad, if you are looking over someone's shoulder reading this book, Mum, David, Donna, Michelle, Danielle and Janice, along with my own sons, Marc and Paul, all asked me to say "Hello".

Your Son

John

Contents

FOREWORD BY EAMONN HOLMES...7

INTRODUCTION...9

SPORTS PERSONALITIES OF THE YEAR 2006–07 11
Raymond van Barneveld *12* ∗ Joe Calzaghe *13* ∗ Darren Clarke *14* ∗ Frankie Dettori *15*
Roger Federer *16* ∗ Lewis Hamilton *17* ∗ Padraig Harrington *18* ∗ Zara Phillips *19*
Cristiano Ronaldo *20* ∗ Beth Tweddle *21*

SPORTS MILESTONES DIARY 2006–07...23
September 2006 *24* ∗ October 2006 *26* ∗ November 2006 *28* ∗ December 2006 *30*
January 2007 *32* ∗ February 2007 *34* ∗ March 2007 *36* ∗ April 2007 *38* ∗ May 2007 *40*
June 2007 *42* ∗ July 2007 *44* ∗ August 2007 *46*

FOOTBALL REVIEW 2006–07...49
Premier League *50* ∗ Champions League *54* ∗ FA Community Shield *57* ∗ UEFA Cup
58 Coca-Cola Championship *60* ∗ Division 1 *62* ∗ Division 2 *64* ∗ FA Cup *66* ∗ Carling
Cup *68* ∗ Nationwide Conference *70* ∗ Non-League Football *72* ∗ Scottish Premier
League *74* Scottish League *76* ∗ Scottish FA Cup *78* ∗ CIS Cup *80* ∗ Scottish Challenge
Cup *81* ∗ Wales *82* ∗ Northern Ireland *83* ∗ Republic of Ireland *84* ∗ Women's Football
85 ∗ Europe *86* ∗ Euro 2008 Qualifiers *88* ∗ Managerial Merry-Go-Round *92* ∗ Transfer
News *96* ∗ European U-21 Championship *98* ∗ Asian Cup *99* ∗ FIFA U-20 World
Cup *100* ∗ Copa America *102* ∗ UEFA Super Cup *103* ∗ New Wembley Stadium *104* ∗
Celebrity News *106*

MAJOR SPORTS REVIEW 2006–07...109
Athletics *110* ∗ Boxing *120* ∗ Cricket *128* ∗ Formula One *154* ∗ Golf *162*
Horse Racing *176* ∗ Rugby League *198* ∗ Rugby Union *206* ∗ Tennis *220*

MISCELLANEOUS SPORTS 2006–07..231
American Football *232* ∗ Australian Rules Football *236* ∗ Badminton *238* ∗ Baseball *240*
Basketball *245* ∗ Bowls *250* ∗ Canoeing *251* ∗ Cycle Racing *252* ∗ Darts *258* ∗ Equestrian
Sports *260* ∗ Gaelic Football *264* ∗ Gymnastics *266* ∗ Handball *269* ∗ Hockey *270*
Hurling *274* ∗ Ice Hockey *276* ∗ Motor Racing *282* ∗ A1GP *282* ∗ IndyCar *284*
NASCAR *285* ∗ Rallying *286* ∗ Speedway *290* ∗ World Touring Cars *292* ∗ Motorcycle
Racing *294* ∗ MotoGP *294* ∗ British Superbikes *297* ∗ World Superbikes *299*
Rowing *302* ∗ Sailing *306* ∗ Figure Skating *310* ∗ Speed Skating *311* ∗ Skiing *312*
Winter Sports *315* ∗ Snooker *317* ∗ Squash *320* ∗ Swimming *321* ∗ Table Tennis *324*
Volleyball *324* ∗ It's a Mad, Mad, Mad, Mad Sports World *325*

OBITUARIES..334
Alan Ball *336* ∗ Trevor Berbick *337* ∗ Desert Orchid *338* ∗ Derek Dougan *339* ∗ Ferenc
Puskas *340* ∗ Clay Regazzoni *341* ∗ Bill Walsh *342* ∗ Bob Woolmer *343* ∗ Other Notable
Sports Deaths in 2006–07 *344*

SPORTS AWARDS..347

SOURCES..350

Foreword by Eamonn Holmes

It gives me enormous pleasure to write the foreword to the first edition of *White's Sports Almanac*. When John first approached me with his idea to write a book covering all the major sporting events around the world taking place between 1 September 2006 and 31 August 2007, I must admit I thought that he had a daunting challenge on his hands. Or should I say at his fingertips. I mean, just how do you manage to cover American football, athletics, boxing, cricket, football, Formula One, golf, horse racing, rugby, sailing, snooker, tennis and winter sports, to mention only a few, in a single book?

Amazingly, John has achieved this truly remarkable feat. Once you pore over the wonderful way he has encapsulated some of the world's greatest sporting tournaments: Manchester United reclaiming the Premiership in 2006–07, their ninth in 15 years; the San Antonio Spurs victory in the 2007 NBA finals; *Team Alinghi* retaining the America's Cup; Lewis Hamilton's fantastic start to his Formula One career; Roger Federer equalling Bjorn Borg's five men's singles titles at Wimbledon; Frankie Dettori's incredible win in the Derby; Padraig Harrington's victory in the 2007 Open Championship at Carnoustie et al. You will be amazed at the amount of detail he has gone into. There are also many interesting quotes from the sporting stars concerned and a generous sprinkling of mind boggling trivia entries that will leave you scratching your head in wonder. And as if all this was not enough, John has a diary section covering the 12-month sporting calendar with many interesting entries for every single day of the year. Unbelievable!

So if you are a sports fanatic like myself or if you just want to know what happened in the world of sport over the last year, then forget about surfing the internet because with this book you don't have to. If it is not in John's book then it definitely wasn't worth watching. I can see that this book will gradually become the standard work of reference for sport lovers and sports journalists alike, a book that anyone can turn to for confirmation of who won what, where, when and how, or just to browse through, unearthing those "Did You Know That?" moments every radio or TV commentator loves to recall.

From the first page to the last you have a sporting cornucopia that would be a gold medal winner at an Olympic Games or the winning goal at Wembley in the FA Cup final. This book is an out and out winner because it is about winners, with occasional stories about the unfortunate runners-up.

So whether you treat yourself to it, your mum or your dad, your brother or your sister, a work colleague or a friend, I can thoroughly recommend it and I have no doubt that it will give you a great deal of reading pleasure as well as keeping you informed as to who's setting the pace among the world's sporting community.

Eamonn Holmes
September 2007

Introduction

So what exactly is *White's Sports Almanac?* Well, it is a book that predominantly covers British sport, with the major emphasis on football, closely followed by cricket, horse racing, rugby and golf. The book is structured around the sporting year, running from 1 September 2006 to 31 August 2007. While I am aware that the end date falls short of the culmination of both the 2007 County Cricket Championship season and the 2007 Formula One season, I have comprehensively covered both competitions in terms of their respective 2006 champions, plus I have included all of the major happenings for both sports up to the publication date.

For football lovers the 2006–07 season is covered in great detail, including a review of the Premier League, FA Cup final, UEFA Cup final, UEFA Champions League final et al., with match reports and statistics for the principle competitions, including a look at who won what elsewhere in Europe. Cricket fans can catch up on the 2006 Ashes series, the 2007 ICC World Cup plus England's 2007 summer Tests and one-day internationals. On the golf front, all four Majors are covered in detail, including tournament reports. Lovers of horse racing can read all about the 2007 flat season including the exploits of Frankie Dettori, the Cheltenham Festival, a National Hunt round-up and a look at the Grand National.

Pugilist connoisseurs can read about the fights involving Messrs Calzaghe, Hatton and Khan, while snooker devotees, rugby-goers, motorcycle racing enthusiasts and followers of water sports can find out who won what, where and when. Tennis is another sport that is included in detail with reports, reviews and statistics for the four Grand Slams, including Wimbledon 2007.

The endeavours of British sportsmen and women across the five continents are all encapsulated within the book, including their exploits in the 2007 Tour de France, athletics meetings and rowing. While wishing to concentrate on the achievements of Britons it is difficult, indeed folly, to compile a book about the world's major sporting events and ignore what happened across the pond. Therefore, baseball fans can enjoy a review of the 2006 World Series, NASCAR lovers can look up who won the key races, including the Indy 500, while American football fans can read about the 2006 NFL season and play-offs, as well as the 2007 Super Bowl.

In addition, throughout the book there is a sprinkling of curious trivia items plus full-page write-ups on the year's back page headline makers, while you can also browse through the Milestones Diary (see pages 23–47) and immediately find out what the big sporting scandal, sensation or story of the day was, every day of the year.

I hope you find something of interest in the book and that this is the first of a long series of *Almanacs* published on an annual basis that will continue to whet the appetite of sports fans everywhere.

John White
September 2007

Sports Personalities
of the Year 2006–2007

Raymond van Barneveld................12
Joe Calzaghe.................................13
Darren Clarke................................14
Frankie Dettori.............................15
Roger Federer...............................16

Lewis Hamilton.............................17
Padraig Harrington.......................18
Zara Phillips.................................19
Cristiano Ronaldo.........................20
Beth Tweddle................................21

Raymond van Barneveld

Raymond van Barneveld was born on 20 April 1967 in The Hague, Netherlands. In 1991 he appeared in his maiden British Darts Organisation (BDO) world championship (Embassy World Professional Darts Championship) but he was beaten in the first round at the Lakeside Country Club by Keith Sullivan from Australia. A disappointing 1992 followed but in 1993 he returned to the Lakeside to participate in the last ever unified World Professional Darts Championship. John Lowe defeated "Barney" 3–2 and went on to be crowned champion. However, shortly after Lowe's victory many of the game's top players left the BDO and formed the World Darts Council (now known as the Professional Darts Council, PDC) but Barney remained with the BDO.

In 1994, he reached his first final, the Finnish Open, losing to Andy Fordham. The following year, while still working as a postman, he reached his first BDO world final but lost 6–3 to Richie Burnett (Wales). In two consecutive years, 1996 and 1997, he exited the BDO world championships in the second round. However, in 1998 he enjoyed an upturn in his fortunes at the oche winning the first of his four BDO world championships, defeating Burnett in what many darts fans consider to be one of the greatest ever darts finals. With the match delicately balanced at 5–5 in sets and 5–5 in legs, the title was decided on a sudden death leg that the Dutchman won. In 1999, he successfully defended his BDO crown beating Ronnie Baxter from England in the final, but was put out of the tournament in 2000 by Chris Mason. In 2001 and 2002 he lost in the quarter-finals.

Barney won his third BDO world title in 2003, beating Richie Davies of Wales 6–3 in the final. In the same year he claimed the International Darts League, the Bavaria World Darts Trophy and the World Cup Singles title; only a slender 7–6 loss to England's Tony West in the final of the Winmau World Masters denied Barney a unique darts Grand Slam. He lost 5–4 at the semi-final stage of the 2004 BDO tournament and then in 2005, claimed his fourth world crown with a 6–2 win over Martin Adams. He reached his sixth BDO world championship final in 2006, hoping to emulate Eric Bristow's record of five world titles, but lost 7–5 to his fellow countryman Jelle Klaasen. In February 2006 he moved across to the PDC. On New Year's Day 2007 the 39-year-old Dutchman beat Phil Taylor, the 13-time world champion, 7–6 in a thrilling final at the Circus Tavern, Purfleet, to claim his first PDC world championship. On 10 June 2007 he retained his Blue Square UK Open title with a comfortable 16–8 win over Dutch compatriot Vincent van der Voort and then on 8 July 2007 he claimed his first Las Vegas Desert Classic title with a 13–6 victory over Terry Jenkins.

Did You Know That?
He is only the second player in the history of the BDO world championships to successfully defend his title, the other being Eric Bristow.

> "What a year it's been for me. I had a good
> preparation for this tournament and it always
> feels special playing here."
> *Raymond van Barneveld after winning the 2007 UK Open*

Joe Calzaghe MBE

Joseph "Joe" Calzaghe was born on 23 March 1972 in Hammersmith, London, to an Italian father and Welsh mother. The family moved to Wales when Joe was two. He still lives in Wales and considers himself Welsh. At his father Enzo's behest, the young Calzaghe took up boxing aged nine at Newbridge Boxing Club. Joe claims he was bullied at secondary school (Oakdale Comprehensive) but during his time at Oakdale (1983–1988) Calzaghe impressed and won three British Schoolboy titles.

Joe was an outstanding amateur boxer, becoming only the second man to win British Amateur Boxing Association (ABA) titles at different weights – welterweight in 1991, light-middleweight in 1992 and middleweight in 1993. In September 1993, Joe signed to the Mickey Duff/Terry Lawless stable of boxing and made his professional debut the following month on the undercard at the Mike Tyson versus Frank Bruno world heavyweight championship fight at Cardiff Arms Park.

Since then, Joe has swept aside all-comers in the ring, having a perfect record of 41 fights, 41 wins with 32 knockouts. In 1995, he was voted Young Boxer of the Year by the Professional Boxing Association and the Boxing Writers' Club Young Boxer of the Year after winning the British championship. However, despite being undefeated there was no sign of a world title shot for the impatient but highly talented Calzaghe so, in November 1996 he left Duff and Lawless and joined Frank Warren's Sports Network.

Three fights later, on 11 October 1997, Calzaghe was crowned the WBO world super-middleweight boxing champion after beating Chris Eubank in Sheffield. Despite many successful title defences Calzaghe had to wait until 5 March 2006 to get the chance of a unification fight with Jeff Lacy. Joe gave the American a lesson over 12 rounds, handing him his first pro defeat. Calzaghe threw and landed more than 1,000 punches to win the IBF world super-middleweight championship at the MEN Arena, Manchester.

Calzaghe was lined up to fight the former light-heavyweight champion, Glen Johnson, at the Millennium Stadium, Cardiff on 8 July, but he had to withdraw when he aggravated a hand injury sustained in 2005. On 14 October 2006, Calzaghe fought and beat Sakio Bika in a brutal fight. On 27 November 2006, Frank Warren announced that Calzaghe had signed a contract to defend his WBO super middleweight title against Peter Manfredo Jr on 27 April 2007 at the Millennium Stadium. Calzaghe had been required to fight Robert Stieglitz, the mandatory IBF challenger next but as HBO refused to screen the fight he chose to fight Manfredo and had to relinquish his IBF super middleweight belt. In December 2006, Calzaghe was named BBC Wales Sports Personality of the Year.

Did You Know That?
In Calzaghe's only loss in 117 bouts as an amateur, his opponent's father was the referee.

> "On the night of the fight, Manfredo is in for the harsh reality of boxing. There's a world of difference between being a reality TV star and a world champion boxer. Manfredo will go from being a star to seeing stars."
> *Calzaghe won in three rounds*

Darren Clarke

Darren Christopher Clarke was born on 14 August 1968 in Dungannon, County Tyrone, Northern Ireland. He showed a talent for golf while still at school and was offered golf scholarships from universities in the United States. He accepted an offer from Wake Forest University in North Carolina – where US Ryder Cup captains Arnold Palmer, Lanny Wadkins and Curtis Strange all attended. Returning to Europe, Clarke first caught the public's attention in amateur tournaments, winning the 1990 Spanish Amateur Open and Irish Amateur championships. He turned professional later that year.

In 1992, he won his native championship, but the Ulster Open was not a European PGA Tour event. He also fired a 60 in the Monte Carlo Open, equalling the record low round in a European Tour event. A year later, Darren claimed his first European PGA Tour victory, in the Alfred Dunhill Open, formerly the Belgian Open. Nine more tour wins followed, plus two on the World Tour, a match-play defeat of Tiger Woods in 2000's Andersen final and the 2003 NEC Invitational. His consistency on the European Tour is summed up by three second-place finishes in the annual Volvo European Order of Merit. Clarke's best finishes in the Majors have come in the British Open, second and third in 1997 and 2001 respectively, but he has enjoyed top-ten finishes in the other three Majors.

Clarke met his wife Heather at a nightclub in Portrush, Northern Ireland, and the couple were soon married. They had two children together, Tyrone and Conor. Sadly there was no happy ending to this love affair because, in 2005, Heather was diagnosed with breast cancer. She fought the disease, but it affected Darren deeply and his form dropped. When the cancer returned early in 2006, Clarke appealed to the European PGA Tour for compassionate leave; it was granted immediately, allowing him to keep his ranking despite not playing. Heather succumbed to cancer on 13 August 2006. His close friend and compatriot Paul McGinley immediately withdrew from the year's last Major, the US PGA Championship, to be by Darren's side.

Determined to resume his career, Darren made himself available for Europe's 2006 Ryder Cup team and was one of captain Ian Woosnam's two wildcard selections for the event, staged at the K-Club in Ireland. Despite having played almost no competitive golf for six months, Darren played his part in Europe's 18½–9½ victory by winning three points. The ovation he received on the first morning was matched only by the cheers that greeted his victory in the singles. Despite the glare of the world's media, he held himself together emotionally until after he had played his final hole. After that, the tears flowed.

Did You Know That?
Darren has played in five European Ryder Cup teams, winning four times, and has represented Ireland in both the World Cup (from 1994–1996) and the Alfred Dunhill Cup (from 1994–1999).

> **"**I found it very difficult to not get ahead of myself and keep my emotions in check when it was obvious it could come down to my putt. I lost myself a few times out there.**"**
> *Clarke talking about his singles win in the 2006 Ryder Cup*

14

Frankie Dettori, MBE

Lanfranco "Frankie" Dettori was born on 15 December 1970 in Milan, Italy, the son of Gianfranco Dettori from Sardinia, a prolific winning jockey and winner of the 2,000 Guineas in 1975 and 1976. When he was eight years old his dad bought him a palomino pony and in 1984 he left school to become a stable boy and apprentice jockey. In 1985, he moved to England to take up the position of an apprentice with trainer Luca Cumani. In the winter of 1986–87 he rode 16 winners in Italy, his first coming on board Rif at Turin on 16 November 1986. Frankie's first win on English soil came on 9 June 1987, riding Lizzy Hare to victory at Goodwood. Aged 19, Cumani appointed Frankie as his stable jockey, replacing Ray Cochrane, after Frankie became champion apprentice in 1989. In 1990, he repaid Cumani's faith riding 141 winners, becoming the first teenager to ride a century of winners since Lester Piggott. He also won his first Group 1 race on Markofdistinction in the Queen Elizabeth II Stakes at Ascot.

In 1991, he won 94 races and his first Derby, the German, on Temporal. In 1992 he claimed his second century of winners (101), which included the French Derby on Polytain. It was around this time that Frankie adopted his low hands riding style that allows him to reduce the pressure on his mount's mouth thereby relaxing the horse. In 1993 he claimed 149 wins to finish runner-up in the champions jockey table but the following year he was crowned the king of the turf with 233 wins. He retained the title in 1995 (216 victories) and in 1996 he rode 123 winners including the "Magnificent Seven" at Ascot on 28 September: Wall Street (Cumberland Lodge Stakes), Diffident (Diadem Stakes), Decorated Hero (Tote Festival Handicap), Mark of Esteem (QEII Stakes), Fatefully (Rosemary Rated Stakes), Lochangel (Blue Seal Conditions Stakes) and Fujiyama Crest (Gordon Carter Handicap). On 2 June 2000, Frankie and Ray Cochrane were aboard a Piper Seneca plane that crashed on take-off from Newmarket, killing the pilot. Kazzia gave him his 100th Group 1 win in the 1,000 Guineas in 2002 and in 2004, Frankie won his third champion jockey title (195 wins).

His 13 Group 1 wins in 2006 included: Ouija Board (Nassau Stakes and Breeders' Cup Filly and Mare Turf), Authorized (Racing Post Trophy), Sixties Icon (St Leger), Sergeant Cecil (Prix du Cadran), Librettist (Prix Jacques le Marois and Prix du Moulin de Longchamp), Kirklees (Gran Criterium), Discreet Cat (Dubai UAE Derby), Electrocutionist (Dubai World Cup) and Red Rocks (Breeders' Cup Turf). Up until his win on Authorized in the 2007 Epsom Derby, it was the only British classic that Frankie had failed to win. The following day he won the French Derby on Lawman. His other Group 1 wins in 2007 included: Ramonti (Queen Anne Stakes), West Wind (Prix de Diane), Sudan (Gran Premio di Milano), Kelly's Landing (Dubai Golden Shaheen) and Authorized, again, (Juddmonte International Stakes).

Did You Know That?

His mother was a professional circus performer whose speciality was to perform back flips while riding astride two horses.

Roger Federer

Roger Federer was born on 8 August 1981 in Basel, Switzerland. When he was a boy Federer was an excellent footballer but he opted for a tennis career, although his formative years in the sport resulted in him throwing many tantrums on the court. He started playing tennis at the age of six, began taking lessons aged nine and then he started to receive personal coaching on a weekly basis from the age of ten. When he was 14 he won the Swiss National Championship for all age groups and in 1996, joined the International Tennis Foundation junior tennis circuit. Two years later he won the 1998 Wimbledon juniors title and was named the ITF World Junior Tennis Champion.

In July 1998, Federer joined the ATP Tour and made his debut for the Swiss Davis Cup team in 1999 before ending the year as the youngest player ranked in the ATP's top 100. During the summer of 2000, he lost in the semi-finals of the tennis tournament at the Olympic Games in Sydney, Australia and then reached his first final as a professional that same year, losing in Marseille, France, to Marc Rosset. He ended the year ranked 29th. His maiden ATP win came in February 2001 in Milan and at Wimbledon he brought Pete Sampras's 31-match unbeaten streak at the championships to an end beating the seven-time champion in the fourth round, before going out in the quarter-finals to Tim Henman. A 13th place ranking was his for 2001 and then his career really started to take off from 2002 onwards.

On 6 July 2003, he won his first Grand Slam event defeating Mark Philippoussis in the Wimbledon final, the first Swiss player to win the coveted prize, and was runner-up to Andy Roddick in the ATP's Champions Race. In 2004, he took a stranglehold of men's tennis winning three of the four Grand Slam singles titles and he won every final he reached. That year he won his first Australian Open to leapfrog Roddick as the number one ranked player in the world (he has attained this ranking ever since), defended his Wimbledon crown and won his first US Open title. His win-loss record for 2004 was 74–6, claiming 11 titles. In 2005, he won his third consecutive Wimbledon singles title and his second US Open.

In 2007, he won his third Australian Open, his fourth Dubai Duty Free Men's Open and the Hamburg Masters, ending Nadal's impressive run of 81 consecutive wins on clay. Nadal exacted revenge by beating him in the French Open final (6–3, 4–6, 6–4, 6–3). In the Wimbledon men's singles final Federer won his fifth consecutive title defeating his nemesis, Nadal, in one of the most exciting finals ever witnessed at the Centre Court (7–6, 4–6, 7–6, 2–6, 6–2). This win equalled the legendary Bjorn Borg's feat of five Wimbledon titles. In total, after claiming a record fourth consecutive US Open, beating Novak Djokovic in straight sets, the Swiss master has won 12 Grand Slam men's singles titles in 34 appearances (all 12 coming in a record 18 consecutive appearances), 3 Tennis Masters Cups and 13 ATP Masters Series titles.

Did You Know That?
On 3 April 2006, he was appointed a Goodwill Ambassador for UNICEF.

Lewis Hamilton

Lewis Carl Hamilton was born on 7 January 1985 in Stevenage, Hertfordshire, England. When he was just two, his parents separated. Lewis remained with his mother until he was ten and then went to live with his father. Lewis fell in love with motor racing when his dad purchased a go-kart for the budding enthusiast as a Christmas present in 1991. However, there was one condition that went with the go-kart – Lewis had to remain focused on his schoolwork. His dad worked as an IT manager at the time and found it difficult to support both the family and his son's racing career. However, knowing how much racing meant to his young son, he took voluntary redundancy and set up his own business as an IT consultant.

When he was eight, Lewis started to participate in organized kart racing and a year later he approached Ron Dennis at a sports award dinner and told the McLaren F1 boss that he would drive for his team in the future. Dennis kept a close eye on Lewis as he raced in the Cadet ranks (1993–96), the Junior Yamaha division (1997) and the Junior Intercontinental A ranks (1998–99). Dennis liked what he saw and, in 1999, signed Lewis for his McLaren driver development support programme. Hamilton's McLaren contract included an option for McLaren to offer him a future F1 seat, thereby effectively making Lewis the youngest ever driver to secure an F1 contract.

In 2000, Dennis's faith in the youngster paid dividends when Lewis won the European Formula A Karting Championship and Formula A World Cup (winning all of his races) and the following year he moved up to racing cars. His achievement was recognized by the British Racing Drivers Club who made him a "Rising Star" member in 2000. The young Speed King then made steady progress through the junior formulae, making his car racing debut in the 2001 Formula Super A World Championship, finishing 15th place overall for TeamMBM.com. In 2002 he raced in Formula Renault UK for Manor Motorsport, finishing third overall and then took the title the following year for the team, claiming ten wins. He also made his debut in the British Formula Three Championship during 2003, racing in the last two races of the season. In 2004 he claimed fifth place overall in the Euroseries driving for Manor Motorsport and took the championship in 2005 driving for the ASM F3 team. When he won the 2006 GP2 Series driving for the ART Grand Prix team, Dennis knew it was time to unleash Lewis in F1. The McLaren boss gave Lewis a seat in his McLaren-Mercedes team as the number two driver to the reigning F1 world champion, Fernando Alonso, for the 2007 F1 season. To say Lewis made an immediate impact on F1 would be a huge understatement. In his maiden F1 season he finished on the podium in his first nine races, winning the Canadian and USA Grands Prix, and led the F1 World Drivers' Championship after ten races.

Did You Know That?
His mother Carmen and father Anthony named him after the nine-time US Olympic gold medal-winning athlete, Carl Lewis.

Padraig Harrington

Padraig Harrington was born on 31 August 1971 in Ballyroan, Dublin, Ireland. After enjoying a fairly successful career as an amateur, including winning the 1995 Walker Cup with the Great Britain & Ireland team and the 1995 Irish Amateur Open Championship and Irish Amateur Closed Championship, he turned professional in late 1995 and in 1996 he joined the PGA European Tour. In his rookie season he won the 1996 Spanish Open, but he then seemed to always be the bridesmaid and never the bride with a string of runners-up positions. However, in 2000 his fortunes, and luck, had a turn for the better. He won two European Tour events, followed by another European Tour win in 2001, the 2002 Dunhill Links Championship, two wins in 2003 and two wins in 2004.

In 2002, he won his first professional tournament in the USA, the non-PGA Tour Target World Championship event hosted by Tiger Woods. He was also runner-up in the prestigous TPC Players' Championship at Sawgrass in 2003 and 2004, and in 2005 he became a member of the PGA Tour. In March 2005, he claimed his first PGA Tour win in the Honda Classic after defeating Vijay Singh and Joe Ogilvie in a sudden death play-off. Then in June 2006, he claimed his second PGA Tour win when he sank a magnificent 65-foot putt on the final hole to beat Jim Furyk to claim the Barclays Classic. He added a second Alfred Dunhill Links Championship in 2006. Padraig has also won the Irish PGA Championship four times (1998, 2004, 2005 and 2007).

Padraig has finished in the top ten of the European Tour's Order of Merit seven times, including two second place finishes (2001 and 2002) and two third place finishes (2003 and 2004), before finally capturing the prize money title in 2006. Indeed, Harrington's 2006 Order of Merit win came after a season-long battle with England's Paul Casey and David Howell. The outcome of the title came down to the final hole on the final day of the final tournament of 2006, when Sergio Garcia bogeyed the last hole of the Volvo Masters, thereby allowing the Irishman to take a share of second place in the event, which was good enough to place him above Casey and Howell in the European money list. As time would tell, this drama on the 72nd hole with Garcia would sensationally surface once again at the 2007 British Open Championship.

Padraig has represented Europe in four Ryder Cups – losing in 1999, with victories in 2002, 2004 and 2006, the latter on home soil at the K Club, Dublin. In 2007 he won the Irish Open but his greatest victory came on 22 July 2007 when he claimed his first Major, the British Open Championship at Carnoustie. His four-hole play-off victory over Spain's Sergio Garcia, his 2006 Ryder Cup team-mate, made him the first Republic of Ireland-born golfer to win the Claret Jug and the first European to win a Major in eight years. At the 2007 US PGA Championship, played at Southern Hills Country Club, Oklahoma, Padraig opened up with a 1-under par 69, but fell behind over the next three days to finish tied for 42nd place.

Did You Know That?
Padraig Harrington is coached by Bob Torrance, father of former Ryder Cup captain Sam.

Zara Phillips, MBE

Zara Anne Elizabeth Phillips was born on 15 May 1981 in London. She is the second child and only daughter of HRH Princess Anne and Captain Mark Phillips, the eldest granddaughter of the Queen and currently 11th in line to the British throne. Her uncle, Prince Charles, named her Zara, a Greek biblical name meaning "bright as the dawn."

After attending a local primary school, Zara was educated at Port Regis Preparatory School, Dorset and at Gordonstoun, Scotland. At school she discovered a deep love of horses and equestrian sports. Phillips also excelled in athletics, gymnastics and hockey. Before going to university Zara took a year out from study, spending three months in Australia and New Zealand. She then attended the University of Exeter and graduated as a physiotherapist, specializing in equine physiotherapy.

Not surprisingly Phillips followed the path of her parents and took up equestrianism. In June 2003, it was announced that she had secured a sponsorship deal with Cantor Index, a spread betting company, to help cover the costs of her equestrian career. This was the first commercial deal involving a member of the Royal Family. At the 2005 European Eventing Championships she emulated her mother by becoming the individual European eventing champion on Toytown and also won gold with the British team. It won her the 2005 *Sunday Times* Sportswoman of the Year award, ahead of Dame Ellen MacArthur and Paula Radcliffe.

Zara and Toytown enjoyed even greater success in 2006, winning the individual gold and team silver medal at the World Equestrian Games in Aachen, Germany, thus becoming only the third rider to hold both the European and world titles simultaneously.

On 10 December 2006, Phillips won the 2006 BBC Sports Personality of the Year, following in the footsteps of her mother, who received the same honour in 1971. "For two members of the same family to win the award for the first time is very special," Zara said on receiving the award. On 15 December 2006, she won the British Equestrian Writers' Association Personality of the Year award and was made an MBE in the 2007 New Year Honours List for "services to equestrianism". Her private life has been closely followed by the world's press. She is currently dating Mike Tindall, a rugby union player for Gloucester and member of the 2003 English World Cup-winning squad.

Did You Know That?

In December 2006, Phillips became the highest ranking member of the Royal Family to appear in an advertisement. She was featured in a mud-splattered Roberto Cavalli dress in a Land Rover advertisement.

> "My mum said when she won it no-one else was in the running! In the build-up to it, I didn't think it would be a big thing for me. I was thinking 'I'd rather have my world gold medal than the Sports Personality of the Year award.' But when it actually came around to the night, and I was up there on the stage, it was unbelievable."
>
> *Phillips on becoming the first second-generation winner of the BBC award*

Cristiano Ronaldo

Cristiano Ronaldo dos Santos Aveiro was born on 5 February 1985 in Funchal, Madeira Islands, Portugal. In 1993, Ronaldo played for his first team, Andorinha, where his father was the kit manager and aged ten he signed for CD Nacional. In season 1999–2000 he helped CD Nacional to the Portuguese Second Division Championship. He then went on a three-day trial with Sporting Lisbon, who signed him. He scored twice on his debut against Moreirense. In 2003 Manchester United travelled to Portugal to play Sporting Lisbon in a match commemorating the official opening of their new Alvalade XXI stadium. The United players were so impressed with Ronaldo's display on both wings in Sporting's 3–1 win that they urged Sir Alex to buy him. Having just lost David Beckham to Real Madrid, United paid Sporting £12.24m to fill the void on the right-hand side of their midfield vacated by the England captain.

When Ronaldo arrived at Old Trafford he asked for the number 28 shirt, his number at Sporting, but Sir Alex handed him the famous red number 7 shirt of United. On the opening day of the 2003–04 Premier League season, Ronaldo made his Manchester United debut at Old Trafford when he came on as a 60th-minute substitute against Bolton Wanderers. United were leading 1–0 at the time and within minutes the new number 7 won a penalty and helped United to win 4–0. In his first season at United he played 39 times and scored 6 goals; in season 2004–05 he made 50 appearances, scoring 9 times and in 2005–06 he played 47 games and scored 12 goals. Ronaldo was named FIFPro Special Young Player of the Year in 2005 and 2006.

Prior to the start of the 2006–07 season, many United fans feared that their star winger might leave the club after he was accused of persuading the referee to send off Wayne Rooney when Portugal knocked England out of the 2006 World Cup finals in a penalty shootout, with Ronaldo scoring the winning spot kick. However, Ronaldo signed a new deal to extend his contract until 2010. During 2006 he was involved in a row with Ruud van Nistelrooy at United's training complex. While the Dutch striker joined Beckham in Madrid, Ronaldo went on to have his best ever season, scoring 23 times from 52 matches, en route to helping the Reds clinch their ninth Premiership crown.

Season 2006-07 also saw Ronaldo win two Barclays Player of the Month awards (November and December), PFA Young Player of the Year award, PFA Players' Player of the Year award, Football Writers' Association Player of the Year award, Portuguese Sports Personality of the Year (2006), Portuguese Player of the Year (2007) and he was named in the PFA Premiership Team of the Year. He also won Manchester United's Player of the Year and Fans' Player of the Year awards.

The 2007–08 season got off to the worst possible start for Ronaldo when he was sent off for violent conduct in United's second Premier League game, against Portsmouth, resulting in an automatic three-match suspension.

Did You Know That?
His parents named him after the former US president, Ronald Reagan.

Beth Tweddle

Elizabeth "Beth" Tweddle was born on 1 April 1985 in Johannesburg, South Africa, to British parents Gerry and Anne. Gerry was working in South Africa at the time, but when Beth was aged 18 months, the family moved back to the UK. Beth began her gymnastic career as a quite reluctant seven-year-old.

In 2001, Beth participated in her first World Championships and performed well on the asymmetric (uneven) bars. The following year she won Britain's first ever medal at a European Championships – bronze on the bars. In 2003, Beth took bronze at the World Championships, another British first for a gymnast. Today she is the most successful British gymnast ever and entered 2007 as the current European and world champion on the asymmetric bars.

Beth's childhood dream came true when she competed at the Olympic Games in Athens in 2004. However, she was unlucky enough to compete in the first subdivision and ended up falling short of qualifying for the bars final. The 19-year-old left Athens determined never to fail again. However, an injury in the early part of 2005 upset her preparations for that year's World Championships but she still managed to claim a bronze medal. The 2007 British Gymnastic Championships held in the Guildford Spectrum over the weekend of 6–8 July saw Tweddle continue to dominate the competition. She convincingly won her seventh consecutive British overall title (her overall score 59.750 was 3.350 points better than her closest rival), eerily claiming this seventh title on a date that can be written 07/07/07. She is now one short of Pat Hurst's eight British titles, between 1947 and 1956.

An ankle injury resulted in Beth missing the Commonwealth Games in Melbourne, Australia, in March 2006, but she was back to full fitness at the European Championships later in the year. Beth performed a brand new and slightly more daring routine on the bars and her almost faultless display wowed the judges who awarded her the gold medal and the title of European champion. On 20 October 2006, the 21-year-old reigning European champion won gold in the uneven bars event at the World Championships in Aarhus, Denmark, to add to the bronze she had won 12 months earlier. It earned Beth enough support to come third in the BBC Sports Personality of the Year voting.

After her disappointment in Athens, Beth has stated that she wants to continue in gymnastics until the 2008 Olympic Games, where she hopes to lead the British team out in Beijing, China. She juggles training with full-time education at Liverpool's John Moores University, where she is studying sport science.

Did You Know That?
Beth's floor routine is the routine used in the Athens 2004 PlayStation® game!

> "All my hard work has finally paid off and I'm absolutely ecstatic. A lot of people told me it would come, but I didn"t think it ever actually would. It hasn't sunk in yet."
> *Beth Tweddle after winning gold in the 2006 world championships.*

Sports Milestones

Diary 2006–2007

September 2006.....................................24
October 2006..26
November 2006....................................28
December 2006....................................30
January 2007..32
February 2007......................................34

March 2007...36
April 2007...38
May 2007...40
June 2007..42
July 2007...44
August 2007..46

September 2006

1. Round 11 of the FIA World Rally Championship began in Japan.
2. Mark Williams beat John Higgins to lift the Pot Black Cup at the Royal Automobile Club in London.
   * Pakistan beat England by 7 wickets in the second NatWest Series one-day match at Lord's.
   * South Africa beat New Zealand 21–20 in Rustenburg, South Africa in the Tri-Nations tournament.
3. Tiger Woods won his fifth straight PGA Tour tournament with a final-round 63 at the Deutsche Bank Championship in Boston, USA.
   * Six athletes shared the £1m IAAF Golden League Jackpot after the season finale in Berlin, Germany. Asafa Powell (JAM, men's 100m), Jeremy Wariner (USA, men's 400m) and Sanya Richards (USA, women's 400m) won all six of their events last year and took US$249,999. Three five-time winners, Tirunesh Dibaba (ETH, women's 5000m), Kenenisa Bekele (ETH, men's 5000m) and Irving Saladino (PAN, men's long jump), each collected US$83,333.
   * Denmark's Martin Pedersen of CSC won the 2006 Tour of Britain cycle race, the third edition of the race. CSC won the team title from Unibet. com and the defending champions QuickStep-Innergetic.
4. Thomas Bjorn heavily criticized the European team captain, Ian Woosnam, after he was left out of Europe's Ryder Cup team to defend the trophy at the K Club.
5. Pakistan beat England by 2 wickets in the third NatWest Series one-day match under the floodlights at Hampshire's Rose Bowl home.

6. Northern Ireland defeated Spain 3–2 at Windsor Park in a Euro 2008 qualifying game.
7. Michelle Wie became only the second female golfer to compete on the European Tour International Schedule when she was invited to play in the Omega European Masters at Crans-sur-Sierre, Crans Montana, Switzerland.
8. England beat Pakistan by 8 wickets in the fourth NatWest Series one-day match at Trent Bridge, Nottingham.
9. South Africa beat Australia 24–16 in Johannesburg in the final game of the Tri-Nations, which was won by New Zealand.
10. England beat Pakistan by 3 wickets in the fifth NatWest Series one-day match at Edgbaston, Birmingham.
    * Michael Schumacher won the Italian Grand Prix at Monza and announced he would retire from motor racing at the end of the season.
11. Frankie Dettori claimed his 100th win of the year in fine style by riding the favourite, Sixties Icon, to victory in the final classic of the season, the Ladbrokes St Leger at York.
12. Andrew Flintoff was named as England's captain for the 2006 Ashes tour and ICC Champions Trophy.
13. Manchester United's Louis Saha scored twice to help his team to a 3–2 victory over Glasgow Celtic in their UEFA Champions League group clash at Old Trafford.
14. After winning five consecutive tournaments the world number one, Tiger Woods, lost 4&3 to Shaun Micheel in the first round of the 2006 World Match Play Championship at Wentworth.

15. Christine Ohuruogu, England's Commonwealth 400m champion, was handed a one-year ban for missing three out-of-competition drug tests.

16. Junior Witter claimed the vacant WBC light welterweight title after a unanimous points win over DeMarcus Corley at Alexandra Palace.

17. Italy's women's tennis team beat Belgium in Charleroi, Belgium, to win their first Federation Cup.
    * Paul Casey beat Shaun Micheel 10&8 to win the HSBC World Match Play Championship at Wentworth.
    * In Gaelic football, Kerry crushed a brave Mayo side 4–15 (27 pts) to 3–5 (14) in the 119th All-Ireland Senior Football final at Croke Park, Dublin.

18. In Beijing, China, the WTA China Open got underway. Svetlana Kuznetsova (Russia) beat top-seeded Amelie Mauresmo (France), 6–4, 6–0.

19. Luton Town manager Mike Newell claimed that Charles Collymore, a freelance football agent, attempted to bribe him by offering him a cut of a player's fee that he tried to negotiate.

20. Following claims made on the BBC's *Panorama* programme, the Football Association and Premier League stated that they would investigate claims made in the documentary concerning the alleged payment of bungs to managers and illegal approaches for players in the game.

21. The opening ceremony of the Ryder Cup was held at the K Club, Straffan, County Kildare, Rep. of Ireland. The Irish president, Mary McAleese, welcomed the players.

22. The 36th Ryder Cup teed off at the K Club.

23. Cricket's County Championships ended in England with Sussex crowned Division One champions and Surrey Division Two champions.

24. Europe beat the USA 18 ½–9 ½ to win the Ryder Cup for the third consecutive time.
    * Denmark's Nicki Pedersen eased to victory in the last Speedway Grand Prix of the season in Bydgoszcz, Poland.

25. Surrey's 37-year-old batsman, Mark Ramprakash, brought Andrew Flintoff's two-year reign to an end when he was named the 2006 PCA Player of the Year.

26. Ashley Cole's agent, Jonathan Barnett, had his licence suspended for 18 months and was fined £100,000 for his role in the tapping-up affair involving the player and Chelsea.

27. Tim Henman, who had lost his three previous matches against Andy Murray, claimed his first victory over the young Scot with a 6–4, 6–2 win in the first round of the Thailand Open in Bangkok.

28. Day one of the WGC-CA Championship teed off at Chandler's Cross, Hertfordshire, with Tiger Woods looking to win his sixth consecutive PGA Tour event.

29. Pakistan cricket captain Inzamam-ul-Haq was cleared of altering the condition of the ball during the controversial Test against England at the Oval following an ICC hearing.

30. The reigning Formula One World Drivers' Champion, Fernando Alonso, took pole position for the Chinese Grand Prix.
    * Japan's Ryuichi Kiyonari (Honda) won the 2006 British Superbikes title.

October 2006

1. Tiger Woods won the WGC-CA Championship at Chandler's Cross, Herts, to claim his sixth consecutive PGA Tour event win. * Michael Schumacher won the Chinese Grand Prix to move ahead of Fernando Alonso in the World Championship for the first time.
   * The 2006–07 A1 Grand Prix season commenced with the Dutch A1GP, Team South Africa won the sprint while Team Germany won the main race at Circuit Park, Zandvoort.

2. The AIG Men's and Women's Japan Opens began in Tokyo, as did the Porsche Women's Grand Prix in Stuttgart and the Tashkent Women's Open in Uzbekistan.

3. David Beckham, the former England captain, was left out of coach Steve McClaren's squad for the forthcoming Euro 2008 qualifiers against Macedonia and Croatia.

4. Andy Murray suffered his third straight defeat on the ATP Tour as he lost to Jiri Novak in the second round of the Japan Open.

5. Following claims made by the Real Madrid president, Ramon Calderon, that Chelsea's spending power could result in overinflating transfer fees for other European clubs, Chelsea hit back claiming it was an open market and sometimes they had to spend high because of who they were.

6. Hull beat Bradford 19–12 to reach their first Super League Grand Final, ending the Bulls' defence of their title.
   * In yachting, Hamish Pepper skippered *New Zealand 8187* to victory in the Wells Fargo Private Bank Sailing World Championships in San Francisco.

7. Scotland beat France 1–0 at Hampden Park in their Euro 2008 qualifying Group B game thanks to a Gary Caldwell goal on 67 minutes.

8. Roger Federer won his ninth title of the year and the 42nd ATP win of his career with a victory over Tim Henman in the Japan Open final.
   * In women's hockey, the Netherlands won its sixth world crown, beating Australia 3–1 in the final in Madrid.
   * Fernando Alonso (Renault) won the Japanese Grand Prix to edge him closer to retaining his world title.

9. Following a battle against cancer, snooker star Paul Hunter died aged 27 in Kirkwood Hospice, Huddersfield.

10. Peterborough Panthers beat Reading Bulldogs to win the 2006 Elite Speedway League title.

11. England lost 2–0 to Croatia in a Euro 2008 qualifying game in Zagreb. Eduardo gave Croatia the lead in the 61st minute, followed by a bizarre own goal by Gary Neville 8 minutes later.

12. The Wembley Conference Centre, host to snooker's Masters Tournament for the past 26 years, was demolished to make way for a new stadium.

13. Bangladesh beat Zimbabwe by 101 runs in their fifth ICC Champions Trophy qualifier game in Jaipur, India.

14. St Helens beat Hull 26–4 to claim their fourth Grand Final victory and a Grand Final, Challenge Cup and League Leaders Shield treble.
   * Tensions ran high when the World Gymnastics Championships opened in Aarhus, Denmark. At the request of China, the organizers removed the official flag of Chinese Taipei that had been put up in error. China has never recognized Taipei.

15. India beat England by 4 wickets in the ICC Champions Trophy in Jaipur.
   * Australia beat New Zealand 30–18 in a spiteful Tri-Nations opening game in Auckland, New Zealand.
16. Pakistan withdrew their fast bowlers Shoaib Akhtar and Mohammad Asif from the ICC Champions Trophy in India after they tested positive for the banned performance-enhancing steroid, nandrolone.
17. Pakistan beat Sri Lanka by 4 wickets in the third ODI of the ICC Champions Trophy played at Jaipur.
18. Andy Murray beat Ivan Ljubicic in round two of the Madrid Masters.
19. The Football Association ended their dispute with Multiplex, the builders of the new Wembley Stadium, and announced that the venue would open early in 2007.
20. Sri Lanka beat New Zealand by 7 wickets in the fifth ODI of the ICC Champions Trophy at Mumbai.
   * Beth Tweddle won Britain's first ever gold medal at the World Gymnastics Championships.
21. Phil "The Power" Taylor won his third PDPA Darts Players Championship title by beating Denis Ovens 3–0 in the CityWest Hotel, Dublin.
   * The St Louis Cardinals defeated the Detroit Tigers 7–2 in game one of the 2006 Baseball World Series.
22. Fernando Alonso (Renault) claimed back-to-back Formula One world titles with a second-place finish in the Brazilian GP.
   * The 2006 World Series was level at 1–1 following the Detroit Tigers 3–1 win over the St Louis Cardinals.
   * Australia beat New Zealand 20–15 in the second Test of the Tri-Nations.

23. Angela Merkel, the new German chancellor, paid tribute to seven-time Formula One champion Michael Schumacher, saying he was one of the biggest German sports stars of all time.
24. In game three of the MLB World Series the Detroit Tigers were simply outclassed at their Busch Stadium home by the St Louis Cardinals losing 5–0 to trail 2–1 in the best of seven games series.
25. New Zealand beat Pakistan by 51 runs at Mohali in the 2006 ICC Champions Trophy.
26. The West Indies beat India by 3 wickets at Ahmedabad in the ICC Champions Trophy.
   * St Louis beat Detroit 5–4 to lead the World Series 3–1.
27. The St Louis Cardinals beat the Detroit Tigers 4–2 to clinch the 2006 World Series.
   * Vladimir Romanov, the majority shareholder of Scottish Premier League side Hearts, issued a warning to his players that they would all be placed on the market for sale if they failed to beat Dunfermline – they drew 1–1.
28. England beat West Indies by 3 wickets at Ahmedabad in the 2006 ICC Champions Trophy.
   * A hat trick from Wayne Rooney against Bolton kept Manchester United top of the FA Premier League.
   * New Zealand beat Great Britain 18–14 in the Lions' opening 2006 Tri-Nations Series game at Christchurch.
29. In the ICC Champions Trophy, India lost to Australia by 6 wickets at Mohali.
   * France's Sebastien Loeb was crowned world rally champion for the third year.

November 2006

_1._ Pakistan fast bowlers Shoaib Akhtar and Mohammad Asif were banned from all international and domestic cricket for failing a drugs test. Shoaib for two years and Asif for one.

_2._ New Zealand was stripped of two Tri-Nations points by the Rugby League International Federation for fielding an ineligible player, the Australian-born Nathan Fien, in their Tri-Nations match against Great Britain.

_3._ Selwyn Bennett, chairman of the New Zealand Rugby League, resigned in the aftermath of the Nathan Fien affair.

_4._ Invasor won the $5 million Breeders' Cup Classic at Churchill Downs, with his jockey, Fernando Jara, becoming the youngest rider to win the classic.
• Great Britain beat Australia 23–12 at Aussie Stadium to secure their first victory in Australia in 14 years and moved a step closer to a place in the Rugby League Tri-Nations final.

_5._ Brazil's Marilson Gomes dos Santos of Brazil became the first South American to win the men's ING New York City Marathon. Latvia's Jelena Prokopcuka retained her women's title.
* Australia beat the West Indies by 8 wickets at the Brabourne Stadium, Mumbai, in the final of the ICC Champions Trophy.

_6._ The Los Angeles Galaxy sensationally confirmed that they were keen to sign David Beckham if the former England captain decided not to renew his Real Madrid contract when it expires in May 2007.

_7._ Paul Azinger was named as the United States' Ryder Cup captain for Valhalla in 2008.

_8._ World number two, Maria Sharapova, notched up her 18th consecutive victory with a 6–4, 6–4 victory over Kim Clijsters in the round robin stage of the season-ending WTA Championships in Madrid.

_9._ The San Francisco 49ers announced that they will construct a new stadium in the Bay Area suburb of Santa Clara after electing not to redevelop Candlestick Park.

_10._ Australia Prime Minister's XI scored 347–5 against England before bowling the tourists out for only 181.

_11._ Despite a score of 122 from their captain Brian Lara, the West Indies lost by 9 wickets to Pakistan in Lahore in the first Test match.

_12._ Ukraine's Wladimir Klitschko, retained his IBF heavyweight champion title after knocking out the previously unbeaten American Calvin Brock in the seventh round of their bout in New York.
* Justine Henin-Hardenne of Belgium beat Amélie Mauresmo of France in the final of the WTA Championships in Madrid, Spain.

_13._ Desert Orchid passed away in his sleep aged 27.
* The ATP Tennis Masters got underway in Shanghai, China.

_14._ Peter Senior of Australia beat Bradley Dredge on the 18th green to win the inaugural Goodwill Trophy for Retief Goosen's International side that defeated Colin Montgomerie's combined Ryder Cup side 6 ½–5 ½.

_15._ WBO featherweight champion Scott Harrison was released from a Spanish jail, where he had been detained since 6 October after being arrested for the attempted theft of a car and assault.

16. Joe Calzaghe, the WBO and IBF world champion, was named British Boxer of the Year at the annual Reebok British Boxing Board of Control awards night in Piccadilly, London. Tshifiwa Munyai, the Commonwealth bantamweight champion, was voted the Overseas Boxer of the Year.

17. In the singles round robin of the Masters Cup in Shanghai, Rafael Nadal beat Nikolay Davydenko 5–7, 6–4, 6–4 and Tommy Robredo beat James Blake 6–2, 3–6 7–5 to progress to the quarter-final stages of the tournament.

18. Ruslan Chagaev from Uzbekistan edged a split decision win over 12 rounds against John Ruiz to earn himself a shot at the WBA title-holder, Nikolay Valuev from Russia.

19. Manny Pacquiao from the Philippines met Erik Morales for the third time and knocked out the Mexican legend in the third round. A massive crowd filled the Thomas & Mack Arena, Las Vegas, to watch the Filipino boxer win the decider in their best of three super featherweight fights.

20. In Canada the British Columbia Lions beat the Montreal Alouettes 25–14 to win the 94th Grey Cup Championship game in Winnipeg, Manitoba, and were crowned the best team of the 2006 Canadian Football League season.

21. Ian Thorpe, the 24-year-old Australian swimmer, announced his retirement during a packed press conference at a Sydney hotel.

22. FIFA's new world football rankings showed Brazil (1,588 points) retained their number one position, with Italy second on 1,560 points and Argentina (1,523 points) up to third place.

23. The first Test of the 2006–07 Ashes Series began at The Gabba, Brisbane, Australia. England, the holders of the urn, took a thrashing on the first day's play with Australia 346–3.

24. Ashes First Test, second day, the home side declared on 602–9 from 155 overs. England replied with 53–3 (17 overs).

25. Ashes First Test, third day, Australia 602–9 declared and 181–1 versus England 157.
   * Australia defeated New Zealand 16–12 in the final of the Tri-Nations at Aussie Stadium, Sydney, in front of 27,325 fans.

26. England's Justin Rose claimed his first European Tour victory in four years after winning the MasterCard Australian Masters at Huntingdale Golf Club, Melbourne.

27. On the final day of the First Test in the Ashes Series, Australia 602–9 declared and 202–1 declared, beat England 157 & 370 by 277 runs.

28. Valencia president Juan Soler informs Chelsea that if they intend to purchase their star striker David Villa they will have to start the bidding at £100 million if they want the Los Che's Spanish international. Villa is under contract at Valencia until 2013 and has a €150 million buy-out clause.

29. Andy Robinson walked out of the Twickenham HQ exit doors for the last time, after officially standing down as England head coach.

30. Australia and England both named unchanged sides for the second Ashes Test in Adelaide beginning on 1 December.

December 2006

1. England finished the first day of the second Test of the Ashes Series, on 266–3 at the Adelaide Oval.
   * Henrik Larsson agreed to join Manchester United on a three-month loan deal.

2. England declared on 551–6 on day two of the Second Ashes Test; Paul Collingwood scored 206.

3. At close of play on day three of the Second Test of the Ashes Series, Australia were 312–5.
   * Ronnie O'Sullivan whitewashed Jimmy White 7–0 to win his third consecutive Premier League title at the Wythenshawe Forum.

4. On day four of the Second Ashes Test, England bowled Australia out for 513.
   * Dubai International Capital (DIC), the investment arm of Dubai's government, confirmed that they were in talks about a possible £450 million buy-out of Liverpool FC.

5. Australia won the Second Test by 6 wickets to go 2–0 up in the Ashes Series.
   * Shoaib Akhtar and Mohammad Asif, who both tested positive for the banned substance nandrolone prior to the start of the ICC Champions Trophy in October, won their appeals to have their suspensions overturned.

6. The McLaren Formula One team asked Renault to release Fernando Alonso from his contract early so that he could test for his new team. Alonso will partner the British rookie driver, Lewis Hamilton, at the team in an all new line-up for the 2007 season.

7. England cricket coach Duncan Fletcher ruled out former captain Michael Vaughan's return to the 2006–07 Ashes Series in Australia.

8. Damien Martyn, the 35-year-old Australian batsman, announced his retirement from all forms of cricket with immediate effect.

9. Gary Speed of Bolton Wanderers became the first man to play in 500 FA Premier League matches; a 4–0 defeat of West Ham United at the Reebok Stadium.
   * Amir Khan won his first professional title, beating Rachid Drilzane in an IBF intercontinental light-welterweight contest.

10. Zara Phillips won the 2006 BBC Sports Personality of the Year.

11. West Ham United sacked their manager Alan Pardew.

12. Qatar revealed that it will bid to stage the 2016 Olympic Games. The winner of which will be awarded in 2009.

13. Alan Curbishley was appointed the manager of West Ham United.
    * The former World Cup downhill champion skier Andreas Schifferer retired aged 32.

14. Ronnie O'Sullivan was trailing Stephen Hendry 4–1 in the quarter-final of the Maplin UK Championship when he suddenly conceded the match.
    * At the end of day one of the third Test of the Ashes Series, England bowled Australia out for 244 in Perth before replying with 51–2.

15. England were dismissed by Australia on day two of the Third Ashes Test for 215. Australia ended the day on 119–1 in Perth, a lead of 148.

16. At the close of play on day three of the Third Ashes Test, Australia declared on 527–5, setting England a daunting score of 556 runs to win, or batting for two full days, to keep their chances of bringing the Ashes home alive.

17. England closed day four of the third Test against Australia on 265–5.
* Peter Ebdon beat Stephen Hendry 10–6 to win the final of the Maplin UK Snooker Championship in York.

18. Australia reclaimed the Ashes after bowling England out for 350 on the final day of the Third Test.
* India recorded their first Test victory in South Africa with a 123-run success on the fourth morning of the Fourth Test in Johannesburg.
* Beth Tweddle, the world uneven bars champion, won the same event at the World Cup final in Brazil.

19. Japan's 2004 Olympic marathon gold medal winner, Mizuki Noguchi, confirmed that she will take part in the 2007 London Marathon.

20. Shane Warne said he would retire from international cricket after the Ashes.

21. England bowler Steve Harmison announced his retirement from one-day internationals just three months before the Cricket World Cup.

22. The Spanish cyclist, Aitor Gonzalez, was handed a two-year doping ban by the Court of Arbitration for Sport. The Court found Gonzalez was personally responsible for taking a food supplement that resulted in him proving positive for a banned steroid at the 2005 Tour of Spain. The ban applies from 28 September 2005 when Gonzalez stopped competing.

23. Michael Vick of the Atlanta Falcons ran for a total of 32 yards to become the first quarterback in NFL history to rush for over 1,000 yards in one season.

24. Charlton Athletic appointed Alan Pardew as their new manager after their head coach, Les Reed, left the club by mutual consent.

25. On the quietest day of the sporting year, England looked forward with nothing but pride to salvage from the Ashes series. The Fourth Test starts on Boxing Day.

26. Shane Warne took his 700th Test wicket as Australia bowled England out for 159 on day one of the Fourth Ashes Test on his home ground.

27. On day two of the Fourth Ashes Test, Australia ended the day on 372–7, a lead of 213 runs over England.

28. Australia won the Fourth Ashes Test by an innings and 99 runs inside only three days in Melbourne.

27. Third seed Dennis Priestley beat Dane Per Laursen to reach the last 16 at the Professional Darts Corporation World Championships in Purfleet.

28. Phil Taylor hammered Chris Mason 4–0 to reach the quarter-finals of the PDC World Championships.

29. Mike Tyson was arrested and charged with driving under the influence of drugs and possession of cocaine.
* Michael Walchhofer from Austria became the first man to win two World Cup double downhills after claiming victory at Bormio.

30. Zara Phillips (MBE), Gareth Edwards (CBE), Ian Woosnam (OBE), Gary Wolstenholme (MBE), Steven Gerrard (MBE), Faye White (MBE) and Ricky Hatton (MBE) were among the sports stars to feature in the New Year Honours List.
* Raymond van Barneveld and Phil Taylor set up a dream final in the PDC World Darts Championship.

31. Sir Alex Ferguson celebrated his 65th birthday going into the new year with Manchester United six points clear at the top of the FA Premier League.

January 2007

1. Naseem Hamed, the former world featherweight boxing champion, was stripped of his MBE after being sent to prison after a conviction for a high-speed crash in his sports car.
   * Raymond van Barneveld won his first PDC World Championship title after defeating the 13-time world champion Phil Taylor, 7–6, in the final.

2. England ended day one of the fifth and final Ashes Test in Sydney on 234–4.

3. On day two of the fifth Ashes Test, England were all out for 291. At the close of play Australia were 188–4.

4. Day three of the fifth Ashes Test ended with Australia 393 all out in their first innings; England's second innings stood on 114–5 at stumps, a lead of just 12 runs.
   * Paul Le Guen sensationally resigned as manager of Glasgow Rangers.

5. Australia whitewashed England 5–0 in the 2006–07 Ashes by beating the tourists on day four of the fifth Test.

6. Andy Murray lost 4–6, 4–6 to second seed Ivan Ljubicic in the Qatar Open final in Doha.

7. Henrik Larsson made his Manchester United debut and scored in United's 2–1 FA Cup third round win over Aston Villa at Old Trafford.
   * Rangers' nightmare season took another downhill lurch when they went out of the Scottish Cup 3–2 to Dunfermline, having trailed 3–0 at one stage, at East End Park.

8. Britain's number one tennis player Andy Murray was ranked 15th in the world, his highest ever world ranking.

9. England played Australia in an International Twenty20 match at Sydney. Australia won by 77 runs.

10. Andy Murray won his first match at the Kooyong Classic beating world number four Ivan Ljubicic 6–4, 6–2, avenging his defeat by the Croatian in the Qatar Open final four days earlier.

11. Walter Smith left his position as Scotland coach to take up the vacant managerial post at Glasgow Rangers.

12. David Beckham signed a lucrative contract with the Los Angeles Galaxy to play his football in the USA's Major League Soccer from season 2007.

13. Andy Roddick recorded his first defeat of Roger Federer since August 2003 to successfully defend his Kooyong Classic victory of 2006 in Melbourne.

14. Europe crushed Asia 12½–3½ at the Amata Spring Golf Club in Bangkok to retain the Royal Trophy.
    * China's Ding Junhui became the youngest snooker player to score a televised maximum 147 break when the 19-year-old defeated Anthony Hamilton 6–3 at the Saga Insurance Masters at Wembley.
    * England's Martin Adams won the 2007 British Darts Organisation World Championships at Frimley Green; Trina Gulliver (England) claimed the women's crown.

15. The Australian Open began in Melbourne, with Roger Federer and Amelie Mauresmo defending their singles titles.

16. Ronnie O'Sullivan refused to talk to the media after beating Ali Carter 6–1 in the first round of the snooker Masters.

17. Boxer Muhammad Ali, self-styled "The Greatest", celebrated his 65th birthday.

18. The FA Premier League agreed a new £625 million deal for overseas TV rights, while the 2007–08 champions will receive £50 million in prize money.

19. UEFA expelled Feyenoord from the 2006–07 UEFA Cup following crowd trouble during their match in France against Nancy on 30 November 2006.

20. Ricky Hatton regained his IBF world light-welterweight championship belt with a points victory over Colombia's Juan Urango in Las Vegas.

21. Paul Casey fired a 7 under par final round of 65 to win golf's European Tour Abu Dhabi Championship.
   * Ronnie O'Sullivan beat Ding Junhui 10–3 to claim his third snooker Masters title.

22. Pakistan (265 & 191–5) beat South Africa (124 & 331) by 5 wickets in the second Test at Port Elizabeth to give them only their second ever Test win in South Africa, to level the series at 1–1.

23. England suffered a humiliating defeat to New Zealand at the Adelaide Oval, a result that left them at the bottom of the Commonwealth Bank Series table.

24. Government ministers stated that the costs of London hosting the 2012 Olympic Games should not be paid for from National Lottery monies or by taxpayers. The MPs made their announcement after learning that the projected costs had risen to £900 million since the bid was made.

25. UEFA awarded Tottenham Hotspur a bye into the last 16 of the UEFA Cup subject to a potential appeal from their scheduled opponents Feyenoord.

26. Tennis history was made at the Australian Open when ladies doubles pairing, Chuang Chia-Jung and Chan Yung-Jan, became the first players from Taiwan to appear in a Grand Slam final; they lost 6–4, 6–7, 6–1 to Zimbabwean Cara Black and South African Liezel Huber.

27. Serena Williams defeated the number one seed Maria Sharapova to win her third Australian Open title.

28. World number one Roger Federer won his third Australian Open with a 7–6 (7–2), 6–4, 6–4 win over Fernando Gonzalez.
   * Ronnie O'Sullivan beat Ding Junhui 10–3 to claim his third snooker Masters title.
   * Team Hungary won the Fencing World Cup epée event in Kuwait City, while Benjamin Kleibrink from Germany won the individual foil Fencing World Cup in Paris.
   * In cycling, Argentina's Francisco Chamorro won the Copa da Republica de Ciclismo – a single day's road racing event in Brazil.

29. Alex McLeish, the former Hibernian and Glasgow Rangers manager, was named the new Scotland coach.

30. Stephen Hendry became the first snooker player in history to make 700 centuries in competitive matches.
   * Olympic gold medallist swimmer, China's Luo Xuejuan, was forced to retire because of a potentially fatal heart problem.
   * The 95th edition of the Six Days of Berlin cycle endurance race ended with Germany's Rolf Aldag and Robert Bartko victorious.
   * The host nation of the 18th Gulf Cup of Nations, United Arab Emirates, beat Oman 1–0 in the final at the Sheikh Zayed Stadium, Abu Dhabi to claim their first title.

31. India beat West Indies by 160 runs in their one-day international played in Vadodara. Sachin Tendulkar hit his 41st one-day century to help India clinch the series 3–1.

February 2007

1. The five-time former MotoGP world champion Valentino Rossi signed a new contract to remain a Yamaha racer until the end of 2008.

2. England claimed their first victory over Australia since the 2005 Ashes in their Commonwealth Bank Series encounter played at Sydney Cricket Ground. Australia, chasing 293, were bowled out for 200 in 38.5 overs giving England (292–7) victory by 92 runs.

3. The 205th Merseyside derby ended in stalemate at Anfield – Liverpool 0 Everton 0.

* France opened their defence of their Six Nations title in sensational form with a crushing 39–3 win over Italy at the Stadio Flaminio, Rome. Meanwhile, England got their campaign off to a flying start with a convincing 42–20 win over Scotland in the Calcutta Cup at Twickenham.

4. Ireland opened their Six Nations campaign with a 19–9 win over Wales at the Millennium Stadium, Cardiff.

5. American tycoons George Gillett and Tom Hicks were close to finalizing their £470m takeover of Liverpool.

6. England 270–7 (50 overs) beat New Zealand 256–8 by 14 runs in their Commonwealth Bank Series one-day encounter in Brisbane, a win that took them into the final against the hosts Australia.

* George Gillett and Tom Hicks reached an agreement to take over Liverpool Football Club.

7. Mervyn King left the British Darts Organisation and joined the increasing band of players who had recently jumped ship to join the rival Professional Darts Corporation.

8. In Deloitte's annual table listing the wealthiest football clubs in the world, Manchester United dropped from second place in 2006 to fourth in 2007, trailing Real Madrid, Barcelona and Juventus (based on revenues generated during the 2005–2006 season). However, United remain the world's most profitable club.

9. England faced Australia in Melbourne in game one of their best-of-three tri-series Commonwealth Bank Series final. England (253–6) beat Australia (252) by 4 wickets to go 1–0 up in the tri-series final.

10. In the Six Nations tournament, England beat Italy 20–7 at Twickenham and Scotland thrashed Wales 21–9 at Murrayfield.

11. Irish rugby history was made at Croke Park, Dublin, when Ireland played their first ever international at the home of the Gaelic Athletic Association. France spoiled the party with a late Vincent Clerc try giving them a 20–17 win in the Six Nations.

* England 246–8 (50 overs) beat Australia 152–8 (33 overs), by 34 runs under the Duckworth/Lewis scoring system to win the Commonwealth Bank Series tournament. England's victory put the visitors 2–0 up in the best-of-three final. England's tournament win was the first time in 14 years that Australia had lost in the finals of their home one-day series and it was also the first time England have won this tournament since 1986–87.

12. Finland's Marcus Gronholm claimed victory in the Rally of Sweden in his Ford Focus to cut Sebastien Loeb's World Rally Car Championship lead to just 2 points.

13. Milan Mandaric, the former owner of Portsmouth, completed his takeover of Leicester City after the Championship outfit's shareholders accepted his offer for the club.

14. In snooker, Shaun Murphy became the first player in the 31-year history of 201 world ranking tournaments to compile four centuries in a row in a best-of-nine match.

15. Vladimir Romanov, the major shareholder of Hearts Football Club, accused Glasgow Celtic and Glasgow Rangers of "buying off" referees and players in Scotland.

16. In the Chappell-Hadlee Trophy, New Zealand (149–0) beat Australia (148) by 10 wickets in Wellington. The Black Caps became the first country to defeat the Aussies by 10 wickets in a one-day international.

17. David Beckham was sent off for Real Madrid at home to Real Betis.

18. Andy Murray fought back from a set down to beat Ivo Karlovic to retain his SAP Open title in San Jose, Calif. His older brother, Jamie, won the men's doubles at the same event partnered by American Eric Butorac.

19. The draw for the WGC–Accenture Match Play Championship, in Tucson, Arizona, was announced. Darren Clarke, the only European player to win the event (beating Tiger Woods in the 2000 final), will face his Ryder Cup team-mate Sergio Garcia in the first round on 21 February.

20. In the UEFA Champions League an official from Lille grabbed the football and invited the Lille players to walk off the pitch shortly after Manchester United scored. United won the game 1–0 thanks to a Ryan Giggs goal.

21. UEFA confirmed that they would be investigating the crush scare involving Manchester United fans at the Champions League tie against Lille.

22. The All England Club announced that the 2007 Wimbledon Championships will give men and women equal prize money for the first time.

23. St Helens were officially crowned the world's best rugby league club side after defeating Australia's best, the Brisbane Broncos, 18–14 in the World Club Challenge match played in Bolton Wanderers' Reebok Stadium.

24. In rugby union, Italy beat Scotland 37–17 at Murrayfield to record their first ever away win in the Six Nations. Ireland beat England 43–13 at Croke Park, England's heaviest ever defeat to the Irish. France beat Wales 32–21 in Paris to lead the table.

25. Chelsea beat Arsenal 2–1 in the Carling Cup Final at the Millennium Stadium, Cardiff. Three players were sent off late in the game.

26. Roger Federer broke Jimmy Connors' 30-year-old record as the longest reigning world number one male tennis player. Federer's reign began on 4 February 2004.
   * The 1997 Tour de France winner Jan Ullrich announced his retirement.

27. Guus Hiddink, coach of the Russian national team, was handed a six-month suspended sentence and fined £30,000 after being found guilty of tax evasion by a Dutch court.

28. FIFA president Sepp Blatter raised serious doubts over England's hopes of staging the FIFA World Cup in 2018.
   * Dame Tanni Grey Thompson, Britain's most successful Paralympian, announced her retirement.

March 2007

1. Nicole Cooke from Wales won cycling's Geelong Tour in Victoria, Australia, her first race of the year. Her victory meant she became the first non-Australian winner.

2. Jimmy White will miss this year's World Professional Snooker Championship after losing 10–4 to Scotland's Jamie Burnett in the qualifying event.

3. In cycling, Spain's Alejandro Valverde won the Tour of Valencia riding for the Caisse D'Epargne team.
   * Ryan Giggs made his 700th appearance for Manchester United in their 1–0 FA Premier League win over Liverpool at Anfield.

4. At the end of day three of the 29th European Indoor Athletics Championships held in Birmingham, the United Kingdom topped the medals table with four gold, three silver and three bronze.
   * Roger Federer won his 41st straight match as he beat Mikhail Youzhny in the final of tennis's Dubai Open.

5. In horse racing, four racing greats were honoured as the first new inductees for nine years into the prestigious Hall of Fame at the Cheltenham Festival: trainers Martin Pipe and David Nicholson and horses Best Mate and Desert Orchid.

6. The Olympic badminton champion, Taufik Hidayat from Indonesia, withdrew from the All England Championships in Birmingham.

7. Sixty Cricket World Cup players had to evacuate their hotel in Trinidad as a result of an explosion caused by a gas leak. At least three members of hotel staff were taken to hospital but no one from the teams was hurt.

8. Richard Vaughan's second-round defeat ended the British interest in the singles at badminton's All England Championships. The Welshman was beaten by China's Bao Chunlai.

9. Multiplex officially handed over the keys to the FA for the new 90,000-seater Wembley Stadium. The stadium cost of £800 million to construct.

10. In the RBS Six Nations Ireland won their third Triple Crown title in four years following a narrow 19–18 victory over Scotland at Murrayfield. Italy beat Wales 23–20 in Rome.

11. An inexperienced England team put their RBS Six Nations campaign back on track with a 26–18 win over France at Twickenham.

12. American golfer Meaghan Francella, playing in only her sixth LPGA event, won her first title after defeating Annika Sorenstam in a play-off in the MasterCard Classic, Mexico City.

13. In National Hunt racing, the 2007 Cheltenham Festival got under way.
   * At Sabina Park, Jamaica, hosts West Indies enjoyed a 54-run victory in the opening match of the ninth Cricket World Cup.

14. At the Cheltenham Festival, Voy Por Ustedes, the 2006 Arkle winner, won the Queen Mother Champion Chase.
   * Andy Murray defeated the world number four Nikolay Davydenko at the Indian Wells Masters Series.

15. Luton Town sacked manager Mike Newell, with the club battling against relegation from the Championship.
   * Tessa Jowell, the Culture Secretary, told MPs that the budget for the 2012 London Olympics had risen to £9.35 billion, nearly four times the original £2.4 billion estimate.

16. On the final day of the Cheltenham Festival the hot favourite Kauto Star, despite a mistake at the last fence, won the Totesport Cheltenham Gold Cup.

17. On St Patrick's Day, Ireland caused one of the greatest ever upsets in the history of cricket by beating Pakistan in their group D World Cup game in Jamaica. In Trinidad there was almost as big a shock as Bangladesh beat India.
    * France won the RBS Six Nations title following their 46–19 victory over Scotland in Paris.

18. Andrew Flintoff was sacked as England vice-captain after he and several team-mates went out drinking following their loss to New Zealand.
    * Pakistan cricket coach Bob Woolmer was found dead in his hotel room in Jamaica.
    * In Formula One, Kimi Raikkonen got his Ferrari career off to a perfect start by winning the Australian Grand Prix at Melbourne. Lewis Hamilton (McLaren) made an impressive F1 debut taking third place.

19. India beat Bermuda by 257 runs after amassing a Cricket World Cup record score of 413–5 in Trinidad.

20. Philip Beard, venue manager of the Millennium Dome, renamed the O2 Arena, announced that it will become a world-class indoor sports venue after receiving a £600 million refit.

21. Vladimir Dyatchin (RUS) took gold in 1 hour, 55 minutes, 32.52 seconds to win the 10km open water race in the World Swimming Championships in Melbourne, Australia.

22. Jamaican Police could not confirm how Bob Woolmer had died and continued to treat his death as "suspicious".

23. India were all but eliminated from the CWC after losing to Sri Lanka.

24. Spain's Dani Pedrosa took pole position on his Honda for Sunday's Spanish MotoGP in Jerez.

25. Michael Phelps led the USA 4 x 100m freestyle relay team to gold at the World Swimming Championships.
    * Valentino Rossi (Yamaha) won the MotoGP in Jerez.

26. Kevin Pietersen rose to the top of the International Cricket Council's world rankings for one-day batsmen.
    * Brendan Hansen (USA) successfully defended his 100m breaststroke title at the World Swimming Championships.

27. Three American swimmers set new world records at the World Championships: Aaron Peirsol (100m back), Michael Phelps (200m free) and Natalie Coughlin (100m back).
    * Australia beat the West Indies in their World Cup Super 8 game in Antigua, meaning the hosts could not reach the semi-finals.

28. Michael Phelps took gold in the 200m butterfly at the World Swimming Championships and bettered his own world record time by 1.7 seconds.

29. Michael Phelps won his fourth gold in the 200m medley at the World Swimming Championships and broke his third world record of the week.

30. Invasor, trained by Kiaran McLaughlin for HH Sheikh Hamdan bin Rashid Al Maktoum and ridden by 19-year-old Fernando Jara, won the £3 million Dubai World Cup at Nad Al Sheba.

31. Great Britain's Victoria Pendleton won the gold medal in the women's sprint at the World Track Cycling Championships in Palma de Mallorca.

April 2007

1. Michael Phelps won a record seventh gold medal at the World Swimming Championships in Melbourne and with it smashed his own 400m individual medley world record.

2. Alexandra Palace in London was chosen ahead of the Circus Tavern, Purfleet (the host for the previous 14 years), to host the 2008 PDC World Darts Championship.

3. The Rugby Football Union (RFU) refused to rule out legal action against the 12 Premiership clubs if they voted to withdraw from the 2007–08 Heineken Cup, based on a similar decision from the French clubs.

4. Sri Lanka beat England by 2 runs in their World Cup Super Eight match in Antigua. England needed 3 runs off the final ball to win, but Ravi Bopara was bowled by Dilhara Fernando.

5. England's top rugby union clubs confirmed they would follow their French counterparts and boycott the European club cups in 2008.

6. At the US Masters in Augusta, Bruce Wetterich (USA) and the 2006 Masters runner-up, Tim Clark (RSA), led after two rounds on 2 under par.

7. Cambridge President Tom James finally became a Boat Race winner at his fourth and final attempt, when the Light Blues beat the Dark Blues in the 153rd University Boat Race.

8. Fernando Alonso secured his first win for McLaren in the Malaysian Grand Prix at Sepang; Lewis Hamilton made it a McLaren one-two.
   * Zach Johnson (USA) won the US Masters on a dramatic final day at Augusta. Johnson fired a 3 under par 69 for a 1 over total of 289, the joint highest winning score in the Masters.

9. New Zealand beat Ireland by 129 runs in their Cricket World Cup Super Eight match played in Guyana.
   * Tony McCoy rode Butler's Cabin to victory in the Powers Whiskey Irish Grand National at Fairyhouse.

10. Trailing 2–1 from the first leg of their UEFA Champions League quarter-final tie with AS Roma, Manchester United beat the Italian side 7–1 at Old Trafford. Chelsea, who drew 1–1 with Valencia in their first leg tie, beat the Spanish side 2–1 away to join United in the semi-finals.

11. Liverpool made it three English clubs in the semi-finals of the UEFA Champions League with a 1–0 home win over PSV Eindhoven for a 4–0 aggregate win; Milan beat Bayern Munich 2–0 in Germany to win their quarter-final tie 4–2 on aggregate.

12. In rugby union, Ireland's Brian O'Driscoll was named the RBS Six Nations man of the tournament for the second successive year.

13. Manchester United's 22-year-old Portuguese winger, Cristiano Ronaldo, signed a new five-year deal.
    * Australia beat Ireland by 9 wickets to secure a semi-final berth in the Cricket World Cup final.

14. Silver Birch, a 33-1 shot, won the John Smiths Grand National at Aintree.
    * Manchester United beat Watford 4–1 in the FA Cup semi-final, to book their appearance in the first FA Cup final at the new Wembley Stadium.

15. Felipe Massa (Ferrari) won the Bahrain Grand Prix from pole position.
    * Chelsea beat Blackburn Rovers 2–1 after extra time to set up an FA Cup final against Manchester United.

16. Robert Cheruiyot and Rita Jeptoo from Kenya won the men's and women's races in the Boston Marathon.

17. The European Greco-Roman, Freestyle and Women's Wrestling Championships opened in Bulgaria's capital, Sofia.

18. Poland and Ukraine were chosen to host the Euro 2012.

19. In winter sports, Janica Kostelic, the first woman in Olympic history to win three alpine gold medals (which she won at the 2002 Salt Lake Games), announced her retirement from skiing due to long-standing injuries.

20. Roger Federer and Rafael Nadal set new personal milestones reaching the semi-finals of the Monte Carlo Masters: Federer claimed his 500th professional victory; Nadal's winning streak on clay reached 65 matches.

21. Brian Lara, the West Indies captain, ended his international career with a 1-wicket defeat to England in a Super Eight match at the Cricket World Cup.
   * The 14-1 shot Hot Weld, ridden by PJ McDonald, won the Scottish Grand National at Ayr.

22. Manchester United's Cristiano Ronaldo won the PFA Player of the Year Award and also scooped the PFA Young Player of the Year Award.
   * Glasgow Celtic won the Scottish Premier League title.
   * In Italy, Inter Milan beat Siena 2–1 to retain their Serie A title.
   * In the 2007 London Marathon, Martin Lel from Kenya won the men's race, while Zhou Chunxiu became the first Chinese female to win the women's race.

23. Bennett King resigned as West Indies coach following the team's exit from the Cricket World Cup.

24. Alan Ball, the youngest member of England's World Cup winning team in 1966, died of a heart attack aged 61.
   * Sri Lanka eased their way into the ICC Cricket World Cup final with a comfortable 81-run victory over New Zealand at Sabina Park.

25. Australia annihilated South Africa in the Cricket World Cup semi-final in St Lucia and will now face Sri Lanka in a rematch of the 1996 final.

26. Liverpool retained the FA Youth Cup, 4–2 on penalties, after winning the second leg 1–0 at Old Trafford; the aggregate score was 2–2.

27. Arthur Milton, the last man to play full internationals at both football and cricket for England, died at his home in Bristol aged 79.

28. In Barbados, Australia were crowned Cricket World Cup champions for the fourth time in farcical conditions, after beating Sri Lanka by 53 runs on the Duckworth-Lewis scoring method. Australia's wicket-keeper/batsman Adam Gilchrist struck 13 fours and 8 sixes on his way to 149 off 104 balls opening the innings.

29. Great Britain made A1GP history after dominating the Brands Hatch sprint race from start to finish thereby becoming the first team to win a home race in the series. A1GP Team Germany won the main race and claimed the overall A1GP 2006–07 championship.

30. Following the shock resignation of Sam Allardyce 24 hours earlier, Sammy Lee was appointed the new manager of Bolton Wanderers.

May 2007

_1._ Liverpool beat Chelsea 4–1 in a penalty shootout at Anfield to reach the UEFA Champions League final.
* Manchester City banned Joey Barton until the end of the season following his training ground bust-up with team-mate Ousmane Dabo.

2. Cricket's MCC announced that Mike Brearley, a former England captain, will become president of the club for the year starting 1 October 2007.
* Milan beat Manchester United 3–0 (5–3 agg.) in the UEFA Champions League semi-final second leg and will meet Liverpool in the final.

_3._ Many legends from the football world joined hundreds of mourners at the funeral of World Cup star Alan Ball.

_4._ _BMW Oracle Racing_ (USA) and _Luna Rossa_ (Italy) were tied at the top of the round robin second stage table racing in sailing's Louis Vuitton Cup, off Valencia. The winners will face the defending champion, _Alinghi_, in the America's Cup, 23 June–4 July.

_5._ With Queen Elizabeth II attending for the first time, Street Sense won the Kentucky Derby at Churchill Downs.

_6._ Manchester United claimed the FA Premier League championship when Chelsea could only draw 1–1 at Arsenal.
* Glenn Roeder resigned as manager of Newcastle United.
* Kim Clijsters, the former world tennis number one, announced her retirement with immediate effect.

_7._ John Higgins overcame Mark Selby 18–13 in one of the most dramatic World Professional Snooker Championship finals ever seen.
* Charlton Athletic became the second club to be relegated from the FA Premier League.

_8._ Ricky Hatton admitted to being "absolutely devastated" upon learning of the death of Diego Corrales, a world boxing champion at two weights, in a motorbike accident in Los Angeles on 7 May.

9. In the America's Cup, _Team New Zealand_ topped the Louis Vuitton Cup round robin standings ahead of rivals _BMW Oracle_ after 11 races.

10. Sky Sports' 1,000th live game was Tottenham Hotspur's 1–1 draw with Blackburn Rovers at White Hart Lane.

11. Rafael Nadal's quarter-final win over Novak Djokovic in the Rome Masters equalled John McEnroe's one-surface record of 75 consecutive wins.

12. Japan's Noriyuki Haga (Yamaha) set a new Monza track record time of 1:44.941 to take pole position for Sunday's World Superbike Championship Grand Prix (Round 6).

13. Manchester United were presented with the FA Premier League Championship trophy after a 1–0 home defeat to West Ham United.
* Sheffield United lost 2–1 at home to Wigan Athletic, a result which saw them drop into the Coca Cola Championship.
* In F1, Felipe Massa (Ferrari) won the Spanish Grand Prix.

14. Stuart Pearce was sacked as manager of Manchester City.
* Paul Jewell resigned as manager of Wigan Athletic one day after helping the club to avoid relegation.
* Scotland's Gary Anderson won the International Darts League title with a 13–9 win over Mark Webster in the final at Nijmegen, Holland.

15. Sam Allardyce, who had recently resigned as Bolton Wanderers' manager, became Newcastle United's boss.

16. Sevilla retained the UEFA Cup with a 3–1 penalty shootout win over FCD Espanyol after a 2–2 (aet) draw.
    * Neil Warnock resigned as the manager of Sheffield United, three days after his team had been relegated from the FA Premier League.

17. Chelsea's Didier Drogba was presented with the FA Premier League Golden Boot award after finishing the 2006–07 season as the leading goal scorer with 20 goals.
    * In cricket, England ended day one of their first Test against the West Indies at Lord's on 200–3 with Alastair Cook on 102 not out, his fifth Test century.

18. Max Mosley, the FIA president, issued a statement proposing an environmentally friendly overhaul of Formula One for the 2011 season.

19. Chelsea beat Manchester United 1–0, after extra time, in the first FA Cup final to be played at the new Wembley Stadium.
    * Rugby Union's London Wasps ended Leicester Tiger's hopes of a treble by beating the Premiership champions and EDF Cup winners 25–9 in the Heineken Cup final played at Twickenham.

20. Rafael Nadal's streak of 81 consecutive wins on clay ended in the Hamburg Masters final where Roger Federer triumphed 2–6, 6–2, 6–0.

21. Rain interrupted play on the final day of the first Test between England and the West Indies at Lord's, with the match declared a draw.

22. Bryan Robson was unveiled as the new manager of Sheffield United.
    * Andy Murray withdrew from the French Open with a wrist injury.

23. AC Milan beat Liverpool 2–1 in Athens to win the 2007 UEFA Champions League.

24. During practice for the Monaco Grand Prix, Lewis Hamilton crashed his McLaren-Mercedes into a tyre barrier but escaped unhurt.

25. England coach Steve McClaren named David Beckham in England's squads to play Brazil in a friendly at Wembley and a Euro 2008 qualifier in Estonia.

26. Celtic beat Dunfermline Athletic 1–0 at Hampden Park to win the Scottish Cup final and complete the double.

27. Fernando Alonso won the Monaco Grand Prix and was followed across the line by his McLaren Mercedes team-mate Lewis Hamilton.
    * Scotland's Dario Franchitti won the Indianapolis 500.

28. Derby County beat West Bromwich Albion 1–0 in the Championship play-off final to earn promotion to the FA Premier League for 2007–08.
    * In cricket, England inflicted the West Indies' heaviest ever defeat with victory by an innings and 283 runs in the second Test at Headingley.

29. Tim Henman lost 6–4, 6–3, 6–2 to Latvia's Ernests Gulbis in the first round of the French Open singles.

30. Ryan Giggs said he was retiring from international football after his 64th appearance for Wales, against the Czech Republic in a Euro 2008 qualifier.

31. Manchester United announced the signings of 19-year-old Anderson from FC Porto and Nani, a 20-year-old Portuguese winger, from Sporting Lisbon. They also confirmed that England midfielder Owen Hargreaves will join them from Bayern Munich on 1 July.

June 2007

1. England drew 1–1 with Brazil at Wembley with David Beckham winning his 95th cap for his country.

2. Frankie Dettori won his first Epsom Derby, at his 15th attempt, on the 5–4 favourite, Authorized.

   * Ryan Giggs made his 64th and last appearance for Wales in their 1–1 draw with the Czech Republic in a Euro 2008 qualifying game at the Millennium Stadium, Cardiff.

3. America's Tyson Gay recorded a blistering 9.76 seconds for the 100m at the Reebok Grand Prix in New York. It would have beaten the world record by 0.01 seconds, but he was denied the title of the fastest human on earth because his time was wind-assisted.

   * In horse racing, 24 hours after his success on Authorized, Frankie Dettori claimed victory in the Prix du Jockey Club (the French Derby) at Chantilly on Lawman.

4. A UEFA report named Liverpool fans as the worst-behaved in Europe.

   * The logo for the 2012 London Olympics was unveiled.

5. In athletics, the new Scottish Executive said it was 110 per cent behind Glasgow's bid to host the 2014 Commonwealth Games.

6. In sailing, Team New Zealand completed a 5–0 whitewash of Italy's Luna Rossa to win the Louis Vuitton Cup and book a place in the 32nd America's Cup final.

7. England's cricketers found it hard going on the first day of the third Test against the West Indies. They ended on 296–7 at Old Trafford.

8. At Old Trafford, England took control of the Third Test by making 370 and bowling out the West Indies for 229.

9. Justine Henin won a third consecutive French Open title, beating Serbia's Ana Ivanovic 6–1, 6–2 in the final.

   * On day three of the third Test the West Indies reached the stumps at Old Trafford on 22–1, requiring an almost impossible 455 for victory.

   * In F1, Lewis Hamilton claimed the first pole position of his career thanks to a brilliant qualifying lap for the Canadian Grand Prix in Montreal.

10. Formula One rookie Lewis Hamilton claimed his maiden Grand Prix victory at Montreal in Canada.

    * West Indies ended day four of the Third Test on 301–5, 154 short of victory at Old Trafford.

11. Despite another century from Shivnarine Chanderpaul, England beat the West Indies by 60 runs in the Third Test. They lead the series 2–0 with one Test to play.

12. In an amazing U-turn, the Jamaican police told the world's media that Pakistan cricket coach Bob Woolmer had not been murdered, but that he had died of natural causes.

    * The LA Galaxy rejected an offer from Real Madrid to buy David Beckham out of his contract.

13. In tennis, Lleyton Hewitt the defending Stella Artois men's singles champion and four-time winner of the event, suffered a shock second round defeat to French qualifier Jo-Wilfred Tsonga at Queen's Club.

14. The 2007–08 football fixture lists were published. Premiership champions, Manchester United, open at home to Reading.

15. The opening day of the final Test between England and the West Indies was rained out at Chester-le-Street.

* Ian Botham got a knighthood in the Queen's Birthday Honours List – one of many sports stars to be honoured.

16. Paul Malignaggi became IBF world light-welterweight champion after a unanimous points defeat of champion Lovemore N'dou in Uncasville, USA.

17. Lewis Hamilton (McLaren-Mercedes) won the USA Grand Prix at the Indianapolis Motor Speedway Circuit.

* The Audi driven by Frank Biela, Marco Werner and Emanuele Pirro won the Le Mans 24-hour race for the second successive year.

* David Beckham was finally a winner in Spain when Real Madrid clinched La Liga title on the season's last day.

18. Arbitration hearing into the Carlos Tevez affair opened in London.

* Francesco Totti of AS Roma won the European Golden Boot award.

* Michael Vaughan resigned as captain of England's one-day side.

19. England's cricketers beat the West Indies by 7 wickets to win the Fourth Test at the Riverside and claim a 3–0 series victory.

* In racing, a revamped Royal Ascot opened with six course records set.

20. England spinner Monty Panesar broke into the top 10 of the world rankings for bowlers for the first time following his superb performances in the 3-0 Test series win over the West Indies.

21. Thaksin Shinawatra, the former prime minister of Thailand, lodged an £81.6m formal takeover bid for Man City.

22. Paul Collingwood was named captain of England's one-day squad for the series against the West Indies.

23. Justine Henin beat Amelie Mauresmo in the final of the International Women's Open in Eastbourne.

* In sailing, Alinghi beat challengers Team New Zealand in the first race of their defence of the America's Cup.

* Boxing's Ricky Hatton knocked out challenger Jose Luis Castillo in Las Vegas in their IBO world light-welterweight championship fight.

24. Derek Dougan, former PFA chairman and Wolverhampton Wanderers and Northern Ireland striker, died aged 69.

* Andy Murray pulled out of Wimbledon because of a wrist injury.

25. Tim Henman's match with Spain's Carlos Moya on the opening day at Wimbledon was suspended at two sets all and 5–5 in the final set.

* Thierry Henry completed his £16.1 million move from Arsenal to Barcelona.

26. In one of the most exciting games ever seen at Wimbledon, Tim Henman defeated Carlos Moya 6–3, 1–6, 5–7, 6–2, 13–11 to reach the second round.

27. The Copa America kicked-off in Venezuela.

28. After his first-round heroics, Tim Henman was involved in another five-set thriller at Wimbledon. In round two, however, he lost in five sets to another Spaniard, Feliciano Lopez.

* Spanish league champions Real Madrid sacked coach Fabio Capello.

29. Tottenham Hotspur signed Charlton Athletic's 23-year-old England striker Darren Bent for a club record £16.5m.

* Team New Zealand's boat blew a spinnaker allowing Team Alinghi to go ahead 3–2 in the America's Cup.

30. Valentino Rossi (Yamaha) won the Dutch MotoGP after starting from 11th place on the grid.

* In Melbourne, Australia beat New Zealand 20–15 in the rugby union Tri-Nations.

July 2007

_1._ In F1, Ferrari's Kimi Raikkonen won the French Grand Prix at Magny-Cours with team-mate Felipe Massa second and Lewis Hamilton third.
 * England's Graeme Storm claimed his maiden European Tour title with a one-shot victory in the Open de France ALSTOM title.

_2._ A cloud of controversy shrouded the first round of qualifying for golf's 2007 Open Championship when eight players had to replay the fourth hole after the pin was repositioned at Sunningdale.

_3._ Sheffield United lost their appeal against relegation from the Premiership.

_4._ Liverpool signed 23-year-old Fernando Torres from Atletico Madrid.
 * In F1, McLaren were at the centre of an alleged spy row involving one of their senior employees and a member of the Ferrari team.

_5._ In rugby union, Bob Carruthers, the owner of Edinburgh, claimed that the Scottish Rugby Union threatened to close down Edinburgh if the club went ahead with court action against the Union for outstanding monies Carruthers said the club was owed.

_6._ Roger Federer, Rafael Nadal, Novak Djokovic and Richard Gasquet made it through to the Wimbledon semi-finals. Meanwhile, Venus Williams and Marion Bartoli will play in the women's final.

_7._ Venus Williams won her fourth Wimbledon women's singles title. She beat France's Marion Bartoli 6–4, 6–1.

_8._ Roger Federer equalled Bjorn Borg's record of five successive Wimbledon men's singles titles, beating Rafael Nadal in an epic five-set final.

• Jamie Murray became the first British champion at Wimbledon for 20 years, winning the mixed doubles with Jelena Jankovic.

_9._ Thomas Daley, a 13-year-old schoolboy from Plymouth, won two titles at the Senior National Diving Championships in Sheffield.

_10._ Great Britain's Marlon Devonish set a new 100m lifetime best of 10.06 seconds at the Lausanne Super Grand Prix, placing him sixth on the UK all-time list.

_11._ England striker David Nugent was transferred from Preston North End to Portsmouth for £6m.

_12._ F1 supremo Bernie Ecclestone announced that there will not be a 2008 US Grand Prix.

_13._ David Beckham was unveiled as a LA Galaxy player at the Home Depot Center, the home of the Californian Major League Soccer team.

_14._ Amir Khan got off the canvas to win the Commonwealth lightweight title, forcing his Scottish opponent Willie Limond to retire with a broken jaw at London's 02 Arena.

_15._ France's Gregory Havret beat Phil Mickelson in a sudden death play-off to win golf's Barclays Scottish Open at Loch Lomond.

_16._ The IAAF warned South African Paralympian, Oscar Pistorius, "to calm down" after the double-amputee accused athletics' governing body of "stuffing-up" his season. The controversy surrounds the blades used by Pistorius and he could be banned from competing at the 2008 Beijing Olympics if the IAAF decides his blades give him an unfair advantage over his competitors.

17. Carlos Tevez's transfer to Manchester United was hampered by the refusal of West Ham to sanction the Argentinean's required medical, pending the resolution of a dispute between the two clubs over his registration as a player.

18. On the eve of the 136th Open at Carnoustie, Gary Player reopened the debate about drug-taking in golf, claiming that performance-enhancing substances were a fact of life on the professional circuit. He alleged that at least ten current players were using steroids or other body-building chemical compounds.

19. Michael Rasmussen, the overall leader of the Tour de France after Stage 11, was dropped by the Danish Cycling Union from Denmark's cycling team for the World Championships in September 2007 and the 2008 Beijing Olympic Games after receiving several warnings for missing drugs tests.

20. Britain's Jenson Button and Rubens Barrichello of Brazil were confirmed as Honda's drivers for the 2008 Formula One campaign.

21. In the Tour de France, Alexandre Vinokourov clawed his way back into contention to win the overall yellow jersey after winning the 54km individual time trial on Stage 13.

22. Padraig Harrington won the 136th Open Championship at Carnoustie defeating Sergio Garcia in a four-hole play-off.

23. England were a single wicket away from beating India in the first Test at Lord's when bad light and rain forced a draw with England on 298 & 282 and India needing 98 runs to win on 201 & 282–9.

24. The International Rugby Board announced that the 2011 Rugby Union World Cup will be held at Auckland's Eden Park in New Zealand.

25. Christian Prudhomme, director of the Tour de France, stated that professional cycling needed a complete overhaul following Alexandre Vinokourov's positive test for blood doping, the latest of several recent drugs scandal to rock the sport.

26. Denmark's Michael Rasmussen, the yellow jersey leader of the Tour de France, was sacked by his Rabobank team and withdrawn from the Tour. Alberto Contador (Discovery Channel) took over the *maillot jaune*. British rider Bradley Wiggins' Tour was also over when his Cofidis team withdrew because his team-mate, Cristian Moreni, failed a drugs test.

27. F1 announced that the 2008 season will comprise 18 Grands Prix, including two new street races in Valencia, Spain, and Singapore.
   • Former British heavyweight boxer James Oyebola died after his life-support machine was switched off. He was shot in the head after a row at a bar on 23 July.

28. Ricky Hatton's father Ray confirmed that a deal had been struck "in principle" for his son to fight Floyd Mayweather later in 2007.

29. Spain's Alberto Contador (Discovery Channel) won the Tour de France at his first attempt.

30. Justin Gatlin attended a two-day hearing he requested trying to get his eight-year doping ban reduced.

31. India beat England by 7 wickets in the second Test at Trent Bridge.

August

1. The British Racing Drivers' Club announced a £25m redevelopment of their Silverstone circuit.

   * James Toseland announced that he was switching from World Superbikes to ride for Yamaha's Tech 3 team in next year's MotoGP Championship.

2. Newcastle United's Joey Barton was charged with assault after an alleged training ground bust-up with a former Manchester City team-mate.

   • Newcastle bought striker Alan Smith from Manchester United for £6 million.

3. British teams were given tough draws in the third qualifying round of the UEFA Champions League; Liverpool drew Toulouse, Arsenal drew Sparta Prague and Celtic, the Scottish champions, face Spartak Moscow.

4. The Football League allowed Leeds United to play in League One in 2007–08, granting the club their Football League Share. But they will start the season with a 15-point deduction after the club failed to agree a Company Voluntary Arrangement (CVA).

   * The Scottish League season kicked-off with Rangers beating Inverness CT 3–0 away. Gretna, in their first ever season in the SPL, lost 4–0 to Falkirk at their temporary Motherwell home.

   * Fernando Alonso (McLaren-Mercedes) was fastest in qualifying for the Hungarian Grand Prix but was stripped of his pole position after he had deliberately delayed team-mate Lewis Hamilton's exit from the pits.

5. Lewis Hamilton (McLaren-Mercedes) won his third Grand Prix of the season, the Hungarian.

   • Manchester United drew 1–1 with Chelsea in the FA Community Shield, then won the penalty shootout 3–0.

* Mexico's Lorena Ochoa won the Women's British Open Championship at the Old Course, St Andrews.

6. Lewis Hamilton admitted that his relationship with team-mate, Fernando Alonso, had hit rock-bottom after the Briton won the Hungarian Grand Prix.

7. In baseball, Barry Bonds of the San Francisco Giants hit his 756th home run to break the all-time Major League record set by Henry Aaron in 1974.

8. The countdown to the 2008 Olympic Games in Beijing began with the Games exactly one year away – 63 official events took place across China.

9. The 2007 USPGA Championship got under way at the Southern Hills Country Club, Tulsa, Oklahoma.

   * In a repeat of the 2007 World Snooker final, Mark Selby got his revenge over John Higgins beating him 5–3 in the Shanghai Masters.

10. Carlos Tevez finally joined Manchester United.

11. The 2007–08 Premiership season kicked off with new boys Sunderland briefly topping the table with a 1–0 home win over Tottenham Hotspur.

12. Manchester United opened their Premier League title defence with a 0–0 against Reading at Old Trafford.

    * Tiger Woods won the USPGA Championship, his 13th Major.

13. On the fifth day of the third NPower Test at The Oval, India (664 & 180–6 dec) drew with England (345 & 369–6) and won the series 1–0.

14. Thailand's Supreme Court issued an arrest warrant for Thaksin Shinawatra after the country's former president – and new owner of Manchester City – failed to attend court in Bangkok to answer corruption charges.

15. Steve McClaren's attempts to persuade Liverpool's Jamie Carragher to reverse his decision not to play any more international football failed.
• David Beckham scored on his debut for LA Galaxy with a trademark free-kick in a 2–0 victory over DC United in the SuperLiga semi-final.

16. Kieron Dyer joined West Ham United from Newcastle United.

17. Doncaster Racecourse, closed in 2005 for a total revamp, reopened following a £32m facelift.

18. Paula Radcliffe engaged the services of pollution experts to assist her quest to win the gold medal in the marathon at the 2008 Olympic Games in Beijing.

19. Durham claimed their first major success with a 125-run win over Hampshire in the Friends Provident Trophy final at Lord's.

20. In his autobiography David Coulthard revealed he suffered from bulimia when he was a teenager trying to break into Formula One.
* Referee Rob Styles was notified he would not be officiating in the Premier League next weekend after awarding Chelsea a controversial penalty in their 1–1 draw with Liverpool the day before.

21. Gabriel Heinze lost his case before a Premier League arbitration panel to force Manchester United to allow him to move to rivals Liverpool.
• The BMW Sauber Formula One team announced that they will retain the services of Nick Heidfeld and Robert Kubica for the 2008 season.
• Sweden's Christian Olsson, the Olympic triple jump champion, was forced to withdraw from the 2007 World Championships in Osaka, Japan, after tearing his left hamstring.

22. Sevilla coach Juande Ramos said he rejected an approach by Tottenham Hotspur to take over as boss even though Martin Jol was still in post.
* At a meeting of the IAAF Congress in Osaka, Japan, Lord Sebastian Coe was elected a vice-president.

23. Tim Henman announced his retirement from professional tennis after Great Britain's Davis Cup tie with Croatia at Wimbledon in September 2007.

24. In F1, McLaren team-mates Lewis Hamilton and Fernando Alonso held "clear the air" peace talks.

25. The IAAF World Championships got under way in Osaka, Japan.
* The NFL gave one of its biggest stars, Atlanta Falcons quarterback Michael Vick, an indefinite suspension without pay after he pleaded guilty to being involved in a dog-fighting operation.
* The World Rowing Championships began in Munich, Germany.

26. Kelly Sotherton won bronze in the heptathlon – Great Britain's first medal at the World Athletics Championships.
• Felipe Massa (Ferrari) won the Turkish GP, his third win of 2007.

27. The US Open tennis tournament opened at Flushing Meadows, New York.

28. Manchester United's Ole Gunnar Solskjaer announced his retirement from football.

29. Christine Ohuruogu claimed Britain's first World Athletics Championships gold medal in the women's 400m. Team-mate Nicola Sanders took silver.

30. Sri Lanka's inspirational spinner, Muttiah Muralitharan, withdrew from the inaugural ICC World Twenty20 tournament with an elbow injury.

31. AC Milan won their fifth UEFA Super Cup, defeating Sevilla 3–1 in Monaco.

Football Review 2006–2007

Premier League	50
FA Community Shield	53
Champions League	54
UEFA Cup	58
Coca Cola Championship	60
Division 1	62
Division 2	64
FA Cup	66
Carling Cup	68
Nationwide Conference	70
Non-League Football	72
Scottish Premier League	74
Scottish League Division 1	76
Scottish League Division 2	77
Scottish League Division 3	78
Scottish FA Cup	79
CIS Cup	80
Scottish Challenge Cup	81
Welsh League	82
Northern Ireland	83
Republic of Ireland	84
Women's Football	85
European Football	86
Euro 2008 Qualifiers	88
Managerial Merry-go-round	92
Transfer News	96
U21 European Championship	98
Asian Cup	99
FIFA U-20 World Cup	100
Copa America	102
The New Wembley Stadium	104
Celebrity News	106

Premier League 2006–07

Chelsea went into the 2006–07 season as the reigning Premiership champions and hoping to equal the feat achieved by Manchester United in 1999, 2000 and 2001, by claiming their third consecutive title. Over the summer both the London team and United had strengthened their squads with Chelsea splashing out big on Andriy Schevchenko (£30m), John Obi Mikel (£16m) and Ashley Cole (£5m plus William Gallas). Michael Ballack arrived at the Bridge on a free transfer from Bayern Munich, although his wage bill for the season unquestionably dwarfed the total transfer spend of many English league clubs. Meanwhile, the Old Trafford outfit added Michael Carrick to their midfield in a £16m transfer from Tottenham Hotspur.

In the end, the season came down to a two-horse race for the title between the blue of Chelsea and the red of United, while Arsenal and Liverpool fought it out for third and fourth places. Beneath the top four places a host of teams fought it out for a UEFA Cup berth next season, while the usual scrap took place at the foot of the table involving two of the three promoted clubs, Sheffield United and Watford. The surprise package of the season came in the shape of Steve Coppell's unfashionable Reading side. They acquited themselves well in their first season in the top flight, finishing a highly respectable eighth, just missing out on European football in season 2007–08. Indeed, Coppell was voted the Manager of the Season by the League Managers' Association.

United came out of the traps early and by October they were top of the table with Chelsea hot on their tail. A sticky winter saw Chelsea drop points in vital games but in the end it was United's consistent performances (they won four games more than Chelsea), harnessed by the dazzling displays of Cristiano Ronaldo, that won United their first title in four seasons and their ninth FA Premier League crown. Chelsea finished six points behind the champions to claim the second automatic 2007–08 UEFA Champions League spot, while Liverpool pipped Arsenal for third place (both clubs going into the Champions League preliminary round). As Chelsea won both the Carling (League) Cup and the FA Cup, it meant that Spurs (fifth), Everton (sixth) and Bolton Wanderers (seventh) all claimed UEFA Cup places for the 2007–08 season. Blackburn Rovers (tenth) qualified for the Intertoto Cup as the highest-placed team who applied for the competition but who failed to earn an automatic UEFA Cup spot, as neither Reading (eighth) or Portsmouth (ninth) applied. Aston Villa missed out on a place in the UEFA Cup via the European Fair Play League draw. Their name was placed in the hat by virtue of Spurs, the 2006–07 FA Premier League Fair Play winners, already having qualified for the competition, but Villa missed out, losing to the representatives from Finland and Norway.

West Ham United, who controversially signed Argentine internationals Carlos Tevez and Javier Mascherano from Corinthians, of Brazil, a deal brokered by Media Sports Invetments (MSI), their management company, left it late to escape from the relegation zone. However, the registrations contravened FA Premier League regulations, and the Hammers were fined £5m. A three-point penalty, demanded by many clubs, would have seen them drop instead of Sheffield United, who joined Charlton and Watford in going down.

Meanwhile, Premiership salaries and bonuses are set to exceed the £1b barrier next season for the first time in the Premier League's history when the new £1.7b television deal for top-flight games comes into effect.

Premier League Championship

Pos	Team	P	W	D	L	GF	GA	Pts
1.	**Manchester United**	38	28	5	5	83	27	89
2.	Chelsea	38	24	11	3	64	24	83
3.	Liverpool	38	20	8	10	57	27	68
4.	Arsenal	38	19	11	8	63	35	68
5.	Tottenham Hotspur	38	17	9	12	57	54	60
6.	Everton	38	15	13	10	52	36	58
7.	Bolton Wanderers	38	16	8	14	47	52	56
8.	Reading	38	16	7	15	52	47	55
9.	Portsmouth	38	14	12	12	45	42	54
10.	Blackburn Rovers	38	15	7	16	52	54	52
11.	Aston Villa	38	11	17	10	43	41	50
12.	Middlesbrough	38	12	10	16	44	49	46
13.	Newcastle United	38	11	10	17	38	47	43
14.	Manchester City	38	11	9	18	29	44	42
15.	West Ham United	38	12	5	21	35	59	41
16.	Fulham	38	8	15	15	38	60	39
17.	Wigan Athletic	38	10	8	20	37	59	38
18.	Sheffield United	38	10	8	20	32	55	38
19.	Charlton Athletic	38	8	10	20	34	60	34
20.	Watford	38	5	13	20	29	59	28

Premiership Top Scorers

Player	Team	Goals
Didier Drogba	Chelsea	20
Benni McCarthy	Blackburn Rovers	18
Cristiano Ronaldo	Manchester Utd	17
Wayne Rooney	Manchester Utd	14
Mark Viduka	Middlesbrough	14
Darren Bent	Charlton Athletic	13
Kevin Doyle	Reading	13
Dimitar Berbatov	Tottenham H	12
Dirk Kuyt	Liverpool	12
Ayegbeni Yakubu	Middlesbrough	12
Nicolas Anelka	Bolton Wanderers	11
Andy Johnson	Everton	11
Robbie Keane	Tottenham H	11
Frank Lampard	Chelsea	11
Obafemi Martins	Newcastle Utd	11
Robin Van Persie	Arsenal	11
Bobby Zamora	West Ham Utd	11

Premiership Attendances

Highest Attendance
76,098 (Old Trafford)   31 March 2007
Manchester United v Blackburn Rovers

Lowest Attendance
13,760 (Vicarage Road)   23 January 2007
Watford v Blackburn Rovers

Trivia

* On 14 October 2006, Chelsea goalkeepers Petr Cech and Carlo Cudicini both sustained head injuries during their match against Reading. Cech underwent surgery for a depressed skull fracture while Cudicini was treated and discharged that evening.

* Manchester United won their ninth FA Premier League title to make it 16 top flight championships, trailing Liverpool's record of 18 titles.

* Season 2006–07 was Reading's first season in top flight football in their 135-year history. The Royals won their inaugural Premiership game, beating Middlesbrough 3–2.

* The 1–1 draw between Tottenham Hotspur and Blackburn Rovers at White Hart Lane on 10 May 2007 was the 1,000th live game to be shown by SKY Sports.

* On 2 August 2006, Ken Bates the Leeds chairman and former chairman of Chelsea, reported the London club to the Football Association, the FA Premier League and FIFA over the alleged tapping up of three Leeds United youth team players.

* On 19 September 2006, Randy Lerner replaced 82-year-old Doug Ellis as the chairman of Aston Villa.

* In September 2006, a BBC *Panorama* programme was shown on television, alleging widespread corruption in the English game.

* When Manchester City lost 1–0 at home to Manchester United on 5 May 2007, they set a new record for the fewest goals scored at home in a season by a club in the top flight – a meagre 10. City had not scored at home since New Year's Day 2007.

* Following Watford's relegation from the Premier League, the club handed Aidy Boothroyd a new three-year contract.

GOLDEN BOOT WINNER

1. Didier Drogba............Chelsea......................20 goals
2. Benni McCarthy.......Blackburn Rovers.............18 goals
3. Cristiano Ronaldo.....Manchester United..........17 goals

Drogba was the first Chelsea player to win the award since Jimmy Floyd Hasselbaink claimed it in 2001.

> "It would be nice to get to ten (league titles), but it would be nicer to get to 11."
>
> **Ryan Giggs,** *winner of a record nine Premier League titles.*

PREMIERSHIP BESTS AND WORSTS 2006–07

Biggest win – Reading 6–0 West Ham Utd	**Highest agg** – Arsenal 6–2 Blackburn R
Most goals for – Manchester United 83	**Fewest goals for** – Man City, Watford 29
Most goals against – Fulham, Charlton 60	**Fewest goals against** – Chelsea 24
Most wins – Manchester United 28	**Fewest defeats** – Chelsea 3
Fewest wins – Watford 5	**Most defeats** – West Ham Utd 21
Most draws – Fulham 15	**Fewest draws** – Man Utd, West Ham 5

FA Community Shield

5 August 2007, Wembley Stadium, London

Manchester United won thanks to a marvellous hat-trick of saves in the penalty shootout by Edwin Van der Sar, after the match finished 1–1. Ryan Giggs, making his tenth Shield appearance, opened the scoring in the 35th minute but Chelsea's new French striker, Florent Malouda, levelled matters on the stroke of half-time. Rio Ferdinand, Michael Carrick and Wayne Rooney were the only players to score from the spot.

Chelsea 1 – 1 Manchester United
Malouda 45'   *Giggs 35'*
(United won 3–0 on penalties)

Chelsea: Cech, Johnson *(Sidwell 78)*, Carvalho, Ben Haim, Ashley Cole *(Diarra 67)*, Wright-Phillips, Essien, Mikel, Lampard, Malouda *(Pizarro 51)*, Joe Cole *(Sinclair 82)*
Subs not used: Cudicini, Hilario, Worley
Booked: Ben Haim, Carvalho, Mikel

Manchester United: Van der Sar, Brown, Vidic, Ferdinand, Evra, Ronaldo, Carrick, O'Shea, Silvestre *(Nani 68)*, Giggs *(Fletcher 81)*, Rooney
Subs not used: Kuszczak, Pique, Bardsley, Martin, Eagles
Booked: Rooney
Att: *80,731*

Trivia

* United won the inaugural FA Charity Shield in 1908.

* Manchester United have played in 24 of the 99 Shields, winning 16 (12 outright and 4 shared) while Ryan Giggs won his sixth winner's medal to equal Ray Clemence's record (five with Liverpool and one with Tottenham Hotspur).

* United drew 1–1 with Chelsea in the 1997 Charity Shield at the "old" Wembley and went on to win 4–2 in the penalty shootout.

"That was a little bit of revenge after we lost to Chelsea in the FA Cup Final."
Edwin van der Sar, *Manchester United's goalkeeping hero at Wembley*

"We controlled the game against the champions so why should we be afraid of the future?"
Jose Mourinho, *Chelsea manager*

UEFA Champions League 2006–07

The 52nd edition of the now-named UEFA Champions League was thrown into chaos with the scandal in Italy. Juventus and Fiorentina were expelled, while Milan were forced to go through the qualifying stages. Former champions Ajax and Red Star Belgrade missed out on the group stages, but once the competition started it was clear that the "usual suspects" would all reach the last 16. Lyon and Bayern Munich were both unbeaten through the group stage. Celtic became the first Scottish club to advance, courtesy of a dramatic win over co-qualifiers Manchester United at Celtic Park. Benfica missed out. Barcelona had a fright, reaching the last 16 only by beating Werder Bremen in their final match. All four English clubs reached the last 16 and they all topped their groups too.

Champions League Group Results

Group A

Chelsea	2–0	Werder Bremen	Barcelona	5–0	Levski Sofia
Levski Sofia	1–3	Chelsea	Werder Bremen	1–1	Barcelona
Werder Bremen	2–0	Levski Sofia	Chelsea	1–0	Barcelona
Levski Sofia	0–3	Werder Bremen	Barcelona	2–2	Chelsea
Werder Bremen	1–0	Chelsea	Levski Sofia	0–2	Barcelona
Chelsea	2–0	Levski Sofia	Barcelona	2–0	Werder Bremen

Group B

Sporting Lisbon	1–0	Internazionale	Bayern Munich	4–0	Spartak Moskva
Spartak Moscow	1–1	Sporting Lisbon	Internazionale	0–2	Bayern Munich
Internazionale	2–1	Spartak Moscow	Sporting Lisbon	0–1	Bayern Munich
Spartak Moscow	0–1	Internazionale	Bayern Munich	0–0	Sporting Lisbon
Internazionale	1–0	Sporting Lisbon	Spartak Moskva	2–2	Bayern Munich
Sporting Lisbon	1–3	Spartak Moscow	Bayern Munich	1–1	Internazionale

Group C

Galatasaray	0–0	Bordeaux	PSV Eindhoven	0–0	Liverpool
Liverpool	3–2	Galatasaray	Bordeaux	0–1	PSV Eindhoven
Bordeaux	0–1	Liverpool	Galatasaray	1–2	PSV Eindhoven
Liverpool	3–0	Bordeaux	PSV Eindhoven	2–0	Galatasaray
Bordeaux	3–1	Galatasaray	Liverpool	2–0	PSV Eindhoven
Galatasaray	3–2	Liverpool	PSV Eindhoven	1–3	Bordeaux

Group D

Roma	4–0	Shakhtar Donetsk	Olympiakos	2–4	Valencia
Shakhtar Donetsk	2–2	Olympiakos	Valencia	2–1	Roma
Valencia	2–0	Shakhtar Donetsk	Olympiakos	0–1	Roma
Shakhtar Donetsk	2–2	Valencia	Roma	1–1	Olympiakos
Valencia	2–0	Olympiakos	Shakhtar Donetsk	1–0	Roma
Olympiakos	1–1	Shakhtar Donetsk	Roma	1–0	Valencia

Group E

Dynamo Kyiv	1–4	Steaua Bucharest
Real Madrid	5–1	Dynamo Kyiv
Steaua Bucharest	1–4	Real Madrid
Real Madrid	1–0	Steaua Bucharest
Steaua Bucharest	1–1	Dynamo Kyiv
Dynamo Kyiv	2–2	Real Madrid

Lyon	2–0	Real Madrid
Steaua Bucharest	0–3	Lyon
Dynamo Kyiv	0–3	Lyon
Lyon	1–0	Dynamo Kyiv
Real Madrid	2–2	Lyon
Lyon	1–1	Steaua Bucharest

Group F

Manchester Utd	3–2	Celtic
Benfica	0–1	Manchester Utd
Celtic	3–0	Benfica
Benfica	3–0	Celtic
Celtic	1–0	Manchester Utd
Manchester Utd	3–1	Benfica

Copenhagen	0–0	Benfica
Celtic	1–0	Copenhagen
Manchester Utd	3–0	Copenhagen
Copenhagen	1–0	Manchester Utd
Benfica	3–1	Copenhagen
Copenhagen	3–1	Celtic

Group G

Porto	0–0	CSKA Moscow
Arsenal	2–0	Porto
CSKA Moscow	1–0	Arsenal
Arsenal	0–0	CSKA Moscow
CSKA Moscow	0–2	Porto
Porto	0–0	Arsenal

Hamburg	1–2	Arsenal
CSKA Moscow	1–0	Hamburg
Porto	4–1	Hamburg
Hamburg	1–3	Porto
Arsenal	3–1	Hamburg
Hamburg	3–2	CSKA Moscow

Group H

Anderlecht	1–1	Lille
AEK Athens	1–1	Anderlecht
Lille	3–1	AEK Athens
AEK Athens	1–0	Lille
Lille	2–2	Anderlecht
Anderlecht	2–2	AEK Athens

Milan	3–0	AEK Athens
Lille	0–0	Milan
Anderlecht	0–1	Milan
Milan	4–1	Anderlecht
AEK Athens	1–0	Milan
Milan	0–2	Lille

Champions League Group Tables

Pos	Team	Pts	
Group A			
1.	Chelsea	13	*Qualify*
2.	Barcelona	11	*Qualify*
3.	Werder Bremen	10	*UEFA Cup*
4.	Levski Sofia	0	

Pos	Team	Pts	
Group C			
1.	Liverpool	13	*Qualify*
2.	PSV Eindhoven	10	*Qualify*
3.	Bordeaux	7	*UEFA Cup*
4.	Galatasaray	4	

Pos	Team	Pts	
Group B			
1.	Bayern Munich	12	*Qualify*
2.	Internazionale	10	*Qualify*
3.	Spartak Moscow	5	*UEFA Cup*
4.	Sporting Lisbon	5	

Pos	Team	Pts	
Group D			
1.	Valencia	13	*Qualify*
2.	Roma	10	*Qualify*
3.	Shakhtar Donetsk	6	*UEFA Cup*
4.	Olympiakos	3	

Champions League continued ...

Champions League Group Tables cont.

Pos	Team	Pts		Pos	Team	Pts	
Group E				**Group G**			
1.	Lyon	14	*Qualify*	1.	Arsenal	11	*Qualify*
2.	Real Madrid	11	*Qualify*	2.	Porto	11	*Qualify*
3.	Steaua Bucharest	5	*UEFA Cup*	3.	CSKA Moscow	8	*UEFA Cup*
4.	Dynamo Kyiv	2		4.	Hamburg	3	
Group F				**Group H**			
1.	Manchester United	12	*Qualify*	1.	Milan	10	*Qualify*
2.	Celtic	9	*Qualify*	2.	Lille	9	*Qualify*
3.	Benfica	7	*UEFA Cup*	3.	AEK Athens	8	*UEFACup*
4.	Copenhagen	7		4.	Anderlecht	4	

Champions League Knockout Stages

Manchester United produced the performance of the knockout rounds, thrashing Roma 7–1 in the quarter-final second leg. Liverpool ended Chelsea's hopes, on penalties, in the semi-final. There would not be an all-English final as Milan beat United 5–3 at the same stage.

ROUND OF 16

First Leg	*Second Leg*	*Result*
Celtic 0–0 Milan	Milan 1–0 Celtic	Milan 1–0
PSV Eindhoven 1–0 Arsenal	Arsenal 1–1 PSV	PSV 2–1
Lille 0–1 Manchester United	Man Utd 1–0 Lille	Man Utd 2–0
Real Madrid 3–2 Bayern Munich	Munich 2–1 R Madrid	Munich 4–4 *(away gls)*
Porto 1–1 Chelsea	Chelsea 2–1 Porto	Chelsea 3–2
Internazionale 2–2 Valencia	Valencia 0–0 Inter	Inter 2–2 *(away gls)*
Barcelona 1–2 Liverpool	Liverpool 0–1 Barcelona	Liverpool 2–2 *(away gls)*
AS Roma 2–0 Lyon	Lyon 1–1 Roma	Roma 3–2

QUARTER-FINALS

First Leg	*Second Leg*	*Result*
Milan 2–2 Bayern Munich	Munich 0–2 Milan	Milan 4–2
PSV Eindhoven 0–3 Liverpool	Liverpool 1–0 PSV	Liverpool 4–0
Roma 2–1 Manchester United	Man Utd 7–1 Roma	Man Utd 8–3
Chelsea 1–1 Valencia	Valencia 1–2 Chelsea	Chelsea 3–2

SEMI-FINALS

First Leg	*Second Leg*	*Result*
Chelsea 1–0 Liverpool	Liverpool 1–0 Chelsea	Liverpool 1–1 *(4–1p)*
Manchester United 3–2 Milan	Milan 3–0 Man Utd	Milan 5–3

UEFA Champions League Final

23 May 2007, Olympic Stadium, Athens, Greece

Milan's seventh Champions League success, leaving them just two behind Real Madrid and two clear of Liverpool, was certainly their most controversial, albeit for the off-field decisions in the courts. They had to come through a qualifying round but, once they were in the group stages, their path to glory opened up nicely.

By winning in Athens, the *Rossoneri* avenged their 2005 Istanbul nightmare against Liverpool. The match was something of a mirror image of the 2005 final but without the incredible drama. Liverpool were clearly the better, more fluid team and they should have won, but their inability to convert good chances throughout the 90 minutes proved fatal.

Three good openings had already gone begging when Milan struck, moments before half-time. Liverpool conceded a silly free-kick close to their penalty area when Kaka was knocked over. Andrea Pirlo drove the ball towards the defensive wall where a couple of Milan players had also congregated. The ball struck Filippo Inzaghi, probably on the hand, and bounced past the wrong-footed Pepe Reina in the Liverpool goal.

In the second half, Liverpool again set the pace, but they could not get the equalizer. It was not until 12 minutes from time that Peter Crouch was introduced, taking over from Javier Mascherano. Reds manager Rafa Benitez was criticized after the match for not changing the Liverpool system when they were behind, but he argued that he had wanted to keep Kaka quiet, a job Mascherano had done very well. And, four minutes after Crouch had come on, Kaka, in much more space than previously, delievered a slide-rule pass into the path of Inzaghi, whose finish was clinical. In the final couple of minutes, Dirk Kuyt reduced the arrears, but it was too late.

Milan 2 – 1 Liverpool
Inzaghi 45' 82'   Kuyt 89'

Milan: Dida, Oddo, Nesta, Maldini, Jankulovski *(Kaladze 79)*, Gattuso, Pirlo, Ambrosini, Seedorf *(Favalli 90)*, Kaka, Inzaghi *(Gilardino 88)*
Subs not used: Kalac, Cafu, Serginho, Brocchi
Booked: Gattuso, Jankulovski

Liverpool: Reina, Finnan *(Arbeloa 88)*, Carragher, Agger, Riise, Pennant, Alonso, Mascherano *(Crouch 78)*, Zenden *(Kewell 59)*, Gerrard, Kuyt
Subs not used: Dudek, Hyypia, Gonzalez, Bellamy
Booked: Mascherano, Carragher
Att: *74,000*

"The defeat two years ago will stay with me for a lifetime, but this is a different story. It's our turn to celebrate now.**"**
Gennaro Gattuso

"I've scored quite a few times in Europe, but scoring in the Champions League final is something special.**"**
Pippo Inzaghi

UEFA Cup 2006–07

The 2006–07 UEFA Cup was the 49th edition of the competition. Unfortunately, events off the field took the shine off the fine feat of Sevilla in retaining the Cup. The Italian entry changed as a result of the match-fixing scandal, while the Greek FA was temporarily suspended by UEFA putting their clubs' participation in jeopardy. When the competition got under way, serious crowd trouble in a group match against Nancy resulted in Feyenoord being expelled. Meanwhile Parma and Livorno played their last 32 matches behind closed doors after the Italian government removed safety certificates from clubs following the murder of a police officer in a Serie A match. Three out of four semi-finalists were Spanish, with Sevilla and Espanyol seeing off Osasuna and Werder Bremen, respectively.

UEFA Cup Group Tables

Group A

Pos	Team	Pts
1.	Glasgow Rangers	10
2.	Maccabi Haifa	7
3.	Livorno	5
4.	Auxerre	4
5.	Partizan Belgrade	1

Group B

Pos	Team	Pts
1.	Tottenham Hotspur	12
2.	Dinamo Bucharest	7
3.	Bayer Leverkusen	4
4.	Besiktas	3
5.	Club Brugge	2

Group C

Pos	Team	Pts
1.	AZ Alkmaar	10
2.	Sevilla	7
3.	Braga	6
4.	Liberec	5
5.	Grasshoppers	0

Group D

Pos	Team	Pts
1.	Parma	9
2.	Osasuna	7
3.	Lens	4
4.	Odense BK	4
5.	Heerenveen	4

Group E

Pos	Team	Pts
1.	Blackburn Rovers	10
2.	AS Nancy	7
3.	Feyenoord	5
4.	Wisla Krakow	3
5.	Basle	2

Group F

Pos	Team	Pts
1.	Espanyol	12
2.	Ajax	7
3.	Zulte-Waregem	6
4.	Sparta Prague	4
5.	Austria Magna	0

Group G

Pos	Team	Pts
1.	Panathinaikos	7
2.	Paris Saint-Germain	5
3.	Hapoel Tel-Aviv	5
4.	Rapid Bucharest	4
5.	Mlada Boleslav	3

Group H

Pos	Team	Pts
1.	Newcastle United	10
2.	Celta Vigo	5
3.	Fenerbahce	4
4.	Palermo	4
5.	Eintracht Frankfurt	3

Knockout Stages

ROUND OF 32 *(two legs)*

Zulte-Waregem 1–4 Newcastle United * Sporting Braga 2–0 Parma*
Lens 3–1 Panathinaikos * Bayer Leverkusen 3–2 Blackburn Rovers
Hapoel Tel-Aviv 2–5 Glasgow Rangers * Livorno* 1–4 Espanyol
Fenerbahçe 5–5 AZ *(away goals)* * Werder Bremen** 4–3 Ajax
Spartak Moscow** 2–3 Celta Vigo * CSKA Moscow** 0–1 Maccabi Haifa
AEK Athens** 0–4 Paris Saint-Germain * Benfica** 3–1 Dinamo Bucharest
Steaua Bucharest** 0–3 Sevilla * Shakhtar Donetsk** 2–1 AS Nancy
Bordeaux** 0–1 Osasuna*(aet)* Feyenoord*** * N/A Tottenham Hotspur

Played their home legs behind closed doors. ** *Third place finisher in UEFA Champions League group.*
*** *Ejected from competition by UEFA.*

ROUND OF 16 *(two legs)*

Newcastle United 4–4 AZ Alkmaar *(away goals)* * Maccabi Haifa 0–4 Espanyol
Glasgow Rangers 1–2 Osasuna * Sporting Braga 4–6 Tottenham Hotspur
Sevilla 5–4 Shakhtar Donetsk *(aet)* * Lens 2–4 Bayer Leverkusen
Paris Saint-Germain 3–4 Benfica * Celta Vigo 0–3 Werder Bremen

QUARTER-FINALS *(two legs)*

AZ Alkmaar 1–4 Werder Bremen * Bayer Leverkusen 0–4 Osasuna
Sevilla 4–3 Tottenham Hotspur * Espanyol 3–2 Benfica

SEMI-FINALS *(two legs)*

Espanyol 5–1 Werder Bremen * Osasuna 1–2 Sevilla

Final – 16 May 2006, Hampden Park, Glasgow

Sevilla retained the UEFA Cup with a 3–1 penalty shootout win over FCD Espanyol after the sides drew 2–2 after extra time. It was an epic final contested between the two La Liga teams, but in the end Sevilla matched Real Madrid's (1985 and 1986) feat to successfully defend the UEFA Cup. Adriano put the holders in front before Alberto Riera drew Espanyol level with a deflected shot. When Espanyol's Moises Hurtado was sent off for a second booking on 68 minutes, Sevilla took advantage and stretched their opponents, but the game ended 1–1. In added time at the end of the first period of extra time, the ex-West Ham United and Tottenham Hotspur striker, Freddie Kanoute, put Sevilla in front. Amazingly the ten men of Espanyol fought back and drew level at 2–2 thanks to a goal from substitute Jonatas. In the resulting penalty shootout Andres Palop saved from Luis Garcia, Jonatas and Marc Torrejon to keep Sevilla on course for a treble of La Liga, Spanish Cup and UEFA Cup.

Espanyol 2 – 2 Sevilla *(aet, Sevilla won 3–1 on penalties)*
Riera 28, Jonatas 115   *Adriano Correia 18, Kanoute 105*
Att: *50,670*   Referee: *Massimo*

Busacca (Switzerland)

Coca-Cola Championship 2006–07

Sunderland won the Coca-Cola Championship despite failing to win any of their opening five games. However, things turned around for the Black Cats after Roy Keane was appointed their manager and their season went from strength to strength under him. Keano's former Old Trafford team-mate, Steve Bruce, guided Birmingham City to runners-up spot and promotion to the Premier League, while Derby County claimed the third promotion place after defeating West Bromwich Albion 1–0 in the play-off final at the new Wembley. Leeds United finished bottom of the table to slide into Football League Division One, with Southend United joining them after two previously successful seasons that earned them successive promotions. Luton Town were also relegated in a season where they found themselves having to off-load some of their best players.

Coca-Cola Championship

Pos	Team	P	W	D	L	GF	GA	Pts
1.	**Sunderland**	46	27	7	12	67	47	88
2.	Birmingham City	46	26	8	12	61	43	86
3.	Derby County	46	25	9	12	60	35	84
4.	West Bromwich Albion	46	22	10	14	82	50	76
5.	Wolverhampton Wanderers	46	22	10	14	59	56	76
6.	Southampton	46	21	12	13	77	53	75
7.	Preston North End	46	22	8	16	64	53	74
8.	Stoke City	46	19	16	11	62	41	73
9.	Sheffield Wednesday	46	20	11	15	70	66	71
10.	Colchester United	46	20	9	17	70	56	69
11.	Plymouth Argyle	46	17	16	13	63	62	67
12.	Crystal Palace	46	18	11	17	59	51	65
13.	Cardiff City	46	17	13	16	57	53	64
14.	Ipswich Town	46	18	8	20	64	59	62
15.	Burnley	46	15	12	19	52	49	57
16.	Norwich City	46	16	9	21	56	71	57
17.	Coventry City	46	16	8	22	47	62	56
18.	Queens Park Rangers	46	14	11	21	54	68	53
19.	Leicester City	46	13	14	19	49	64	53
20.	Barnsley	46	15	5	26	53	85	50
21.	Hull City	46	13	10	23	51	67	49
22.	Southend United	46	10	12	24	47	80	42
23.	Luton Town	46	10	10	26	53	81	40
24.	Leeds United*	46	13	7	26	46	72	36

*Deducted 10 points for going into administration

Play-off Semi-finals

First leg: Southampton 1–2 Derby County
Second leg: Derby County 2–3 Southampton (4–4 on aggregate)
Result: Derby County won 4–3 on penalties after extra time

First leg: Wolverhampton Wanderers 2–3 West Bromwich Albion
Second leg: West Bromwich Albion 1–0 Wolverhampton Wanderers
Result: West Bromwich Albion won 4–2 on aggregate

Play-off Final

Wembley Stadium, Monday, 28 May 2007; Att: 74,993

Derby County 1 – 0 West Bromwich Albion
Pearson 61

Derby: Bywater, Mears, Leacock, Moore, McEveley, Fagan *(Edworthy 83)*, Oakley, Seth Johnson *(Jones 87)*, Pearson, Howard, Peschisolido *(Barnes 58)*
Subs not used: Camp, Macken
Booked: Peschisolido, Mears, Bywater, Oakley, Jones

West Brom: Kiely, McShane *(Ellington 71)*, Perry, Sodje *(Clement 81)*, Robinson, Koumas, Greening, Gera *(Carter 71)*, Koren, Kamara, Phillips
Subs not used: Daniels, Chaplow
Booked: Sodje, McShane, Perry

Coca-Cola Championship Top Scorers

Player	Team	Goals	Player	Team	Goals
Cureton	Colchester	23	Howard	Derby	16
Chopra	Cardiff	22	Lee	Ipswich	16
Kamara	West Brom	20	Nugent	Preston	15
Earnshaw	Norwich	18	Gray	Burnley	14
Iwelumo	Colchester	18	McSheffrey	Birmingham	14
Rasiak	Southampton	18			

Coca-Cola Championship Attendances

Highest Attendance
44,448 (Stadium of Light)   27 April 2007
Sunderland v Burnley

Lowest Attendance
4,249 (Layer Road)   12 August 2006
Colchester United v Barnsley

Coca-Cola Football League One 2006–07

The 2006–07 Football League Division One season saw three teams, who had all enjoyed football in higher divisions in their history, promoted to the Coca Cola Championship. Champions Scunthorpe United returned to the Championship after languishing in English football's lower divisions since the early 1960s. Bristol City returned to the second tier after almost a decade of near misses, while Blackpool beat Yeovil Town 2–0 in the play-off final at the new Wembley Stadium, to claim the third promotion place. Bradford City, who played in the FA Premier League from 1999–2001, suffered relegation to Division Two along with Brentford (finished bottom), Chesterfield and Rotherham United. An era ended at Gresty Road when it was announced that Dario Gradi would be standing down as manager of Crewe Alexandra.

Coca-Cola Football League One

Pos	Team	P	W	D	L	GF	GA	Pts
1.	**Scunthorpe United**	**46**	**26**	**13**	**7**	**73**	**35**	**91**
2.	Bristol City	46	25	10	11	63	39	85
3.	Blackpool	46	24	11	11	76	49	83
4.	Nottingham Forest	46	23	13	10	65	41	82
5.	Yeovil Town	46	23	10	13	55	39	79
6.	Oldham Athletic	46	21	12	13	69	47	75
7.	Swansea City	46	20	12	14	69	53	72
8.	Carlisle United	46	19	11	16	54	55	68
9.	Tranmere Rovers	46	18	13	15	58	53	67
10.	Millwall	46	19	9	18	59	62	66
11.	Doncaster Rovers	46	16	15	15	52	47	63
12.	Port Vale	46	18	6	22	64	65	60
13.	Crewe Alexandra	46	17	9	20	66	72	60
14.	Northampton Town	46	15	14	17	48	51	59
15.	Huddersfield Town	46	18	17	15	60	69	59
16.	Gillingham	46	17	8	21	56	77	59
17.	Cheltenham Town	46	15	9	22	49	61	54
18.	Brighton & Hove Albion	46	14	11	21	49	58	53
19.	Bournemouth	46	13	13	20	50	64	52
20.	Leyton Orient	46	12	15	19	61	77	51
21.	Chesterfield	46	12	11	23	45	53	47
22.	Bradford City	46	11	14	21	47	65	47
23.	Rotherham United*	46	13	9	24	58	75	38
24.	Brentford	46	8	13	25	40	79	37

*Deducted 10 points for going into administration

Play-off Semi-finals

First leg: Oldham Athletic 1–2 Blackpool
Second leg: Blackpool 3–1 Oldham Athletic
Result: Blackpool won 5–2 on aggregate

First leg: Yeovil Town 0–2 Nottingham Forest
Second leg: Nottingham Forest 2–5 Yeovil Town
Result: Yeovil Town won 5–4 on aggregate

Play-off Final

Wembley Stadium, 27 May 2007, Att: 59,313
Blackpool 2 – 0 Yeovil Town
Williams 43, Parker 52

Yeovil: Mildenhall, Lindegaard (Lynch 77), Forbes, Guyett, Jones, Gray, Barry, Cohen (Kalala 40), Davies, Stewart, Morris (Knights 72)
Subs not used: Skiverton, Rose
Booked: Barry, Morris

Blackpool: Rachubka, Barker, Jackson, Evatt, Williams, Forbes (Fox 78), Jorgensen, Southern, Hoolahan (Vernon 86), Parker (Gillett 90), Morrell
Subs not used: Coid, Burgess
Booked: Barker

Coca-Cola Football League One Top Scorers

Player	Team	Goals	Player	Team	Goals
Sharp	Scunthorpe	30	Maynard	Crewe	16
Constantine	Port Vale	22	Beckett	Huddersfield	15
Porter	Oldham	21	Byfield	Millwall	15
Trundle	Swansea	18	Holt	Nottm Forest	14
Greenacre	Tranmere	17	Odejayi	Cheltenham	13
Varney	Crewe	17	Sodje	Port Vale	13

Coca-Cola Football League One Attendances

Highest Attendance
27,875 (City Ground)   9 April 2007
Nottingham Forest v Rotherham United

Lowest Attendance
3,036 (Whaddon Road)   16 January 2007
Cheltenham Town v Scunthorpe United

"You have to believe to achieve and it's about everyone believing something can happen."
*Scunthorpe United manager **Nigel Adkins***

Coca-Cola Football League Two 2006–07

At the end of the 2005–06 season, Hartlepool United (21st), Milton Keynes Dons (22nd), Swindon Town (23rd) and Walsall (24th) were all relegated from League Division One to Division Two. One year later, Walsall returned to Division One after being crowned champions of Division Two, Hartlepool were promoted after claiming the runners-up spot, Swindon Town finished third and were also promoted, while the MK Dons finished fourth but lost out on promotion via the play-offs that saw Bristol Rovers beat Shrewsbury Town 3–1 at the new Wembley. At the other end of the table, Torquay United finished bottom and dropped into the Conference along with Boston United, who announced they were going into administraton two minutes from the end of their final match, when it became clear they would not get the victory that would enable them to avoid the drop.

Coca-Cola Football League Two

Pos	Team	P	W	D	L	GF	GA	Pts
1.	**Walsall**	**46**	**25**	**14**	**7**	**66**	**34**	**89**
2.	Hartlepool United	46	26	10	10	75	50	88
3.	Swindon Town	46	25	10	11	58	38	85
4.	Milton Keynes Dons	46	25	9	12	76	58	84
5.	Lincoln City	46	21	11	14	70	59	74
6.	Bristol Rovers	46	20	12	14	49	42	72
7.	Shrewsbury	46	18	17	11	68	46	71
8.	Stockport County	46	21	8	17	65	54	71
9.	Rochdale	46	18	12	16	70	50	66
10.	Peterborough United	46	18	11	17	70	61	65
11.	Darlington	46	17	14	15	52	56	65
12.	Wycombe Wanderers	46	16	15	16	52	47	62
13.	Notts County	46	16	14	16	55	53	62
14.	Barnet	46	16	11	19	55	70	59
15.	Grimsby Town	46	17	8	21	57	73	59
16.	Hereford United	46	14	13	19	45	53	55
17.	Mansfield Town	46	14	12	20	58	63	54
18.	Chester City	46	13	14	19	40	48	53
19.	Wrexham	46	13	12	21	43	65	51
20.	Accrington Stanley	46	13	11	22	70	81	50
21.	Bury	46	13	11	22	46	61	50
22.	Macclesfield Town	46	12	12	22	55	77	48
23.	Boston United*	46	12	10	24	51	80	46
24.	Torquay United	46	7	14	25	36	63	35

*Boston United underwent financial restructuring after the season's end and were demoted to the Conference North division

Play-off Semi-finals

First leg: Bristol Rovers 2–1 Lincoln City
Second leg: Lincoln City 3–5 Bristol Rovers
Result: Bristol Rovers won 7–4 on aggregate

First leg: Shrewsbury Town 0–0 MK Dons
Second leg: MK Dons 1–2 Shrewsbury Town
Result: Shrewsbury Town won 2–1 on aggregate

Play-off Final

Wembley Stadium, 27 May 2007; Att: 61,589

Bristol Rovers 3 – 1 Shrewsbury Town
Walker 21, 35, Igoe 90   *Drummond 3*

Bristol Rovers: Phillips, R Green, Anthony, Elliott, Carruthers, Haldane *(Rigg 64)*,
Disley, Campbell, Igoe, Lambert, Walker
Subs not used: M Green, Lines, Sandell, Lescott
Booked: Campbell, Walker

Shrewsbury: MacKenzie, Herd *(Burton 84)*, Hope, Langmead, Tierney, Asamoah, Hall,
Drummond, Ashton, Cooke *(Humphrey 73)*, Symes *(Fortune-West 80)*
Subs not used: Esson, Leslie
Sent off: Tierney (89); **Booked:** Cooke, Tierney

Coca-Cola Football League Two Top Scorers

Player	Team	Goals	Player	Team	Goals
Barker	Hartlepool	21	Dagnall	Rochdale	15
McLeod	Milton Keynes Dons	21	Lee	Notts County	15
Murray	Rochdale	18	Bishop	Bury	14
Platt	Milton Keynes Dons	18	Elding	Stockport	14
Easter	Wycombe	17	Mullin	Accrington Stanley	14
Forrester	Lincoln City	17	Stallard	Lincoln City	14

Coca-Cola Football League Two Attendances

Highest Attendance
14,731 (County Ground)   5 May 2007
Swindon Town v Walsall

Lowest Attendance
1,234 (Fraser Eagle Stadium) 16 Jan 2007
Accrington Stanley v Mansfield Town

"I genuinely felt we would have a chance of a good season.**"**
*Walsall manager **Richard Money**, after clinching promotion*

FA Cup 2006–07

The first shock of the competition came in round two when Bury were expelled from the competition for fielding an ineligible player, Stephen Turnbull (on loan from Hartlepool United), during a 2–1 win at Chester City, who took their place in round three.

Manchester United made it to the final having played an Premiership side in every round and after having played at home in every round up to the semi-finals: R3 Aston Villa 2–1, R4 Portsmouth 2–1, R5 Reading 1–1 and 3–2 (away), QF Middlesbrough 2–2 (away) and 1–0 at home, SF Watford 4–1 at Villa Park.

Chelsea began their FA Cup campaign with a 6–1 win at League Two Macclesfield Town and followed up with a 3–0 win over League One side Nottingham Forest in round four. In the fifth round the Blues swept aside Norwich City from the Coca-Cola Championship 3–0 at Stamford Bridge to set up an all-London quarter-final encounter with Tottenham Hotspur. Spurs gave Chelsea a shock by taking a 3–1 lead at the Bridge, but two goals from Frank Lampard and an 86th-minute equalizer from Soloman Kalou earned them a replay at White Hart Lane. In the replay Chelsea won 2–1 and then saw off stiff competition from Blackburn Rovers, Arsenal's conquerors in the last 16, winning 2–1 after extra time at Old Trafford. Watford crept through the competition almost unnoticed until they were in the last four. The semi-final at Villa Park pitted the champions elect and the club destined to finish rock bottom. The result went with form, although United's 4–1 wins was a little flattering. Nontheless, it set up a final between England's two top teams.

Quarter-finals

Manchester United 2–2 Middlesbrough *(replay 1–0)*
Blackburn Rovers 2–0 Manchester City
Chelsea 3–3 Tottenham Hotspur *(replay 2–1)*
Plymouth Argyle 0–1 Watford

Semi-finals

Manchester United 4–1 Watford, Villa Park, Birmingham
Chelsea 2–1 Blackburn Rovers *(aet)*, Old Trafford, Manchester

FA Cup Final – 19 May 2007, Wembley Stadium, London

Despite the fact that the two best teams in the country were contesting the first FA Cup final to be played at the new Wembley Stadium, this was a disappointing game from start to finish. Indeed, the parade of FA Cup final legends from 1957–2000 prior to kick-off proved the most entertaining spectacle of the day. The only action of a dour first-half was Paulo Ferreira's effort on goal just after the half hour mark and when the second-half failed to provide any fireworks, extra time was played. A Didier Drogba goal in the 116th minute prevented the spectre of a third successive FA Cup final being decided on penalties. So, while the pre-match hype was all about Jose Mourinho's missing dog, it was his "Drog" who settled the affair with his first ever goal against United.

Chelsea 1 – 0 Manchester United
Drogba 116

Chelsea: Cech, Ferreira, Essien, Terry, Bridge,
Mikel, Makelele, Lampard, Wright-Phillips *(Kalou 93)*,
Drogba, Joe Cole *(Robben 46)*, Robben *(Ashley Cole 108)*
Subs not used: Cudicini, Diarra
Booked: Makelele, Ferreira, Ashley Cole, Kalou

Manchester United: Van der Sar, Brown, Ferdinand, Vidic, Heinze,
Fletcher *(Smith 92)*, Scholes, Carrick *(O'Shea 112)*, Ronaldo,
Rooney, Giggs *(Solskjaer 112)*
Subs not used: Kuszczak, Evra
Booked: Scholes, Vidic, Smith
Att: 89,826

Trivia

* Chelsea enjoy the unique distinction of having won the last FA Cup final at the old Wembley (2000) and the first FA Cup at the new Wembley.

* It was the eighth FA Cup final in succession involving a London club. (Manchester United beat Newcastle United 2-0 in 1999.)

* Ryan Giggs went into the game seeking his fifth FA Cup winners' medal, while Ashley Cole won his fourth.

* Ryan Giggs was the only player on the pitch when the two sides last met in the FA Cup final in 1994. United won 4–0.

* Between Watford's 4–1 third round win over Stockport and the 4–1 semi-final defeat against Manchester United, they recorded three 1–0 wins.

* The 2007 FA Cup final was only the third time the top two teams in the country have contested the Cup (Aston Villa v Sunderland 1913 and Everton v Liverpool 1986).

* The 2007 FA Cup final was the first time that the Premier League champions met the League Cup winners from the same season in the final.

* Bury were expelled from the Cup for fielding a loan player in their replay against Chester City. Chester were reinstated.

* Brighton & Hove Albion had the biggest win in the competition proper beating Northwich Victoria 8–0 in round 1.

* A record total of 687 teams entered the 2006-07 FA Cup competition.

"It has been exceptional what my players have been through – we just couldn't cross the line.**"**
Sir Alex Ferguson

"I won't be throwing this one away, it means a lot, it's the FA Cup and it's the first one for me.**"**
Jose Mourinho

Carling Cup 2006–07

The Carling Cup started with a bang as League new-boys Accrington Stanley knocked out five-time winners Nottingham Forest in round one. Watford needed penalties to see them off in the next round. Fellow League Two members Wycombe Wanderers reached the last four and pushed Chelsea all the way over two legs. Arsenal continued to field youngsters and fringe first-teamers and despite not playing at home until the semi-final second-leg, reached the final. They knocked out three Premiership rivals, including Liverpool 6–3 in the quarter-final at Anfield – Julio Baptista scoring four times – and Tottenham Hotspur in the semi-final.

Quarter-finals

Liverpool (1) 3 **Arsenal** (4) 6
Newcastle (0) 0 **Chelsea** (0) 1
Tottenham Hotspur (0) 1 Southend (0) 0 *(aet)*
Charlton (0) 0 Wycombe (1) 1

Semi-finals

SEMI-FINAL FIRST LEG
Wycombe (0) 1 **Chelsea** (1) 1
Tottenham Hotspur (2) 2 **Arsenal** (0) 2

SEMI-FINAL SECOND LEG
Chelsea (2) 4 Wycombe (0) 0
Arsenal (0) 3 Tottenham Hotspur (0) 1 *(aet, 1–1 after 90 minutes)*

Carling Cup Final, 25 February 2007, Millennium Stadium, Cardiff

Arsenal came flying out of the blocks from the opening kick-off and really took the game to their bitter London rivals and in the 12th minute Theo Walcott, aged 17, gave the Gunners the lead, his first goal for Arsenal and a goal that meant he became the second youngest player ever to score in an English domestic cup final. Eight minutes later Didier Drogba equalised, although TV replays showed that he may have been fractionally offside.

Arsenal began the second half in similar fashion to the first, taking the game to Chelsea. Midway through the second half Chelsea lost their skipper, John Terry, when he received a kick on the chin from Diaby as he tried to get on the end of an Arjen Robben corner. In the 84th minute Robben's floated cross picked out Drogba and he headed past Almunia. The game ended in a mass brawl when John Obi Mikel clashed with Kolo Toure, resulting in players from both teams, as well as both managers, becoming embroiled in an ugly fracas on the pitch. When order was restored, referee Howard Webb showed red cards to Obi Mikel, Toure and Emmanuel Adebayor as well as yellows to Cesc Fabregas and Frank Lampard. Thus Chelsea claimed the first piece of silverware of the season in what was the last League Cup final to be played in the Millennium Stadium.

Chelsea 2 – 1 Arsenal
Drogba 20, 84   Walcott 12

Chelsea: Cech, Diarra, Terry *(Mikel 63)*, Carvalho, Bridge,
Makelele *(Robben 46)*, Lampard, Ballack, Essien,
Shevchenko *(Kalou 90)*, Drogba
Subs not used: Hilario, Ashley Cole
Sent off: Mikel (90)
Booked: Essien, Carvalho, Diarra, Lampard

Arsenal: Almunia, Hoyte, Toure, Senderos, Traore *(Eboué 66)*,
Walcott, Fabregas, Denilson, Diaby *(Hleb 68)*,
Aliadiere *(Adebayor 80)*, Julio Baptista
Subs not used: Poom, Djourou
Sent off: Toure (90), Adebayor (90)
Booked: Denilson, Eboue, Fabregas
Att: 70,073

Trivia

* From the inaugural Football League Cup competition in season 1960–61 up to and including the 1965–66 competition, the final of the League Cup was played over two legs home and away.

* Wembley hosted its first League Cup final in season 1966–67 with Queens Park Rangers beating West Bromwich Albion 3–2. Since season 2000–01 the League Cup final has been played at the Millennium Stadium, Cardiff.

* Liverpool were the first club to win the League Cup after a penalty shootout. In the 2001 final Liverpool and Birmingham City drew 1–1 before Liverpool triumphed 5–4 on penalties.

* In season 1993–94 Manchester United were chasing the first ever domestic treble. However, despite going on to win the double of the FA Premier League and FA Cup, the Red Devils fell at the first hurdle when Aston Villa beat them 3–1 in the final.

* In season 1981–82 the League Cup was sponsored for the first time, with Liverpool lifting the Milk Cup following their 3–1 extra-time win over Tottenham Hotspur. Since then, the League Cup has been sponsored by Littlewoods, Rumbelows, Coca-Cola, Worthington and today's sponsors, Carling.

Milk Cup
(1981–82 to 1985–86)
Littlewoods Challenge Cup
(1986–87 to 1989–90)
Rumbelows Cup
(1990–91 and 1991–92)
Coca-Cola Cup
(1992–93 to 1997–98)
Worthington Cup
(1998–99 to 2002–03)
Carling Cup
(2003–04 to present)

Nationwide Conference 2006–07

Oxford United's early season charge sputtered and died in the dog days of winter allowing Dagenham & Redbridge, an amalgam of half-dozen famous amateur clubs to waltz away with the title. In the play-offs, Exeter City saw off Oxford United, but fell to Morecambe.

Nationwide Conference National Championship

Pos	Team	P	W	D	L	GF	GA	Pts
1.	**Dagenham & Redbridge**	**46**	**28**	**11**	**7**	**93**	**48**	**95**
2.	Oxford Utd	46	22	15	9	66	33	81
3.	Morecambe	46	23	12	11	64	46	81 P
4.	York City	46	23	11	12	65	45	80
5.	Exeter City	46	22	12	12	67	48	78
6.	Burton Albion	46	22	9	15	52	47	75
7.	Gravesend & Northfleet	46	21	11	14	63	56	74
8.	Stevenage Borough	46	20	10	16	76	66	70
9.	Aldershot Town	46	18	11	17	64	62	65
10.	Kidderminster Harriers	46	17	12	17	43	50	63
11.	Weymouth	46	18	9	19	56	73	63
12.	Rushden & Diamonds	46	17	11	18	58	54	62
13.	Northwich Victoria	46	18	4	24	51	69	54
14.	Forest Green Rovers	46	13	18	15	59	64	57
15.	Woking	46	15	12	19	56	61	57
16.	Halifax Town	46	15	10	21	55	62	55
17.	Cambridge United	46	15	10	21	57	66	55
18.	Crawley Town	46	17	12	17	52	52	53
19.	Grays Athletic	46	13	13	20	56	55	52
20.	Stafford Rangers	46	14	10	22	49	71	52
21.	Altrincham*	46	13	12	21	53	67	51
22.	Tamworth	46	13	9	24	43	61	48
23.	Southport	46	11	14	21	57	67	47
24.	St Albans	46	10	10	26	57	89	40

Because Boston United were demoted from League Two to the Conference North division, Altrincham were saved from relegation.

Play-offs

SEMI-FINAL *(two legs, aggregate score)*
Exeter City 2–2 Oxford United
(Exeter won 4–3 on penalties)
Morecambe 2–1 York City

FINAL *Wembley Stadium, 20 May Att: 40,043*
Morecambe 2 – 1 Exeter City
Thompson 42,   Phillips 8
Carlton 82

Nationwide Conference North

Pos	Team	P	W	D	L	GF	GA	Pts
1.	**Droylsden**	42	23	9	10	85	55	78
2.	Kettering Town	42	20	13	9	75	58	73
3.	Workington	42	20	10	12	61	46	70
4.	Hinckley United	42	19	12	11	68	54	69
5.	Farsley Celtic	42	19	11	12	58	51	68
6.	Harrogate Town	42	18	13	11	58	41	67

Play-offs

SEMI-FINAL *(two legs, aggregate score)*
Farsley Celtic 1 – 1 Kettering Town
(Farsley won 4–3 on penalties)
Hinckley United 2 – 1 Workington

FINAL *Pirelli Stadium, Burton, 15 May*
Farsley Celtic 4 – 3 Hinckley Utd
Grant 15, Crossley 87,   Shilton 19,
Reeves 79, 89 (pen)   Cartwright 21, 83

Nationwide Conference South

Pos	Team	P	W	D	L	GF	GA	Pts
1.	**Histon**	42	30	4	8	85	44	94
2.	Salisbury City	42	21	12	9	65	37	75
3.	Braintree Town	42	21	11	10	51	38	74
4.	Havant & Waterlooville	42	20	13	9	75	46	73
5.	Bishops Stortford	42	21	10	11	72	61	73
6.	Newport County	42	21	7	14	82	54	70

Play-offs

SEMI-FINAL *(two legs, aggregate score)*
Braintree Town 2 – 2 Havant &
Waterlooville
(Braintree won 4–2 on penalties)
Salisbury City 4 – 2 Bishops Stortford

FINAL
Broadhall Way, Stevenage, 14 May
Salisbury City 1 – 0 Braintree Town
Tubbs 85

"When I came here five years ago I said I wanted
to bring league football in ten years. Five years on,
we're a league higher than I expected.**"**
Salisbury City manager
Nick Holmes

71

Non-League Football 2006–07

Wembley Stadium hosted the two non-league cup finals over one weekend in early May. First was the FA Trophy, where more than 53,000 spectators were on hand to watch as Stevenage Borough came back from a two-goal half-deficit to beat Kidderminster Harriers, Steve Morison netting the winner just two minutes from time.

Scoring first did not bring success in the FA Vase final 24 hours later either when Truro City overcame AFC Totton. Danny Potter's goal for the Hampshire club was cancelled out Kevin Willis just before half-time. Willis got his second after 57 minutes and Joe Broad added a third six minutes from time to give Cornwall its first ever Wembley winner.

FA Trophy Final – 12 May 2007, Wembley Stadium, London

Stevenage Borough 3 – 2 Kidderminster Harriers
Cole 51, Dobson 74, Morison 88   *Constable 32, 37*

Stevenage Borough: Julian, Fuller, Nutter, Oliver, Santos Gaia, Miller, Cole, Guppy *(Dobson, 63)*, Henry, Morison, Beard
Subs: Potter *(GK)*, Slabber, Nurse, McMahon

Kidderminster Harriers: Bevan, Kenna, Hurren, Creighton, Whitehead, Blackwood, Russell, Penn, Smikle *(Reynolds, 90)*, Christie *(White, 76)*, Constable
Subs: Taylor *(GK)*, Sedgemore, McGrath
Att: 53,262

FA Vase Final – 13 May 2007, Wembley Stadium, London

AFC Totton 1 – 3 Truro City
Danny Potter 28   *Kevin Wills 45, 57, Joe Broad 84*

AFC Totton: Brunnschweiler, Reacord, Troon *(Stevens, 61)*, Potter *(Gregory, 82)*, Bottomley, Austen, Roden, Gosney, Hamodu *(Goss, 89)*, Osman, Byres
Subs: Zammit, McCormack *(GK)*

Truro City: Stevenson, Ash, Power, Smith, Martin *(Pope, 86)*, Broad, Wills, Gosling, Yetton, Watkins, Walker *(Ludlam, 90)*
Subs: Butcher *(GK)*, Tolley, Routledge, Reski
Att: 27,754

Trivia

* Hoddesdon Town were the inaugural FA Vase winners in 1974–75, defeating Epsom & Ewell 2–1 at Wembley.

* No Vase winner has reached the Football League; two, Forest Green and Tamworth, reached the Conference.

* Truro City got £15,000 for winning the Vase.

* Just four teams have won the Vase more than once.

Ryman (Isthmian) League Premier Division

Pos	Team	P	W	D	L	GF	GA	Pts
1.	Hampton & Richmond B.	42	24	10	8	77	53	82
2.	Bromley	42	23	11	8	83	43	80
3.	Chelmsford City	42	23	8	11	96	51	77
4.	Billericay Town	42	22	11	9	71	42	77
5.	AFC Wimbledon	42	21	15	6	76	37	75
6.	Margate	42	20	11	11	79	48	71

PLAY-OFF FINAL
Bromley   **1 − 1**   **Billericay Town** *(Bromley won 4–2 on penalties)*

British Gas Business (Southern) League Premier Division

Pos	Team	P	W	D	L	GF	GA	Pts
1.	**Bath City**	42	27	10	5	84	29	91
2.	Team Bath	42	23	9	10	66	42	78
3.	King's Lynn	42	22	10	10	69	40	76
4.	Maidenhead United	42	20	10	12	58	36	70
5.	Hemel Hempstead Town	42	19	12	11	79	60	69
6.	Halesowen Town	42	18	13	11	66	53	67

PLAY-OFF FINAL
Team Bath   **0 − 1**   **Maidenhead United**

Unibond (Northern Premier) League Premier Division

Pos	Team	P	W	D	L	GF	GA	Pts
1.	**Burscough**	42	23	12	7	80	37	80
2.	Witton Albion	42	24	8	10	90	48	80
3.	AFC Telford	42	21	15	6	72	40	78
4.	Marine	42	22	8	12	70	53	74
5.	Matlock Town	42	21	9	12	70	43	72
6.	Guiseley	42	19	12	11	71	49	69

PLAY-OFF FINAL
Witton Albion   **0 − 1**   **AFC Telford**

Scottish Premier League 2006–07

The Scottish Premier League championship race was pretty much over and done with by mid-September. Rangers, under new manager Paul LeGuen, were struggling to string results together, Hearts were riven by off-field turmoil and neither Aberdeen, nor any other contenders were close to matching Celtic's metronomic efficiency. The Bhoys could actually have wrapped up the title by beating Rangers at Parkhead in mid-March. However, Rangers who had replaced LeGuen with Walter Smith, were a different proposition and they stretched the race into April. The final margin was 12 points, with Rangers 10 clear of Aberdeen, and Hearts in fourth. Dunfirmline, despite a great Scottish Cup run, were bottom of the table most of the season and ended up four points behind 11th-placed St. Mirren. The Saints were favourites to make an immediate return to the First Division, but they started the season well and just hung on to their SPL place.

Scottish Premier League Championship

Pos	Team	P	W	D	L	GF	GA	Pts
1.	**Celtic**	**33**	**24**	**6**	**3**	**59**	**25**	**78**
2.	Rangers	33	19	8	6	54	25	65
3.	Aberdeen	33	17	6	10	46	33	57
4.	Heart of Midlothian	33	15	9	9	40	30	54
5.	Kilmarnock	33	13	7	13	43	49	46
6.	Hibernian	33	12	8	13	49	37	44
7.	Falkirk	33	12	4	17	40	42	40
8.	Dundee United	33	10	10	13	39	53	40
9.	Inverness Caledon'n Thistle	33	8	12	13	36	45	36
10.	Motherwell	33	10	6	17	35	49	36
11.	St Mirren	33	5	12	16	24	47	27
21.	Dunfermline Athletic	33	5	8	20	19	49	23

Scottish Premier League Top Scorers

Player	Team	Goals
Boyd	Rangers	19
McDonald	Motherwell	14
Killen	Hibernian	13
Naismith	Kilmarnock	13
Mackie	Aberdeen	12
Nish	Kilmarnock	12
Robson	Dundee Utd	11
Vennegoor of Hesselink	Celtic	11
Adam	Rangers	10
Dargo	Inverness CT	10
Hunt	Dundee Utd	10
Nakamura	Celtic	9
Sutton	St Mirren	9
Crawford	Dunfermline	8
Lovell	Aberdeen	8

Trivia

* Celtic's early season form was so dominating that the Irish bookmakers, Paddy Power, paid out on 4 November 2006 on all bets placed for Celtic to win the 2006–07 SPL. Amazingly, only 13 league games had been played.

* Celtic won their 41st Scottish League Championship following a 2–1 win over Kilmarnock, which left the Bhoys 13 points clear of Rangers with only four matches to play.

* Since the inception of the Scottish Premier League in season 1998–99 only seven teams have been ever present: Aberdeen, Dundee United, Heart of Midlothian, Glasgow Celtic, Glasgow Rangers, Kilmarnock and Motherwell.

* Henrik Larsson (Celtic 1998–2004) is the all-time leading SPL goal scorer with 173 goals. He also scored the most goals in a season, with 55 in 2000–01.

* Dunfermline Athletic hold the record for the fewest number of SPL away wins in a single season, failing to win any of their games on the road in 1998–99.

* Celtic hold the record for the most SPL goals in a season with 105 (2003–04), while Aberdeen has conceded the most (83 in 1999–2000).

* Courtesy of the late-season Premier League split, top-half Hibernian finished sixth but Falkirk, who were seventh, collected one more point.

SPL PLAYER OF THE YEAR 2006–07
Shansuke Nakamura   Glasgow Celtic

SCOTTISH FOOTBALL WRITERS' PLAYER OF THE YEAR 2006–07
Shansuke Nakamura   Glasgow Celtic

Scottish Premier League Attendances

Club	Average	Highest	Club	Average	Highest
Celtic	57,928	59,659	Kilmarnock	6,807	13,506
Rangers	49,955	50,488	Dunfermline Athletic	6,106	8,561
Hearts	16,937	17,369	Motherwell	5,877	11,745
Hibernian	14,587	16,747	St Mirren	5,609	10,251
Aberdeen	12,475	20,045	Falkirk	5,387	7,245
Dundee United	7,147	12,329	Inverness CT	4,879	7,522

"The best team won the league. There is a difference between the best individuals and the best team. My players just don't like getting beat. We have players here, like Neil Lennon, who set the standard."
Gordon Strachan, *after Celtic had clinched the title.*

Scottish Football Leagues 2006–07

Scottish Football League Division 1 Championship

Gretna were First Division champions, courtesy of a late winner in the season's final match at Ross County. Bankrolled by multi-millionaire businessman Brooks Mileson, the Borders club, who were in England's Unibond League until 2002, made it three consecutive divisional titles with this success. They had led the division by 12 points until a slump in form gave St Johnstone a glimmer of hope. But James Grady's 89th-minute strike – which coincidentally condemned County to relegation – clinched the title.

Pos	Team	P	W	D	L	GF	GA	Pts
1.	**Gretna**	**36**	**19**	**9**	**8**	**70**	**40**	**66**
2.	St Johnstone	36	19	8	9	65	42	65
3.	Dundee	36	16	5	15	48	42	53
4.	Hamilton Academical	36	14	11	11	46	47	53
5.	Clyde	36	11	14	11	46	35	47
6.	Livingston	36	11	12	13	41	46	45
7.	Partick Thistle	36	12	9	15	47	63	45
8.	Queen of the South	36	10	11	15	34	54	41
9.	Airdrie United	36	11	7	18	39	50	40
10.	Ross County	36	9	10	17	40	57	37

Play-offs

`SEMI-FINAL *(two legs, aggregate score)*
Airdrie United 6-1 Brechin City
Stirling Albion 3-1 Raith Rovers

FINAL
1st Leg: Stirling Albion 2–2 Airdrie Utd
2nd Leg: Airdrie United 2–3 Stirling Alb
Stirling Albion win 5–4 on aggregate

Scottish Football League Division 1 Top Scorers

Player	Team	Goals	Player	Team	Goals
McMenamin	Gretna	24	Lyle	Dundee	12
Scotland	St Johnstone	17	Arbuckle	Clyde	10
Roberts	Partick	15	Hardie	St Johnstone	10
Offiong	Hamilton	13	Twigg	Airdrie Utd	10

> "Over the two legs, I think we deserved it and I am just delighted for all the players concerned."
> **Allan Moore**, *Stirling Albion manager*

Scottish Football League Division 2 Championship

Champions Greenock Morton finished eight points clear of Stirling Albion, who went on to gain promotion through the play-offs. At the bottom, Forfar Athletic had a miserable season, collecting just 19 points from 36 matches; their relegation was confirmed with a 9–1 hammering at Morton. There was quite a battle to avoid the relegation/promotion play-off place. Stranraer were the losers – and eventually went down – but Peterhead, Alloa Athletic and Cowdenbeath all left it late to achieve safety.

Pos	Team	P	W	D	L	GF	GA	Pts
1.	**Greenock Morton**	**36**	**24**	**5**	**7**	**76**	**32**	**77**
2.	Stirling Albion	36	21	6	9	67	39	69
3.	Raith Rovers	36	18	8	10	50	33	62
4.	Brechin City	36	18	6	12	61	45	60
5.	Ayr United	36	14	8	14	46	47	50
6.	Cowdenbeath	36	13	6	17	59	56	45
7.	Alloa Athletic	36	11	9	16	47	70	42
8.	Peterhead	36	11	8	17	60	62	41
9.	Stranraer	36	10	9	17	45	74	39
10.	Forfar Athletic	36	4	7	25	37	90	19

Play-offs

SEMI-FINAL *(two legs, aggregate score)*
Queen's Park 4–1 Arbroath
East Fife 4–2 Stranraer

FINAL
1st Leg: Queen's Park 4–2 East Fife
2nd Leg: East Fife 0–3 Queen's Park
Queen's Park win 7–2 on aggregate

Scottish Football League Division 2 Top Scorers

Player	Team	Goals
Russell	Brechin	21
Buchanan	Cowdenbeath	20
Weatherson	Morton	15
Cramb	Stirling	14
Clarke	Cowdenbeath	13
Moore	Stranraer	13
Linn	Morton	12
Templeman	Morton	12
Bavidge	Peterhead	11
Gribben	Forfar	11
McGowan	Morton	11
Hamilton	Stranraer	10

"I was lucky enough to win things as a player, but this brings different feelings and is even better as you're responsible for the whole team.**"**
*Queen's Park manager **Billy Stark***

Scottish Football League Division 3 Championship

Berwick Rangers won a close title race, which saw the top four – Berwick, Arbroath, Queen's Park and East Fife, respectively – separated by just eight points. Queen's Park emerged from the play-offs to take the second promotion spot. The remainder of the table was well spread out. East Stirlingshire were again wooden-spoonists, winning just six games out of 36. Following a ruling by the Scottish Football League, they will be reduced to Associate Members with a similar finish in 2008.

Pos	Team	P	W	D	L	GF	GA	Pts
1.	**Berwick Rangers**	36	24	3	9	51	29	79
2.	Arbroath	36	22	4	10	61	33	70
3.	Queen's Park	36	21	5	10	57	28	68 P
4.	East Fife	36	20	7	9	59	37	67
5.	Dumbarton	36	18	5	13	52	37	59
6.	Albion Rovers	36	14	6	16	56	61	48
7.	Stenhousemuir	36	13	5	18	53	63	44
8.	Montrose	36	11	4	21	42	62	37
9.	Elgin City	36	9	2	25	39	69	29
10.	East Stirling	36	6	3	27	27	78	21

Play-offs

SEMI-FINAL *(two legs, aggregate score)*
Queen's Park 4–1 Arbroath
East Fife 4–2 Stranraer

FINAL
1st Leg: Queen's Park 4–2 East Fife
2nd Leg: East Fife 0–3 Queen's Park
Queen's Park win 7–2 on aggregate

Scottish Football League Championship Division 3 Top Scorers

Player	Team	Goals	Player	Team	Goals
Chaplain	Albion	18	Dobbie	Dumbarton	10
Johnston	Elgin	18	Jablonski	East Fife	10
Weatherston	Queen's Park	16	Rogers	Montrose	10
O'Reilly	East Fife	13	Walker	Albion	10
Ferry	Queen's Park	11	Wood	Berwick	10

Trivia

* When Dunfermline beat Celtic in the 1961 Scottish Cup final, their manager was the future Celtic legend Jock Stein.

* Apart from Celtic (34) and Rangers (31), only Queen's Park have won the Scottish Cup as often as 10 times.

Scottish FA Cup 2006–07

Dunfermline Athletic shocked Rangers in round three, winning 3–2. St Mirren, Aberdeen and Kilmarnock also fell at that stage. Non-League Deveronvale reached the last 16 after winning 5–4 against Elgin City. Celtic nearly lost at Inverness Caley Thistle in the quarter-finals, but scored in the 89th and 90th minutes to win 2–1. The other last-eight ties pitted SPL teams against Division One rivals; Hibernian and Dunfermline won, but Motherwell lost to Partick Thistle. For Hibs, the wait for a first Scottish Cup triumph since 1902 goes on after losing to Dunfermline in a semi-final replay, so the Pars faced Celtic in the final.

Quarter-Final

Inverness Caledonian Thistle 1–2 Celtic
Queen of the South 1–2 Hibernian
Motherwell 1–2 St Johnstone
Dunfermline Athletic 2–0 Partick Thistle

Semi-Final

Dunfermline Athletic 0–0 Hibernian
Replay: Dunfermline Athletic 1–0 Hibernian
Celtic 2–1 St Johnstone

Scottish FA Cup Final – 26 May 2007, Hampden Park, Glasgow

Celtic won the Scottish Cup for the 34th time in the club's history, thanks to a goal from defender Jean-Joel Perrier Doumbe in the 84th minute. Having already clinched the SPL title Celtic achieved the Scottish double with this victory over relegated Dunfermline Athletic at Hampden Park in what can only be described as a dour finale to the season.

Celtic 1 – 0 Dunfermline Athletic
Perrier Doumbe 85

Celtic: Boruc, Perrier Doumbe, McManus, Pressley, Naylor, Nakamura, Lennon *(Caldwell 66)*, Hartley, McGeady, Miller *(Beattie 56)*, Vennegoor of Hesselink
Subs not used: McGovern, Riordan, Bjarnason
Booked: McGeady, Perrier Doumbe, Pressley

Dunfermline: De Vries, Shields, Wilson, Bamba, Muirhead, Scott Morrison *(Crawford 72)*, Young, McCunnie, Hammill, Burchill *(Williamson 89)*, McIntyre *(Hamilton 80)*
Subs not used: McKenzie, McGuire
Booked: Burchill
Att: 49,600

CIS Insurance Cup Final 2007

The CIS Insurance Cup had no Old Firm representation after the quarter-finals when – despite home ties – Celtic and Rangers went out, to Falkirk on penalties and 2–1 to St Johnstone, respectively. Third Division Queen's Park pulled off the biggest shock, knocking out Aberdeen on penalties in round two.

Quarter-Finals

Celtic 1–1 Falkirk *(aet. Falkirk won 5–4 on penalties)*
Kilmarnock 3–2 Motherwell
Hibernian 1–0 Heart of Midlothian
Rangers 0–2 St Johnstone

Semi-Finals

Kilmarnock 3–0 Falkirk *(at Fir Park, Motherwell)*
St Johnstone 1–3 Hibernian *(aet, at Tynecastle Park, Edinburgh)*

CIS Cup Final – 18 March 2007, Hampden Park, Glasgow

Former Celtic, Everton, Fulham, AS Monaco and Scottish international play-maker John Collins, now the manager of Hibernian, watched with delight as his young guns swept aside Kilmarnock 5–1. It ended a run of 16 trophyless years for the Easter Road club. Hibs took the lead in the 28th minute through Rob Jones and led 1–0 at the interval. In the second-half, Abdessalam Benjelloun made it 2–0 after 59 minutes, while Steven Fletcher made it 3–0 seven minutes later. A goal from Kilmarnock's Gordon Greer 13 minutes served only to spur on the Edinburgh club forward and they scored two more goals, through Benjelloun, after 85 minutes, and Fletcher, two minutes later, to complete a comprehensive victory.

Hibernian 5 – 1 Kilmarnock
Jones 28, Benjelloun 59, 85, Fletcher 66, 87   *Greer 77*

Hibernian: McNeil, Whittaker *(Martis 90)*, Hogg *(McCann 90)*, Jones, Murphy, Sproule *(Zemmama 79)*, Scott Brown, Beuzelin, Stevenson, Benjelloun, Fletcher
Subs not used: Simon Brown, Stewart

Kilmarnock: Combe, Frazer Wright, Greer, Ford, Hay, Di Giacomo *(Locke 76)*, Johnston, Fowler, Leven *(Wales 57)*, Nish, Naismith
Subs not used: Smith, Murray, O'Leary
Booked: Hay, Di Giacomo
Att: 52,000

Scottish Challenge Cup 2006–07

The Scottish Challenge Cup is open only to the 30 clubs outside the Scottish Premier League. Introduced in 1990 as part of the Scottish League's centenary, it is an early-season competition. The first round is regionalized – North & East and South & West, with two teams receiving byes – after which it is national.

Quarter-finals

Albion Rovers 3–3 Arbroath 3 *(aet. Albion won 5–3 pens)*
Clyde 1–0 Ayr United
Greenock Morton 3–2 St Johnstone
Ross County 3–2 Gretna *(aet)*

Semi-finals

Ross County 4–1 Albion Rovers
Clyde 3–1 Greenock Morton

Scottish Challenge Cup Final, 12 November, McDiarmid Park, Perth

Ross County goalkeeper Craig Sampson was the hero of the Stags' first trophy since joining the Scottish League. He saved two efforts in the penalty shoot-out as the Dingwall team won 5–4. Clyde, who dominated much of the match, took the lead two minutes before half-time, Roddy Hunter side-footing home. The Bully Wee sat on their lead and paid for it when Andy Dowie headed an equaliser ten minutes from time. Three minutes into extra time Clyde's Eddie Malone was sent off. Neither team was perfect in the shoot-out, but Sampson saved from Chris Higgins and then Neil McGregor. The pressure was on susbstitute Jason Crooks, and he made no mistake.

Ross County 1 – 1 Clyde
Dowie 80   Hunter 43
After extra time: Ross County won 5–4 on penalties

Ross County: Samson, Gary Irvine, McKinlay, Dowie, Keddie, Gardyn, Adams, Cowie *(Robertson 102)*, Scott *(Anderson 117)*, Caimi *(Crooks 115)*, Gunn
Subs not used: McCulloch, Malin
Booked: Caimi, Scott, Dowie

Clyde: Hutton, McKeown, McGregor, Higgins, Bryson, Ryan McCann, McHale, O'Donnell, Malone, Hunter (McKenna 78), Ferguson (Bradley 78)
Subs not used: Smith, Murray, O'Leary
Booked: O'Donnell, Malone, Ryan McCann, Higgins, McGregor
Sent off: Malone (93)
Att: 4,062

Welsh Football 2006–07

Welsh Premier League Championship

The name may have changed, but the results didn't. The New Saints, formerly Total
Network Solutions, of Llansantffraid, were again champions, completing a hat-trick
of titles, finishing seven points clear of Rhyl. With the league one club short, only the
bottom team was relegated. It turned out to be founder members and inaugural champions
Cwmbran Town who suffered that fate.

Pos	Team	P	W	D	L	GF	GA	Pts
1.	The New Saints*	32	24	4	4	81	20	76
2.	Rhyl	32	20	9	3	67	35	69
3.	Llanelli	32	18	9	5	72	33	63
4.	Welshpool Town	32	17	9	6	54	33	60
5.	Connah's Quay Nomads	32	16	8	8	49	40	56
6.	Port Talbot Town	32	15	6	11	42	39	51
7.	Carmarthen Town	32	14	8	10	57	50	50
8.	Aberystwyth Town	32	13	9	10	47	37	48
9.	Bangor City	32	14	6	12	55	47	48
10.	Haverfordwest County	32	10	9	13	49	46	39
11.	Porthmadog	32	8	11	13	40	52	32
12.	Airbus UK	32	7	8	17	40	67	29
13.	Cefn Druids	32	7	7	18	41	66	28
14.	Caersws	32	6	9	17	34	59	27
15.	Caernarfon Town	32	6	8	18	41	73	26
16.	Newtown	32	6	6	20	30	63	24
17.	Cwmbran Town	32	4	8	20	36	75	20

*The New Saints FC completed the Welsh double having already won the FAW Premier Cup.

FAW Premier Cup Final, 21 March 2007

The New Saints FC 1–0 Newport County

Welsh Cup Final, 6 May 2007

Carmarthen Town 3–2 Afan Lido

Loosemores Challenge Cup Final, 18 March 2007

Rhyl 1–1 Caersws *(aet) Caersws won 3–1 on penalties*

Northern Irish Football 2006–07

Northern Ireland Championship

Champions Linfield won their 47th title by eight points from cross-Belfast rivals Glentoran. They were utterly dominant and lost just the once all season. Belfast clubs controlled the league, with the city's four representatives all occupying top-six spots. At the bottom, Loughgall enjoyed a solitary victory and finished 14 points adrift of Glenavon of Lurgan and 15 from Larne.

Pos	Team	P	W	D	L	GF	GA	Pts
1.	**Linfield**	**30**	**21**	**8**	**1**	**73**	**19**	**71**
2.	Glentoran	30	20	3	7	76	33	63
3.	Cliftonville	30	18	7	5	47	26	61
4.	Portadown	30	17	7	6	49	26	58
5.	Lisburn Distillery	30	14	6	10	50	39	48
6.	Crusaders	30	14	5	11	50	42	47
7.	Coleraine	30	13	6	11	55	50	45
8.	Dungannon Swifts	30	13	5	12	41	41	44
9.	Ballymena United	30	12	7	11	46	40	43
10.	Limavady United	30	10	5	15	39	54	35
11.	Armagh City	30	11	2	17	42	68	35
12.	Newry City	30	8	7	15	39	52	31
13.	Donegal Celtic	30	6	9	15	33	51	27
14.	Larne	30	7	5	18	33	60	26
15.	Glenavon	30	5	10	15	40	58	25
16.	Loughgall	30	1	8	21	23	77	10

Irish Cup Final Final, 5 May 2007

Linfield 2–2 Dungannon Swifts *(aet) Linfield won 3-2 on penalties and clinched the double*

Setanta Cup 2006–07

SEMI-FINALS	FINAL
St Patrick's Ath 0-1 Drogheda Utd *(aet)*	Linfield 1-1 Drogheda Utd
Linfield 1-0 Cork City	*McAreavy* *Grant 77*
	Drogheda United won the penalty shootout 4–3

"Great credit must go to Dungannon. They fought their eye-strings out but we knew it was going to be difficult."

Linfield manager **David Jeffrey**

Republic of Ireland Football 2006–07

Republic of Ireland Championship (2006)

The league season runs March–November. The 2006 champions were Shelbourne, who finished level on points with Northern Ireland-based Derry City, but had a superior points difference. Dublin City withdrew after 17 games and basement-dwellers Waterford lost a play-off, but were reprieved when Shelbourne were refused a 2007 license for financial reasons. Derry took Shelbourne's Champions League spot.

Pos	Team	P	W	D	L	GF	GA	Pts
1.	**Shelbourne***	**30**	**18**	**8**	**4**	**60**	**27**	**62**
2.	Derry City	30	18	8	4	46	20	62
3.	Drogheda United	30	16	10	4	37	23	58
4.	Cork City	30	15	11	4	37	15	56
5.	Sligo Rovers	30	11	7	12	33	42	40
6.	University College Dublin	30	9	11	10	26	26	38
7.	St Patrick's Athletic	30	9	10	11	32	29	37
8.	Longford Town	30	8	10	12	23	27	34
9.	Bohemians	30	9	5	16	29	34	29
10.	Bray Wanderers	30	3	8	19	22	64	17
11.	Waterford United	30	2	6	22	20	58	12
	Dublin City	withdrew; all matches annulled						

*Shelbourne were denied a Premier Division license for 2007 due to problems paying their players (who have been sold or made free agents as per FAI rules). The UEFA Champions League 1st Qualifying Round-place was awarded to runners-up Derry City.

League of Ireland Cup 2006

SEMI-FINALS

Shamrock Rovers 0 - 2 **St Patrick's Athletic**
Sligo Rovers 0 - 0 **Derry City**
Replay
Derry City 5 - 0 Sligo Rovers

FINAL

3 December 2006, Lansdowne Road, Dublin
St Patrick's Athletic 3 - 4 **Derry City** *(aet)*

Dave Mulcahy 20,	*David Forde 25*
Trevor Molloy 75,	*Clive Delany 85*
Sean O'Connor 103	*Peter Hutton 107*
	Stephen Brennan 110og

Women's Football League 2006–07

FA Women's Premier League

On 3 April 2007, Arsenal Ladies won their fourth consecutive league title with a 5–1 win at Chelsea, their ninth title. Goals from Lianne Sanderson and Katie Chapman in both halves and a goal from Rachel Yankey secured Arsenal's third trophy of the season. The Gunners had already claimed the FA Premier League Cup (their ninth) and the London County Cup (their sixth). This was the second major trophy (excludes the London County Cup) of a historic four the London team were attempting to win in their 20th anniversary season. Amazingly, the Arsenal Ladies won all 22 of their league games during the season, netting 119 goals on their path to the title. Indeed, their last loss in the league was against Charlton Athletic on 15 October 2003.

Arsenal Ladies reached their first UEFA Women's Cup final in season 2006–07 and faced a tricky away first leg against the Swedish side, Umea IK, winners of the trophy on two occasions in the past four seasons and Europe's only full-time professional women's team. The game looked set to be heading for a draw only for Arsenal's England full back, Alex Scott, to drive home a superb shot in injury time to seal a 1–0 win in the Gammliavallen Stadium. Eight days later on 29 April, the Gunners played the second leg at Borehamwood FC's Meadow Park and following a tense 0–0 draw, Arsenal Ladies became the first British club to win the UEFA Women's Cup with a 1–0 aggregate victory.

On 7 May 2007, Arsenal made history in the women's game by beating Charlton Athletic to win the FA Cup (their eighth) and complete a historic quadruple. A crowd of 24,529 fans poured into Nottingham Forest's City Ground to watch the final, almost double the crowd of any previous women's FA Cup final (13,824 in 2001). The Gunners went 1–0 down inside 2 minutes, but their strength and determination came through as they led 3–1 at the interval. In the second half, the Gunners added a fourth to wrap up the quad with a 4–1 win. Season 2006–07 was undoubtedly the finest in the club's history.

Pos	Team	P	W	D	L	GF	GA	Pts
1.	**Arsenal Ladies**	**22**	**22**	**0**	**0**	**119**	**10**	**66**
2.	Everton Ladies	22	17	1	4	56	15	52
3.	Charlton Women	22	16	2	4	63	32	50
4.	Bristol Academy	22	13	1	8	53	41	40
5.	Leeds Utd Ladies	22	12	1	9	50	44	37
6.	Blackburn Ladies	22	10	2	10	37	36	32
7.	Birmingham Ladies	22	8	4	10	34	29	28
8.	Chelsea Ladies	22	8	4	10	33	34	28
9.	Doncaster Rovers Belles	22	7	2	13	29	54	23
10.	Cardiff Ladies	22	3	3	16	26	64	12
11.	Sunderland Ladies	22	3	2	17	15	72	11
12.	Fulham Ladies	22	1	2	19	12	96	5

European League Football 2006–07

The Italian championship was delayed a week as the match-fixing saga rumbled on. In the end only Juventus were relegated, while Milan (eight points), Lazio (three), Fiorentina (15) and Reggina (11) all had points deducted, but none were relegated. Lazio were third and Milan fourth, but they were a long way behind runners-up Roma. Internazionale were champions by 22 points. Juventus were Serie B champions.

In Spain, Sevilla, Barcelona and Real Madrid all had chances to win the title on the last day, with Madrid favourites on head-to-head results with Barça. Real beat Majorca to clinch the title and end the Galacticos era on a high note. Both Roberto Carlos and David Beckham – the first and last of the Galacticos – moved on at season's end, Ronaldo having joined Milan in January.

In Germany, Bayern Munich failed to win the title and didn't even qualify for the Champions League. The championship went to Stuttgart, with Schalke second and Werder Bremen third. France's domination by Lyon, coached by former Liverpool supremo Gerard Houllier, continued as they finished 17 points clear of Marseille. PSV Eindhoven took the Dutch crown for the third consecutive season, while the Belgian title was retained by Anderlecht and Porto reigned again in Portugal. Moscow clubs occupied the top three spots in Russia, CSKA heading Spartak and Lokomotiv.

European League Champions 2006–07

Country	Champions	Runners-up	Champions League Qualifiers
Albania	**KF Tirana**	KS Teuta*	
Andorra	**FC Ranger's**	Santa Colomax	
Armenia *(2006)*	**FC Pyunik**	FC MIKA*	
Austria	**FC Salzburg**	SV Ried*	
Azerbaijan	**Khazar Lenkoran**	PFC Neftchi*	
Belarus *(2006)*	**BATE Borisov**	Dinamo Minsk*	
Belgium	**Anderlecht**	Genk	
Bosnia	**FK Sarajevo**	NK Zrinjski*	
Bulgaria	**Levski Sofia**	CSKA Sofia*	
Croatia	**Dinamo Zagreb**	Hajduk Split*	
Cyprus	**APOEL**	Omonia Nicosia*	
Czech Republic	**Sparta Prague**	Slavia Prague	
Denmark	**FC Kobenhavn**	Midtjylland*	
Estonia	**Levadia Tallinn**	JK Trans Narva*	
Faroe Islands *(2006)*	**HB Torshavn**	EB/Streymur*	
Finland *(2006)*	**Tampere United**	HJK Helsinki*	
France	**Olympique Lyonnais**	Marseille	Toulouse
Georgia	**Olimpi Rustavi**	Dinamo Tbilisi*	
Germany	**VfB Stuttgart**	Schalke 04	Werder Bremen
Greece	**Olympiakos**	AEK Athens	

Country	Champions	Runners-up	Champions League Qualifiers
Gibraltar	FC Newcastle**	Manchester United**	
Holland	PSV Eindhoven	Ajax	
Hungary	Debreceni VSC	MTK Budapest*	
Iceland	Hafnarfjordur	KR Keflavik*	
Israel	Beitar Jerusalem	Maccabi Netanya*	
Italy	Internazionale	AS Roma	Lazio, Milan
Kazakhstan *(2006)*	FK Astana	FK Aktobe*	
Kosovo	Besax	Prishtinax	
Latvia *(2006)*	FK Ventspils	Skonto Riga*	
Lithuania *(2006)*	FBK Kaunas	FK Ekranas*	
Luxembourg	F91 Dudelange	Etzella Ettelbruck*	
Macedonia	FK Pobeda	FK Rabotnicki*	
Malta	Marsaxlokk FC	Sliema Wanderers*	
Moldova	FC Sheriff	Zimbru Chisinau*	
Montenegro	FK Zeta	Buducnost Podborica*	
Norway *(2006)*	Rosenborg	SK Brann*	
Northern Cyprus	Cetinkaya Turk**	Lapta**	
Poland	Zaglebie Lubin	Beichatow*	
Portugal	FC Porto	Sporting Clube	Benfica
Romania	Dinamo Bucharest	Steaua Bucharest	
Russia	CSKA Moscow	Spartak Moscow	
San Marino	S.S. Murata	SP Libertas*	
Serbia	Crvena Zvezda *(Red Star)*	Partizan Belgrade*	
Slovakia	MSK Zilina	Artmedia Bratislava*	
Slovenia	NK Domžale	NK Gorica*	
Spain	Real Madrid	Barcelona	Sevilla, Valencia
Sweden *(2006)*	IF Elfsborg	AIK Solna*	
Switzerland	FC Zürich	Basel*	
Turkey	Fenerbahce	Besiktas	
Ukraine	Dynamo Kyiv	Shakhtar Donetsk	

*Qualified for the UEFA Cup. All other clubs qualified for the UEFA Champions League.
**These league winners and/or runners-up do not qualify for UEFA competitions.
(2006) = Countries' seasons end in late summer/autumn, so these are the 2006 champions.
There is no league in Liechtenstein, only a cup. The UEFA Cup qualifiers are winners Vaduz.

European Golden Boot Award

Francesco Totti of AS Roma won the 2006–07 award. The 30-year-old Italian striker scored 26 league goals in Serie A for his club to push Ruud van Nistelrooy into second place. Van Nistelrooy scored 25 goals in La Liga for Real Madrid. Totti gained 52 points in the scoring system used by UEFA that awards 2 points per goal scored to those players in Europe's top leagues. Luca Toni of Fiorentina won it in 2005–06 with 31 goals.

Euro 2008 Qualifiers *(to 22 August 2007)*

England

2 September 2006 England 5–0 Andorra	*24 March 2007* Israel 0–0 England
6 September 2006 FYR Macedonia 0–1 England	*28 March 2007* Andorra 0–3 England
7 October 2006 England 0–0 FYR Macedonia	*6 June 2007* Estonia 0–3 England
11 October 2006 Croatia 2–0 England	

England v Germany – Friendly International

22 August 2007; Wembley Stadium, London;
England 1–2 Germany

Germany, the last visiting winners at old Wembley, became the first overseas team to win at new Wembley, their fifth straight triumph at the venue. England took an early lead though Frank Lampard, but an error from goalkeeper Paul Robinson gifted Kevin Kuranyi an equaliser. The winner came from debutant Christian Panders just before half-time.

Scotland

2 September 2006 Scotland 6–0 Faroe Islands	*24 March 2007* Scotland 2–1 Georgia
6 September 2006 Lithuania 1–2 Scotland	*28 March 2007* Italy 2–0 Scotland
7 October 2006 Scotland 1–0 France	*6 June 2007* Faroe Islands 0–2 Scotland
11 October 2006 Ukraine 2–0 Scotland	

Trivia

* In early 2007, Alex McLeish replaced Walter Smith to become the 20th manager of the national side. Scotland beat Georgia 2–1 in his first game in charge, making him only the third Scotland manager to begin his reign with a win.

Wales

2 September 2006
Czech Republic 2–1 Wales

24 March 2007
Republic of Ireland 1–0 Wales

7 October 2006
Wales 1–5 Slovakia

28 March 2007
Wales 0–0 San Marino

11 October 2006
Wales 3–1 Cyprus

2 June 2007
Wales 0–0 Czech Republic

Trivia

* Ryan Giggs played his 64th and final game for Wales in the draw against the Czechs.

Northern Ireland

2 September 2006
Northern Ireland 0–3 Iceland

24 March 2007
Liechtenstein 1–4 Northern Ireland

6 September 2006
Northern Ireland 3–2 Spain

28 March 2007
Northern Ireland 2–1 Sweden

7 October 2006
Denmark 0–0 Northern Ireland

22 August 2007
Northern Ireland 3–1 Liechtenstein

11 October 2006
Northern Ireland 1–0 Latvia

Trivia

* David Healey has scored 11 of Northern Ireland's 13 goals.

Republic of Ireland

2 September 2006
Germany 1–0 Republic of Ireland

7 February 2007
San Marino 1–2 Republic of Ireland

7 October 2006
Cyprus 5–2 Republic of Ireland

24 March 2007
Republic of Ireland 1–0 Wales

11 October 2006
Republic of Ireland 1–1 Czech Republic

28 March 2007
Republic of Ireland 1–0 Slovakia

15 November 2006
Republic of Ireland 5–0 San Marino

Qualifying Groups Standings *(to 22 August 2007)*

Group A

Team	P	W	D	L	F	A	Pts
Poland	9	6	1	2	15	7	19
Finland	9	5	2	2	11	6	17
Portugal	8	4	3	1	16	6	15
Serbia	8	4	2	2	12	7	14
Belgium	9	3	1	5	8	12	10
Armenia	8	2	2	4	4	8	8
Kazakhstan	9	1	3	5	6	13	6
Azerbaijan	8	1	2	5	4	17	5

Group B

Team	P	W	D	L	F	A	Pts
France	7	6	0	1	15	2	18
Italy	7	5	1	1	13	6	16
Scotland	7	5	0	2	13	6	15
Ukraine	6	4	0	2	8	6	12
Lithuania	7	2	1	4	4	7	7
Georgia	8	2	0	6	13	14	6
Faroe Islands	8	0	0	8	2	27	0

Group C

Team	P	W	D	L	F	A	Pts
Greece	7	6	0	1	12	5	18
Bosnia & Herz	7	4	1	2	14	14	13
Turkey	6	4	1	1	16	6	13
Norway	7	4	1	2	17	6	13
Hungary	7	2	0	5	7	14	6
Malta	7	1	1	5	5	15	4
Moldova	7	0	2	5	4	15	2

Group D

Team	P	W	D	L	F	A	Pts
Germany	7	6	1	0	29	4	19
Czech Rep	7	4	2	1	15	4	14
Rep of Ireland	7	4	1	2	12	8	13
Slovakia	7	3	0	4	16	13	9
Wales	6	2	1	3	8	9	7
Cyprus	7	2	1	4	10	16	4
San Marino	7	0	0	6	1	37	0

Group E

Team	P	W	D	L	F	A	Pts
Croatia	7	5	2	0	16	4	17
Israel	8	5	2	1	17	7	17
Russia	7	4	3	0	11	1	15
England	7	4	2	1	12	2	14
FYRMacedonia	7	2	1	4	6	7	7
Estonia	8	1	0	7	2	15	3
Andorra	8	0	0	8	2	30	0

Group F

Team	P	W	D	L	F	A	Pts
Sweden	7	5	0	1	14	4	18
N Ireland	7	5	1	1	13	8	16
Spain	7	5	0	2	13	6	15
Denmark	6	3	1	1	9	2	10
Liechtenstein	8	1	1	6	5	21	4
Iceland	7	1	1	5	5	15	4
Latvia	6	1	0	5	4	7	3

Group G

Team	P	W	D	L	F	A	Pts
Romania	7	5	2	0	14	4	17
Bulgaria	7	4	3	0	11	4	15
Netherlands	6	4	2	0	8	2	14
Albania	7	2	3	2	8	6	9
Belarus	7	2	1	4	10	15	7
Slovenia	7	1	1	5	5	12	4
Luxembourg	7	0	0	7	1	14	0

"I am delighted with the players' performances and their attitude. The squad has knuckled down and when it was time to deliver, we did. We should not be afraid of anybody.**"**

*England coach, **Steve McClaren**, after the 3–0 defeat of Russia at Wembley in September 2007*

Trivia

* On 2 June 2007, the Group F game between Sweden and Denmark in Copenhagen was abandoned in the 89th minute after a fan attacked the referee. The two teams were level at 3–3 and when the referee awarded Sweden a penalty the Danish fan ran on to the pitch. The referee took both teams off, he refused to return and play out the remainder of the game and awarded Sweden a 3-0 win. UEFA also ordered Denmark to play their next two home games outside Copenhagen.

* In Group A the two games between Armenia and Azerbaijan were cancelled by UEFA when the two sides failed to agree over where the matches would be played. Armenia were content to play Azerbaijan home and away but Azerbaijan made it clear that the Armenians were not welcome in their country. No points were awarded to either nation.

Euro 2008 Finals – Facts

DATE: 7–29 June 2008

VENUES: Austria – Innsbruck, Klagenfurt, Salzburg, Vienna; Switzerland – Basel, Berne, Geneva, Zurich

QUALIFIED TEAMS: Austria and Switzerland (automatically qualify as co-hosts)

TEAMS: 16 from 52 football associations across Europe

MATCHES: 31

Trivia

* Euro 2008 will have co-hosts for only the second time in the tournament's history. Belgium and the Netherlands we co-hosts in 2000. Euro 2012 will be in Poland and Ukraine.

* When England met Israel on 24 March 2007 in a Euro 2008 qualifier played at the National Stadium, Tel Aviv, Israel, it was only the third time in history that the two sides had met. England have won one with two draws.

* Irish football history was made on 24 March 2007 when the Gaelic Athletic Association allowed the Republic of Ireland to play football at Croke Park for the first time in the stadium's 94-year history while Lansdowne Road was being rebuilt.

* The 2008 European Championships will see Austria's first appearance in the finals.

Managerial Merry-Go-Round 2006–07

England

Date	Club	Div	Outgoing	Incoming	Date
30/8/06	Doncaster Rovers	CCL1	Dave Penney	Sean O'Driscoll	9/9/06
7/9/06	Brighton & Hove Alb	CCL1	Mark McGhee	Dean Wilkins	8/9/06
9/9/06	AFC Bournemouth	CCL1	Sean O'Driscoll	Kevin Bond	12/10/06
18/9/06	West Bromwich Alb[16]	CCL1	Bryan Robson	Tony Mowbray	18/10/06
20/9/06	Leeds United[7]	CCC	Kevin Blackwell	Dennis Wise	25/10/06
20/9/06	Queens Park Rangers	CCC	Gary Waddock	John Gregory	20/9/06
25/9/06	Millwall	CCL1	Nigel Spackman	Willie Donachie	25/9/06
30/9/06	Darlington[6]	CCL2	David Hodgson	Dave Penney	30/10/06
30/9/06	Macclesfield Town	CCL2	Brian Horton	Paul Ince	23/10/06
1/10/06	Norwich City[11]	CCC	Nigel Worthington	Peter Grant	16/10/06
19/10/06	Sheffield Wednesday[13]	CCL1	Paul Sturrock	Brian Laws	6/11/06
24/10/06	Swindon Town[15]	CCL2	Dennis Wise	Paul Sturrock	7/11/06
6/11/06	Scunthorpe United	CCL2	Brian Laws	Nigel Adkins	6/11/06
6/11/06	Grimsby Town	CCL2	Graham Rodger	Alan Buckley	9/11/06
13/11/06	Charlton Athletic	PL	Iain Dowie	Les Reed	14/11/06
18/11/06	Brentford	CCL1	Leroy Rosenior	Scott Fitzgerald	18/11/06
21/11/06	Barnsley	CCC	Andy Ritchie	Simon Davey	21/11/06
27/11/06	Torquay United	CCL2	Ian Atkins	Lubos Kubik	28/11/06
4/12/06	Hull City	CCC	Phil Parkinson	Phil Brown	4/12/06
11/12/06	West Ham United	PL	Alan Pardew	Alan Curbishley	13/12/06
17/12/06	Rochdale	CCL2	Steve Parkin	Keith Hill	18/12/06
19/12/06	Mansfield Town[9]	CCL2	Peter Shirtliff	Bill Dearden	28/12/06
20/12/06	Northampton Town[10]	CCL2	John Gorman	Stuart Gray	2/1/07
24/12/06	Charlton Athletic	PL	Les Reed	Alan Pardew	24/12/06
11/1/07	Wrexham	CCL2	Denis Smith	Brian Carey	12/1/07
15/1/07	Peterborough United[12]	CCL2	Keith Alexander	Darren Ferguson	21/1/07
17/1/07	Coventry City[5]	CCC	Mickey Adams	Iain Dowie	19/2/07
5/2/07	Torquay United	CCL2	Lubos Kubik	Keith Curle	7/2/07
12/2/07	Bradford City[2]	CCL1	Colin Todd	Stuart McCall	22/5/07
15/2/07	Swansea City[14]	CCL1	Kenny Jackett	Roberto Martinez	27/2/07
1/3/07	Rotherham United	CCL1	Alan Knill	Mark Robins	1/3/07
6/3/07	Huddersfield Town[1]	CCL1	Peter Jackson	Andy Ritchie	11/4/07
12/3/07	Chesterfield	CCL1	Roy McFarland	Lee Richardson	12/3/07
15/3/07	Luton Town	CCC	Mike Newell	Kevin Blackwell	27/3/07
9/4/07	Brentford[3]	CCL1	Scott Fitzgerald	Terry Butcher	7/5/07
10/4/07	Fulham	PL	Chris Coleman	Laurie Sanchez	11/4/07
11/4/07	Leicester City[8]	CCC	Robert Kelly	Martin Allen	25/5/07
29/4/07	Bolton Wanderers	PL	Sam Allardyce	Sammy Lee	30/4/07
30/4/07	Chester City[4]	CCL2	Mark Wright	Bob Williamson	11/5/07

Date	Club	Div	Outgoing	Incoming	Date
6/5/07	Newcastle United	PL	Glenn Roeder	Sam Allardyce	15/5/07
14/5/07	Wigan Athletic	PL	Paul Jewell	Chris Hutchings	18/5/07
14/5/07	Manchester City	PL	Stuart Pearce	Sven-Goran Eriksson	5/7/07
15/5/07	Sheffield United	PL	Neil Warnock	Bryan Robson	22/5/07
17/5/07	Torquay United	CCL2	Keith Curle	Leroy Rosenior	17/5/07
17/5/07	Torquay United*	CCL2	Leroy Rosenior	Paul Buckle	2/6/07
25/5/07	Milton Keynes Dons	CCL2	Martin Allen	Paul Ince	25/6/07
27/5/07	Boston United	CCL2	Steve Evans	Tommy Taylor	13/7/07
25/6/07	Macclesfield Town	CCL2	Paul Ince	Ian Brightwell	29/6/07
1/7/07	Crewe Alexandra	CCL1	Dario Gradi	Steve Holland	1/7/07
13/8/07	Carlisle United[17]	CCL1	Neil McDonald	*No appointment yet*	
29/8/07	Leicester City[18]	CCC	Martin Allen	*No appointment yet*	

*Leroy Rosenior was appointed manager of Torquay United on 17 May but, following a takeover on the same day, he was dismissed 10 minutes after accepting the job – the shortest-ever managerial tenure in English football.

[1] Gerry Murphy Huddersfield Town caretaker 6/3–11/4/07
[2] Dave Weatherall Bradford City caretaker 12/2–22/5/07
[3] Barry Quinn Brentford caretaker 10/4–7/5/07
[4] Simon Davies Chester City caretaker 30/4–11/5/07
[5] Adrian Heath Coventry City caretaker 17/1–19/2/07
[6] Neil Maddison and Martin Gray Darlington joint caretakers 30/9–30/10/06
[7] John Carver caretaker 20/9–23/10/06, David Geddis caretaker 23/10–25/10/06
[8] Nigel Worthington caretaker 11/4–25/5/07
[9] Paul Holland caretaker 19/12–28/12/06
[10] Jim Barron and Ian Sampson joint caretakers 20/12/06–2/1/07
[11] Martin Hunter caretaker 1/10–15/10/06
[12] Tommy Taylor caretaker 15/1–20/1/07
[13] Sean McAuley caretaker 19/10–6/11/06
[14] Kevin Nugent caretaker 15/2–27/2/07
[15] Adrian Williams and Barry Hunter joint-caretakers 25/10–7/11/06
[16] Nigel Pearson caretaker 19/9–16/10/06, Craig Shakespeare caretaker 16/10–17/10/06
[17] Gregg Abbott caretaker 13/8–date/07. McDonald was sacked two days after drawing the season-opener at Walsall
[18] Martin Allen's stint at Leicester ended after just four competitive matches

Managers of the Month 2006–07

PREMIER LEAGUE

Month	Manager	Team
August	Sir Alex Ferguson	Manchester United
September	Steve Coppell	Reading
October	Sir Alex Ferguson	Manchester United
November	Steve Coppell	Reading
December	Sam Allardyce	Bolton Wanderers
January	Rafael Benitez	Liverpool
February	Sir Alex Ferguson	Manchester United
March	Jose Mourinho	Chelsea
April	Martin O'Neill	Aston Villa
Manager of the year	Sir Alex Ferguson	Manchester United

Scotland

Date	Club	Div	Outgoing	Incoming	Date
1/9/06	Raith Rovers	SFL2	Gordon Dalziel	Craig Levein	5/9/06
12/10/06	Hibernian[E]	SPL	Tony Mowbray	John Collins	31/10/06
21/10/06	Cowdenbeath	SFL2	Mixu Paatelainen	Brian Welsh	30/10/06
25/10/06	Dunfermline Athletic[B]	SPL	Jim Leishman	Stephen Kenny	10/11/06
29/10/06	Dundee United	SPL	Craig Brewster	Craig Levein	30/10/06
29/10/06	Peterhead	SFL2	Iain Stewart	Steve Paterson	30/10/06
30/10/06	Raith Rovers	SFL2	Craig Levein	John McGlynn	20/11/06
1/11/06	Stenhousemuir	SFL3	Des McKeown	Campbell Money	10/11/06
13/11/06	Airdrie United	SFL1	Sandy Stewart	Kenny Black	17/11/06
17/12/06	Elgin City[C]	SFL3	Brian Irvine	R Williamson	11/1/07
4/1/07	Rangers	SPL	Paul Le Guen	Walter Smith	10/1/07
17/1/07	Montrose	SFL3	David Robertson	Jim Weir	8/2/07
26/2/07	Ayr United[A]	SFL2	Bobby Connor	Neil Watt	22/3/07
19/3/07	Forfar Athletic[D]	SFL2	George Shaw	Jim Moffatt	7/4/07
20/03/07	Heart of Midlothian[++]	SPL	Valdas Ivanauskas	Kestutis Latoza	20/3/07
3/07	Gretna[**]	SFL1	Rowan Alexander	Davie Irons	3/07
27/3/07	Partick Thistle[H]	SFL1	Dick Campbell	Ian McCall	25/5/07
15/4/07	Livingston[F]	SFL1	John Robertson	Mark Proctor	23/5/07
28/4/07	Queen of the South	SFL1	Ian McCall	Gordon Chisholm	7/5/07
28/4/07	Ross County	SFL1	Scott Leitch	Dick Campbell	17/5/07
8/5/07	Albion Rovers	SFL3	Jim Chapman	J McCormack	31/5/07
25/5/07	Clyde	SFL1	Joe Miller	Colin Hendry	11/6/07
1/6/07	Motherwell[G]	SPL	Maurice Malpas	Mark McGhee	18/6/07
20/8/07	Inverness Caley Thistle	SPL	Charlie Christie	Craig Brewster	27/8/07

[++] Heart of Midlothian manager Vadas Ivanauskas was stood down because of health reasons by majority shareholder Vladimir Romanov and was absent from 23/10 to 1/12. He was replaced, at this time, by Eduard Malofeev. After Ivanauskas left in March both Kestutis Latoza and Anotoly Korobochka are recorded as interim managers. No permanent appointment has been made.

[**] Gretna manager Rowan Alexander stood down because of ill health; his successor, Davie Irons, has been caretaker manager in Alexander's absence. The move was made permanent late in the summer.

[A] Mark McGeown, Brian Reid, Tom Tait & Alex Ingram Ayr United caretakers 26/2–22/3/07

[B] Craig Robertson Dunfermline caretaker 25/10–10/11/06

[C] Graham Tatters Elgin City caretaker 26/12/06–11/01/07

[D] Paul Tosh Forfar caretaker 19/3–26/3/06; Alan Rattray Forfar caretaker 26/3–11/4/07

[E] Mark Proctor and John Park Hibernian caretakers 13/10–31/10/06

[F] David Bowman Livingston caretaker 15/4–16/5/07

[G] Scott Letich Motherwell caretaker 1/6–18/6/07

[H] Jim Bone Partick Thistle caretaker 27/3–25/5/07

Scottish PFA Manager of the Year 2006–07

SCOTTISH PREMIER LEAGUE

Manager	Team
Gordon Strachan	Glasgow Celtic

National Teams

Date	Club	Outgoing	Incoming	Date
10/1/07	Scotland	Walter Smith	Alex McLeish	29/1/07
25/1/07	England U21	Peter Taylor	Stuart Pearce	1/2/07
11/5/07	N. Ireland	Lawrie Sanchez	Nigel Worthington	1/6/07

European Clubs

Club	Outgoing	Incoming	Last club (country)
SPAIN			
Real Betis	Luis Fernandez	Hector Cupar	Mallorca
Athletic Bilbao	Jose Manuel Esnal	Joaquin Caparros	Deportivo Coruna
Deportivo Coruna	Joaquin Caparros	Miguel A. Lotina	Real Sociedad
Getafe	Bernd Schuster	Michael Laudrup	Brondby *(Den)*
Recreativo Huelva	Marcelino Garcia	Victor Munoz	Panathinaikos *(Gre)*
Levante	Juan Ramon Lopez Caro	Abel Resino	Murcia
Real Madrid	Fabio Capello	Bernd Schuster	Getafe
Murcia	Abel Resino	Luis Alcaraz	Xerez
Racing Santander	Miguel Angel Portugal	Marcelino Garcia	Recreativo Huelva
Real Sociedad	Miguel Angel Lotina	Chris Coleman	Fulham *(Eng)*
Celta Vigo	Fernando Vazquez	Hristo Stoichkov	Bulgaria *(national)*
ITALY			
Atalanta	Stefano Colantuono	Luigi Del Neri	Chievo
Catania	Pasquale Marino	Silvio Bandini	Lecce
Juventus	Didier Deschamps	Claudio Ranieri	Parma
Livorno	Danieli Arrigoni	Fernando Orsi	*(first head coach job)*
Palermo	Francesco Guidolin	Stefano Colantuono	Atalanta
Parma	Claudio Ranieri	Domenico Di Carlo	Mantova
Reggina	Walter Mazzarri	Massimo Ficcadenti	Verona
Sampdoria	Walter Novellino	Walter Mazzarri	Reggina
Siena	Mario Beretta	Andrea Mandorlini	Padova
Torino	Gianni Di Biasi	Walter Novellino	Sampdoria
Udinese	Alberto Malesani	Pasquale Marino	Catania
GERMANY			
Hertha Berlin	Falko Gotz	Lucien Favre	FC Zurich *(Swi)*
Arminia Bielefeld	Frank Geideck	Ernst Middendorp	Kaizer Chiefs *(SA)*
Borussia Dortmund	Jurgen Rober	Thomas Doll	Hamburg
Hamburg	Thomas Doll	Huub Stevens	Roda *(Neth)*
Bayern Munich	Felix Magath	Ottmar Hitzfeld	Bayern (2004)
Wolfsburg	Klaus Augenthaler	Felix Magath	Bayern Munich

Transfer News 2006–07

Manchester United were the biggest off-season spenders, bringing in England international Owen Hargreaves from Bayern Munich, Portuguese starlet Nani from Sporting Lisbon and Brazilian Anderson from FC Porto, for a combined total approaching £50 million. Their attempts to sign West Ham's Argentine star Carlos Tevez were resolved with the transfer to go through in 2008 after he spends the 2007–08 season on loan.

Tottenham broke their club record by spending £16.6 million on striker Darren Bent from Charlton Athletic. Local rivals Arsenal received a similar sum for French striker Thierry Henry as he left London for Barcelons.

Welsh captain Craig Bellamy left Liverpool after just one season and joined West Ham United. The fee was £7.5 million – significantly less than the Reds will have spent on Israeli Yossi Benayoun, who went the other way. Liverpool's big-money deals brought Atletico Madrid striker Fernando Torres for £30 million and Ajax and Holland under-21 star Ryan Babel for £11.5 million

No summer would be complete without big-money moves involving Chelsea. They signed Lyon and France international Florent Malouda and sold Arjen Robben to Real Madrid.

Championship club West Bromwich Albion missed out on promotion in the play-off final, but their coffers were swollen by more than £10 million as Welsh international Jason Koumas joined Wigan Athletic and Senegalese striker Diomansy Kamara went to Fulham.

Headline Transfers 2006–07

Month	Player	From	To	Fee
Oct 06	Henrik Larsson	Helsingborg	Manchester Utd	Loan*
Jan 07	Milan Baros	Aston Villa	Lyon	Undisclosed
Jan 07	Luis Boa Morte	Fulham	West Ham Utd	Undisclosed
Jan 07	John Carew	Lyon	Aston Villa	Undisclosed
Jan 07	Calum Davenport	Tottenham Hotspur	West Ham Utd	Undisclosed
Jan 07	Alvaro Arbeloa	Deportivo La Coruna	Liverpool	£2.6m
Jan 07	Edgar Davids	Tottenham Hotspur	Ajax	Undisclosed
Jan 07	Simon Davies	Everton	Fulham	Undisclosed
Jan 07	Clint Dempsey	NE Revolution	Fulham	Undisclosed
Jan 07	David Dunn	Birmingham	Blackburn	Undisclosed
Jan 07	Ugo Ehiogu	Middlesbrough	Rangers	Free
Jan 07	Lauren	Arsenal	Portsmouth	Undisclosed
Jan 07	Javier Mascherano	West Ham Utd	Liverpool	Undisclosed
Jan 07	Lucas Neill	Blackburn	West Ham Utd	Undisclosed
Jan 07	Nigel Quashie	WBA	West Ham Utd	£1.5m
Jan 07	Claudio Reyna	Manchester City	NY Red Bulls	Free
Jan 07	Ricardo Rocha	Benfica	Tottenham	Undisclosed
Jan 07	Ronaldo	Real Madrid	Milan	£5.2m
Jan 07	Alexi Smertin	Dynamo Moscow	Fulham	Undisclosed
Jan 07	Ben Thatcher	Manchester City	Charlton	£500,000

Month	Player	From	To	Fee
Jan 07	Kevin Thomson	Hibernian	Rangers	£2m
Jan 07	Matthew Upson	Birmingham	West Ham Utd	£6m
Jan 07	Ashley Young	Watford	Aston Villa	£9.65m
May 07	Anderson	FC Porto	Manchester Utd	Undisclosed
May 07	Nani	Sporting Clube	Manchester Utd	Undisclosed
June 07	David Beckham	Real Madrid	LA Galaxy	Bosman
June 07	Darren Bent	Charlton Athletic	Tottenham	£15.5m
June 07	Gio. van Bronckhorst	Barcelona	Feyenoord	Free
June 07	Roberto Carlos	Real Madrid	Fenerbahce	Bosman
June 07	Diego Forlan	Villareal	Atletico Madrid	£14.16m
June 07	Owen Hargreaves	Bayern Munich	Manchester Utd	£17m
June 07	Thierry Henry	Arsenal	Barcelona	£18m
July 07	Luis Garcia	Liverpool	Atletico Madrid	Undisclosed
July 07	Geremi	Chelsea	Newcastle Utd	Free
July 07	Fernando Torres	Atletico Madrid	Liverpool	Undisclosed
Aug 07	Keiran Dyer	Newcastle Utd	West Ham Utd	£6m
Aug 07	Elano	Shakhtor Donetsk	Manchester City	£8m
Aug 07	Craig Gordon	Heart of Midlothian	Sunderland	£9m
Aug 07	Mido	Tottenham Hotspur	Middlesbrough	£6m
Aug 07	Arjen Robben	Chelsea	Real Madrid	Undisclosed
Aug 07	Alan Smith	Manchester Utd	Newcastle Utd	£6m
Aug 07	Yakubu	Middlesbrough	Everton	£11.25m

Larsson's loan began in January 2007 and ended in March 2007. He was offered the chance to extend the contract but declined.

Trivia

* The biggest deal of the offseason saw David Beckham join MLS club LA Galaxy from Real Madrid on a Bosman.

* Roberto Ayala left Valencia to join Villareal on a summer 2007 Bosman deal. Before Argentina's captain had even trained with them, he joined Real Zaragoza.

* Almost unnoticed, Ronaldo ended his six-year spell with Real Madrid joining Milan for around £5 million in January.

* Real Madrid signed Brazilian defender Pepe from Porto for £20.3m, while they signed Argentina striker Javier Saviola from Barcelona on a Bosman.

* Another big-money defender deal saw Argentina's Gabriel Milito go from Real Zaragoza to Barcelona for £13.5m.

* The largest deal in Italy saw Honduras striker David Suazo join Internazionale from Cagliari for £9.47 million.

* On the final day of transfer activity (31 August 2007) Fulham signed Shefki Kuqi, Danny Murphy and Dejan Stefanovic, making it a Premier League record 15 signings by Lawrie Sanchez.

European Under-21 Championships 2007

DATE: 10–23 June *VENUE:* Holland

Holland easily retained their title after hammering Serbia 4–1. Goals from Otman Bakkal, Ryan Babel and Maeco Ritgers put the Dutch in command before Dragan Mrdja scored for Serbia, who had Aleksandar Kolarov sent off. Luigi Bruins sealed the victory for the host nation with their fourth goal late in the one-sided affair. Rigters's strike was his fourth of the competition and was enough to put him one ahead of England's Leroy Lita to win the Golden Boot as the top goal scorer.

England's Group Matches

Date	Location	Opponents	Result
11 June	Arnhem	Czech Republic	0–0
14 June	Arnhem	Italy	2–2
17 June	Nijmegan	Serbia	2–0

Group A	P	W	D	L	F	A	Pts	Group B	P	W	D	L	F	A	Pts
Holland	3	2	1	0	5	3	7	Serbia	3	2	0	1	2	2	6
Belgium	3	1	2	0	3	2	5	England	3	1	2	0	4	2	5
Portugal	3	1	1	1	5	2	4	Italy	3	1	1	1	4	1	4
Israel	3	0	0	3	0	6	0	Czech Rep.	3	0	1	2	4	3	1

Olympic Qualifying Play-Off Match*

Portugal 0 (3)   Italy 0 (4) *(decided on penalties)*

*Top two from each group qualify as of right for the 2008 Olympics,
but England do not send a national team so were not eligible.

Semi-finals

DATE: 20 June *VENUE:* Heerenveen
Holland 1 England 1 *(Holland won 13–12 on penalties – an EU21 record of 32 were taken)*
Serbia 2 Belgium 0

Final

DATE: 23 June *VENUE:* Euroborg, Groningen

Holland 4 – 1 Serbia
Bakkal 17, Babel 60, Ritgers 67, Bruins 87   Mrdja 79

Holland: Waterman, Zuiverloon, Kruiswijk, Donk, Pieters *(Jong-a-Pin)*, Maduro, Drenthe *(Beerens)*, De Ridder, Bakkal, Ritgers, Babel *(Bruins)*. Coach: Foppe de Haan.
Serbia: Kahriman, Rukavina, Ivanovic, Tosic D., Kolarov, Smiljanic, Drincic *(Tosic Z.)*, Basta *(Babovic)*, Milvanovic, Jankovic, Rakic *(Mrdja)*. Coach: Miroslav Djukic.

The AFC Asian Cup 2007

DATE: 7-29 July *CO-HOST NATIONS:* Indonesia, Malaysia, Thailand, Vietnam

The AFC Asian Cup is Asia's most prestigious football competition with the winners automatically earning qualification to the FIFA Confederations Cup. The inaugural competition was held in Hong Kong in 1956 (winners, Korea Republic) and has been held every four years since. However, when Beijing, China won the right to host the 2008 Olympic Games the organisers of the Asian Cup decided to bring the 2008 competition forward one year. Iraq, playing in their maiden Asian Cup Final, beat the 3-times winners and 2-times beaten finalists, Saudi Arabia 1-0 to win the 2007 AFC Asian Cup.

Semi-Finals

Iraq 0–0 South Korea *(Iraq won 4-3 on penalties after extra-time)*
Bukit Jalil Stadium, Kuala Lumpur, Malaysia

Saudi Arabia 3 – 2 Japan
My Dinh National Stadium, Hanoi, Vietnam

Third Place Play-Off

Korea 0 – 0 Japan *(South Korea won 6-5 on penalties after extra-time)*
Jakabaring Stadium, Palembang, Indonesia

Final

DATE: 29 July *VENUE:* Bung Karno Stadium, Jakarta; Attendance: 60,000
Iraq 1 – 0 Saudi Arabia
Younis Mahmoud 76

Iraq: Noor Sabri Abbas, Jassim Gholam, Bassim Abbas *(Ali Abbas)*, Haidar Abdul Amer, Ali Hussein Rehema, Nashat Akram, Hawar Mohammed, Karrar Jassim *(Ahmed Menajed)*, Mahdi Karim *(Ahmed Abid Ali)*, Qusay Munir, Younis Mahmoud.
Saudi Arabia: Yaser Al Mosailem, Osama Hawsawi, Kamil Al Mousa, Waleed Jahdali, Saud Khariri, Ahmed Al Bahari *(Saad Al Harthi)*, Khaled Aziz, Taiseer Al Jassam *(Abdoh Autef)*, Abdulrahman Al Qahtani *(Ahmed Al Mousa)*, Malek Maaz, Yasser Al Qahtani.

Top Goal Scorer – 4: Younis Mahmoud *(Iraq)*, Naohiro Takahara *(Japan)*,
Yasser Al-Qahtani *(Saudi Arabia)*

Most Valuable Player: Younis Mahmoud *(Iraq)*

Trivia

*Ali Daei of Iran holds the record for the most goals in the AFC Asian Cup, 14.

FIFA Under-20 World Cup 2007

30 June–22 July; Six host cities, Canada

Canada hosted the 52-match FIFA Under-20 World Cup, the biggest single-sport event in Canadian history. The matches were held at six venues: Victoria, Burnaby, Edmonton, Toronto, Ottawa and Montreal. The six group-winners and runners-up, plus the four best third-placed teams progressed to the knockout stages. The hosts and Scotland, the only British interest, failed to win a single point. Brazil lost to Spain in the first knockout stage. In the quarter-finals, Austria beat the USA 2–1 (aet), Czech Republic drew 1–1 with Spain (aet) but won 5–4 on penalties, Chile beat Nigeria 4–0 (aet) and Argentina defeated Mexico 1–0. Chile beat Austria for third place. Argentina strolled to the final conceding one goal in six games, where they met the Czechs, who won only two of their six games in 90 minutes.

Group Tables

Team	P	W	D	L	F	A	Pts
Group A							
1. Chile	3	2	1	0	6	0	7
2. Austria	3	1	2	0	2	1	5
3. Congo	3	1	1	1	3	4	4
4. Canada	3	0	0	3	0	6	0
Group B							
1. Spain	3	2	1	0	8	5	7
2. Zambia	3	1	1	1	4	3	4
3. Uruguay	3	1	1	1	3	4	4
4. Jordan	3	0	1	2	3	6	1
Group C							
1. Mexico	3	3	0	0	7	2	9
2. Gambia	3	2	0	1	3	4	6
3. Portugal	3	1	0	2	4	4	3
4. New Zealand	3	0	0	3	1	5	0

Team	P	W	D	L	F	A	Pts
Group D							
1. USA	3	2	1	0	9	3	7
2. Poland	3	1	1	1	3	7	4
3. Brazil	3	1	0	2	4	5	3
4. South Korea	3	0	2	1	4	5	2
Group E							
1. Argentina	3	2	1	0	7	0	7
2. Czech Rep.	3	1	2	0	4	3	5
3. North Korea	3	0	2	1	2	3	2
4. Panama	3	0	1	2	1	8	1
Group F							
1. Japan	3	2	1	0	4	1	7
2. Nigeria	3	2	1	0	3	0	7
3. Costa Rica	3	1	0	2	2	3	3
4. Scotland	3	0	0	3	2	7	0

Round of 16

11 July	Edmonton	Austria	2–1	Gambia
11 July	Toronto	USA	2–1 *aet*	Uruguay
11 July	Burnaby	Spain	4–2 *aet*	Brazil
11 July	Victoria	Japan	2–2 *(3–4p)*	Czech Rep.
12 July	Edmonton	Chile	1–0	Portugal
12 July	Ottawa	Zambia	1–2	Nigeria
12 July	Toronto	Argentina	3–1	Poland
12 July	Montreal	Mexico	3–0	Congo

Quarter-finals

14 July	Toronto	Austria	2–1 *aet*	USA
14 July	Edmonton	Spain	1–1 *(3–4p)*	Czech Rep.
15 July	Montreal	Chile	4–0 *aet*	Nigeria
15 July	Ottawa	Argentina	1–0	Mexico

Semi-finals

18 July	Edmonton	Austria	0–2	Czech Republic
19 July	Toronto	Chile	0–3	Argentina

Third-place Play-off

22 July	Toronto	Austria	0–1	Chile

Final – 22 July 2007

National Soccer Stadium, Toronto, Canada

Argentina successfully defended their title to claim a sixth FIFA Under-20 World Cup. They were hot favourites to retain the the cup, but they were made to work very hard for their success. The first-half was notable for 29 fouls and six yellow cards issued by Spanish referee Alberto Undiano Mallenco. However, both goalkeepers, Radek Petr and Sergio Romero, distinguished themselves with some fine saves. After 60 minutes, Martin Fenin shocked Argentina by firing a first-time shot past Romero to give the Czech Republic the lead. It lasted only two minutes, because Sergio Aguero sprinted between two defenders to slide home a through ball from Ever Banega for the equalizer. Aguero, who was a member of Argentina's successful 2005 team and would be named player of tournament and winner of the Golden Boot in Canada, became the second man to win two Under-20 World Cups when Mauro Zarate rifled a 20-yarder into the net after 86 minutes.

Czech Republic 1 – 2 Argentina
Fenin 60   Aguero 62, Zarate 86

Czech Republic: Petr, Kuban, Mazuch, Simunek, Kudela, Fenin,
Mares *(Gecov, 76)*, Micola, Strestik *(Pekhart, 83)*, Suchy, Kalouda
Subs not used: Dohnalek, Valenta, Held, Oklestek, Frydrych, Cihlar, Frystak
Booked: Kuban, Mazuch, Simunek, Kudela, Fenin, Micola

Argentina: Romero, Fazio, Insua, Mercado, Banega, Sigali,
Moralez *(Cabral, 90)*, Sanchez, Zarate, Aguero, Piatti *(Acosta, 80)*
Subs not used: Escudero, Garcia, Voboril, Gomez, Di Maria, Centeno
Booked: Mercado, Banega, Sanches, Zarate
Att: 4,062

Copa America 2007

26 June–15 July 2007; Nine host cities in Venezuela

The opening day of the 42nd Copa America brought with it the first shock when Uruguay were surprisingly beaten by Peru. The following day an even greater shock occurred when Brazil, the defending champions, lost 2–0 to Mexico. Meanwhile, the favourites, Argentina, beat the USA 4–1 in their opening game. The hosts, Venezuela, drew their opening game 2–2 with Bolivia but when they beat Peru 2–0 it was their first Copa America win in 40 years to take top spot in Group A, eventually winning the group.

Mexico continued their good start and won Group B with Brazil runners-up, while Argentina were the only nation to win all three of their group games. The quarter-finals brought Brazil and Chile together again. After beating them 3–0 in their group encounter, Brazil hammered their opponents 6–1. Uruguay beat Venezuela 4–1, Mexico beat Paraguay 6–0 and Argentina cruised into the semi-finals with a 6–0 thrashing of Paraguay. In the semi-finals, Argentina disposed of Mexico 3–0 while Brazil scraped past Uruguay 5–4 on penalties after the game ended 2–2. Mexico beat Uruguay 3–0 in the third place play-off.

GROUP A	Pts	GROUP B	Pts	GROUP C	Pts
1. Venezuela	5	1. Mexico	7	1. Argentina	9
2. Peru	4	2. Brazil	6	2. Paraguay	6
3. Uruguay*	4	3. Chile*	4	3. Colombia	3
4. Bolivia	2	4. Ecuador	0	4. USA	0

*At the end of the group matches the two teams with the best third placed finishes progressed to the quarter-finals with the three group winners and runners-up.

Quarter-final

Venezuela 1–4 Uruguay
Chile 1–6 **Brazil**
Mexico 6–0 Paraguay
Argentina 4–0 Peru

Semi-final

Uruguay 2 (4)–2 (5) **Brazil**
(decided on penalties)
Mexico 0–3 **Argentina**

Final – 15 July 2007, Estadio Jose Pachencho Romero, Maracaibo

Brazil retained the Copa America following a comfortable 3–0 victory over the favourites Argentina. With just four minutes gone, Brazil were 1–0 up when the former Arsenal striker, Julio Baptista, fired past Roberto Abbondanzieri into the Argentina net. Then in the 40th minute, Roberto Ayala inadvertently deflected Daniel Alves' cross into his own net to give the Brazilians a 2–0 half-time lead. Then Alves scored Brazil's third in the 69th minute to give A Selecao (meaning "The Selection") their eighth Copa America title, denying their arch-rivals a record 15th crown. Brazil's victory was all the more impressive without superstars Kaka and Ronaldinho who had both stayed at home.

Brazil 3 – 0 Argentina
Baptista 4, Ayala 40 (o.g.), Alves 69

Brazil: Doni, Maicon, Alex, Gilberto, Juan Silveira dos Santos, Josué, Mineiro, Elano *(Daniel Alves, 34)*, Julio César Baptista, Robinho *(Diego Ribas da Cunha, 90+1)*, Vagner Love *(Fernando, 90)*

Argentina: Roberto Abbondanzieri, Roberto Ayala, Gabriel Heinze, Gabriel Milito, Javier Mascherano, Javier Aldemar Zanetti, Juan Roman Riquelme, Juan Sebastian Verón *(Luis Oscar González, 67)*, Esteban Cambiasso *(Pablo Aimar, 59)*, Lionel Andrés Messi, Carlos Alberto Tevez
Att: 40,000

Third-place Play-off	Top Scorer of the Tournament
Uruguay 1–3 Mexico	Robinho *(Brazil)* 6 goals

"We came to rescue the self-esteem of the Brazilian worker, who wakes up in the morning and returns home late at night, whose only satisfaction in life is seeing Brazil win a football match."
Brazil coach
Dunga

"We knew we had to be awake today, but instead we were caught falling asleep. It makes you angry being unable to win and close out an exceptional tournament."
Argentina
Carlos Tevez

UEFA Super Cup 2007

31 August 2007; Stade Louis II, Monaco; AC Milan 3–1 Sevilla

AC Milan, the 2007 UEFA Champions League winners, beat the 2007 UEFA Cup winners, Sevilla, 3–1 in the Super Cup final. The Sevilla players, still shocked at the death of their team-mate Antonio Puerta just three days earlier, were looking to become only the second team to defend the trophy, thereby equalling the achievement of their opponents. Sevilla took the lead on 14 minutes with a goal from Renato, but three second-half strikes from Filippo Inzaghi (55), Marek Jankulovski (62) and Kaka (87), the UEFA Club Footballer of the Year 2007, gave the Rossoneri their fifth Super Cup – a record.

"We don't know how we will feel tomorrow. To pay tribute to him [Antonio Puerta], we will play the best we can. We know a victory or a defeat will not have the same meaning."
Milan player Massimo Ambrosini

"All this has become a bit meaningless."
Milan coach Carlo Ancelotti on the eve of the game

The New Wembley Stadium

The last ever match played at the original Wembley Stadium took place on 7 October 2000 when England lost their opening 2002 World Cup qualifying game against Germany. Dietmar Hamann scored the only goal of the game to give the Germans a 1–0 win under the famous old twin towers. The defeat marked the end of Kevin Keegan's 20-month reign as England manager as he immediately resigned following the loss.

The new stadium was designed by the architects HOK Sport and Foster and Partners, Mott MacDonald were the appointed engineers while the Australian company, Multiplex, were awarded the contract to construct English football's new home. The plan was to commence demolition work of the old stadium soon after the Germany game so that the new Wembley would be ready in time to stage the 2003 FA Cup final, 80 years after the old stadium hosted its maiden FA Cup final. However, a succession of delays meant that work only began in September 2002, with the official opening delayed until the 2006 FA Cup final.

In October 2002, piling work commenced while the pitch area was excavated with the new pitch level set at 4 metres below the old one. Mid-2003 saw the assembly of what is today an iconic image on the London landscape, the Wembley arch, a circular section lattice arch measuring 133 by 315 metres and weighing 1.65 tonnes. The stadium's signature feature supports the entire weight of the north roof and 60 per cent of the weight of the retractable roof on the southern side. This engineering masterpiece is the world's longest unsupported roof structure. However, the arch was not without its own problems, ultimately leading to Cleveland Bridge, the company sub-contracted to construct the arch, being removed from the project in 2003. Problems concerning design changes, rising costs and a construction delay were attributed to their dismissal. They were replaced by Hollandia, a company based in the Netherlands. In early 2004, work on the terracing supports and units commenced and by mid-2004, the arch was rotated into place to permit the work on the southern side of the stadium to be completed and the roof structure put in place – the roof stands 52 metres above pitch level. Away from the building site, the cultivation of Wembley's new surface got underway.

Around mid-2005, the construction of the roof was completed with the sliding roof panels installed to allow the southern roof to partially retract. Meanwhile, the arch was de-propped from its supports and fixed to the roof. Outside the stadium, the bridge link to Olympic Way was rebuilt. Towards the end of 2005 the roof was completed and the under-pitch heating and drainage system were installed, leading Richard Caborn, the sports minister, to announce in October 2005: "They say the FA Cup final (2006) will be there, barring six feet of snow or something like that." Despite a number of financial difficulties and various legal wrangles that plagued the contract to build the stadium, Multiplex were confident that the stadium would be officially opened on 13 May 2006 for the FA Cup final.

However, further problems and concerns over the completion date followed, with Multiplex admitting that there was a "material risk" that the stadium might not be completed in time for the Cup final, resulting in the FA announcing that the 2006 showpiece event would be played at the Millennium Stadium, Cardiff, the competition's temporary home since 2001. On 20 March 2006, around 3,000 workers had to evacuate the stadium when a steel rafter collapsed. Three days later sewers beneath the stadium buckled due to ground movement, with the repair work estimated to take months. These setbacks resulted in a Wembley Stadium announcement on 31 March 2006 confirming that all events scheduled to be held at the stadium in 2006 were cancelled. All of this now meant that the official opening was delayed until 2007. The new Wembley turf was laid on 19 June 2006 and on 19 October 2006, Multiplex breathed a huge sigh of relief announcing that they had settled their dispute with the FA (centred around possible penalty payments because of late completion) and the stadium would be ready in early March 2007.

The keys to the "new" Wembley Stadium were handed over to their owners, the Football Association, on 9 March 2007. The unexpected hiccups during the construction phase resulted in the stadium exceeding its original budget (£757m) and in the end it cost a whopping £1 billion, (£798m to build and £200m to improve the existing transport infrastructure and the cost of financing) making it the most expensive stadium ever constructed in the world. The project was funded by the FA, Sport England, Wembley National Stadium Limited, the London Development Agency and the Department for Culture, Media and Sport.

However, despite its astronomic cost it truly is a magnificent stadium and a fitting successor to the original Wembley Stadium. Fans approaching the front of the stadium are greeted by a statue of Bobby Moore, England's 1966 World Cup-winning captain. The new stadium can accommodate 90,000 fans and with a built-in sliding roof it makes it the largest roof-covered seating capacity in the world. The stadium can also be used as an athletics stadium by means of erecting a temporary platform over the lowest tier of seating, although the capacity is reduced by up to 20,000 seats.

The stadium's first major event was the 2007 FA Cup final, on 19 May, between Chelsea and Manchester United, at which Prince William officially declared the stadium open. The Football League play-offs followed later in the month. England's first ever game at their new home took place on 1 June 2007, a 1–1 draw with Brazil. Welcome to the new Wembley!

Trivia

* It took 1,750 tonnes of British steel to make the arch, equivalent to 10 jumbo jets or 275 double-decker buses.

* Mark Bright scored the first goal at the new stadium in the first game it hosted – Geoff Thomas Foundation Charity XI versus the Wembley Sponsors Allstars on 17 March 2007.

* The first player to score in a FIFA-sanctioned match was Italy's Under-21 player Giampaolo Pazzini in a 3–3 draw

with England Under-21. Pazzini scored all three of Italy's goals, making him the first player to score a hat-trick at Wembley Stadium since Paul Scholes in 1999. The first English player to score in a FIFA-sanctioned game was England Under-21 David Bentley in the same game.

* Exeter City's Matthew Gill was the first player sent off at the new Wembley, given the red card during the 2007 Nationwide Conference play-offs.

Celebrity News

Matches of the Day

On Friday 15 June 2007 John Terry (26), captain of Chelsea and England, married Toni Poole (24) at Blenheim Palace, Oxfordshire. To protect the event from the eyes of the public and the paparazzi, vast canvas screens were erected. There were rumours that the couple had agreed a £1m exclusive deal with *OK!* magazine to photograph their big day.

The day after, Saturday 16 June, three England international footballers married their girlfriends in a series of lavish ceremonies across the country. First up was the Liverpool captain, Steven Gerrard (26) who married Alex Curran (24) at Cliveden House Hotel in Berkshire. Manchester United's captain, Gary Neville (32), married girlfriend Emma Hadfield (24) at Manchester Cathedral, while his Old Trafford team-mate, Michael Carrick (25) wed Lisa Roughhead (25) at St Peter's Church in Wymondham, Leicestershire. With three weddings taking place on the same day there was the inevitable dilemma of whose wedding to attend. Particular speculation surrounded Wayne Rooney and his fiancée, Coleen McLoughlin, who were believed to have been invited to all three weddings. Rumours were rife that they were going to travel by helicopter and attend at least two of the weddings. In reality, Rooney attended only his skipper Neville's wedding.

Did You Know That?
The total cost of the four WAG weddings was around £3 million.

The Beckhams Go Stateside

In mid-July 2007 Becks moved from Real Madrid to the Los Angeles Galaxy, a team in Major League Soccer (MLS), that has won the MLS Cup and the MLS Supporters' Shield twice. So, Posh and the boys packed their bags and left Madrid to head to Tinsel Town, Hollywood. If the Beckhams thought the paparazzi attention was intense when they were Madrilènes, life in LA will be one huge celebrity goldfish bowl.

In true Hollywood fashion the Beckhams took America by storm with a "Welcome to LA" party hosted by Tom Cruise, Katie Holmes, Will Smith and Jada Pinkett-Smith at the LA Museum of Contemporary Art. When Becks was "unveiled" to the Galaxy fans at the team's stadium in Carson, California, the paparazzi went into a camera-clicking frenzy and the lenses were not just pointing at the former England captain. Posh turned up wearing a £990 pink Robert Mouret moon dress, with a matching pink ostrich skin Hermes Birkin bag, Balenciaga court shoes and, yes, you guessed it, those oversized trademark thick black sunglasses.

David Beckham wants to change the American public's opinion of professional soccer while Posh hopes to change the American opinion of her. Indeed, Posh went to work quickly and signed-up for a cameo appearance on the hit TV show *Ugly Betty*.

When The WAGs Took Over

On 15 August 2007, the Sunderland manager Roy Keane, no stranger to controversy himself during his high profile career as a footballer with Manchester United, laid into a new vice that he feels is seeping into the game – WAG's shopping. The Black Cats' boss was enraged when a number of the players he attempted to sign before the 2007–08 Premier League season got underway turned down a move to the Stadium of Light because their WAGs complained that the city lacked attractive shopping opportunities. "If a player doesn't want to come to Sunderland then all well and good. But if he decides he doesn't want to come because his wife wants to go shopping in London, then it's a sad state of affairs."

There was a time when managers had to be on the look out for their players indulging in binge drinking or gambling to pass the time between games, but now it seems that more and more players are being dragged to the trendy boutiques and shops; less of an immediate worry for the manager but a worrying trend when a footballer decides what club he will join based on the designer label shops in the city's High Street. "It's different with Chelsea, Arsenal or maybe Tottenham, but if players are starting to go to clubs just because they're in London and they're not even that big a club, it's clearly down to the shops. We had a player who didn't even ring us back [about a contract offer] this summer because his wife wanted to move to London – and, yes, shopping was mentioned. To me it's wrong to sign for a club with half the crowds and less attention [than Sunderland]," added the former United and Republic of Ireland captain Keane.

World's Richest Clubs

In February 2006, Real Madrid dethroned Manchester United as the world's richest club in the table compiled annually by Deloitte, the second largest professional services firm in the world. In 2007, United, who had topped the table for eight consecutive years, slipped a further two places to fourth. Eight English clubs made the top twenty.

Football's Rich List 2006

		2005–06	2004–05
1.	(1) Real Madrid	€292.2m	€275.7m
2.	(6) Barcelona	259.1	207.9
3.	(4) Juventus	251.2	229.4
4.	(2) Manchester United	242.6	246.4
5.	(3) AC Milan	238.7	234.0
6.	(5) Chelsea	221.0	220.8
7.	(9) Inter Milan	206.6	177.2
8.	(7) Bayern Munich	204.7	189.5
9.	(10) Arsenal	192.4	171.3
10.	(8) Liverpool	176	181.2
11.	(15) Lyon	127.7	92.9
12.	(11) AS Roma	127	131.8
13.	(12) Newcastle United	124.3	128.9
14.	(14) Schalke 04	122.9	97.4
15.	(13) Tottenham Hotspur	107.2	104.5

Source: Deloitte Football Money League

Major Sports Review 2006–07

Athletics	110	Horse Racing (Flat)	176
Boxing	120	Horse Racing (National Hunt)	188
Cricket	128	Rugby League	198
Formula One	154	Rugby Union	206
Golf	162	Tennis	220

Athletics

European Athletics Indoor Championships 2007

DATE: 2–4 March *VENUE:* Birmingham National Indoor Arena

Day 1: Highlights

Sweden's Carolina Klüft defended her title despite a magnificent challenge from Britain's Kelly Sotherton. In the men's 60m hurdles final, Gregory Sedoc from the Netherlands got off to a flyer and led home a shock one-two for the Dutch with his close friend Marcel van der Westen taking silver. Mikulas Konopka won the first gold of the championships, and the first ever gold medal for Slovakia in a European Indoor Championship, in the men's shot put.

Day 2: Highlights

Nicola Sanders took Britain's first gold of the 2007 games in the women's 400m. In the men's 400m, Ireland's David Gillick confirmed his status as European number one by winning in 45.52. Britain's Phillips Idowu added the European Indoor triple jump crown to his Commonwealth title.

Day 3: Highlights

On the third and final day of the meeting Europe's fastest man and woman, Jason Gardener (UK) and Kim Gevaert (BEL) retained their European indoor 60m titles. In the 1500m the Spanish trio of Juan Carlos Higuero (gold), Sergio Gallardo (silver) and Arturo Casado (bronze) claimed the first ever 1500m clean sweep at the European Athletics Indoor Championships. In the women's equivalent, Poland's Lidia Chojecka made history by becoming the first athlete to complete the 1500m and 3000m double. In the women's 4 x 400m relay, two outstanding performances by the Usovich sisters, firstly by Svetlana on the third leg and then by her younger sibling Ilona on the final leg, gave Belarus its first ever gold medal of the European Athletics Indoor Championships. The championships ended in dramatic fashion when Germany was disqualified from first place in the men's 4 x 400m after Russia lodged a protest claiming they were pushed. The judges awarded the gold medal to the UK that put them at the top of the medals table.

MEDALS TABLE (TOP 5)

Pos.	Nation	Gold	Silver	Bronze	Total
1.	United Kingdom	4	3	3	10
2.	Italy	3	1	2	6
3.	Sweden	3	1	0	4
4.	Russia	2	9	4	15
5.	Spain	2	4	3	9

"The pressure does get to you. I knew that if I didn't win, questions would be asked, so I'm absolutely thrilled."
Nicola Sanders, 400m gold medal winner

Paralympic World Cup 2007

DATE: 7–13 May 2007 *VENUE:* Regional Arena, Manchester

A total of 47 countries sent 340 of the world's best Paralympic athletes to compete for 143 medals in four sports (athletics, swimming, track Cycling and wheelchair basketball). The week's action saw five new world records set, while Great Britain's Tanni Grey-Thompson, a 15-time Paralympic medallist, brought the curtain down on her distinguished career by finishing second in her favourite event, the T53 200m. In the men's T36 200m, Ben Rushgrove aged 19, became the first Paralympic athlete to go below 25 seconds in the race, with a time of 24.86 seconds, winning gold. Three world records were set in the Manchester Velodrome, all by Britons, with Jody Cundy, Darren Kenny and Rik Waddon obliterating their own team sprint world record with a time of 52.096 seconds in the heats on their way to claiming the gold medal. The fifth world record came in the pool with Greece's Ioannis Kostakis winning the men's multi-disability 100m freestyle in 1.41.08.

Norwich Union British Grand Prix 2007

DATE: 15 July 2007 *VENUE:* Don Valley Stadium, Sheffield, England

The USA's Tyson Gay overcame the very wet conditions to win the 100m in 10.13s, with Great Britain's Marlon Devonish second in 10.23. It was Devonish's second race of the meeting having earlier finished fifth in the 200m behind the winner, Wallace Spearmon (USA) who won in 20.08ss. In the women's 200m Allyson Felix (USA) beat her compatriot Sanya Richards to win in 22.35s while Ethiopia's Kenenisa Bekele dominated the 3000m setting a new UK all-comers' record and personal best time of 7:26.69. The biggest upset came in the men's 400m when the world and Olympic champion Jeremy Wariner stumbled out of the blocks and watched another American, Angelo Taylor, win. However, the South African Paralympian, Oscar Pistorius, struggled in the wet, finishing last, before being disqualified for running out of his lane. Great Britain's Andy Baddeley won the 1500m in a new personal best time of 3:34.74 while Nicola Sanders, the European Indoor champion, set a season's best time of 51.01s to win the 400m.

Norwich Union Super Grand Prix 2007

DATE: 3 August 2007 *VENUE:* Crystal Palace National Sports Centre, London

The men's world number one, Tyson Gay (USA), stormed to victory in the 100m final, easing over the line in 10.02s, ahead of Francis Obikwelu and Britain's Marlon Devonish and Craig Pickering. Meanwhile Mark Lewis-Francis put his marker on the table for the third 100m place in Britain's World Championship team, coming home fifth in 10.31s. However, it was a sad end to Jason Gardener's outdoor career as he failed to make the final. Laura Turner won the women's 100m in 11.37s, ahead of Jeanette Kwakye, the UK champion. Veronica Campbell, the Olympic gold medallist, blew her opponents away to win the 200m in 22.55s while Jamaica's Usain Bolt won the men's 200m in 20.06s.

World Triathlon Championships

31 August–2 September 2007
Hamburg, Germany

The Corus Great Britain team sent a strong contingent to Hamburg – Tim Don, the defending champion; Will Clarke, the world and European under-23 champion, making his maiden bow in a senior championship and 19-year-old Alistair Brownlee, the European champion, who was out to defend his world crown in the junior boys race. Other British European champions in the team were Hollie Avil (junior girls), Ritchie Nicholls (under-23 men) and Rosie Clarke (under-23 women).

GB TEAM

Senior men: Will Clarke, Tim Don, Oliver Freeman, Stuart Hayes
Senior women: Michelle Dillon, Andrea Whitcombe, Kerry Lang
Under-23 men: Dann Brook, Philip Graves, Ritchie Nicholls
Under-23 women: Rosie Clarke
Junior boys: Alistair Brownlee, Jonathan Brownlee, Aaron Harris
Junior girls: Hollie Avil, Kirsty McWilliam, Jodie Stimpson

Vanessa Fernandes from Portugal, runner-up in 2006, claimed the gold medal in the elite women's race. Great Britain's leading female was Andrea Whitcombe in 25th place, while Michelle Dillon finished 29th and Kerry Lang 51st.

Daniel Unger from Germany claimed the world title in front of his home crowd. Great Britain's three men all finished in the top ten with Will Clarke best of all in fifth. Suart Hayes managed eighth place, while Tim Don was a disappointing tenth.

ELITE WOMEN'S RESULTS

1. Vanessa Fernandes *(Por)*	01:53:27
2. Emma Snowsill *(Aus)*	01:54:31
3. Laura Bennett *(USA)*	01:54:37
4. Emma Moffatt *(Aus)*	01:54:54
5. Ricarda Lisk *(Ger)*	01:54:59
6. Anja Dittmer *(Ger)*	01:55:04
7. Magali Di *(Swe)*	01:55:09
marco Messmer	
8. Joelle Franzmann *(Ger)*	01:55:15
9. Jessica Harrison *(Fra)*	01:55:26
10. Sarah Haskins *(USA)*	01:55:27

ELITE MEN'S RESULTS

1. Daniel Unger *(Ger)*	01:43:18
2. Javier Gomez *(Spa)*	01:43:22
3. Brad Kahlefeldt *(Aus)*	01:43:36
4. Simon Whitfield *(Can)*	01:43:40
5. William Clarke *(GB)*	01:43:45
6. Jan Frodeno *(Ger)*	01:43:57
7. Terenzo Bozzone *(Nzl)*	01:44:04
8. Stuart Hayes *(GB)*	01:44:07
9. Bevan Docherty *(Nzl)*	01:44:22
10. Tim Don *(GB)*	01:44:27

Great Britain did have some success at the world championships, in the younger age groups. Hollie Avil was crowned the women's world junior champion and in the men's junior event Alistair Brownlee won a silver medal. In the Under-23 events, Richie Nicholls and Rosie Clarke both finished just out of the medals in fourth postion. Nicholls was 15 seconds behind the race winner, while Clarke was four seconds from third place.

Modern Pentathlon World Championships 2007

14–22 August; Olympic Park, Berlin, Germany

This was the sixth time Germany had played host to the World Championships (1965, 1970, 1983, 1987 and 1993) but 2007 was the first time Berlin had staged the event. Great Britain had four women in the individual final – Heather Fell, Georgina Harland, Katy Livingston and Mhairi Spence. However, the British men failed to reach their final with Ben McLean, Sam Weale and Nick Woodbridge all missing out.

MEN'S INDIVIDUAL		**WOMEN'S INDIVIDUAL**	
Gold	Viktor Horvath *(Hun)*	Gold	Amelia Caze *(Fra)*
Silver	IIia Frolov *(Rus)*	Silver	Lena Schöneborn *(Ger)*
Bronze	Robert Nemeth *(Hun)*	Bronze	Laura Asadauskaite *(Lit)*

MEN'S TEAM		**WOMEN'S TEAM**	
Gold	Germany	Gold	Belarus
Silver	Czech Republic	Silver	Germany
Bronze	Hungary	Bronze	Russia

MEN'S TEAM RELAY *(non-Olympic event)*		**WOMEN'S TEAM RELAY** *(non-Olympic event)*	
Gold	Germany	Gold	Great Britain
Silver	China	Silver	Poland
Bronze	Czech Republic	Bronze	Germany

London Marathon 2007

22 April

Martin Lel, the London Marathon winner in 2005, claimed his second victory winning the 2007 Flora London Marathon. The Kenyan's superb final sprint gave him the title in a time of 2 hours, 7 minutes and 41 seconds. In the women's race Zhou Chunxiu became the first Chinese woman to win the London Marathon. Her winning time was 2 hours, 21 minutes and 38 seconds. Great Britain's David Weir successfully defended his wheelchair title while Shelly Woods won the women's wheelchair race.

RESULTS

Men's Top 5

1. Martin Lel *(Ken)*	2:07:41
2. Abderrahim Goumri *(Mor)*	2:07:44
3. Felix Limo *(Ken)*	2:07:47
4. Jaouad Gharib *(Mor)*	2:07:54
5. Hendrick Ramaala *(RSA)*	2:07:56

Women's Top 6

1. Chunxiu Zhou *(Chn)*	2.20:38
2. Gete Wami *(Eth)*	2:21:45
3. Constantina Tomescu-Dita *(Rom)*	2:23:55
4. Salina Kosgei *(Rom)*	2:24:13
5. Lornah Kiplagat *(NL)*	2:24:46
6. Mara Yamauchi *(GB)*	2:25:41

World Championships 2007

DATE: 25 August–2 September; *VENUE:* Nagai Stadium, Osaka, Japan

A fast track produced close races and good times, although no world records were set. Highlights included Tyson Gay's supreme sprinting in the 100 and 200m, a tight women's 100m narrowly won by Jamaica's Veronica Campbell, a dominant Jeremy Wariner in the 400m and a masterclass in elegant sprinting in the 200m by Allyson Felix. Roman Sebrle claimed gold in the decathlon, the only title he was missing and Liu Xiang won the 110m hurdles from lane 9. One of the more extraordinary victories was Donald Thomas of the Bahamas in the high jump – he took up the sport less than two years ago after being dared to try it by a friend.

Great Britain's team won five medals and achieved thirteen top eight finishes. Britain's only gold medal was won by Christine Ohuruogu, a remarkable victory considering she had only just finished serving a one-year ban for missing three out-of-competition drugs tests. Nicola Sanders made it a British one-two. Kelly Sotherton worked hard for her bronze in the heptathlon and Jessica Ennis finished behind her in fourth. The men's 4 x 100m relay bronze was testament to the time and resources that have been put into this event in recent years, and there was more success for the women's team in the 400m relay, winning bronze. Ohuruogu led off, followed by Marilyn Okoro and Lee McConnell, but it took a magnificent final sprint from Sanders to snatch third place from the Russians.

MEN'S RESULTS

100m	Tyson Gay USA 9.85	Derrick Atkins BAH 9.91 (NR)	Asafa Powell JAM 9.96
200m	Tyson Gay USA 19.76 (CR)	Usain Bolt JAM 19.91	Wallace Spearmon USA 20.05
400m	Jeremy Wariner USA 43.45	LaShawn Merritt USA 43.96 (PB)	Angelo Taylor USA 44.32
800m	Alfred Kirwa Yego KEN 1:47.09	Gary Reed CAN 1:47.10	Yuriy Borzakovskiy RUS 1:47.39
1500m	Bernard Lagat USA 3:34.77	Rashid Ramzi BRN 3:35.00 (SB)	Shedrack Kibet Korir KEN 3:35.04
5000m	Bernard Lagat USA 13:45.87	Eliud Kipchoge KEN 13:46.00	Moses Ndiema Kipsiro UGA 13:46.75
10,000m	Kenenisa Bekele ETH 27:05.90 (SB)	Sileshi Sihine ETH 27:09.03	Martin Irungu Mathathi KEN 27:12.17
110m Hurdles	Xiang Liu CHN 12.95	Terrence Trammell USA 12.99	David Payne USA 13.02 (PB)
400m Hurdles	Kerron Clement USA 47.61	Felix Sanchez DOM 48.01 (SB)	Marek Plawgo POL 48.12 (NR)
3000m Steeplechase	Brimin Kiprop Kipruto KEN	Ezekiel Kemboi KEN 8:16.94	Richard Kipkemboi Mateelong KEN

Event			
20km Race Walk	8:13.82 Jefferson Perez ECU 1:22:20	Francisco Javier Fernandez ESP 1:22:40	8:17.59 Hatem Ghoula TUN 1:22:40
50km Race Walk	Nathan Deakes AUS 3:43:53	Yohan Diniz FRA 3:44:22 (SB)	Alex Schwazer ITA 3:44:38
Marathon	Luke Kibet KEN 2:15:59	Murbarak Hassan Shami QAT 2:17:18	Viktor Rothlin SUI 2:17:25
4 x 100m Relay	USA 37.78	Jamaica 37.89 (NR)	GB & NI 37.90 (SB)
4 x 400m Relay	USA 2:55.56	Bahamas 2:59.18 (SB)	POL 3:00.05 (SB)
Shot Put	Reese Hoffa USA 22.04	Adam Nelson USA 21.61 (SB)	Andrei Mikhnevich BLR 21.27 (SB)
Discus Throw	Gerd Kanter EST 68.94	Robert Harting GER 66.68	Rutger Smith NED 66.42
Hammer Throw	Ivan Tsikhan BLR 83.63	Primoz Kozmus SLO 82.29	Libor Charfreitag SVK 81.60 (SB)
Javelin Throw	Tero Pikamaki FIN 90.33	Andreas Thorkildsen NOR 88.61	Breaux Greer USA 86.21
Pole Vault	Brad Walker USA 5.86	Romain Mesnil FRA 5.86 (SB)	Danny Ecker GER 5.81a
Long Jump	Irving Saladino PAN 8.57 (AR)	Andrew Howe ITA 8.47 (NR)	Dwight Phillips USA 8.30
Triple Jump	Nelson Evora POR 17.74 (NR)	Jadel Gregorio BRA 17.59	Walter Davis USA 17.33 (SB)
High Jump	Donald Thomas BAH 2.35	Yaroslav Rybakov RUS 2.35	Kyriakos Ioannou CYP 2.35
Decathlon	Roman Sebrle CZE 8676 pts	Maurice Smith JAM 8644 pts	Dmitriy Karpov KAZ 8586 pts

MEDALS TABLE – TOP TEN

	Country	Gold	Silver	Bronze	Total
1.	USA	14	4	8	26
2.	Kenya	5	3	5	13
3.	Russia	4	9	3	16
4.	Ethiopia	3	1	0	4
5.	Germany	2	2	3	7
6.	Czech Republic	2	1	0	3
7.	Australia	2	0	0	2
8.	Jamaica	1	6	3	10
9.	Bahamas	1	2	0	3
10.	Great Britain & NI	1	1	3	5

WOMEN'S RESULTS

100m	Veronica Campbell JAM 11.01	Lauryn Williams USA 11.01 (SB)	Carmelita Jeter USA 11.02 (PB)
200m	Allyson Felix USA 21.81	Veronica Campbell JAM 22.34 (SB)	Susanthika Jayasinghe SRI 22.63
400m	Christine Ohuruogu GB 49.61 (PB)	Nicola Sanders GB 49.65 (PB)	Novlene Williams JAM 49.66 (SB)
800m	Janeth Jepkosegi KEN 1:56.04	Hasna Behassi MAR 1:56.99	Mayte Martinez ESP 1:57.62
1500m	Maryam Yusuf Jamal BRN 3:58.75	Yelena Soboleva RUS 3:58.99	Iryna Lishchynska UKR 4:00.69 (SB)
5000m	Meseret Defar ETH 14:57.91	Vivian Cheruiyot KEN 14:58.50	Priscah Jepleting Cherono KEN 14:59.21
10,000m	Tirunesh Dibaba ETH 31:55.41 (SB)	Elvan Abeylegesse TUR 31:59.40	Kara Goucher USA 32:02.05
100m Hurdles	Michelle Parry USA 12.46	Perdita Felicien CAN 12.49 (SB)	Delloreen Ennis-London JAM 12.50 (PB)
400m Hurdles	Jana Rawlinson AUS 53.31 (SB)	Yuliya Pechenkina RUS 53.50 (SB)	Anna Jesien (POL)53.92

Trivia

* Kelly Sotherton has said that the 2008 Beijing Olympics may be her last heptathlon. Keen to stay injury free and compete in the 2012 Olympics, she is considering retraining in kayaking or track cycling.

* Sotherton's bronze medal came with a season's best 6,510 points. Meanwhile fourth-placed Jessica Ennis recorded a lifetime best with her 6,469.

* Sweden''s Carolina Kluft dominated the heptathlon. She was further ahead of bronze medalist Kelly Sotherton than Kelly was of the 20th-placed finisher.

* Christine Ohuruogu is the first British woman to win a World Championship track event since 1993, when Sally Gunnell won gold in the 400m hurdles.

* The one-two achieved by Christine Ohuruogu and Nicola Sanders is a rare feat by British athletes in World Championships. The last time it happened was in 1993 when Colin Jackson and Tony Jarrett finished first and second in the 110m hurdles.

* The British men's 4 x 100m relay time of 37.90 is the third fastest ever by a British team.

3000m Steeplechase	Yekaterina Volkova RUS 9:06.57 (CR)	Tatyana Petrova RUS 9:09.19 (PB)	Eunice Jepkorir KEN 9:20.09
20km Race Walk	Olga Kaniskina RUS 1:30:09	Tatyana Shemyakina RUS 1:30:42	Maria Vasco ESP 1:30:47
Marathon	Catherine Ndereba KEN 2:30:37 (SB)	Chunxiu Zhou CHN 2:30:45	Reiko Tosa JPN 2:30:55 (SB)
4 x 100m Relay	USA 41.98	Jamaica 42.01 (SB)	Belgium 42.75 (NR)
4 x 400m Relay	USA 3:18.55	Jamaica 3:19.73 (NR)	GB & NI 3:20.04 (NR)
Shot Put	Valerie Vili NZ 20.54	Nadzeya Ostapchuk BLR 20.48 (SB)	Nadine Kleinert GER 19.77 (SB)
Discus Throw	Franka Dietzsch GER 66.61	Darya Pishchalnikova RUS 65.78 (PB)	Yarelis Barrios CUB 63.90 (PB)
Hammer Throw	Betty Heidler GER 74.76	Yipsi Moreno CUB 74.74	Wenxiu Zhang CHN 74.39
Javelin Throw	Barbora Spotakova CZE 67.07	Christina Obergfoll GER 66.46	Steffi Nerius GER 64.42
Pole Vault	Yelena Isinbeova RUS 4.80	Katerina Badurova CZE 4.75 (NR)	Svetlana Feofanova RUS 4.75
Long Jump	Tatyana Lebedova RUS 7.03	Lyudmila Kolchanova RUS 6.92	Tatyana Kotova RUS 6.90 (SB)
Triple Jump	Yargelis Savigne CUB 15.28	Tatyana Lebedeva RUS 15.07	Hrysopiyi Devetski GRE 15.04
High Jump	Blanka Vlasic CRO 2.05	Antonietta Di Martino ITA 2.03 (NR) Anna Chicerova RUS 2.03 (PB)	–
Heptathlon	Carolina Kluft SWE 7032 pts	Lyudmila Blonska UKR 6832 pts (NR)	Kelly Sotherton GB 6510 pts (SB)

KEY TO ABBREVIATIONS

WR = World Record
CR = Competition Record
NR = National Record
SB = Season's Best (for that athlete)
PB = Personal Best

"Never in a million years did I think I would win three golds."
Tyson Gay, *who emulated Maurice Greene in winning the 100m, 200m and 4x100m in Osaka.*

London Olympics 2012

As far back as 6 July 2005, the International Olympic Committee (IOC) announced that London had won the vote to host the Games of the XXX Olympiad in 2012. London won a two-way fight with Paris by 54 votes to 50 at the IOC meeting in Singapore, after bids from Moscow, New York and Madrid were eliminated. Prime Minister Tony Blair called the win "a momentous day" for Britain, who will play host to its third Olympiad (1908 and 1948). However, since the IOC announcement one controversy after the other appears to have dogged the lead-up to the "Greatest Show On Earth".

On 20 April 2006, the IOC sent a 17-strong inspection team to London for a close-up view of preparations for the 2012 Games. The IOC held meetings over two days with the London Organising Committee of the Games (LOCOG). The IOC members visited the proposed site of the Olympic Park in London's East End and various other event venue sites. Olympics Minister Tessa Jowell said London was going "hell for leather" to stay on schedule for what she said was "a once in a lifetime opportunity for the capital". In March 2007, Jowell announced that the cost of London hosting the 2012 Games would be in the region of £9.35 billion as opposed to the original estimate of £2.35 billion.

On 4 June 2007, the logo for the Games of the London 2012 Olympics and Paralympics was unveiled in a star-studded ceremony in London. For the first time, the same logo will be used for both the Olympic and Paralympic Games. The logo, designed by Wolff Ollins, depicts a jagged emblem based on the date 2012. The word "London" appears in the first digit of the 2012 date, while the five Olympic rings are included in the second digit. "This is the vision at the very heart of our brand. It will define the venues we build and the Games we hold and act as a reminder of our promise to use the Olympic spirit to inspire everyone and reach out to young people around the world. It is an invitation to take part and be involved. We will host a Games where everyone is invited to join in because they are inspired by the Games to either take part in the many sports, cultural, educational and community events leading up to 2012 or they will be inspired to achieve personal goals," said Lord Coe (chairman of the London 2012 Organising Committee). "London 2012 will be a great sporting summer but will also allow Britain to showcase itself to the world," added Tony Blair. The logo sparked a fierce response, with many negative opinions being expressed. On 5 June 2007, a part of the animated footage used to promote the London Olympics in 2012 was removed from the Games organizers' website after it raised concerns that it could actually trigger epileptic seizures. The "offending" footage showed a diver diving into a pool followed by a multi-colour ripple effect. The charity Epilepsy Action said it had received calls from people who had suffered seizures after seeing it.

On 27 June 2007, Jowell said that profit from 312 hectares of Olympic Park land in Stratford, East London, bought for the London 2012 Olympics, will reimburse National Lottery funds that are helping to pay for the Games. The lottery donated an extra £675m to help cover the Olympics' ever spiralling budget while the London Development Agency (LDA) predicted the land would be sold for up to £800m after the Games. On 2 July 2007, the LDA assumed legal ownership of the Olympic Games site in East London thereby allowing the LDA to enforce compulsory purchase orders on the remaining businesses which have yet to relocate from the site. The vast majority of the 208 traders concerned have already acquired new premises. The relocation plan also included 425 residents, 35 traveller families and 64 allotment holders. The LDA was given a £625m compensation budget to cover the eviction process.

Gordon Brown reaffirmed his backing for the London Olympics on 5 July 2007, promising "total support" from his government and stated that he had written to the IOC president, Jacques Rogge, advising him that "robust" funding was in place. Six days later Lord Coe, the Games chairman, confirmed that the energy company, EDF, had been accepted as a major sponsor for the Games, joining Lloyds TSB as the second major corporate partner to back London 2012. The mayor of London, Ken Livingstone, welcomed the news that demolition of the site for the Olympic Park was given the green light on 24 July 2007, with the area equalling the size of Hyde Park. Two days later he said that it would be a "defeat" if the final bill to host the 2012 Games exceeded £7b.

Did You Know That?
£1 in every £5 of lottery money spent on good causes goes towards the cost of the 2012 Olympics and has done since 2005.

Beijing Olympics 2008 Controversy

OLYMPIC FIRM GUILTY OF USING CHILD LABOUR
On 13 June 2007, Lekit Stationery, a Chinese company producing merchandise related to the Beijing 2008 Olympic Games, admitted that it had used the services of children in their factories despite having denied the allegation when it was first made against the company. According to the company, children as young as 12 and 13 were used by one of its sub-contracted companies (Leter Stationery) although Lekit Stationery maintains that the children did not work on any Olympic Games merchandise. Michael Lee, a manager at Lekit Stationery, told the BBC that Leter Stationery had employed the services of school children from Dongguan city, where Lekit is based, in the winter of 2006 paying them as little as 20 Yuan (about £1.10) per day (from 07.30 to 22.30). An investigation was launched into Lekit Stationery by Dongguan city officials following complaints lodged against it by child action groups. "We didn't know that they would hire children. We will not use them again, and in future we will make sure that all sub-contractors are qualified," said Mr Lee, despite the fact that Leter Stationery is situated directly opposite the premises of Lekit Stationery. It is believed the children made labels for products and did some packaging of the merchandise. The swift action taken by Dongguan officials, including the publication of an official report into the matter, is seen as China wishing to avoid any unwanted adverse publicity in the lead-up to the Beijing Games.

Trivia

* On 31 August 2007, Dennis Spurr, owner of the Fantastic Sausage Factory in Weymouth, Dorset, was instructed by the organizers of London 2012 to take down a sign he had put up in his shop depicting five sausage rings in the shape of the Olympic logo. The Fantastic Sausage Factory is famous for its own home-made showbiz sausages such as the Tom Jones sausage (pork and leek) and the Beckham (pork and "posh spices").

Boxing

Big Fights

Joe Calzaghe v Peter Manfredo, Jr
DATE: 7 April 2007; VENUE: Millennium Stadium, Cardiff

Joe Calzaghe, aged 34 from Newbridge, Wales, went into this fight as the undefeated super-middleweight champion of the world with a stunning record (42–0, 31 KOs). Up against the Welsh Warrior was the new boxing sensation, Peter Manfredo, Jr (26–3, 12 KOs) from Providence, Rhode Island. The 25-year-old American was co-trained for the fight by the legendary Sugar Ray Leonard, who was at ringside in Cardiff. However, on the night the devastating Calzaghe, cheered on by a partisan 35,000 audience, was simply too good for his young challenger and the referee, Terry O'Connor, stepped in and ended the fight inside the third round of a one-sided contest. Amazingly, it was Calzaghe's 20th defence of his WBO super-middleweight championship belt.

Did You Know That?
Peter Manfredo, Jr was the runner-up in the US reality TV series *The Contender*.

Amir Khan v Steffy Bull
DATE: 7 April 2007; VENUE: Millennium Stadium, Cardiff

Amir Khan (11–0, 8 KOs) took on fellow Britain, Steffy Bull (24–4–1, 5 KOs), at the Millennium Stadium, Cardiff as an under-card scheduled ten-round lightweight bout ahead of Joe Calzaghe's fight with Peter Manfredo, Jr. It was anticipated to be Khan's toughest test yet, fighting a more experienced and rugged southpaw. However, Khan fought like a veteran belying his tender age of 20, and he had his 29-year-old opponent on the canvas after 1 minute, 45 seconds of the first round. Khan continued to hurt Bull with savage body blows in the second round before referee Marcus McDonnell waved the contest off in round three.

Floyd Mayweather v Oscar De La Hoya
DATE: 5 May 2007; VENUE: MGM Grand, Las Vegas, USA

Floyd Mayweather took six-weight world champion Oscar de la Hoya's light-middleweight crown after an absorbing fight which came down to the judges' scorecards and a split decision. Mayweather remains unbeaten in 38 professional fights, while De la Hoya's record now reads 38 wins and 5 defeats. The fight was the richest ever in boxing history, grossing $120m (£60m), to beat the $112m (£56m) of Mike Tyson and Lennox Lewis' heavyweight encounter in 2002.

Shannon Briggs v Sultan Ibrigamov
DATE: 2 June 2007; VENUE: Boardwalk Hall, Atlantic City, USA

This WBO world heavyweight championship fight was originally scheduled to take place on 10 March 2007, but was cancelled when Briggs, the defending champion, fell ill with a bout of pneumonia. Ibrigamov fought Javier Mora instead and knocked him out in 46 seconds, the quickest knockout in a main event held at Madison Square Garden.

Briggs went into this fight with Ibrigamov in confident mood having captured the title from Sergei Liakhovich in his previous bout. The champion started the contest well, winning the first round, but after that it was all downhill for him as he clearly lacked the stamina, and on occasion the will-power, to handle his younger more aggressive opponent. Briggs looked content to wade his way through the contest in the hope that somehow the decision might just go his way. However, it was a plan doomed to failure as Ibrigamov constantly laid into the champion at every opportunity. Sultan took the title following a unanimous points decision and improved his record to 21–0–1.

Did You Know That?
Ibrigamov became only the fifth southpaw heavyweight champion in history following Michael Moorer, Corrie Sanders, Chris Byrd and Ruslan Chagaev.

Ricky Hatton v Jose Luis Castillo
DATE: 23 June 2007; VENUE: Tommy & Mack Center, Las Vegas, USA

With an estimated 10,000 British fans in the hall, Hatton entered the ring wearing a sombrero and poncho in the colours of Manchester City for his IBO world light-welterweight championship fight against Jose Luis Castillo from Mexico. Wayne Rooney of Manchester United and Mexican boxing legend, Marco Antonio Barrera, carried his two championship belts (IBF and IBO light-welterweight) into the ring. A lot of pressure was placed on the 28-year-old champion from Manchester, with the American media claiming he would follow other British trans-Atlantic flops like the Spice Girls and Oasis if he failed to beat the 33-year-old Mexican. However, The Hitman started aggressively and in the fourth round landed a savage left shot to the Mexican's kidney that sent him to the floor. Castillo was clearly in pain as the referee began the 10-second count and when his gumshield hung from his mouth Joe Cortez waved his arms in the air bringing the fight to an end. It was the first time in Castillo's 17-year professional career that he had been sent to the canvas and he left the ring with a 55 wins and 8 defeats record, while Hatton went 43 and 0. Hatton's impressive win may now earn him a long awaited super-fight with Floyd Mayweather.

> "Sometimes I have tried too hard to put on a show and that has got me in trouble in the past. I think I've definitely proved the fat man is back. I hit him with a left and then another left and it just about cut him in half. I was going for the body from the first round and I've got him with one of the best shots I've ever thrown."
>
> *Ricky Hatton*

Amir Khan v Willie Limond
DATE: 14 July 2007; VENUE: O2 Arena, London

Amir Khan (12–0, 9 KOs) made it 13 wins out of 13 beating Scotland's Willie Limond in this scheduled 12-rounder for the Commonwealth lightweight title. However, it was almost "unlucky 13" for the Bolton man as his 28-year-old opponent hurt him badly, sending him to the canvas in the sixth round for the first time in his professional career. As always, Khan started at a ferocious pace, laying into his opponent at every opportunity but Limond, a seasoned campaigner who had lost only one of his previous 29 professional bouts, stayed calm and weathered the early hurricane. It was evident early on that Khan was not going to finish the Scot off quickly and after Khan had won the first two rounds, the third went to the defending champion. Little separated the pair over the next two rounds before Khan hit the deck in the sixth. Somehow, he managed to hold on until the bell and battered Limond in rounds seven and eight. At the start of the ninth, Limond's corner called the contest off with their man suffering from a broken jaw and nose. Many called it the "Fight of the Year".

David Diaz v Erik Morales
DATE: 4 August 2007; VENUE: AllState Arena, Chicago, USA

Erik Morales entered the ring seeking to become the first Mexican to win world titles at four different weights. The 30-year-old Mexican fighter had previously claimed belts at super-bantamweight, featherweight and super-featherweight. Here he was seeking to become the WBC world lightweight champion. However, David Diaz, fighting in his home city, proved one bridge too far for Morales, unanimously outpointing him 114–113, 115–113, 115–112 in his first title defence. Morales had the champion on the canvas in the first round but the 31-year-old Diaz knocked Morales to the floor in the second round before unleashing a non-stop onslaught on his opponent.

Bernard Dunne v Kiko Martinez
DATE: 25 August 2007; VENUE: Point Arena, Dublin, Republic of Ireland

Spain's Kiko Martinez flew at Bernard Dunne from the opening bell of the Irish fighter's third defence of his European super-bantamweight belt. Dunne was knocked to the canvas twice in the opening 60 seconds and the fight was all over inside 90 seconds when the referee, Terry O'Connor, stepped in to prevent Dunne receiving further punishment. Martinez could now boast an impressive record of 14 knock-outs from his 17 wins – from 17 fights – while Dunne suffered the first defeat of his professional career, in his 25th contest. "I got hit with a punch that I didn't see coming and from there I was in trouble. I'm just so disappointed for myself and everyone in the team and I feel that I have let the people down. Now I have to go away from this and watch the tape and see where I went wrong. It's hard to take but that's boxing. I know that I have the character to come back from this and I'll prove that. I can come back even stronger," said the temporarily down-hearted dethroned champion.

World Championship Contests 2006–07

HEAVYWEIGHT

WBC	10/12/06	O Maskaev *(Rus)*	P Okhello *(Uga)*	w pts 12	Moscow
WBA	7/10/06	N Valuev *(Rus)*	M Barrett *(USA)*	w rsf 11	Rosemont, IL
WBO	4/11/06	S Briggs *(USA)*	S Lyahovich *(Rus)*	w ko 12	Phoenix
IBF	11/11/06	W Klitschko *(Ukr)*	C Brock *(USA)*	w rsf 7	New York
WBA	20/1/07	N Valuev	J McCline *(US)*	w rsf 3	Basel
IBF	10/3/07	W Klitschko	R Austin *(US)*	w rsf 2	Mannheim
WBO	2/6/07	S Ibragimov *(Rus)*	S Briggs	w pts 12	Atlantic City
WBA	14/4/07	R Chagaev *(Uzb)*	N Valuev	w pts 12	Stuttgart
IBF	7/7/07	W Klitschko	L Brewster *(USA)*	w rsf 6	Cologne

CRUISERWEIGHT

WBO*	14/10/06	E Maccarinelli *(Wal)*	M Hobson *(Eng)*	w rsf 1	Manchester
IBF*	25/11/06	K Wlodarczyk *(Pol)*	S Cunningham *(US)*	w pts 12	Warsaw
WBA/					
WBC	17/3/07	M Mormeck *(Fra)*	O'N Bell *(Jam)*	w pts 12	Levallois
WBO	7/4/07	E Maccarinelli	B Gunn *(USA)*	w rsf 1	Cardiff
IBF	26/5/07	S Cunningham	K Wlodarczyk	w pts 12	Katowice
WBA*	16/6/07	F Arslan *(Ger)*	V Brudov *(Rus)*	w pts 12	Budapest
WBO	21/7/07	E Maccarinelli	W Braithwaite *(USA)*	w pts 12	Cardiff

LIGHT-HEAVYWEIGHT

IBF	2/9/06	C Woods *(Eng)*	G Johnson *(Jam)*	w pts 12	Bolton
WBC	7/10/06	T Adamek *(Pol)*	P Briggs *(Aus)*	w pts 12	Rosemont
WBO	27/1/07	Z Erdei *(Hun)*	D Santiago *(USA)*	w rsf 8	Dusseldorf
WBC	3/2/07	C Dawson *(USA)*	T Adamek	w pts 12	Kissimmee
WBA	28/4/ 07	S Drews *(Cro)*	S Branco *(Ita)*	w pts 12	Oberhausen
WBC	9/6/07	C Dawson	J Ruiz *(Mex)*	w tko 6	Hartford
IBO	16/6/07	Z Erdei	G Blades *(USA)*	w rsf 11	Budapest

SUPER-MIDDLEWEIGHT

IBF/					
WBO	14/10/06	J Calzaghe *(Wal)*	S Bika *(Cmr)*	w pts 12	Manchester
WBA/					
WBC	14/10/06	M Kessler *(Den)*	M Beyer *(Ger)*	w ko 3	Copenhagen
IBF*	3/3/07	A Berrio *(Col)*	R Stieglitz *(Ger)*	w rsf 3	Rostock
WBA/					
WBC	24/3/07	M Kessler	L Andrade *(Mex)*	w pts 12	Copenhagen
WBO	7/4/07	J Calzaghe	P Manfredo *(USA)*	w rsf 3	Cardiff
WBA*	27/6/07	A Mundine *(Aus)*	P Nievas *(Arg)*	w pts 12	Broadbeach

MIDDLEWEIGHT

IBF	23/9/06	A Abraham *(Arm)*	E Miranda *(Col)*	w pts 12	Wetzlar

WBA	2/12/06	M Carrera *(Arg)*	J Castillejo *(Spa)*	nd 11	Berlin
(Carrera won the bout, but failed a drugs test so Castillejo was reinstated and fight called a no decision)					
WBC /WBO	9/12/06	J Taylor *(USA)*	K Ouma *(Uga)*	w pts 12	Little Rock
WBA	28/4/07	F Sturm *(Ger)*	J Castillejo	w pts 12	Oberhausen
WBC	19/5/07	J Taylor	C Spinks *(USA)*	w pts 12	Memphis
IBF	26/5/07	A Abraham	S Demers *(Can)*	w ko 3	Bamberg
WBA	30/6/07	F Sturm	N T G Alcoba *(Uru)*	w pts 12	Stuttgart
IBF	18/8/07	A Abraham	K Ghevor *(Arm)*	w ko 11	Berlin

LIGHT-MIDDLEWEIGHT

WBO	21/10/06	S Dzinziruk *(Ukr)*	A Nadirbegov *(Rus)*	w pts 12	Halle
WBA	6/1/07	T Simms *(US)*	J Rivera *(USA)*	w rsf 9	Hollywood
IBF	3/2/07	C Spinks *(US)*	R Jones *(USA)*	w pts 12	Kissimmee
WBC	5/5/07	F Mayweather *(USA)*	O De La Hoya *(USA)*	w pts 12	Las Vegas
WBO	19/5/07	S Dzinziruk	C Nascimento *(Bra)*	w ko 12	Hamburg
WBA	7/7/07	J Alcine (Hti)	T Simms	w pts 12	Bridgeport
WBC*	28/7/07	V Forrest *(USA)*	C Baldomir *(Arg)*	w pts 12	Tacoma

WELTERWEIGHT

IBF*	28/10/06	K Cintron *(PR)*	M Suarez *(USA)*	w rsf 6	Palm Beach
WBC	4/11/06	F Mayweather *(USA)*	C Baldomir *(Arg)*	w pts 12	Las Vegas
WBA*	2/12/06	M Cotto *(PR)*	C Quintana *(PR)*	w rtd 5	Atlantic City
WBO	2/12/06	A Margarito *(USA)*	J Clottey *(Gha)*	w pts 12	Atlantic City
WBC	10/2/07	S Mosley *(USA)*	L Collazo *(USA)*	w pts 12	Las Vegas
WBA	3/3/07	M Cotto	O Urkal *(Ger)*	w rsf 11	San Juan
IBF	14/7/07	K Cintron	WD Matthysse *(Arg)*	w ko 2	Atlantic City
WBO	14/7/07	P Williams *(USA)*	A Margarito	w pts 12	Carson

LIGHT-WELTERWEIGHT

WBA*	2/9/06	S M'Baye *(Fra)*	R Balbi *(Arg)*	w rsf 4	Bolton
WBC*	15/9/06	J Witter *(Eng)*	DeM Corley *(USA)*	w pts 12	London
WBO*	18/11/06	R Torres *(Col)*	M Arnaoutis *(Gre)*	w pts 12	Las Vegas
IBF	20/1/07	R Hatton *(Eng)*	J Urango *(Col)*	w pts 12	Las Vegas
WBC	20/1/07	J Witter	A Morua *(Mex)*	w rsf 9	London
IBF*	4/2/07	L N'Dou *(Aus)*	N Ben Rabah *(Aus)*	w ret 11	Homebush
WBA	10/3/07	S M'Baye	A Kotelnik *(Ukr)*	drew 12	Liverpool
WBO	28/4/07	R Torres	A Morua	w pts 12	Barranquilla
IBF	16/6/07	P Malignaggi *(USA)*	L N'Dou	w pts 12	Uncasville
WBA	21/7/07	G Rees *(Wal)*	S M'Baye	w pts 12	Cardiff
WBO	1/9/07	R Torres	K Holt *(USA)*	w rsf 11	Barranquilla

LIGHTWEIGHT

WBC*	7/10/06	J Casamayor *(Cub)*	D Corrales *(USA)*	w pts 12	Las Vegas
WBA	4/11/06	J Diaz *(US)*	F Angulo *(Ecu)*	w pts 12	Phoenix

IBF	3/2/07	J Diaz *(Mex)*	J Chavez *(Mex)*	w ko 3	Kissimmee
WBO*	17/2/07	M Katsidis *(Aus)*	G Earl *(Eng)*	w ret 5	London
WBA/					
WBO	28/4/07	J Diaz	A Freitas *(Bra)*	w ret 8	Mashantucket
WBA*	11/5/07	J M Cotto *(PR)*	P Singwangcha *(Th)*	draw 12	Salinas
WBC*	4/8/07	D Diaz *(USA)*	E Morales *(Mex)*	w pts 12	Rosemont
WBO*	21/7/07	M Katsidis	C Amansot *(Phil)*	w pts 12	Las Vegas

SUPER-FEATHERWEIGHT

WBC	16/9/06	M A Barrera *(USA)*	R Juarez *(USA)*	w pts 12	Las Vegas
WBO	16/9/06	J Guzman *(DR)*	J Barrios *(Arg)*	w pts 12	Las Vegas
IBF	4/11/06	M Klassen *(SA)*	G St Clair *(Guy)*	w pts 12	Kempton Park
WBO	12/12/06	J Guzman	A Davis *(USA)*	w pts 12	SantoDomingo
WBA	3/1/07	E Valero *(Ven)*	M Lozada *(Mex)*	w rsf 1	Tokyo
WBC	17/3/07	J M Marquez *(Mex)*	M A Barrera	w pts 12	Las Vegas
IBF	20/4/07	M Fana *(SA)*	M Klassen	w pts 12	Khayelitsha
WBA	3/5/07	E Valero	N Honmo *(Jap)*	w rsf 8	Tokyo
IBF*	21/7/07	A Arthur	K Gogladze *(Geo)*	w rsf 10	Cardiff
IBF	31/8/07	M Fana	JO Alvarez *(Arg)*	w ko 9	Klerksdorp

FEATHERWEIGHT

WBA	9/9/06	C John *(Indo)*	R Acosta *(Pan)*	w pts 12	Jakarta
IBF	4/11/06	O Salido *(Mex)*	R Guerrero *(USA)*	w pts 12	Las Vegas

(Salido was stripped of the title after testing positive for a banned substance. Title declared vacant)

WBO	25/11/06	J M Marquez *(Mex)*	J Jaca *(Phil)*	w ko 9	Hidalgo
WBC	17/12/06	In-jin Chi *(Kor)*	R Lopez *(Mex)*	w pts 12	Seoul
IBF	23/2/07	R Guerrero	S Abazi *(Den)*	w rsf 9	Copenhagen
WBA	3/3/07	C John ·	J Rojas	w pts 12	Jakarta
WBO*	14/7/07	S Luevano *(USA)*	N Cook *(GB)*	w ko 11	London
WBC*	21/7/07	J Linares *(Ven)*	O Larios *(Mex)*	w rsf 10	Las Vegas
WBA	19/8/07	C John	Z Takemoto *(Jap)*	w ret 9	Kobe

SUPER-BANTAMWEIGHT

WBC	16/9/06	I Vazquez *(Mex)*	J Gonzalez *(Mex)*	w rsf 10	Las Vegas
WBA	4/10/06	C Caballero *(Mex)*	S Sithchatchawal	w rsf 3	Nakornratchasima
WBO	21/10/06	D Ponce de Leon *(Mx)*	Al Seeger *(USA)*	w rsf 8	El Paso
IBF	10/11/06	S Molitor *(Can)*	M Hunter *(Eng)*	w ko 5	Hartlepool
WBC	3/3/07	R Marquez *(Mex)*	I Vazquez	w rtd 7	Carson
WBA	16/3/07	C Caballero	R Castillo *(Mex)*	w dq 9	Hollywood
WBO	17/3/07	D Ponce de Leon	G Penalosa *(Phil)*	w pts 12	Las Vegas
IBF	14/7/07	S Molitor	T Ndlovu *(SAf)*	w rsf 7	Orillia
WBC	4/8/07	I Vazquez	R Marquez	w rsf 6	Hidalgo
WBA	4/8/07	C Caballero	J Lacierva *(Mex)*	w pts 12	Hidalgo
WBO	11/8/07	D Ponce de Leon	R Bautista *(Phil)*	w rsf 1	Sacramento

BANTAMWEIGHT

WBC	13/11/06	H Hasegawa *(Jap)*	G Garcia *(Mex)*	w pts 12	Tokyo
WBA	17/3/07	W Sidorenko*(Ukr)*	R Cordoba *(Pan)*	drew 12	Stuttgart
WBO	30/3/07	J Gonzalez *(Mex)*	I Pacheco *(Col)*	w rsf 9	Tucson
WBC	3/5/07	H Hasegawa *(Jap)*	S Vetyeka *(SA)*	w pts 12	Tokyo
WBA	29/6/07	W Sidorenko	J Arnould *(Fra)*	w ko 12	Marseille
IBF*	7/7/07	L A Perez (Nic)	G Garcia	w ko 7	Bridgeport
WBO	30/3/07	J Gonzalez	G Penalosa *(Phil)*	w ko 7	Sacramento

SUPER-FLYWEIGHT

WBC*	18/9/06	C Mijares *(Mex)*	K Kawashima *(Jap)*	w pts 12	Yokohama
WBC	17/11/06	C Mijares	R Lopez *(Col)*	w pts 12	Torreon
WBA	2/12/06	N Nashiro *(Jap)*	M Castillo *(Mex)*	w rsf 10	Higashiosaka
WBC	3/1/07	C Mijares	K Kawashima	w rsf 10	Tokyo
WBO	4/2/07	F Montiel *(Mex)*	Z Gorres *(Phi)*	w pts 12	Cebu
WBC	14/4/07	C Mijares	J Arce *(Mex)*	w pts 12	San Antonio
WBA	3/5/07	A Munoz *(Ven)*	N Nashiro	w pts 12	Tokyo
WBC	13/7/07	C Mijares	T Kikui *(Jap)*	w rsf 10	Durango
WBO	14/7/07	F Montiel	C Santis *(Mex)*	w rsf 10	Sonora

FLYWEIGHT

IBF	7/10/06	V Darchinyan *(Arm)*	G Donaire *(Phil)*	w tdec 6	Las Vegas
WBO	14/10/06	O Narvaez *(Arg)*	W Ramos *(Col)*	w pts 12	Buenos Aires
WBC	17/11/06	P Wonjongkam *(Tha)*	M Myekeni *(SA)*	w pts 12	Nakornratchasima
WBA	2/12/06	R Vasquez *(Pan)*	T Sakata *(Jap)*	w pts 12	Paris
IBF	3/3/07	V Darchinyan	V Burgos *(Mex)*	w rsf 12	Carson, CA
WBO	10/3/07	O Narvaez	B Asloum *(Fra)*	w pts 12	Le Cannet
WBA	19/3/07	T Sakata	L Parra *(Ven)*	w rsf 3	Tokyo
WBC	6/4/07	P Wonjongkam	T Shimizu *(Jap)*	w rsf 7	Saraburi
WBA	1/7/07	T Sakata	R Vasquez	w pts 12	Tokyo
IBF	7/7/07	N Donaire *(Phil)*	V Darchinyan	w ko 5	Bridgeport
WBC	18/7/07	D Naito *(Jap)*	P Wonjongkam	w pts 12	Tokyo

LIGHT-FLYWEIGHT

WBO	30/9/06	H Cazares *(Mex)*	N Dieppa *(PR)*	w rsf 10	Caguas
WBC	18/11/06	O Nino *(Mex)*	B Viloria *(Haw)*	nd 12	Las Vegas
(Nino tested positive for a banned substance and was stripped of the title)					
WBA	20/12/06	K Kameda *(Jap)*	J J Landaeta *(Ven)*	w pts 12	Tokyo
IBF	25/1/07	U Solis *(Mex)*	W Grigsby *(USA)*	w rtd 8	Las Vegas
WBC*	14/4/07	E Sosa *(Mex)*	B Viloria	w pts 12	San Antonio
WBO	4/5/07	H Cazares	W Perez *(Col)*	w rsf 2	Las Vegas
IBF	19/5/07	U Solis	J A Aguirre *(Mx)*	w rsf 9	Guadalajara
WBA*	22/6/07	J C Reveco *(Arg)*	N Sasiprapa *(Thai)*	w ko 8	Las Heras
WBC	14/4/07	E Sosa *(Mex)*	L A Lazarte	w dq 10	Canccun

| IBF | 4/8/07 | U Solis | R Mayol *(Phil)* | w ko 10 | Rosemont |
| WBO | 25/8/07 | I Calderon *(PR)* | HF Cazares | w pts 12 | Bayamon |

STRAWWEIGHT

WBO	21/10/06	I Calderon *(PR)*	J L Varela *(Ven)*	w pts 12	Barranquilla
WBA*	7/11/06	K Takayama *(Jap)*	C Melo *(Pan)*	w rsf 9	Tokyo
WBC	13/11/06	E Kyowa *(Jap)*	L Trejo *(Mex)*	w pts 12	Tokyo
IBF	23/12/06	M Rachman *(Id)*	B Sorolla *(Phil)*	w rsf 7	Jakarta
WBA	7/4/07	Y Niida *(Jap)*	K Takayama	w pts 12	Tokyo
WBO	28/4/07	I Calderon	R Barrera *(Col)*	w pts 12	Barranquilla
WBC	4/6/07	E Kyowa	A Yaegashi *(Jap)*	w pts 12	Kanagawa
WBC	7/7/07	F Condes *(Phil)*	M Rachmani	w pts 12	Jakarta
WBA	1/9/07	Y Niida	E Gejon *(Phil)*	w pts 12	Tokyo

KEY

* =	Fight for a vacant title
IBF =	International Boxing Federation
WBA =	World Boxing Association
WBC =	World Boxing Council
WBO =	World Boxing Organization

Where more than one governing body was listed for a fight, it was a unification bout.

Trivia

* There are 17 weight classifications, from straw to heavyweight. In the Olympics, there is also a super-heavyweight class.

* Nikolai Valuev of Russia, at 7ft and 323lbs (23st 1lb), is the biggest man ever to be a world boxing champion.

British & Commonwealth Champions (as at 31 August 2007)

Weight	British	Commonwealth
Heavyweight	Danny Williams	Matt Skelton
Cruiserweight	John Keaton	Troy Ross
Light-heavyweight	Tony Oakey	Julius Francis
Super-middleweight	Carl Froch	Carl Froch
Middleweight	Harold Eastman	Scott Dann
Light-middleweight	Jamie Moore	Bradley Pryce
Welterweight	Kevin Anderson	Kevin Anderson
Light-welterweight	Colin Lynes	Ajose Olusegun
Lightweight	Jonathan Thaxton	Amir Khan
Super-lightweight	Carl Johanneson	Leva Kirakosyan
Featherweight	John Simpson	Jackson Asiku
Super-bantamweight	Esham Pickering	Argie Ward
Bantamweight	Ian Napa	Tshifhiwa Munyai
Flyweight	*vacant*	Lee Haskins

Cricket

The Ashes Series 2006–07 Review

Australia defeated England 5–0 to avenge their Ashes defeat in England in 2005, after they had held the most famous urn in sport for 16 years. In winning back the Ashes, the Australians also completed their first Ashes whitewash in 86 years, last achieved by Warwick Armstrong's 1920–21 Australians. The Aussies, led by their inspirational captain and man of the series, Ricky Ponting, claimed their twelfth consecutive Test victory, in humiliating England with a 10-wicket win oin the final Test. This match also signalled the inernational retirement of three of Australia's greatest players, Justin Langer, Glenn McGrath and Shane Warne, joining Damien Martyn who exited after the second Test.

The increasing gap in class between Australia and England was never more evident than in the fourth Test, at Melbourne, where England's demoralised troops were brushed aside by an innings and 99 runs. This humiliating loss prompted the England skipper and hero of their 2005 Ashes victory, Andrew Flintoff, to state, "We don't want to leave this country having been turned over 5–0. We want to win a game of cricket." However, the troops did not rally and England capitulated inside four days. "Australia has hit back with unstoppable force after its shame in coughing up the urn it had come to regard as its own" said the *Sydney Morning Herald*. More praise was lavished on the victorious Australian side by the *Daily Telegraph*, claiming that Australia had built one of the top two dynasties in world cricket history.

In defence of England, they arrived in Australia underprepared and they were also without a number of key members of their 2005 Ashes team, including skipper Michael Vaughan and fast bowler Simon Jones. From the moment Steve Harmison's first ball of the First Test ended up, untouched, in second slip's hands, England fans knew it was going to be difficult. Ponting's 196 set up the Australians for a massive first innings score and England's pitiful reply ensured another winning start for the men in the baggy green caps. What was most disappointing, however, was that in the last four Tests, England were competititve for much of the first innings, only to be blown away later. At Adelaide, Paul Collingwood's 206 and Kevin Pietersen's 158 gave England the platform for a score of 551, but Ponting was dropped on 49 and he added another 93 as Australia conceded a first-innings deficit of 38. A second innings collapse gave Australia the chance to win and they grabbed it. At Perth, England trailed by only 29 runs after the first innings, only for Australia to clincally and ruthlessly put the result beyond doubt, Adam Gilchrist being particularly brutal on the England attack with a 59-ball century. In Melbourne, Australia were 84–5 on day two in reply to England's miserable 159, but they escaped to 419 and an innings victory. A perfect illustration of the series came in Sydney; England's last six first-innings wickets put on 46 runs, Australia's last five added 203. England's second innings failure left Australia a target of just 46 runs to complete this most painful of whitewashes.

Series Results

1st Test: England lost by 277 runs   **4th Test:** England lost by an innings and 99 runs
2nd Test: England lost by 6 wickets   **5th Test:** England lost by 10 wickets
3rd Test: England lost by 206 runs

The Ashes 2006–07

FIRST TEST, 23–27 NOVEMBER 2006, GABBA, BRISBANE
AUSTRALIA WON BY 277 RUNS. *UMPIRES:* BF BOWDEN, SA BUCKNOR

Australia

JL Langer	c Pietersen	b Flintoff	82	not out	100
ML Hayden	c Collingwood	b Flintoff	21	run out (Anderson/Jones)	37
RT Ponting	lbw	b Hoggard	196	not out	60
DR Martyn	c Collingwood	b Giles	29		
MEK Hussey		b Flintoff	86		
MJ Clarke	c Strauss	b Anderson	56		
AC Gilchrist	lbw	b Hoggard	0		
SK Warne	c Jones	b Harmison	17		
B Lee	not out		43		
SR Clark		b Flintoff	39		
GD McGrath	not out		8		
Extras	(b 2, lb 8, w 8, nb 7)		25	(lb 4, nb 1)	5
TOTAL	(for 9 wickets dec)		602	(for 1 wicket dec)	202

1/79, 2/141, 3/198, 4/407, 5/467   *1/83*
6/467, 7/500, 8/528, 9/578

Bowling: *First Innings:* Harmison 30–4–123–1, Hoggard 31–5–98–2,
Anderson 29–6–141–1, Flintoff 30–4–99–4, Giles 25–2–91–1, Bell 1–0–12–0,
Pietersen 9–1–28–0. *Second Innings:* Hoggard 11–2–43–0, Anderson 9–1–54–0,
Flintoff 5–2–11–0, Harmison 12.1–1–54–0, Giles 5–0–22–0, Pietersen 3–0–14–0.

England

AJ Strauss	c Hussey	b McGrath	12	c sub (RA Broad)	b Clark	11
AN Cook	c Warne	b McGrath	11	c Hussey	b Warne	43
IR Bell	c Ponting	b Clark	50	lbw	b Warne	0
PD Collingwood	c Gilchrist	b Clark	5	st Gilchrist	b Warne	96
KP Pietersen	lbw	b McGrath	15	c Martyn	b Lee	92
A Flintoff	c Gilchrist	b Lee	0	c Langer	b Warne	16
GO Jones	lbw	b McGrath	19		b McGrath	33
AF Giles	c Hayden	b McGrath	24	c Warne	b Clark	23
MJ Hoggard	c Gilchrist	b Clark	0	c Warne	b Clark	8
SJ Harmison	c Gilchrist	b McGrath	0	c McGrath	b Clark	13
JM Anderson	not out		2	not out		4
Extras	(b 2, lb 8, w 2, nb 6)		18	(b 8, lb 10, w 2, nb 11)		31
TOTAL	(all out)		157	(all out)		370

1/28, 2/28, 3/42, 4/78, 5/79   *1/29, 2/36, 3/91, 4/244, 5/271*
6/126, 7/149, 8/153, 9/154, 10/157   *6/293, 7/326, 8/346. 9/361, 10/370*

Bowling: *First Innings:* Lee 15–3–51–1, McGrath 23.1–8–50–6, Clark 14–5–21–3,
Warne 9–0–25–0. *Second Innings:* Lee 22–1–98, McGrath 19–3–53–1,
Clark 24.1–6–72–4, Warne 34–7–124–4, Hussey 1–0–5–0

The Ashes 2006–07

SECOND TEST, 1–5 DECEMBER 2006, THE OVAL, ADELAIDE
AUSTRALIA WON BY 6 WICKETS. *UMPIRES:* RE KOERTZEN, SA BUCKNOR

England

AJ Strauss	c Martyn	b Clark	14	c Hussey	b Warne	34
AN Cook	c Gilchrist	b Clark	27	c Gilchrist	b Clark	9
IR Bell	c & b	Lee	60	run out (Clarke/Warne)		26
PD Collingwood	c Gilchrist	b Clark	206	not out		22
KP Pietersen	run out (Ponting)		158		b Warne	2
A Flintoff	not out		38	c Gilchrist	b Lee	2
GO Jones	c Martyn	b Warne	1	c Hayden	b Lee	10
AF Giles	not out		27	c Hayden	b Warne	0
MJ Hoggard					b Warne	4
SJ Harmison				lbw	b McGrath	8
JM Anderson				lbw	b McGrath	1
Extras	(lb 10, w 2, nb 8)		20	(b 3, lb 5, w 1, nb 2)		11
TOTAL	(6 wickets declared)		551	(all out)		129

1/32, 2/45, 3/158, 4/468, 5/489, 6/491

*1/31, 2/69, 3/70, 4/73, 5/77
6/94, 7/97, 8/105. 9/119, 10/129*

Bowling: *First Innings:* Lee 34–1–139–1, McGrath 30–5–107–0, Clark 34–6–75–3, Warne 53–9–167–1, Clarke 17–2–53–0. *Second Innings:* Lee 18–3–35–2, McGrath 10–6–15–2, Warne 32–12–49–4, Clark 13–4–22–1.

Australia

JL Langer	c Pietersen	b Flintoff	4	c Bell	b Hoggard	7
ML Hayden	c Jones	b Hoggard	12	c Collingwood	b Flintoff	18
RT Ponting	c Jones	b Hoggard	142	c Strauss	b Giles	49
DR Martyn	c Bell	b Hoggard	11	not out		61
MEK Hussey		b Hoggard	91	c Strauss	b Flintoff	5
MJ Clarke	c Giles	b Hoggard	124	not out		21
AC Gilchrist	c Bell	b Giles	64			
SK Warne	lbw	b Hoggard	43			
B Lee	not out		7			
SR Clark		b Hoggard	0			
GD McGrath	c Jones	b Anderson	1			
Extras	(b 4, lb 2, w 1, nb 7)		14	(b 2, lb 2, w 1, nb 2)		7
TOTAL	all out		513	(4 wickets)		168

*1/8, 2/35, 3/65, 4/257, 5/286
6/384, 7/502, 8/505, 9/507, 10/513*

1/14, 2/33, 3/116, 4/121

Bowling: *First Innings:* Hoggard 42–6–109–7, Flintoff 26–5–82–1, Harmison 25–0–96–0, Anderson 21.3–3–85–1, Giles 42–7–103–1, Pietersen 9–0–32–0. *Second Innings:* Hoggard 4–0–29–1, Flintoff 9–0–44–2, Giles 10–0–46–1, Harmison 4–0–15–0, Anderson 3.5–0–23–0, Pietersen 2–0–7–0.

The Ashes 2006-07

Australia

JL Langer		b Panesar	37		b Hoggard	0
ML Hayden	c Jones	b Hoggard	24	c Collingwood	b Panesar	92
RT Ponting	lbw	b Harmison	2	c Jones	b Harmison	75
MEK Hussey	not out		74	c Jones	b Panesar	103
MJ Clarke	c and b	Harmison	37	not out		135
A Symonds	c Jones	b Panesar	26	c Collingwood	Panesar	2
AC Gilchrist	c Bell	b Panesar	0	not out		102
SK Warne	c Jones	b Panesar	25			
B Lee	lbw	b Panesar	10			
SR Clark		b Harmison	3			
GD McGrath	c Cook	b Harmison	1			
Extras	(w 1, nb 4)		5	(lb 15, w 2, nb 1)		18
TOTAL	**(all out)**		**244**	**(5 wickets declared)**		**527**

1/47, 2/54, 3/69, 4/121, 5/172   *1/0, 2/144, 3/206, 4/357, 5/365*
6/172, 7/214, 8/234, 9/242, 10/244

Bowling: *First Innings:* Hoggard 12-2-40-1, Flintoff 9-2-36-0, Harmison 19-4-48-4, Panesar 24-4-92-5, Mahmood 7-2-28-0. *Second Innings:* Hoggard 20-4-85-1, Flintoff 19-2-76-0, Harmison 24-3-116-1, Panesar 34-3-145-3, Mahmood 10-0-59-0, Pietersen 5-1-31-0.

England

AJ Strauss	c Gilchrist	b Clark	42	lbw	b Lee	0
AN Cook	c Langer	b McGrath	15	c Gilchrist	b McGrath	116
IR Bell	c Gilchrist	b Lee	0	c Langer	b Warne	87
PD Collingwood	c Hayden	b McGrath	11	c Gilchrist	b Clark	5
KP Pietersen	c Symonds	b Lee	70	not out		60
A Flintoff	c Warne	b Symonds	13	(7)	b Warne	51
GO Jones	c Martyn	b Symonds	0	(8) run out (Ponting)		0
SI Mahmood	c Gilchrist	b Clark	10	(9) lbw	b Clark	4
MJ Hoggard	c Hayden	b Warne	4	(6)	b McGrath	0
SJ Harmison	c Lee	b Clark	23	lbw	b Warne	0
MS Panesar	not out		15		b Warne	1
Extras	(w 1, nb 10)		11	(b 11, lb 4, w 6, nb 5)		26
TOTAL	**(all out)**		**215**	**(all out)**		**350**

1/36, 2/37, 3/55, 4/82, 5/107   *1/0, 2/170, 3/185, 4/261, 5/261*
6/114, 7/127, 8/155, 9/175, 10/215   *6/336, 7/336, 8/345. 9/346, 10/350*

Bowling: *First Innings:* Lee 18-1-69-2, McGrath 18-5-48-2, Clark 15.1-3-49-3, Warne 9-0-41-1, Symonds 4-1-8-2. *Second Innings:* Lee 22-3-75-1, McGrath 27-9-61-2, Clark 25-7-56-2, Warne 39.2-6-115-4, Symonds 9-1-28-0.

The Ashes 2006–07

FOURTH TEST, 26–28 DECEMBER 2006, MCG, MELBOURNE
AUSTRALIA WON BY INNINGS & 99 RUNS. *UMPIRES:* RE KOERTZEN, ALEEM DAR

England

AJ Strauss		b Warne	50	c Gilchrist	b Lee	31
AN Cook	c Gilchrist	b McGrath	11		b Clark	20
IR Bell	lbw	b Clark	7	lbw	b McGrath	2
PD Collingwood	c Ponting	b Lee	28	(5) c Langer	b Lee	16
KP Pietersen	c Symonds	b Warne	21	(4)	b Clark	1
A Flintoff	c Warne	b Clark	13	lbw	b Clark	25
CMW Read	c Ponting	b Warne	3	not out		26
SI Mahmood	c Gilchrist	b McGrath	0	lbw	b Warne	0
SJ Harmison	c Clarke	b Warne	7	lbw	b Warne	4
MS Panesar	c Symonds	b Warne	4	c Clarke	b Lee	14
MJ Hoggard	not out		9		b Lee	5
Extras	(b 2, lb 1, nb 3)		6	(lb 12, w 1, nb 4)		17
TOTAL	**(all out)**		**159**	**(all out)**		**161**

1/23, 2/44, 3/101, 4/101, 5/122   *1/41, 2/48, 3/49, 4/75, 5/90*
6/135, 7/136, 8/145, 9/146, 10/159   *6/108, 7/109, 8/127. 9/146, 10/161*

Bowling: *First Innings:* Lee 13–0–36–2, McGrath 20–8–37–1, Clark 17–6–27–2, Symonds 7–2–17–0, Warne 17.2–4–39–5. *Second Innings:* Lee 18.5–6–47–4, McGrath 12–2–26–1, Clark 16–6–30–3, Warne 19–3–46–2.

Australia

JL Langer	c Read	b Flintoff	27
ML Hayden	c Read	b Mahmood	153
B Lee	c Read	b Flintoff	0
RT Ponting	c Cook	b Flintoff	7
MEK Hussey		b Hoggard	6
MJ Clarke	c Read	b Harmison	5
A Symonds	c Read	b Harmison	156
AC Gilchrist	c Collingwood	b Mahmood	1
SK Warne	not out		40
SR Clark	c Read	b Mahmood	8
GD McGrath	c Bell	b Mahmood	0
Extras	(lb 6, w 1, nb 9)		16
TOTAL	**(all out)**		**419**

1/44, 2/44, 3/62, 4/79, 5/84
6/363, 7/365, 8/383, 9/417, 10/419

Bowling: Hoggard 21–6–82–1, Flintoff 22–1–77–3, Harmison 28–6–69–2, Mahmood 21.3–1–100–4, Panesar 12–1–52–0, Collingwood 3–0–20–0, Pietersen 1–0–13–0.

The Ashes 2006–07

FIFTH TEST, 2–5 JANUARY 2007, SCG, SYDNEY
AUSTRALIA WON BY 10 WICKETS. *UMPIRES:* BF BOWDEN, ALEEM DAR

England

AJ Strauss	c Gilchrist	b Lee	29	lbw	b Clark	24
AN Cook	c Gilchrist	b Clark	20	c Gilchrist	b Lee	4
IR Bell		b McGrath	71	c Gilchrist	b Lee	28
KP Pietersen	c Hussey	b McGrath	41	c Gilchrist	b McGrath	29
PD Collingwood	c Gilchrist	b McGrath	27	c Hayden	b Clark	17
A Flintoff	c Gilchrist	b Clark	89	st Gilchrist	b Warne	7
CMW Read	c Gilchrist	b Lee	2	(8) c Ponting	b Lee	4
SI Mahmood	c Hayden	b Lee	0	(9)	b McGrath	4
SJ Harmison	lbw	b Clark	2	(10) not out		16
MS Panesar	lbw	b Warne	0	(7) run out (Symonds)		0
JM Anderson	not out		0	c Hussey	b McGrath	5
Extras	(lb 5, w 3, nb 2)		10	(b2, lb 3, w 1, nb 3)		9
TOTAL	**(all out)**		**291**	**(all out)**		**147**

1/45, 2/58, 3/166, 4/167, 5/245   *1/5, 2/55, 3/64, 4/98, 5/113*
6/245, 7/258, 8/282, 9/291, 10/291   *6/114, 7/114, 8/122. 9/123, 10/147*

Bowling: *First Innings:* McGrath 29–8–67–3, Lee 22–5–75–3, Clark 24–6–62–3, Warne 22.4–1–69–1, Symonds 6–2–13–0. *Second Innings:* Lee 14–5–39–3, McGrath 21–11–38–3, Clark 12–4–29–2, Warne 6–1–23–1, Symonds 5–2–13–0.

Australia

JL Langer	c Read	b Anderson	26	not out	20
ML Hayden	c Collingwood	b Harmison	33	not out	23
RT Ponting	run out (Anderson)		45		
MEK Hussey	c Read	b Anderson	37		
MJ Clarke	c Read	b Harmison	11		
A Symonds		b Panesar	48		
AC Gilchrist	c Read	b Anderson	62		
SK Warne	st Read	b Panesar	71		
B Lee	c Read	b Flintoff	5		
SR Clark	c Pietersen	b Mahmood	35		
GD McGrath	not out		0		
Extras	(lb 10, w 4, nb 6)		20	(lb 3)	3
TOTAL	**(all out)**		**393**	**(0 wickets)**	**46**

1/34, 2/100, 3/118, 4/155, 5/190
6/260, 7/318, 8/325, 9/393, 10/393

Bowling: *First Innings:* Flintoff 17–2–56–1, Anderson 26–8–98–3, Harmison 23–5–80–2, Mahmood 11–1–59–1, Panesar 19.3–0–90–2. *Second Innings:* Anderson 4–0–12–0, Harminson 5–1–13–0, Mahmood 1.5–0– 18–0.

Commonwealth Bank ODI Series 2006/07

12 January 2006–9 February 2007, Australia

Australia entered the 2006–07 competition as hot favourites, having whitewashed England in the Ashes just six days before the tournament began. New Zealand made up the trio of participants.

The tournament opened in Melbourne on 12 January, with the home side beating England by 8 wickets, their sixth consecutive win over their old rivals. Two days later the Aussies won again, this time defeating New Zealand by 105 runs at Hobart. Having failed to win any of their previous 11 games during their current Tour down under, England finally notched up their first win in game three, defeating the Kiwis by 3 wickets, also in Hobart. However, England then lost again to Australia, this time by 4 wickets in Brisbane. The Aussies clinched their place in the final with a fourth consecutive win of the tournament, a 2-wicket victory over the Kiwis in Sydney in game five. England then lost games six and seven, both in Adelaide, by 90 runs to New Zealand and by a disastrous 9 wickets to Australia respectively. Game 12 became a showdown between England and New Zealand to see who would face Australia in the final. England were the victors.

England faced Australia in Melbourne in game one of their best-of-three final. England beat Australia by four wickets to go 1–0 up. Two days later, the two sides moved on to Sydney for game two and, once again, England beat their old rivals to win their first major overseas one-day tournament since 1997.

Qualifying Matches

FINAL TABLE

Team	P	W	L	NR	BP	Pts	Net R/R
Australia	**8**	**7**	**1**	**0**	**4**	**32**	**0.67**
England	8	3	5	0	1	13	−0.61
New Zealand	8	2	6	0	1	9	−0.01

Final Series

GAME ONE – 9 FEBRUARY 2007, MELBOURNE

Australia 252 (48.3 overs) lost to England 253–6 (49.3 overs) by four wickets

Hayden	82	Collingwood	120
Ponting	75	Bell	65
Flintoff	3–41	Lee	3–41

GAME TWO – 11 FEBRUARY 2007, SYDNEY

England 246–8 (50 0 overs) beat Australia 152–8 (27 overs) by 34 runs (D/L method)

Collingwood	70	Hodge	49
Loye	45	Plunkett	3–43
Flintoff	42		

England win the series 2–0 (game 3 not played)

ICC Cricket World Cup 2007

13 March–28 April, West Indies

The ICC Cricket World Cup witnessed a number of highlights – some good and some bad. Some of the venues were not complete by the time the opening ceremony took place on 11 March and at the newly constructed north stand in Sabina Park, a number of seats had to be removed following safety concerns. Meanwhile, both Australia and South Africa raised concerns over the quality of the practice facilities on offer. A total of 51 matches were played, three fewer than at the 2003 World Cup and despite the fact that the 2007 tournament had 16 teams as opposed to 14 in 2003. The 16 competing nations were divided into four groups, with the top two teams from each group progressing to a Super Eight format. Australia, Bangladesh, England, Ireland, New Zealand, South Africa, Sri Lanka and the hosts, West Indies, formed the Super Eight.

In the first semi-final, Sri Lanka beat New Zealand by 81 runs, while the Australians tore apart South Africa, the number one ranked ICC side in the world, winning by a comfortable 7 wickets. On St Patrick's Day, 17 March, Ireland caused one of the biggest upsets in the history of cricket by beating one of the pre-tournament favourites, Pakistan, a result which put Pakistan out of the World Cup. The following day Bob Woolmer, the Pakistan coach was found dead in his hotel room (see page 343).

The World Cup organizers were criticized early on for being over-commercialized with too much emphasis on security restrictions, which meant fans were not permitted to bring in their own food, musical instruments, signs and even the wearing of replica kits was banned. Ticket prices were also very high, resulting in a large number of the local population not being able to afford to watch many of the games.

Glenn McGrath retired after the final bringing the curtain down on his illustrious career by being named man of the tournament. The 37-year-old Australian finished the tournament with a record 25 wickets.

AUSTRALIA V SRI LANKA – WORLD CUP FINAL
DATE: 28 APRIL 2007; *VENUE:* KENSINGTON OVAL, BRIDGETOWN, BARBADOS
RESULT: AUSTRALIA WON BY 53 RUNS (D/L)
TOSS: AUSTRALIA WON THE TOSS AND DECIDED TO BAT

Forty-six days after it all began, Australia were crowned World Cup champions for the fourth time. Australia (281–4, 38 overs) beat Sri Lanka (215–8, 36 overs) by 53 runs on the Duckworth-Lewis scoring method. After a rain delay, Australia maximized the early good conditions and, unlike the Sri Lankans, they knew exactly how many overs they would face. Opener Adam Gilchrist tore into the Sri Lankan bowling, scoring 149, the highest ever made in a World Cup final. By taking just 72 balls to notch up his century, Gilchrist equalled the third fastest ever made in the World Cup, while it was also the 11th highest individual score in the 22-year history of the tournament. When Sri Lanka came in to bat they had to better the Aussies' score of 281–4 but that proved an impossible task.

Man of the match: Adam Gilchrist   **Man of the tournament:** Glenn McGrath

ICC Cricket World Cup 2007

GROUP MATCHES
GROUP A (St Kitts)
Australia 334/6 (50); Scotland 131 (40.1). *Australia won by 203 runs.*
South Africa 353/3 (40); Netherlands 132/9 (40). *South Africa won by 221 runs* (40 over match).
Australia 358/5 (50); Netherlands 129 (26.5). *Australia won by 229 runs.*
Scotland 186/8 (50); South Africa 188/3 (23.2). *South Africa won by 7 wickets.*
Scotland 136 (34.1); Netherlands 140/2 (23.5). *Netherlands won by 8 wickets.*
Australia 377/6 (50); South Africa 294 (48). *Australia won by 83 runs.*

Team	P	W	L	T	Pts
Australia	3	3	0	0	6
South Africa	3	2	1	0	4
Netherlands	3	1	2	0	2
Scotland	3	0	3	0	0

"The last two balls landed in the right areas for me to have a go and luckily I didn't miscue either of them."
South Africa's **Hrschelle Gibbs** *who hit six 6s in an over against the Netherlands.*

GROUP B (Trinidad)
Sri Lanka 321/6 (50); Bermuda 78 (24.4). *Sri Lanka won by 243 runs.*
India 191 (49.3); Bangladesh 192/5 (48.3). *Bangladesh won by 5 wickets.*
India 413/5 (50); Bermuda 156 (43.1). *India won by 257 runs.*
Sri Lanka 318/4 (50); Bangladesh 112 (37/46). *Sri Lanka won by 198 runs (D/L method).*
Sri Lanka 254/6 (50); India 185 (43.3). *Sri Lanka won by 69 runs.*
Bermuda 94/9 (21); Bangladesh 96/3 (17.3). *Bangladesh won by 7 wickets (D/L method – match reduced to 21 overs).*

Team	P	W	L	T	Pts
Sri Lanka	3	3	0	0	6
Bangladesh	3	2	1	0	4
India	3	1	2	0	2
Bermuda	3	0	3	0	0

"We've dominated this tournament, no team has dominated one before. We've never really been tested."
Aussie skipper, **Ricky Ponting**

GROUP C (St Lucia)
Canada 199 (50); Kenya 203/3 (43.2). *Kenya won by 7 wickets.*
England 209/7 (50); New Zealand 210/4 (41). *New Zealand won by 6 wickets.*
England 279/6 (50); Canada 228/7 (50). *England won by 51 runs.*
New Zealand 331/7 (50); Kenya 183 (49.2). *New Zealand won by 148 runs.*
New Zealand 363/5 (50); Canada 249 (49.2). *New Zealand won by 114 runs.*
Kenya 177 (43/43); England 178/3 (33/43). *England won by 7 wickets.*

Team	P	W	L	T	Pts
New Zealand	3	3	0	0	6
England	3	2	1	0	4
Kenya	3	1	2	0	2
Canada	3	0	3	0	0

"The umpires said we had to play three overs. We found out later they had got it wrong."
Sri Lanka captain **Mahela Jayawardene** *after the final*

GROUP D (Jamaica)

West Indies 241/9 (50); Pakistan 187 (47.2). *West Indies won by 54 runs.*
Ireland 221/9 (50); Zimbabwe 221 (50). *Match tied.*
Pakistan 132 (45.4/50); Ireland 133/7 (41.4/47). *Ireland won by 3 wickets (D/L method).*
Zimbabwe 202/5 (50); West Indies 204/4 (47.5). *West Indies won by 6 wickets.*
Pakistan 349 (49.5/50); Zimbabwe 99 (19.1/20). *Pakistan won by 93 runs (D/L method).*
Ireland 183/8 (48/48); West Indies 190/2 (38.1/48). *West Indies won by 8 wickets (D/L).*

Team	P	W	L	T	Pts
West Indies	3	3	0	0	6
Ireland	3	1	1	1	3
Pakistan	3	1	2	0	2
Zimbabwe	3	0	2	1	1

"Congrats Australia!"
The scoreboard at the
Kensington Oval

Super Eights

Each team played the two qualifiers from the other three groups. The group match results between the two qualifiers were carried over and included in the Super Eights table. Thus, although playing only six matches, each team is listed as having played seven.

Antigua Australia 322/6 (50); West Indies 219 (45.3). *Australia won by 103 runs.*
Guyana Sri Lanka 209 (49.3); South Africa 212/9 (48.2). *South Africa won by 1 wicket.*
Antigua West Indies 177 (44.4); New Zealand 179/3 (39.2). *New Zealand won by 7 wkts.*
Guyana England 266/7 (50); Ireland 218 (48.1). *England won by 48 runs.*
Antigua Bangladesh 104/6 (22); Australia 106/0 (13.5). *Australia won by 10 wkts* (22 over match).
Guyana Sri Lanka 303/5 (50); West Indies 190 (44.3). *Sri Lanka won by 113 runs.*
Antigua Bangladesh 174 (48.3); New Zealand 178/1 (29.2). *New Zealand won by 9 wkts.*
Guyana Ireland 152/8 (35); South Africa 165/3 (31.3). *South Africa won by 7 wkts (D/L method – match reduced to 35 overs).*
Antigua Sri Lanka 235 (50); England 233/8 (50). *Sri Lanka won by 2 runs.*
Guyana Bangladesh 251/8 (50); South Africa 184 (48.4). *Bangladesh won by 67 runs.*
Antigua England 247 (49.5); Australia 248/3 (47.2). *Australia won by 7 wkts*
Guyana New Zealand 263/8 (50); Ireland 134 (37.4). *New Zealand won by 129 runs.*
Grenada South Africa 356/4 (50); West Indies 289/9 (50). *South Africa won by 67 runs.*
Barbados Bangladesh 143 (37.2); England 147/6 (44.5). *England won by 4 wkts.*
Grenada New Zealand 219/7 (50); Sri Lanka 222/4 (45.1). *Sri Lanka won by 6 wkts.*
Barbados Ireland 91 (30); Australia 92/1 (12.2). *Australia won by 9 wkts.*
Grenada South Africa 193/7 (50); New Zealand 196/5 (48.2). *New Zealand won by 5 wkts.*
Barbados Ireland 243/7 (50); Bangladesh 169 (41.2). *Ireland won by 74 runs.*
Grenada Sri Lanka 226 (49.4); Australia 232/3 (42.4). *Australia won by 7 wckts*
Barbados England 154 (48); South Africa 157/1 (19.2). *South Africa won by 9 wckts.*
Grenada Ireland 77 (27.4); Sri Lanka 81/2 (10). *Sri Lanka won by 8 wckts.*
Barbados West Indies 230/5 (50); Bangladesh 131 (43.5). *West Indies won by 99 runs.*
Grenada Australia 348/6 (50); New Zealand 133 (25.5). *Australia won by 215 runs.*
Barbados West Indies 300 (49.5); England 301/9 (49.5). *England won by 1 wicket.*

SUPER EIGHTS TABLE

Team	P	W	L	T	Pts
Australia	7	7	0	0	14
Sri Lanka	7	5	2	0	10
New Zealand	7	5	2	0	10
South Africa	7	4	3	0	8
England	7	3	4	0	6
West Indies	7	2	5	0	4
Bangladesh	7	1	6	0	2
Ireland	7	1	6	0	2

Sri Lanka had a better run rate than New Zealand (1.483 to 0.253).
Bangladesh had a better run rate than Ireland (−1.514 to −1.730).

> "There's no secret we had a few drinks... there was water involved and a pedalo as well. But I don't think my life was in danger."
>
> *Andrew Flintoff, after an evening escapade went too far.*

SEMI-FINALS

24 APRIL 2007, SABINA PARK, KINGSTON, JAMAICA

Sri Lanka 289–5 (50 overs) beat New Zealand 208 (41.4 overs) by 81 runs.

Jayawardene	115 *not out*	Fulton	46
Tharanga	73	Styris	37
Dilshan	30	Muralitharan	4–31
Franklin	2–46	Dilshan	2–22

25 APRIL 2007, BEAUSEJOUR CRICKET GROUND, GROS ISLET, ST LUCIA.

South Africa 149 (43.5 overs) lost to Australia 153–3 (31.3 overs) by 7 wickets

Kemp	49 *not out*	Clarke	60 *not out*
Gibbs	39	Hayden	41
Tait	4–39	Ponting	22
McGrath	3–18	Pollock	1–16

Trivia

* The fastest World Cup 100 was scored by Matthew Hayden off of 66 balls during the match between Australia and South Africa.

* Australia's victory over Sri Lanka in the final means that the Aussies have now gone undefeated in 29 consecutive World Cup matches, a remarkable winning streak dating back to the 1999 World Cup.

* Ireland's leading batsman in the qualifying competition for 2007, Ed Joyce, played for England in finals.

* Although the organizers of the 2007 World Cup failed to meet the target revenue of US$42m, the actual revenue from ticket sales was double the ticket sales revenue from the 2003 World Cup and the highest ticketing revenue for a Cricket World Cup.

* In the eyes of most of England's critics, the performance in the World Cup was very disappointing. In fact, going by the ICC World Standings, England excelled because, although ranked seventh in the world, they finished fifth in the Super Eights.

FINAL

SUNDAY 28 APRIL 2007, KENSINGTON OVAL, BARBADOS

UMPIRES: SA BUCKNOR (WEST INDIES), ALEEM DAR (PAKISTAN). *TOSS:* AUSTRALIA (BAT).

AUSTRALIA WON BY 53 RUNS *(DUCKWORTH/LEWIS METHOD)*.

AUSTRALIA

				balls	*4s*	*6s*
Gilchrist	c Silva	b Fernando	149	104	13	8
Hayden	c Jayawardene	b Malinga	38	55	3	1
Ponting	run out (Jayawardene)		37	42	1	1
Symonds	not out		23	21	2	0
Watson		b Malinga	3	3	0	0
Clarke	not out		8	6	1	0
Extras	(lb 4, nb 3, w 16)		23			
TOTAL	**38 overs (for 4 wickets)**		**281**			

Bowling: Vaas 8–0–54–0 (nb2, w1), Malinga 8–1–49–2, Fernando 8–0–74–1 (nb1, w4), Muralitharan 7–0–44–0 (w2), Dilshan 2–0–23–0 (w1), Jayasuriya 5–0–33–0.

FoW: 1/172 (Hayden), 2/224 (Gilchrist), 3/261 (Ponting), 4/266 (Watson). *PP1: 1–13; PP2 19–24.*

SRI LANKA

				balls	*4s*	*6s*
Tharanga	c Gilchrist	b Bracken	6	8	1	0
Jayasuriya		b Clarke	63	67	9	0
Sangakkara	c Ponting	b Hogg	54	52	6	1
Jayawardene	lbw	b Watson	19	19	1	0
Silva		b Clarke	21	22	1	1
Dilshan	run out (Clarke/McGrath)		14	13	2	0
Arnold	c Gilchrist	b McGrath	1	2	0	0
Vaas	not out		11	22	0	0
Malinga	st Gilchrist	b Symonds	10	6	0	1
Fernando	not out		1	5	0	0
Extras	(lb 1, w 14)		15			
TOTAL	**36 overs (for 8 wickets)**		**215**			

Bowling: Bracken 6–1–34–1 (w1), Tait 6–0–42–0 (w2), McGrath 7–0–31–1 (w1), Watson 7–0–49–1 (w3), Hogg 3–0–19–1, Clarke 5–0–33–2 (w2), Symonds 2–0–6–1.

FoW: 1/7 (Tharanga), 2/123 (Sangakkara), 3/145 (Jayasuriya), 4/156 (Jayawardene), 5/188 (Dilshan), 6/190 (Silva), 7/194 (Arnold), 8/211 (Malinga). *PP: 1–13; PP2 11–15.*

"It's been a long career and I've loved every minute of it, but I'll miss playing out on field and all the celebrations, as well as the amazing supporters and everyone who's come to the grounds (around the world) and back in Australia.**"**

Glenn McGrath

"I've played four balls in four World Cups and that's probably four too many.**"**

Glenn McGrath

England v West Indies – First Test

DATE: **17–21 MAY 2007;** *VENUE:* **LORD'S CRICKET GROUND, LONDON**
RESULT: **MATCH WAS DRAWN;** *TOSS:* **WEST INDIES WON THE TOSS AND DECIDED TO FIELD**

England First Innings
553–5 (142.0 overs)

England Second Innings
284–8 (66.5 overs)

West Indies First Innings
437 all out (116.1 overs)

West Indies Second Innings
89–0

Alastair Cook, Paul Collingwood, Matt Prior and Ian Bell all hit centuries, the first time four Englishmen had done so in one innings of a Test since 1938, Prior becoming the first England wicket-keeper to hit a century on his debut. England set the West Indies (437 all out and 7–0) a target of 394 for victory. However, rain ruined day five, the visitors only managing to add 82 runs to their overnight score before the game was declared a draw.

England v West Indies – Second Test

DATE: **25–28 MAY 2007;** *VENUE:* **HEADINGLEY CRICKET GROUND, LEEDS**
RESULT: **ENGLAND WON BY AN INNINGS AND 283 RUNS;**
TOSS: **ENGLAND WON THE TOSS AND DECIDED TO BAT**

England First Innings
570–7 dec (122.3 overs)

West Indies First Innings
146–9 (37.0 overs)

West Indies Second Innings
141–9 (42.1 overs)

On the fourth day England bowled the West Indies out for 141 to win by an innings and 283 runs. The victory margin was England's biggest over the Windies and the tourists' heaviest ever Test defeat. England's Ryan Sidebottom ended the Test with an impressive 8–86 to give England a 1–0 lead in the series going into the third Test at Old Trafford on 7 June.

England v West Indies – Third Test

DATE: **7–11 JUNE 2007;** *VENUE:* **OLD TRAFFORD CRICKET GROUND, MANCHESTER**
RESULT: **ENGLAND WON BY 60 RUNS;**
TOSS: **ENGLAND WON THE TOSS AND DECIDED TO BAT**

England First Innings
370 all out (105.1 overs)

England Second Innings
313 all out (85.3 overs)

West Indies First Innings
229 all out (52.4 overs)

West Indies Second Innings
394 all out (132.5 overs)

England set the West Indies what would have been a record winning total of 455. Much of the credit for their 60-run win goes to Monty Panesar who claimed his first 10-wicket haul in a Test match. England's win meant that they took an unassailable 2–0 lead in the series. Michael Vaughan was extremely proud to become the most successful England Test captain ever, passing Peter May's 20 wins, in what was his 35th match as captain. "It's great to pass so many legends of the game in victories but it's special because we've won the series. We got asked a lot of questions. They pushed us every single day," said Vaughan.

Trivia

* West Indies score of 394 was the eighth highest in a defeat:

  451: NZ v Eng 2002
  445: Ind v Aus 1978
  440: NZ v Eng 1973
  417: Eng v Aus 1977
  411: Eng v Aus 1924
  402: Aus v Eng 1981
  397: Ind v Eng 2002
  394: WI v Eng 2007
  376: Ind v Eng 1959
  370: Eng v Aus 1921
  370: Eng v Aus 2006

* Leading England Captains

  Michael Vaughan (2003–):
  21 wins in 35 Tests *(60% won)*
  Peter May (1955–61):
  20 in 41 *(48.78%)*
  Mike Brearley (1977–81):
  18 in 31 *(58.06%)*
  Nasser Hussain (1999–2003):
  17 in 45 *(37.77%)*
  Michael Atherton (1993–2001):
  13 in 54 *(24.07%)*

England v West Indies – Fourth Test

DATE: **15–19 JUNE 2007;** *VENUE:* **RIVERSIDE GROUND, CHESTER-LE-STREET, DURHAM**
RESULT: **ENGLAND WON BY 7 WICKETS;**
TOSS: **ENGLAND WON THE TOSS AND DECIDED TO FIELD**

West Indies First Innings	West Indies Second Innings
287 all out (97.1 overs)	222 all out (64.0 overs)

England First Innings	England Second Innings
400 all out (100.0 overs)	111 for 3 (21.4 overs)

Day one of the fourth and final Test was washed out with heavy rain at Chester-le-Street. When play finally got underway at 2pm on day two, the West Indies batted well and ended the day on 132–4 at stumps. England bowled the Windies out for 287 (Chanderpaul notched up his 16th Test century) on day three before reaching 121–4 by close of play with Kevin Pietersen caught off the last ball for a duck. By the close of play on day four England were all out for 400. Paul Collingwood's 128 was the first Test century by a Durham player on home turf. The West Indies scored 83–3 at stumps while England bowled the tourists out for 222 runs on day five and then smacked 111 runs for the loss of 3 wickets to win the fourth Test and claim an emphatic 3–0 series victory.

England v India – First Test

DATE: **19–23 JULY 2007;** *VENUE:* **LORD'S CRICKET GROUND, LONDON**
RESULT: **DRAW;** *TOSS:* **ENGLAND WON THE TOSS AND DECIDED TO BAT**

England First Innings	England Second Innings
298 all out (91.2 overs)	282 all out (78.3 overs)

India First Innings	India Second Innings
201 all out (77.2 overs)	282 for 9 (96.0 overs)

A combination of bad light and rain on day five of the first Test against India at Lord's denied England victory over the visitors. India (201 & 137–3) started the final day chasing 380 runs for victory. When Sourav Ganguly (40) and Dinesh Karthik (60) fell in the morning, it left India on 145–5 chasing 235 runs for a win. However, V. V. S. Laxman and Mahendra Dhoni added 86 to their tally before poor visibility forced an early tea with the players not reappearing, resulting in a draw.

England v India – Second Test

DATE: **27–31 JULY 2007;** *VENUE:* **TRENT BRIDGE, NOTTINGHAM**
RESULT: **INDIA BEAT ENGLAND BY 7 WICKETS;**
TOSS: **INDIA WON THE TOSS AND DECIDED TO FIELD**

England First Innings	England Second Innings
198 all out (65.3 overs)	355 all out (104.0 overs)

India First Innings	India Second Innings
481 all out (158.5 overs)	73 for 3 (24.1 overs)

India finished off England on the final day's play at Trent Bridge to claim a 7-wicket victory, which gave the tourists a 1–0 lead in the three-match series. India began the day on 10–0 requiring just 73 runs for victory and they achieved their target in 94 minutes. Chris Tremlett took all three of the fallen wickets.

Trivia

* The only Indian batsman to score a century against England in the series was spinner Anil Kumble, who scored 110 not out in the first innings of the final Test at The Oval. In India's total of 664 all out, every other batsman reached double figures and extras contributed another 54, including 33 byes.

* The new drainage system at Lord's showed its value on the second day of the opening Test. A heavy rainstorm left the ground under water at 12.30, yet play resumed less than two hours later. Sadly, the drainage system can't do anything about bad light, which thwarted England one wicket from victory on the last day.

England v India – Third Test

DATE: **9–13 AUGUST 2007;** *VENUE:* **THE OVAL, LONDON**
RESULT: **DRAW;** *TOSS:* **ENGLAND WON THE TOSS AND DECIDED TO BAT**

India First innings	India Second innings
664 all out (170.0 overs)	180 for 6 (58.0 overs)

England First innings	England Second innings
345 all out (103.1 overs)	369 for 6 (110.0 overs)

Despite Kevin Pietersen hitting his tenth Test century, it wasn't enough to give England the win they needed against India. On day five at the Brit Oval in the third NPower Test England batted through to stumps to force a draw with India, but India won the series 1–0. It was India's first Test series victory on English soil since 1986.

ICC Team Rankings – Test matches

DATE: **13 AUGUST 2007**

1. Australia	*4.* Sri Lanka	*7.* New Zealand
2. England	*5.* South Africa	*8.* West Indies
3. India	*6.* Pakistan	*9.* Bangladesh

N.B. Zimbabwe has not played enough Test matches over the current rating period to be eligible.

ICC Test Player Rankings

DATE: **9 AUGUST 2007**

LEADING TEST BATSMEN

1. Ricky Ponting (Australia)	*6.* Michael Hayden (Australia)
2. Mohammad Yousuf (Pakistan)	*7.* Jaques Kallis (South Africa)
3. Kumar Sangakkara (Sri Lanka)	*8.* Younis Khan (Pakistan)
4. Kevin Pietersen (England)	*9.* Shivnarine Chanderpaul (West Indies)
5. Michael Hussey (Australia)	*10.* Ashwell Prince (South Africa)

LEADING TEST BOWLERS

1. Muttiah Muralitharan (Sri Lanka)	*6.* Mohammad Asif (Pakistan)
2. Makhaya Ntini (South Africa)	*7.* Anil Kumble (India)
3. Shaun Pollock (South Africa)	*8.* Matthew Hoggard (England)
4. Shane Bond (New Zealand)	*9.* Shoaib Akhtar (Pakistan)
5. Stuart Clark (Australia)	*10.* Zaheer Khan (India)

England v West Indies – One-day International Matches

Nat West One-day Series – three matches

MATCH 1

DATE: **1 JULY 2007**; *VENUE:* **LORD'S, LONDON**

TOSS: **WEST INDIES (FIELD)** *RESULT:* **ENGLAND WON BY 79 RUNS (1–0)**

England	West Indies
225 (49.5 overs)	146 (39.5 overs)

MATCH 2

DATE: **4 JULY 2007**; *VENUE:* **EDGBASTON, BIRMINGHAM**

TOSS: **ENGLAND (FIELD)** *RESULT:* **WEST INDIES WON BY 61 RUNS (1–1).**

West Indies	England
278–5 (50.0 overs)	217 (46 overs)

MATCH 3

DATE: **7 JULY 2007**; *VENUE:* **TRENT BRIDGE, NOTTINGHAM.**

TOSS: **WEST INDIES (BAT)** *RESULT:* **WEST INDIES WON BY 93 RUNS (2–1)**

West Indies	England
289–5 (50.0 overs)	196 (44.2 overs)

NatWest International Twenty20 Series – two matches

MATCH 1

DATE: **28 JUNE 2007**; *VENUE:* **THE OVAL, LONDON**

TOSS: **WEST INDIES (BAT)** *RESULT:* **WEST INDIES WON BY 15 RUNS (1–0)**

West Indies	England
208–8 (20.0 overs)	193–7 (20.0 overs)

MATCH 2

DATE: **29 JUNE 2007**; *VENUE:* **THE OVAL, LONDON;**

TOSS: **WEST INDIES (BAT)** *RESULT:* **ENGLAND WON BY 5 WICKETS (1–1).**

West Indies	England
169–7 (20.0 overs)	173–5 (19.3 overs)

England v India – NatWest One-day Series – seven matches

MATCH 1   *DATE:* 21 AUGUST 2007 ; *VENUE:* ROSE BOWL, HAMPSHIRE
TOSS: INDIA (FIELD) *RESULT:* ENGLAND BEAT INDIA BY 104 RUNS (1–0)

England	India
288–2 (50.0 overs)	184 all out (50.0 overs)

MATCH 2   *DATE:* 24 AUGUST 2007; *VENUE:* COUNTY GROUND, BRISTOL
TOSS: INDIA (BAT) *RESULT:* INDIA WON BY 9 RUNS (1–1)

India	England
329–7 (50.0 overs)	320–8 (50.0 overs)

MATCH 3   *DATE:* 27 AUGUST 2007; *VENUE:* EDGBASTON, BIRMINGHAM
TOSS: INDIA (FIELD) *RESULT:* ENGLAND WON BY 42 RUNS (2–1)

England	India
281–8 (50.0 overs)	239 all out (48.1 overs)

MATCH 4   *DATE:* 30 AUGUST 2007; *VENUE:* OLD TRAFFORD, MANCHESTER
TOSS: INDIA (BAT) *RESULT:* ENGLAND WON BY 3 WICKETS (3–1)

India	England
212 all out (49.4 overs)	213–7 (48.0 overs)

MATCH 5   *DATE:* 2 SEPTEMBER 2007; *VENUE:* HEADINGLEY, LEEDS
TOSS: ENGLAND (FIELD) *RESULT:* INDIA WON BY 38 RUNS (2–3)

India	England
324–6 (50.0 overs)	242–8 (39.0 overs)

MATCH 6   *DATE:* 5 SEPTEMBER ; *VENUE:* THE OVAL, LONDON
TOSS: ENGLAND (BAT) *RESULT:* INDIA BEAT ENGLAND BY 2 WICKETS (3–3)

England	India
316-6 (50 overs)	317-8 (49.4 overs)

MATCH 7   *DATE:* 8 SEPTEMBER ; *VENUE:* LORD'S, LONDON
TOSS: INDIA (BAT) *RESULT:* ENGLAND BEAT INDIA BY 7 WICKETS (4–3)

India	England
187 all out (47.3 overs)	188 for 3 (36.2 overs)

County Championship 2006

The 2006 Liverpool Victoria County Championship began on 18 April 2006 and ended on 23 September 2006. The season belonged to Sussex who claimed their second County Championship, three years after winning their first. Their star player, Mushtaq Ahmed, continued to ensure his name would forever be remembered as one of the county's greatest players, with countless match-winning displays and 102 wickets. Lancashire lost more games than any team in the division, and finished 18 points behind Sussex. If they had turned five of those losses into draws, their 69-year wait for the title would have ended.

The relegation battle saw Yorkshire and Durham avoiding the drop by one and half a point, respectively. Nottinghamshire joined Middlesex in the bottom two. Division Two champions were Surrey, for whom Mark Ramprakash scored 2,278 runs and averaged 103.54, one of the six best averages ever compiled. Somerset collected the wooden spoon.

DIVISION ONE

		P	W	D	L	Pen	Bat	Bowl	Pts
1.	Sussex	16	9	2	5	0	49	47	242
2.	Lancashire	16	6	1	9	0	58	46	224
3.	Hampshire	16	6	3	7	1	48	48	207
4.	Warwickshire	16	6	5	5	0	42	43	189
5.	Kent	16	4	4	8	0	43	44	175
6.	Yorkshire	16	3	6	7	0	43	41	154
7.	Durham	16	4	8	4	0.5	39	43	153.5
8.	Nottinghamshire*	16	4	7	5	0	40	37	153
9.	Middlesex*	16	1	7	8	1.5	47	42	133.5

Relegated to Division Two

DIVISION TWO

		P	W	D	L	Pen	Bat	Bowl	Pts
1.	Surrey*	16	10	4	2	0	62	44	262
2.	Worcestershire *	16	8	4	4	0	58	43	229
3.	Essex	16	7	5	4	0	62	40	220
4.	Leicestershire	16	5	7	4	0.5	47	41	185.5
5.	Derbyshire	16	4	8	4	1.5	51	41	178.5
6.	Northamptonshire	16	3	8	5	0	52	37	163
7.	Gloucestershire	16	3	7	6	1.5	51	36	155.5
8.	Glamorgan	16	2	7	7	1.5	51	41	146.5
9.	Somerset	16	3	4	9	1	43	40	140

Promoted to Division One

Second XI Championship *Winners:* Kent II	**Minor Counties Championship** *Winners:* Devon
Second XI Trophy *Winners:* Warwickshire II	**MCCA Knockout Trophy** *Winners:* Northumberland

County Championship 2007

The 2007 Liverpool Victoria County Championship season began on 18 April and ended 22 September. Sussex were the defending champions and they made a very good fist of it too, leading the table with four matches left to play. Surrey, the 2006 Division Two champions, struggled to make an impact, while Worcestershire, the other promoted team, seemed certain to return to the lower division sfter one of the wettest seasons in living memory. Worcestershire were particularly hard hit, with their New Road county ground being left flooded on mon more than one occasion. Warwickshire were almost as hard hit as their Midlands rivals, as nine

Somerset seemed certain to fill one of the two promotion spots, with Essex or one of the two relegated teams in 2006 – Nottinghamshire and Middlesex – taking the runners-up spot. Glamorgan's plight at the bottom of the division matches that of Worcestershire and they were soon startng to build for the 2008 campaign.

The following tables reflect the division standings as at 22 August 2007.

DIVISION ONE

		Pld	W	D	T	L	Aban	Pts
1.	Sussex	12	5	5	0	2	0	149
2.	Yorkshire	13	3	7	0	3	0	145
3.	Durham	12	4	4	0	4	0	136.5
4.	Hampshire	11	4	6	0	1	0	131
5.	Warwickshire	13	2	9	0	2	0	129
6.	Lancashire	11	3	6	0	1	1	127
7.	Kent	12	2	5	0	4	1	113
8.	Surrey	12	2	6	0	4	0	109
9.	Worcestershire	12	1	4	0	5	2	79

DIVISION TWO

		Pld	W	D	T	L	Aban	Pts
1.	Somerset	12	7	4	0	1	0	190
2.	Nottinghamshire	12	4	6	0	2	0	159.5
3.	Essex	12	3	6	0	3	0	127
4.	Middlesex	10	4	5	0	1	0	116.5
5.	Northamptonshire	11	3	4	0	4	0	113
6.	Derbyshire	12	2	7	0	3	0	112
7.	Gloucestershire	12	2	6	0	4	0	105
8.	Leicestershire	12	2	5	0	4	1	103
9.	Glamorgan	11	1	3	0	6	1	70

Trivia

* On 22 July, Durham bowler Otis Gibson took all ten Hampshire wickets in an innings, returning figures of 10–47.

* Middlesex made 600–4 in their first innings against Somerset at Taunton, but the cider county replied with 850–7.

One-Day Cricket

Friends Provident Trophy 2007 Semi-finals

DATE: **20 JUNE 2007;** *VENUE:* **THE ROSE BOWL, HAMPSHIRE**
TOSS: **HAMPSHIRE (BAT)** *RESULT:* **HAMPSHIRE BEAT WARWICKSHIRE BY 40 RUNS;**

Hampshire Hawks	Warwickshire Bears
206–7 (50 overs)	166 all out (43.3 overs)

The Warwickshire Bears paid a heavy price for their decision to leave out Ian Bell. Shane Warne won the toss for the Hampshire Hawks and batted first. John Crawley led the way with 65, but their total of 206 was eminently gettable. Australian Test star Stuart Clark took three early wickets and the Bears struggled to 166, Kumar Sangakkara top-scoring with only 44.

DATE: **20 JUNE 2007;** *VENUE:* **RIVERSIDE GROUND, DURHAM**
TOSS: **DURHAM (FIELD)** *RESULT:* **DURHAM BEAT ESSEX BY 3 WICKETS;**

Durham Dynamoes	Essex Eagles
72–7 (19 overs)	71 all out (22.1 overs)

Otis Gibson, Neil Killeen and Liam Plunkett ripped apart the Essex Eagles batting line-up in the rain-delayed semi-final at the Riverside. Plunkett, bowling as second change, finished with 4–15, this after Gibson and Killeen had reduced Essex to 26–6. Andy Bichel, with 24, and Graham Napier, 14, were the only batsman to reach double figures. Bichel then took 4–22 to leave Durham struggling on 38–7 (Scott Styris 16), before Plunkett became the hero with the bat. Gibson was dropped by Danesh Kaneria, but he and Plunkett (30 off 35 balls) saw Durham home by three wickets. The match lasted only 41.1 overs.

Final

DATE: **17–18 AUGUST 2007;** *VENUE:* **LORD'S, LONDON**
TOSS: **HAMPSHIRE (FIELD)** *RESULT:* **DURHAM BEAT HAMPSHIRE BY 125 RUNS.**

Durham Dynamoes	Hampshire Hawks
206–7 (50 overs)	166 all out (43.3 overs)

The Durham Dynamoes made their first Lord's final appearance a memorable one, crushing the Hampshire Hawks by 125 runs in a one-sided match played over two days because of rain. Put into bat, Durham lost Michael di Venuto for 12 and Phil Mustard for 49 to leave them on 69–2, but Shivnarine Chanderpaul, Kyle Coetzer and Dale Benkenstein all struck rapid half-centuries as the Hampshire attack toiled. Warne went for only 46 off his 10 overs but seamer Daren Powell had figures of 2–80. When Hampshire batted, Otis Gibson, who had taken all 10 Hampshire wickets in a County Championship match a few weeks earlier, ripped out Michael Lumb and Stuart Ervine with the first two balls of the innings. Kevin Pietersen survived the hat-trick ball, but Gibson, Liam Plunkett and England one-day skipper Paul Collingwood ensured the result was never in doubt with three wickets each.

Twenty20 Cup – Group Stage

MID/WEST/WALES DIV				NORTH DIVISION				SOUTH DIVISION			
Team	*P*	*W*	*Pts*	*Team*	*P*	*W*	*Pts*	*Team*	*P*	*W*	*Pts*
1. Warwicks	8	5	11	Notts	8	4	11	Sussex	8	5	11
2. Gloucs	8	4	10	Lancashire	8	3	10	Kent	8	4	10
3. Worcs	8	3	9	Yorkshire	8	4	9	Surrey	8	4	8
4. Northants	8	2	7	Leicester	8	2	9	Essex	8	3	7
5. Somerset	8	3	6	Durham	8	1	5	Middlesex	8	2	7
6. Glam	8	1	5	Derbys	8	0	4	Hants	8	1	5

Quarter-finals

Bristol: Worcestershire 123–6 (17) lost to Gloucestershire 131–3 (14.1) by 7 wickets *(D/L)*

Nottingham: Nottinghamshire 138 (20) lost to Kent 139–1 (19.5) by 9 wickets

Hove: Sussex 193–5 (20) beat Yorkshire 155 (19.5) by 38 runs

Birmingham: Lancashire 193–5 (20) beat Warwickshire 187–7 (20) by 6 runs

Finals Day – 4 August 2007, Edgbaston, Birmingham

Semi-finals

TOSS: **GLOUCESTERSHIRE (FIELD)** *RESULT:* **GLOUCESTERSHIRE BEAT LANCASHIRE BY 8 WKTS**

Gloucestershire Gladiators	Lancashire Lightning
152–2 (16.5 overs)	148–6 (20 overs)

Underdogs Gloucestershire shocked an all-star Lancashire side by taking early wickets and restricting them to 148 before strolling to an easy victory, Craig Spearman scoring 86.

TOSS: **SUSSEX (BAT)** *RESULT:* **KENT BEAT SUSSEX BY 5 WICKETS.**

Kent Spitfires	Sussex Sharks
141–5 (19.2 overs)	140 (19.4 overs)

South Division runners-up Kent bowled out favourites Sussex for 140 and skipper Rob Key smashed 68 as Kent won with four balls to spare.

Final

TOSS: **KENT (FIELD)** *RESULT:* **KENT BEAT GLOUCESTERSHIRE BY 4 WICKETS;**

Kent Spitfires	Gloucestershire Gladiators
147–6 (19.3 overs)	146–8 (20 overs)

Kent won an enthralling Twenty20 Cup final by four wickets over Gloucestershire with three balls remaining. Ryan McLaren was named man of the match after taking a hat-trick, dismissing Hamish Marshall – top-scorer in the final with 65 – Steve Adshead and Ian Fisher, and returning figures of 3–22 off his four overs. Matt Walker hit 45 for Kent.

Pro40 Championship 2006

The Pro40 Championship is the successor to the old John Player Sunday League that was first contested in the late 1960s. The competition, however, is barely recognizable from the one of four decades ago because games are played on all days of the week, sometimes under floodlights, and always with coloured kits.

The Essex Eagles won the 2006 championship by the narrowest possible margin, on run-rate, after finishing level on points with the Northamptonshire Steelbacks. Suffering automatic relegation were the Durham Dynamoes and the Middlesex Crusaders, who thus went down in both the four-day and 40-over leagues in the same season.

The Gloucestershire Gladiators and Worcestershire Royals took the two automatic promotions spots, with Hampshire Hawks third. Both Yorkshire Phoenix and Derbyshire Phantoms managed to collect only one win all season.

The final promotion/relegation spot was decided in a play-off at the Rose Bowl, the Hawks' home. It was a one-sided affair, with Hampshire making 265–9, of which Chris Bentham contributed 158 from 130 balls. Sean Ervine took a wicket with the second ball of the innings and he returned figures of 4–24. The Dragons were dismissed for 114 in only 25 overs to lose by 151 runs, David Harrison top-scoring with just 28.

DIVISION ONE

		P	W	L	NR	T	Pts	RR	Runs For	Runs Conceded
1.	Essex	8	5	2	1	0	11	+1.233	1563	1343
2.	Northamptonshire	8	5	2	1	0	11	-0.037	1318	1344
3.	Sussex	8	5	3	0	0	10	+0.145	1515	1536
4.	Nottinghamshire	8	4	3	1	0	9	+0.062	1277	1248
5.	Warwickshire	8	3	4	1	0	7	-0.162	1260	1298
6.	Lancashire	8	2	3	3	0	7	+0.414	1028	963
7.	Glamorgan**	8	2	3	2	1	7	-0.484	1075	1181
8.	Durham*	8	2	4	1	1	6	-0.309	1428	1449
9.	Middlesex*	8	2	6	0	0	4	-0.781	1428	1530

*Relegated automatically to Division Two. **Relegated to Division Two after losing a playoff game.*

DIVISION TWO

		P	W	L	NR	T	Pts	RR	Runs For	Runs Conceded
1.	Gloucestershire*	8	6	2	0	0	12	+0.283	1687	1762
2.	Worcestershire*	8	6	2	0	0	12	+1.032	1626	1381
3.	Hampshire**	8	5	2	1	0	11	+0.550	1308	1172
4.	Surrey	8	5	2	1	0	11	+0.333	1670	1548
5.	Kent	8	5	3	0	0	10	+0.777	1629	1399
6.	Leicestershire	8	3	5	0	0	6	+0.106	1677	1595
7.	Somerset	8	2	6	0	0	4	-0.840	1474	1794
8.	Derbyshire	8	1	6	1	0	3	-0.860	1502	1624
9.	Yorkshire	8	1	6	1	0	3	-1.463	1327	1625

*Promoted automatically to Division One. **Promoted to Division One after winning a play-off game.*

World Test Cricket 2006–07

India's Tour of South Africa

India toured South Africa for three Test matches and five ODIs from 16 November 2006–6 January 2007. The home side won the Test series 2–1 and also claimed victory in the ODI series winning 4–0, India's first ODI series without a victory since 1997. India's 123-run win in the first Test was their first ever Test victory on South African soil. India went home with another victory, winning the solitary Twenty20 international played. South Africa's Ashwell Prince was the leading Test scorer with 306 runs, while India's Shanthakumaran Sreesanth claimed the most Test wickets, 18.

Sri Lanka's Tour of New Zealand

Sri Lanka toured New Zealand for the third consecutive season from 30 November 2006–9 January 2007 and played three Tests, five ODIs and two Twenty20 internationals. The sides were too evenly matched for either to claim overall victory with the Test series ending all-square at 1–1, the ODIs finished 2–2 (the fifth ODI scheduled for 9 January was abandoned) and both claimed a Twenty20 victory. Sri Lanka's Kumar Sangakkara was the leading Test scorer with 268 runs while the master bowler, Muttiah Muralitharan, claimed the most Test wickets, 17.

Pakistan's Tour of South Africa

Pakistan toured South Africa for three Test matches, five ODIs and one Twenty20 international from 6 January–14 February 2007. The hosts won the Test series 2–1, claimed a 3–1 victory in the

ODI series, with one game ending as a "no result", and won the Twenty20 international by 10 wickets. South Africa's Jacques Kallis was the leading Test scorer with 272 runs while South Africa's Makhaya Ntini and Mohammad Asif shared the most Test wickets taken, 19.

India's Tour of Bangladesh

India toured Bangladesh for two Test matches and three ODIs from 10–29 May 2007. India won the Test series 1–0 and claimed a 2–0 ODI series victory (the third ODI was abandoned as a result of cyclone Akash, which had struck south Bangladesh earlier that day) over Bangladesh less than two months after their opponents shocked India and the cricket world by defeating them by 5 wickets in the ICC World Cup. India's Sachin Tendulkar was the leading Test scorer with 254 runs and their bowler Zaheer Khan took the most Test wickets, 8. Dav Whatmore announced his retirement as coach of Bangladesh.

Bangladesh's Tour of Sri Lanka

Bangladesh toured Sri Lanka for three Test matches and three ODIs from 20 June–24 July 2007. Sri Lanka took a clean sweep of all three Test matches and repeated the feat in the ODIs, for an impressive record of played six, won six. Just as the pair had dominated the Kiwis in their tour of New Zealand, once again it was Sri Lanka's Kumar Sangakkara and Muttiah Muralitharan who grabbed all the headlines. Sangakkara was the leading Test scorer with 428 runs while Muralitharan claimed a staggering 26 Test wickets.

World Domestic Cricket 2006–07

Australia

The Australian cricket season began on 11 October 2006 and ended on 28 April 2007.

ROLL OF HONOUR
International Series
Rose Bowl – Australia Women beat New Zealand Women 5–0 in five-game ODI series.
Champions Trophy – Australia beat West Indies by 8 wickets in the final.
Chappell-Hadlee Trophy – New Zealand beat Australia 3–0 in three-game ODI series.

DOMESTIC COMPETITIONS
Pura Cup Final – Tasmania Tigers (340 & 460) beat New South Wales Blues (230 & 149) by 421 runs (Tasmania's first title after 25 years in the competition).
Ford Ranger One-day Cup Final – Queensland Bulls (274–5) beat Victoria Bushrangers (253–9) by 21 runs.
KFC Twenty20 final – Victoria Bushrangers (160–6) beat Tasmania Tigers (150–8) by 10 runs.
Women's National Cricket League Final – New South Wales Breakers beat Victoria Spirit 2–1 in three-game series.
Cricket Australia Cup (2nd XI competition) top 3 – New South Wales 24 pts, Western Australia 14 pts, Tasmania 12 pts.

New Zealand

ROLL OF HONOUR
State Championship Final – Northern Districts Knights (319 & 258–2) drew with Canerbury Wizards (443–8d & 249–6d) to win the title.
State Shield Competition Final – Auckland Aces (120–5) beat Otago Volts (119) by 5 wkts.
State Shield Twenty20 Final – Auckland Aces (211–4) beat Otago Volts (151) by 60 runs.

India

ROLL OF HONOUR
Ranji Trophy Super League Final – Mumbai (320 & 294) beat Bengal (143 & 339) by 132 runs.
Ranji Trophy Plate League Final – Himachal Pradesh (477 & 58–1) beat Orissa (317 & 216) by 9 wickets.
Ranji Trophy One-Day Trophy Final – Mumbai (287–6) beat Rajasthan (215) by 72 runs.
Inter-State Twenty20 Trophy *(inaugural event)* – Tamil Nadu 135–8 beat Punjab (134–8) by 2 wickets.
Deodhar Trophy top 3 – West Zone 19 pts, Central Zone 8 pts, East Zone 6 pts.
Duleep Trophy final – North Zone (636 & 87–2) beat Sri Lanka A (296 & 426) by 8 wkts.

South Africa

ROLL OF HONOUR
SuperSport Series top 3 – Nashua Titans 149.240 pts, Highveld Lions 107.180 pts,
Gestetner Eagles 95.720 pts.
MTN Domestic Championship Final – Nashua Cape Cobras (213–9) beat Fidentia
Warriors (195) by 18 runs
Pro20 Series final – Highveld Lions (148–4) beat Nashua Cape Cobras (147–9) by 8 wickets.

Pakistan

ROLL OF HONOUR
ABN-AMRO Patron's Trophy Championship – Habib Bank 18 pts, Khan RL 9 pts,
WAPDA 9 pts, Zarai TBL 0 pts.
Quaid-e-Azam Trophy Final, Gold League – Karachi Urban 403 beat Sialkot 183 & 288
by 8 wickets.
ABN-AMRO Cup Gold League Final – Peshawar Panthers (138–2) beat Sialkot
Stallions (137) by 8 wickets at Karachi.
ABN-AMRO Patron's Cup Final – National Bank of Pakistan (206–7) beat Habib Bank
Limited (205) by 3 wickets.
ABN-AMRO Twenty20 Cup Final – Sialkot Stallions (151) beat Karachi Dolphins
(137–7) by 14 runs.
Pentangular Cup top 3 – Habib Bank 24 pts, Punjab 15 pts, Khan Research Labs 9 pts.

West Indies

ROLL OF HONOUR
Carib Beer Challenge Final – Trinidad & Tobago (304 & 200) beat Barbados (229 &
226) by 49 runs.
KFC Cup Final – Trinidad & Tobago (210–8) beat Windward Islands (205) by 5 runs.

Women's Cricket – England v India 2006 / England v New Zealand 2007

ENGLAND V INDIA TEST SERIES: India won two-match series 1–0.

ENGLAND V INDIA ODI SERIES: England won five-match series 4–0.

ENGLAND V INDIA TWENTY20 INTERNATIONAL: India won by 8 wickets.

ENGLAND V NEW ZEALAND ODI SERIES: NZ won six-match series 3–2.

ENGLAND V INDIA TWENTY20 SERIES: England won three match series 2–1.

Formula One

Overview of the 2006 F1 Season

Going into the 2006 season, Ferrari were unsure how things would pan out for the Scuderia. During 2005 the Ferrari/Bridgestone package could only manage one Grand Prix victory – Michael Schumacher's triumph in the ninth GP of the season, the US, – while towards the end of 2004 the team found it increasingly difficult to score points. In contrast, Renault and McLaren-Mercedes were on the ascendancy having won the other 18 GPs between them (Renault eight, McLaren-Mercedes ten). Fernando Alonso (Renault), the reigning world champion, began the 2006 season where he left off in 2005 by winning a GP, in this case Bahrain, and went on to retain his title.

Drivers' World Championship 2006

Pos	Name	Car	Nationality	Points
1.	**Fernando Alonso**	**Renault**	**Spanish**	**134**
2.	Michael Schumacher	Ferrari	German	121
3.	Felipe Massa	Ferrari	Brazilian	80
4.	Giancarlo Fisichella	Renault	Italian	72
5.	Kimi Raikkonen	McLaren-Mercedes	Finnish	65
6.	Jenson Button	Honda	British	56
7.	Rubens Barichello	Honda	Brazilian	30
8.	Juan Pablo Montoya	McLaren-Mercedes	Colombian	26
9.	Nick Heidfeld	Sauber-BMW	German	23
10.	Ralf Schumacher	Toyota	German	20
11.	Pedro de la Rosa	McLaren-Mercedes	Spanish	19
12.	Jarno Trulli	Toyota	Italian	15
13.	David Coulthard	RBR-Ferrari	British	14
14.	Mark Webber	Williams-Cosworth	Australian	7
15.	Jacques Villeneuve	Sauber-BMW	Canadian	7
16.	Robert Kubica	Sauber-BMW	Polish	6
17.	Nico Rosberg	Williams-Cosworth	German	4
18.	Christian Klein	RBR-Ferrari	Austrian	2
19.	Vitantonio Liuzzo	Toro Rosso-Cosworth	Italian	1
20.	Scott Speed	Toro Rosso-Cosworth	American	0
21.	Tiago Monteiro	MF1-Toyota	Portuguese	0
22.	Christijan Albers	MF1-Toyota	Dutch	0
23.	Takuma Sato	Super Aguri-Honda	Japanese	0
24.	Robert Doornbos	RBR-Ferrari	Dutch	0
25.	Yuji Ide	Super Aguri-Honda	Japanese	0
26.	Sakon Yamamoto	Super Aguri-Honda	Japanese	0
27.	Franck Montagny	Super Aguri-Honda	French	0

Constructors' Championship 2006

Pos	Team	Points	Pos	Team	Points
1.	Renault	206	7.	Red Bull Racing–Ferrari	16
2.	Ferrari	201	8.	Williams–Cosworth	11
3.	McLaren–Mercedes	110	9.	STR–Cosworth	1
4.	Honda	86	10.	MF1–Toyota	0
5.	Sauber–BMW	36	11.	Super Aguri–Honda	0
6.	Toyota	35			

2006 F1 Season Review

Bahrain
12 March
Fernando Alonso
Renault

Malaysia
19 March
Giancarlo Fisichella
Renault

Australia
2 April
Fernando Alonso
Renault

San Marino
23 April
Michael Schumacher
Ferrari

Europe
7 May
Michael Schumacher
Ferrari

Spain
14 May
Fernando Alonso
Renault

Monaco
28 May
Fernando Alonso
Renault

Great Britain
11 June
Fernando Alonso
Renault

Canada
25 June
Fernando Alonso
Renault

United States
2 July
Michael Schumacher
Ferrari

France
16 July
Michael Schumacher
Ferrari

Germany
30 July
Michael Schumacher
Ferrari

Hungary
6 August
Jenson Button
Honda

Turkey
27 August
Felipe Massa
Ferrari

Italy
10 September
Michael Schumacher
Ferrari

China
1 October
Michael Schumacher
Ferrari

Japan
8 October
Fernando Alonso
Renault

Brazil
22 October
Felipe Massa
Ferrari

"I have to say that it means more to be the double champion now and win these titles while Michael Schumacher was racing than any other time."
Fernando Alonso, F1 World Champion in 2005 and 2006

155

Michael Schumacher Retrospective

Michael Schumacher was born on 3 January 1969 in Hurth-Hermulheim, Germany. With the most World Championships, most Grand Prix victories, most pole positions and most World Championship points, it is hard to argue with those (outside the Ayrton Senna camp) who say that Schumi is the greatest racing driver the sport has ever seen. A man with a steely determination, bravery beyond belief, a tactical genius and the desire to go even faster, he was the ultimate driving machine.

Michael began his racing career driving karts aged just 4½, and in 1987 he won the German Karting Championship. In 1988, Schumi competed in both the Formula Ford and Formula Three series, and in 1990 he won the German Formula Three Championship. During 1990 he also raced in the World Sportscar Championships for Mercedes, winning in Mexico City and at Autopolis. In 1991 he finished second in the Japanese Formula 3000 race and, on 25 August 1991, he made his F1 debut driving for Jordan-Ford in the Belgian Grand Prix. Shortly after his maiden F1 race, he was poached by Benetton and in his first race for the team, the 1991 Italian Grand Prix, he finished in fifth place to win his first World Championship points.

In 1992 Michael (Benetton-Ford) won the 1992 Belgian Grand Prix to record his first GP victory and finished third in the Drivers' Championship. The following year saw Schumi, still with Benetton, win in Portugal and record eight other top three finishes to rank fourth overall in the Drivers' Championship. In 1994 Schumacher won the first of his seven World Championships in 1994, winning eight of the 16 GPs for Benetton-Ford. In 1995 Michael and Benetton were practically unstoppable as he won nine GPs to claim back-to-back world titles. Ferrari lured Michael to the Scuderia in 1996, but his car was no match for the Williams-Renault of Damon Hill. An otherwise unblemished career was spoilt in the final Grand Prix of the 1997 season when he deliberately swerved his Ferrari into Jacques Villeneuve's Williams-Renault at the Japanese Grand Prix, and despite recording five wins and 78 points, he was ranked last overall in the World Drivers' Championship after being disqualified for his unsportsmanlike behaviour. In 1998 he lost out in the final Grand Prix of the season, the Japanese, to Mika Hakkinen (McLaren-Mercedes).

Michael's 1999 season was cut short after he broke his leg in the British Grand Prix, but he bounced back in 2000 to record nine wins and take his third world title, his first for Ferrari. From 2000 onwards, Schumacher and Ferrari simply blasted the opposition away as he won consecutive titles in 2001, 2002, 2003 and 2004. Fernando Alonso (Renault) finally stopped Schumacher's monopoly of F1 in 2005. Michael retired from racing after the 2006 season, finishing second to Alonso (Renault) in a closely fought Drivers' Championship.

Michael Schumacher Career Stats

Grand Prix starts 250
Grand Prix wins 91
Pole positions 68
F1 World Championships ...... 7 *(1994–95, 2000–04)*

2007 F1 Season Progress Report

Australian Grand Prix

Date: 18 March; **Venue:** Albert Park, Melbourne
Result

1.	Kimi Raikkonen	*Fin*	Ferrari	1.25:28.770
2.	Fernando Alonso	*Spa*	McLaren-Mercedes	+7.2s
3.	Lewis Hamilton	*GB*	McLaren-Mercedes	+18.5s

Fastest lap: Raikkonen, 1:25.235, lap 41   **Pole position:** Raikkonen, 1:26.072

Malaysian Grand Prix

Date: 8 April; **Venue:** Sepang, near Kuala Lumpar
Result

1.	Fernando Aloso	*Spa*	McLaren-Mercedes	1.32:14.930
2.	Lewis Hamilton	*GB*	McLaren-Mercedes	+17.557s
3.	Kimi Raikkonen	*Fin*	Ferrari	+18.339

Fastest lap: Hamilton, 1:36.701, lap 22   **Pole position:** Alonso, 1:35.043

Bahrain Grand Prix

Date: 15 April; **Venue:** Sakhir Circuit, Manama
Result

1.	Felipe Massa	*Bra*	Ferrari	1.33:27.515
2.	Lewis Hamilton	*GB*	McLaren-Mercedes	+2.360s
3.	Kimi Raikkonen	*Fin*	Ferrari	+10.839s

Fastest lap: Massa, 1:34.067, lap 42   **Pole position:** Massa, 1:32.652

Spanish Grand Prix

Date: 13 May; **Venue:** Catalunya Circuit, Barcelona
Result

1.	Felipe Massa	*Bra*	Ferrari	1.31:36.230
2.	Lewis Hamilton	*GB*	McLaren-Mercedes	+6.790s
3.	Fernando Alonso	*Spa*	McLaren-Mercedes	+17.456s

Fastest lap: Massa, 1:22.680, lap 14   **Pole position:** Raikkonen, 1:26.072

Monaco Grand Prix

Date: 27 May; **Venue:** Monaco Circuit, Monte Carlo
Result

1.	Fernando Alonso	*Spa*	McLaren-Mercedes	1.40:29.329
2.	Lewis Hamilton	*GB*	McLaren-Mercedes	+4.095s
3.	Felipe Massa	*Bra*	Ferrari	+1:09.114

Fastest lap: Alonso, 1:15.284 seconds, lap 44   **Pole position:** Alonso, 1:15.726

Canadian Grand Prix

Date: 10 June; **Venue:** Gilles Villeneuve Circuit, Montreal
Result

1.	Lewis Hamilton	*GB*	McLaren-Mercedes	1.44:11.292
2.	Nick Heidfeld	*Ger*	Sauber	+4.343s
3.	Alexander Wurz	*Aut*	Williams	+5.325s

Fastest lap: Fernando Alonso, 1:16.367, lap 46   **Pole position:** Hamilton, 1:15.707

United States Grand Prix

Date: 17 June; **Venue:** Indianapolis Motor Speedway, Indianapolis
Result

1.	Lewis Hamilton	*GB*	McLaren-Mercedes	1.31:09.965
2.	Fernando Alonso	*Spa*	McLaren	+1.518s
3.	Felipe Massa	*Bra*	Ferrari	+12.842s

Fastest lap: Kimi Raikkonen, 1:13.117, lap 49   **Pole position:** Hamilton, 1:12.331

French Grand Prix

Date: 13 July; **Venue:** Magny-Cours Circuit, Magny-Cours
Result

1.	Kimi Raikkonen	*Fin*	Ferrari	1.30:54.200
2.	Felipe Massa	*Bra*	Ferrari	+2.414s
3.	Lewis Hamilton	*GB*	McLaren-Mercedes	+32.153s

Fastest lap: Massa, 1:16.099 seconds, lap 42   **Pole position:** Massa, 1:15.034

British Grand Prix

Date: 8 July; **Venue:** Silverstone, Northamptonshire
Result

1.	Kimi Raikkonen	*Fin*	Ferrari	1.21:43.074
2.	Fernando Alonso	*Spa*	McLaren-Mercedes	+2.459s
3.	Lewis Hamilton	*GB*	McLaren-Mercedes	+39,373s

Fastest lap: Raikkonen, 1:20.638, lap 17   **Pole position:** Hamilton, 1:19.197

European Grand Prix

Date: 22 July; **Venue:** Nurburgring, Nurburg, Germany
Result

1.	Fernando Alonso	*Spa*	McLaren-Mercedes	2.06:26.358
2.	Felipe Massa	*Bra*	Ferrari	+8.155s
3.	Mark Webber	*Aus*	Red Bull	+1:05.674

Fastest lap: Massa,, 1:32.853, lap 34   Pole position: Raikkonen, 1:31.450

Hungarian Grand Prix

Date: 5 August; **Venue:** Hungaroring, Budapest
Result

1.	Lewis Hamilton	*GB*	McLaren-Mercedes	1.35:52.991
2.	Kimi Raikkonen	*Fin*	Ferrari	+0.715s
3.	Nick Heidfeld	*Ger*	Sauber	+43.129s

Fastest lap: Raikkonen, 1:20.047, lap 70   Pole position: *Hamilton, 1:19.781

* Fernando Alonso was fastest in qualifying but was put back to sixth on the grid after he had delayed his team-mate Lewis Hamilton in the pits, denying him a final qualifying lap.

Turkish Grand Prix

Date: 26 August; **Venue:** Istanbul Circuit, Istanbul
Result

1.	Felipe Massa	*Bra*	Ferrari	1.26:42.161
2.	Kimi Raikkonen	*Fin*	Ferrari	+2.275s
3.	Fernando Alonso	*Spa*	McLaren-Mercedes	+23.906s

Fastest lap: Raikonnen, 1:27.295, lap 57   Pole position: Massa, 1:27.329

Italian Grand Prix

Date: 9 September; **Venue:** Monza Circuit, Monza
Result

1.	Fernando Alonso	*Spa*	McLaren-Mercedes	1.18:37.806
2.	Lewis Hamilton	*GB*	McLaren-Mercedes	+6.062s
3.	Kimi Raikkonen	*Fin*	Ferrari	+27.325s

Fastest lap: Alonso, 1:22.871, lap 15   Pole position: Alonso, 1:21.997

Drivers' World Championship 2007 (after 13 races)

Pos	Name	Car	Nationality	Points
1.	Lewis Hamilton	McLaren-Mercedes	British	92
2.	Fernando Alonso	McLaren-Mercedes	Spanish	89
3.	Kimi Raikkonen	Ferrari	Finnish	74
4.	Felipe Massa	Ferrari	Brazilian	69
5.	Nick Heidfeld	BMW Sauber	German	52
6.	Robert Kubica	BMW Sauber	Polish	33
7.	Heikki Kovalainen	Renault	Finnish	21
8.	Giancarlo Fisichella	Renault	Italian	17
9.	Alexander Wurz	Williams-Toyota	Austrian	13
10.	Nico Rosberg	Williams-Toyota	German	12
11.	Mark Webber	Red Bull-Renault	Australian	8
12.	David Coulthard	Red Bull-Renault	British	8
13.	Jarno Trulli	Toyota	Italian	7
14.	Ralf Schumacher	Toyota	German	5
15.	Takuma Sato	Super Aguri-Honda	Japanese	4
16.	Jenson Button	Honda	British	2
17.	Sebastian Vettel	Toro Rosso-Ferrari	German	1

Constructors' Cup 2007 (after 13 races)*

Pos	Team	Pts
1.	Ferrari	143
2.	BMW Sauber	85
3.	Renault	38
4.	Williams-Toyota	25
5.	Red Bull-Renault	16
6.	Toyota	12
7.	Super Aguri-Honda	4
8.	Honda	2
9.	Toro Rosso-Ferrari	1
10.	Spyker-Ferrari	0

"To lead in my first Grand Prix was a fantastic feeling. It's pretty tough when you have a two-times world champion behind you."

Lewis Hamilton, after the 2007 Australian Grand Prix

* = McLaren-Mercedes had their 2007 points removed as a result of the Spy games scandal (see opposite). At the time their points total was 166, which took account of a 15-point deduction as a result of the incident at qualifying for the Hungarian Grand Prix when Fernando Alonso delayed his departure from the pits to deny Lewis Hamilton the opportunity to set a fastest qualifying lap. Hamilton won the race and Alonso was fourth, but before the race started the FIA ruled that any points collected by McLaren-Mercedes in Hungary would be removed.

F1 Spy Games

On 4 July 2007 McLaren Mercedes were at the centre of an alleged "F1 Spy Row" involving one of their senior employees, Mike Coughlan, and Ferrari's performance director Nigel Stepney. The Scuderia claimed that McLaren had obtained confidential team documents. Coughlan was subsequently suspended after a 780-page technical dossier was found at his home. Nine days later the International Automobile Federation (FIA) charged McLaren with breaking the sport's rules following claims that Coughlan illegally received information from their bitter rivals.

The hearing took place in Paris on 26 July 2007 and McLaren were not given any immediate penalty. A World Motorsport Council (WMSC) employee stated that "there was insufficient evidence" that the rules breach had made any impact on the 2007 race for the title. However, the WMSC made it clear to McLaren that there was still the possibility of a Championship ban if any future information proved that they had gained an unfair advantage from the documents. The official statement from the WMSC read: "The WMSC is satisfied that Vodafone McLaren Mercedes was in possession of confidential Ferrari information and is therefore in breach of Article 151c of the International Sporting Code. However, there is insufficient evidence that this information was used in such a way as to interfere improperly with the FIA Formula One World Championship. We therefore impose no penalty."

Ferrari were furious with the WMSC's verdict. "This decision legitimizes dishonest behaviour in F1 and sets a very serious precedent. We feel this is highly prejudicial to the credibility of the sport," said a Ferrari statement. Four days after the Paris hearing a still seething Ferrari F1 team accepted that they could not appeal against the decision not to penalize McLaren. However, a Ferrari statement made it clear that the Scuderia were "evaluating all possible options" in their search for justice and maintained that Ferrari had not ruled out further court action.

On 5 September 2007 the WMSC of the FIA announced that its Court of Appeal would meet on 13 September 2007 to examine new evidence in the spy row. The FIA statement read as follows: "Following the receipt of new evidence, the WMSC has been reconvened for a hearing in Paris on 13 September. In accordance with its decision of 26 July, representatives of McLaren have been invited to attend the hearing. The FIA president Max Mosley's referral of the matter to the International Court of Appeal has been withdrawn." McLaren made it clear that they would co-operate fully with the FIA.

At the 13 September hearing, McLaren was stripped of their points in the 2007 Formula One Constructors' Championship and handed a record fine of $100m (£49.2m). However, the team breathed a huge sigh of relief when their drivers, Fernando Alonso and Lewis Hamilton, were allowed to retain their points in the Drivers' Championship.

> "We believe we have grounds for appeal but, of course, we are going to wait for the findings of the FIA which are going to be published. The most important thing is that we go motor racing this weekend, the rest of the season and next season."
>
> *Ron Dennis, head of McLaren-Mercedes after the point-deduction, but not expulsion penalties were announced*

Golf

The Ryder Cup 2006

Europe went into the 2006 Ryder Cup looking for their third successive victory in the tournament. Never before in the history of the Ryder Cup, dating back to 1927, had the Americans lost three consecutive Samuel Ryder trophies. Although they were playing at the K Club, Straffan, County Kildare, Ireland, they were playing on a course designed by the legendary Arnold Palmer and their team captain, Tom Lehman, felt that the 18 holes better suited their style of play over their European opponents. How wrong they were as the story of this quite remarkable, emotionally charged Ryder Cup unfolded. Inspired by their team captain, the fiery little Welshman Ian Woosnam, the European players, that included their on-course general Colin Montgomerie and Darren Clarke, who was still grieving from the loss of his wife Heather to breast cancer six weeks earlier, totally dominated their opponents from across the pond.

On the final day, Woosnam sent out Montgomerie at the top of the order hoping that the big Scot would set his team-mates an example they would all follow. Monty did not let his team down and made a nerve-racking up-and-down birdie from the bunker at the 18th hole to close out a 1-hole win over David Toms. Amazingly, it was Monty's eighth consecutive Ryder Cup singles match without loss. Team Europe were buoyed by Monty's win as Paul Casey beat Jim Furyk 2&1 and David Howell's 5&4 win over Brett Wetterich edged Europe a step closer to retaining the Ryder Cup. It was England's Luke Donald, playing in the fifth match out, who ensured Europe won the trophy outright when he completed a 2&1 victory over Chad Campbell on the 17th green. However, the one defining moment of the 2006 Ryder Cup was when the huge crowds around the 16th green gave Darren Clarke, who was about to complete an emotionally-charged 3&2 victory over Johnson, a deafening reception that echoed around every hole of the K Club. After sinking the final putt, Clarke looked up to the sky in memory of Heather, broke down in tears and was immediately embraced by Woosnam, Lehman and Woods.

When all 12 singles matches were played the scoreboard told the truth – Europe annihilated the USA 18½–9½. Champagne flooded the 18th green at the Palmer Course as Team Europe, their caddies, their wives and girlfriends, their captain and their fans danced with delight. Fittingly, every one of the 12 European players contributed to the points tally during the first two days of fourballs and foursomes, and when it came to the singles on Sunday, they showed the world just how strong the European Tour really is when they defeated their opponents on the day by 8½ points to 3½.

"I'll miss this when it's gone. That's eight now and I don't know if I am due a ninth."

Colin Montgomerie

"This is as good as it gets. The support I've had is something I will cherish forever."

Darren Clarke

Results

22–24 September 2006, K Club, Ireland – Europe beat the USA 18½ – 9½

EUROPE	USA
Captain: Ian Woosnam	**Captain:** Tom Lehman
Vice Captains: Peter Baker & Des Smyth	**Assistant Captains:** Corey Pavin &
Assistant Captains: Sandy Lyle &	Loren Roberts
David Russell	*Wild Card entries*

	EUROPE			USA
1.	David Howell	(England)	1.	Tiger Woods
2.	Paul Casey	(England)	2.	Phil Mickelson
3.	Luke Donald	(England)	3.	Jim Furyk
4.	Sergio Garcia	(Spain)	4.	Chad Campbell
5.	Colin Montgomerie	(Scotland)	5.	David Toms
6.	Henrik Stenson	(Sweden)	6.	Chris DiMarco
7.	Robert Karlsson	(Sweden)	7.	Vaughn Taylor
8.	Padraig Harrington	(Rep of Ireland)	8.	J.J. Henry
9.	Paul McGinley	(Rep of Ireland)	9.	Zach Johnson
10.	Jose Maria Olazabal	(Spain)	10.	Brett Wetterich
11.	Darren Clarke*	(Northern Ireland)	11.	Stewart Cink*
12.	Lee Westwood*	(England)	12.	Scott Verplank*

Day 1: *Four-balls* Woods/Furyk (US) beat Harrington/Montgomerie (Eur) 1-up. Cink/Henry (US) halved with Casey/Karlsson (Eur). Garcia/Olazabal (Eur) beat Toms/Wetterich (US) 3&2. Clarke/Westwood (Eur) beat Mickelson/DiMarco (US) 1-up. *Foursomes* Campbell/Johnson (US) halved with Harrington/McGinley (Eur). Cink/Toms (US) halved with Howell/Stenson (Eur). Mickelson/DiMarco (US) halved with Westwood/Montgomerie (Eur). Donald/Garcia (Eur) beat Woods/Furyk (US) 2-up.

Day 2: *Four-balls* Cink/Henry (US) halved with Casey/Karlsson (Eur). Garcia/Olazabal (Eur) beat Mickelson/DiMarco 3&2. Clarke/Westwood (Eur) beat Woods/Furyk (US) 3&2. Verplank/Johnson (US) beat Stenson/Harrington (Eur) 2&1. *Foursomes* Garcia/Donald (Eur) beat Mickelson/Toms (US) 2&1. Campbell/Taylor (US) halved with Montgomerie/Westwood (Eur). Casey/Howell (Eur) beat Cink/Johnson (US) 5&4. Furyk/Woods (US) beat Harrington/McGinley (Eur) 3&2.

Day 3: *Singles* Montgomerie (Eur) beat Toms (US) 1-up. Cink (US) beat Garcia (Eur) 4&3. Casey (Eur) beat Furyk (US) 2&1. Woods (US) beat Karlsson (Eur) 3&2. Donald (Eur) beat Campbell (US) 2&1. Henry (US) halved with McGinley (Eur). Clarke (Eur) beat Johnson (US) 3&2. Stenson (Eur) beat Taylor (US) 4&3. Howell (Eur) beat Wetterich (US) 5&4. Olazabal (Eur) beat Mickelson (US) 2&1. Westwood (Eur) beat DiMarco (US) 2-up. Verplank (US) beat Harrington (Eur) 4&3

Trivia

* As Tiger Woods eyed up a putt on the 7th green in his singles match against Robert Karlsson on the final day of the 2006 Ryder Cup, his caddy dropped his 9-iron into the water. Steve Williams had the club in his hand, along with a towel and when he reached down to wet the towel to clean the club, the 9-iron fell from his grasp into the water.

* Thomas Bjorn heavily criticized the European team captain, Ian Woosnam, after he was left out of Europe's Ryder Cup team to defend the trophy at the K Club. Woosnam opted for Darren Clarke and Lee Westwood as his two wild card picks ahead of Bjorn, resulting in the Dane describing the Welshman as "the worst captain I have ever seen". However, despite a sincere apology from Bjorn, who believed Woosnam should have told him personally that he was left out of the team as opposed to learning the news by watching TV, was fined £10,000 by the European Tour.

* Tiger Woods put his first shot of the 2006 Ryder Cup into the River Liffey at the K Club in the morning four-balls of the first day's play. However, Tiger's partner, Jim Furyk, was in fine form and the Americans beat Colin Montgomerie and Padraig Harrington 1-up.

* A record £8 million was gambled on day one of the 2006 Ryder Cup according to bookmakers Ladbrokes. The sum bet works out at approximately £12,500 for every minute of play, beating all previous betting records for a golf event.

* Europe's victory over the USA was their third consecutive victory in the competition, the first time the United States had lost three consecutive Ryder Cup tournaments.

FUTURE RYDER CUP VENUES

2008	Valhalla GC, Louisville, Kentucky, USA
2010	Celtic Manor Resort, Newport, Wales
2012	Medinah CC, Medinah, Illinois, USA
2014	Gleneagles, Auchterarder, Scotland
2016	Hazeltine National GC, Chaska, Minnesota, USA
2018	Continental Europe (TBA)
2020	Whistling Straits, Sheboygan, Wisconsin, USA

"I need to just tip my hat completely to the European team. I don't know if there has ever been a European team that has played better."
Tom Lehman, *USA team captain gracious in defeat*

"Can I have 12 wild cards and just take this team over? Just give them a cat's lick, some deodorant and clean shirts and just start over!"
Incoming 2008 European team captain
Nick Faldo

US Masters 2007

Date: 5–8 April; *Venue:* Augusta, Georgia, USA

The US Masters began with Arnold Palmer hitting the customary first tee shot, making the golf legend the seventh honorary starter in US Masters' history. England's Justin Rose carded a majestic 3 under 69 to claim a share of the first round lead along with Bruce Wetterich (USA). Rose, who putted only 20 times, posted the only bogey-free round on a testing opening day. Wetterich was trying to become the first debutant Masters winner, and only the fourth debutant in history, since Fuzzy Zoeller's victory in 1979. When Jeev Milkha Singh carded a level score of 72, he became the first Indian to play in the Masters in its 73-year history, while Gary Player carded a score of +11 in his 50th appearance at Augusta.

Brett Wetterich (USA) shot a 1 over par 73 to stay at the top of the leaderboard at the halfway stage with a 2 under par total. Justin Rose, the overnight co-leader, slipped to level par after 72 holes, while Wetterich was joined on 2 under par by the 2006 green jacket runner-up Tim Clark of South Africa, who carded a 1 under par 71. Wetterich and Clark's 142 is the highest score for the 36 hole leaders since 1982 when Craig Stadler (1982 Masters champion) and Curtis Strange shot 144. Meanwhile, Wetterich became only the sixth Masters' rookie to lead or co-lead after the first and second rounds.

Australia's Stuart Appleby led the field by 1 shot after the third round while the second round co-leaders, Tim Clark and Brett Wetterich, carded an 80 and an 83 respectively. The average score on an unusually chilly April day in Augusta was 77.35. Appleby was seeking to become the first Australian to win a green jacket, the only Major an Aussie player has never won, while Greg Norman was the last Australian to lead the Masters after 54 holes (1996, lost to Nick Faldo).

Zach Johnson from the USA carded a 3 under par 69 on a dramatic final day's play at to score a 1 over total of 289, enough to earn the 31-year-old from Iowa City the green jacket. His +1 score is the joint highest winning score in US Masters history, while his win was only his second victory on the PGA Tour. Tiger Woods, chasing his fifth green jacket, finished two shots back in joint second place, along with the South African pair of Retief Goosen and Rory Sabbatini. Justin Rose, the co-leader after the first round, finished in a tie for fifth place with Jerry Kelly. Johnson picked up the $664,000 winner's cheque along with the most famous blazer in sport.

Final Leaderboard

1	Zach Johnson (USA) +1		T7	Padraig Harrington (Ire),
T2	Rory Sabbatini (SA),			Stuart Appleby (Aus) +5
	Retief Goosen (SA),		T9	David Toms (USA) +6
	Tiger Woods (USA) +3		T10	Paul Casey (Eng),
T5	Jerry Kelly (USA),			Luke Donald (Eng),
	Justin Rose (Eng) +4			Vaughn Taylor (USA) +7

US Open Championship 2007

Date: 14–17 June; *Venue:* Oakmont CC, Oakmont, Pennsylvania, USA

Nick Dougherty fired a superb 68 (-2) to claim the first round lead. One shot behind lay Argentina's Angel Cabrera who was the only other player to record a score under par on a tough course set by the USGA. "I didn't play all that well from tee to green but my short game was red hot, as it has been lately, and I putted solidly," said Dougherty.

Angel Cabrera birdied the 18th hole to claim a one shot lead at the halfway mark of the tournament. Bubba Watson from the USA was alone in second place on +1, while Justin Rose shared in a four-way tie for third on +2. Paul Casey scored a magnificent four under 66 after a +7 on the opening day, to occupy seventh place by himself on +3. Phil Mickelson missed the cut (+10) carding a 77 to place him on +11.

Australia's Aaron Baddeley took a 2 shot lead into the final round with Tiger Woods in his shadow just 2 shots adrift. Paul Casey and Justin Rose were in a four-way tie for third on +5, while the overnight leader, Angel Cabrera, slipped to +6. "I hit a lot of good putts that just grazed the edge. This round put me right in the tournament," said Woods, the world number one. However, with the leader going from -2 on day one to +2 on day three, it was clear that Oakmount's difficult set-up was proving to be the winner.

Angel Cabrera held off stiff resistance from the American pair of Jim Furyk and Tiger Woods to win by a single stroke. He fired a 1 under 69 to set a +5 target that first Furyk and then Woods just could not reach. Despite winning 12 majors, Woods has still failed to win a Major coming from behind. However, Cabrera almost threw it all away when he hit bogies at 16 and 17 after holding a 3 shot lead after the 15th hole. However Cabrera, ranked number 44 in the world going into the tournament, held on for a much deserved victory.

Final Leaderboard

1 Angel Cabrera (Arg) +5
T2 Jim Furyk (USA),
Tiger Woods (USA) +6
4 Niclas Fasth (Swe) +7
T5 David Toms (USA),
Bubba Watson (USA) +9
T7 Nick Dougherty (Eng),
Scott Verplank (USA),
Jerry Kelly (USA) +10
T10 Justin Rose (Eng),
Paul Casey (Eng),
Stephen Ames (Can) +11
T13 Lee Janzen (USA),
Hunter Mahan (USA),
Steve Stricker (USA),
Aaron Baddeley (Aus)

Trivia

* The inaugural US Open in 1895 saw ten professionals and one amateur start the 36-hole competition, which meant four trips around the nine-hole Newport course on the same day. The surprise winner was a 21-year-old English professional named Horace Rawlins who was the assistant at the host course. Rawlins scored 91-82 – 173 using a gutta-percha ball.

* In 1933, John Goodman became the fifth and last amateur to win the US Open. The others were Francis Ouimet (1913), Jerome D. Travers (1915), Charles Evans Jr., (1916) and Bobby Jones (1923, 1926, 1929, 1930).

British Open 2007

Date: 19–22 July 2007; *Venue:* Carnoustie Golf Links, Carnoustie, Scotland

Spain's Sergio Garcia went into the final round of the 136th Open Championship with a 3-shot lead, having led the first three rounds. He was hoping to emulate Major victories by his compatriots Seve Ballesteros and Jose Maria Olazabal. But it was Ireland's Padraig Harrington who squeezed past the Spaniard, his 2006 Ryder Cup team-mate, in a four-hole play-off to win. Harrington's victory was the first by European in a Major since Paul Lawrie won a play-off to win the 1999 Open on the same course.

In another dramatic ending to an Open, Harrington blew a one-shot lead at the 18th by twice finding the Barry Burn – recalling Jean van de Velde's infamous collapse at Carnoustie in 1999. With Harrington in the clubhouse after carding a 67 to finish on 7 under par, Garcia approached the 18th needing a par 4 to clinch the Open and his first Major. But he bunkered his second shot and took a 5, this after parring the hole in the first three rounds. It meant a four-hole play-off with Harrington. Sergio had played in the final group in two previous Majors but lost both times to Tiger Woods – at the 2002 US Open at Bethpage and the 2006 Open at Hoylake.

The play-off comprised holes 1, 16, 17 and 18. At the first, Harrington, 2006's European Order of Merit winner, holed an 8-foot birdie putt, while Garcia made a bogey five. The pair then halved the next two holes. Harrington was two shots up with one hole to play, so he cautiously decided to lay-up at the last, Garcia had to go for broke with his driver. He hit a good drive, then fired a 6-iron 203 yards from light rough on the left into the heart of the green. Harrington's approach ended outside Garcia's ball and his first putt rolled three feet past the hole. Garcia had a putt to force a sudden death play-off. However, like so many during his final round, it shaved the hole but didn't drop, though he made his par. Harrington bent over his ball knowing that if he made the putt he would be the Open champion. The ball smacked into the centre of the cup to send the travelling Irish fans wild with delight. It was a good Open all round for Ireland as 18-year-old Rory McIlroy from Holywood, Northern Ireland, won the silver medal as the leading amateur, tying for 42nd place.

Final Open Standings

-7	Padraig Harrington	(Ire)*	69	73	68	67	277
	Sergio Garcia	(Spa)	65	71	68	73	277
-6	Andres Romero	(Arg)	71	70	70	67	278
-5	Ernie Els	(SA)	72	70	68	69	279
	Richard Green	(Aus)	72	73	70	64	279
-4	Hunter Mahan	(USA)	73	73	69	65	280
	Stewart Cink	(USA)	69	73	68	70	280
-3	Steve Stricker	(USA)	71	72	64	74	281
	KJ Choi	(S Kor)	69	69	72	71	281
	Mike Weir	(Can)	71	68	72	70	281
	Ben Curtis	(USA)	72	74	70	65	281

Won by one stroke after four-hole play-off.

Trivia

* It was Harrington's 37th attempt to win a Major.

* Harrington won the Dunhill Links Championship in 2002 and 2006 on the Carnoustie Course.

* Harrington became the first Open winner from Ireland since Fred Daly.

British Open Champions (1966–2007)

Year	Venue	Champion (Country)
1966	Muirfield	Jack Nicklaus (United States)
1967	Royal Liverpool	Roberton DeVicenzo (Argentina)
1968	Carnoustie	Gary Player (South Africa)
1969	Royal Lytham & St Annes	Tony Jacklin (England)
1970	St Andrews	Jack Nicklaus (United States)
1971	Royal Birkdale	Lee Trevino (United States)
1972	Muirfield	Lee Trevino (United States)
1973	Royal Troon	Tom Weiskopf (United States)
1974	Royal Lytham & St Annes	Gary Player (South Africa)
1975	Carnoustie	Tom Watson (United States)
1976	Royal Birkdale	Johnny Miller (United States)
1977	Turnberry	Tom Watson (United States)
1978	St Andrews	Jack Nicklaus (United States)
1979	Royal Lytham & St Annes	Seve Ballesteros (Spain)
1980	Muirfield	Tom Watson (United States)
1981	Royal St George's	Bill Rogers (United States)
1982	Royal Troon	Tom Watson (United States)
1983	Royal Birkdale	Tom Watson (United States)
1984	St Andrews	Seve Ballesteros (Spain)
1985	Royal St George's	Sandy Lyle (Scotland)
1986	Turnberry	Greg Norman (Australia)
1987	Muirfield	Nick Faldo (England)
1988	Royal Lytham & St Annes	Seve Ballesteros (Spain)
1989	Royal Troon	Mark Calcavecchia (United States)
1990	St Andrews	Nick Faldo (England)
1991	Royal Birkdale	Ian Baker-Finch (Australia)
1992	Muirfield	Nick Faldo (England)
1993	Royal St George's	Greg Norman (Australia)
1994	Turnberry	Nick Price (Zimbabwe)
1995	St Andrews	John Daly (United States)
1996	Royal Lytham & St Annes	Tom Lehman (United States)
1997	Royal Troon	Justin Leonard (United States)
1998	Royal Birkdale	Mark O'Meara (United States)
1999	Carnoustie	Paul Lawrie (Scotland)
2000	St Andrews	Tiger Woods (United States)
2001	Royal Lytham & St Annes	David Duval (United States)
2002	Muirfield	Ernie Els (South Africa)
2003	Royal St George's	Ben Curtis (United States)
2004	Royal Troon	Todd Hamilton (United States)
2005	St Andrews	Tiger Woods (United States)
2006	Royal Liverpool	Tiger Woods (United States)
2007	Carnoustie	Padraig Harrington (Republic of Ireland)

US PGA Championship 2007

Date: 9-12 August 2007; *Venue:* Southern Hills CC, Tulsa, Oklahoma

Tiger Woods went into the 89th US PGA Championship as the defending champion but Major-less in 2007. However, at the end of four days play he emerged with his fourth Wanamaker Trophy (also won in 1999, 2000, 2006), his 13th Major title, to close within five of Jack Nicklaus's all-time record of 18 Majors. He now tied second overall with the legendary Bobby Jones.

England's Graeme Storm, the 2007 French Open winner, carded an opening five-under 65 to take the lead in the 89th US PGA Championship. Temperatures reached 38C (100F) as many of the players struggled in the stifling humidity in Tulsa. However, John Daly, the 1991 USPGA champion, finished his opening round on -3, closely followed by Arron Oberholser, Woody Austin and Stephen Ames who all shot a two-under 68 while the defending champion, Tiger Woods, was +1. The 2007 British Open champion, Padraig Harrington, shot a 69 but amazingly the 2007 US Open champion, Angel Cabrera, had a terrible day, carding an 11-over round of 81.

As the sweltering sun made playing conditions difficult for the players it was Tiger Woods who scorched the Southern Hills course with a near faultless round of 63 to lead by two shots at the halfway mark, -6. On the 18th Woods had a birdie putt opportunity to etch his name into the history books by carding the lowest ever score in a Major, but he gasp in frustration as it lipped out of the cup. His score put him two clear of the local hero, Oklahoma's Scott Verplank (66) and three clear of Stephen Ames (69) and Geoff Ogilvy (68).

Tiger Woods was poised to end his Major drought in 2007 after carding a 69 to take a three-shot lead (-7) over Canada's Stephen Ames going into the final round. Chasing the frontrunners were Woody Austin (USA) who ended the day -3, Australia's John Senden (-2) and Ernie Els (SA) on -1.

Cheered on by his wife Elin and daughter Sam, Woods claimed back-to-back USPGA Championships in the steamy Tulsa heat. However, he was made to fight hard for his 13th Major victory as Woody Austin and Els chased him hard all day long. The world No.1 began the final day three shots clear of his nearest challenger and at one point led the field by five strokes before he hit a rocky patch, eventually carding a 60 for a -8 score, one clear of Austin (67) and two clear of Els (66). England's Simon Dyson carded a superb 64, the best round of the day, and was tied for sixth place on level par.

Final Leaderboard

-8 T Woods *(US)*
-6 W Austin *(US)*
-5 E Els *(RSA)*
-1 A Oberholser *(US)*
-1 J Senden *(Aus)*
E S Dyson *(Eng)*
E Tr Immelman *(RSA))*
E G Ogilvie *(Aus)*

"This one feels so much more special than the other majors. The British Open last year was different but this one felt so right to have Elin and Sam there."

Tiger Woods

US PGA Tour 2007

Date	Event	Purse	Venue	Winner
7 Jan	Mercedes-Benz Champ.	$5.5m	Maui, Hawaii	Vijay Singh
14 Jan	Sony Open in Hawaii	$5.2m	Honolulu, Hawaii	Paul Goydos
21 Jan	Bob Hope Chrysler Classic	$5m	California	Charley Hoffman
28 Jan	Buick Invitational	$5.2m	San Diego, California	Tiger Woods
4 Feb	FBR Open	$6m	Scottsdale, Arizona	Aaron Baddeley
11 Feb	AT&T National Pro-Am	$5.5m	Pebble Beach, Cal.	Phil Mickelson
18 Feb	Nissan Open	$5.2m	Pacific Palisades, Cal.	Charles Howell III
25 Feb	Mayakoba Golf Classic	$3.5m	Riviera Maya, Mex	Fred Funk
25 Feb	WGC–Accenture Matchplay	$8m	Tucson, Arizona	Henrik Stenson
4 Mar	The Honda Classic	$5.5m	Palm Beach, Florida	Mark Wilson
11 Mar	PODS Championship	$5.3m	Palm Harbor, Florida	Mark Calcavecchia
18 Mar	Arnold Palmer Invitational	$5.5m	Bay Hill, Florida	Vijay Singh
25 Mar	GC–CA Championship	$8m	Doral, Miami, Fla	Tiger Woods
1 Apr	Shell Houston Open	$5.5m	Humble, Texas	Adam Scott
8 Apr	Masters Tournament	$7m	Augusta, Georgia	Zach Johnson
15 Apr	Verizon Heritage	$5.4m	Hilton Head, S.C.	Boo Weekley
22 Apr	Classic of New Orleans	$6.1m	Avondale, Louisiana	Nick Watney
29 Apr	Byron Nelson Championship	$6.3m	Irving, Texas	Scott Verplank
6 May	Wachovia Championship	$6.3m	Charlotte, N.C.	Tiger Woods
13 May	The Players Championship	$9m	Sawgrass, Florida	Phil Mickelson
20 May	AT&T Classic	$5.4m	Duluth, Georgia	Zach Johnson
27 May	The Invitational at Colonial	$6m	Ft. Worth, Texas	Rory Sabbatini
3 Jun	The Memorial Tournament	$6m	Dublin, Ohio	K.J. Choi
10 Jun	St. Jude Championship	$6m	Memphis, Tennessee	Woody Austin
17 Jun	US Open Championship	$7m	Oakmont, Penn.	Angel Cabrera
24 Jun	Travelers Championship	$6m	Cromwell, Conn.	Hunter Mahan
1 Jul	Buick Open	$4.9m	Grand Blanc, Mich.	Brian Bateman
8 Jul	AT&T National	$6m	Bethesda, Maryland	K.J. Choi
15 Jul	John Deere Classic	$4.1m	Silvis, Illinois	Jonathan Byrd
22 Jul	US Bank Championship	$4m	Milwaukee, Wis.	Joe Ogilvie
22 Jul	British Open Championship	$8.6m	Carnoustie, Scotland	Padraig Harrington
29 Jul	Canadian Open	$5m	Markham, Ontario	Jim Furyk
5 Aug	Reno-Tahoe Open	$3m	Reno, Nevada	Steve Flesch
5 Aug	WGC Bridgestone Inv.	$8m	Akron, Ohio	Tiger Woods
12 Aug	PGA Championship	$7m	Southern Hills, Ok.	Tiger Woods
19 Aug	Wyndham Championship	$5m	Greensboro, N.C.	Brandt Snedeker
26 Aug	The Barclays	$7m	Harrison, New York	Steve Stricker
3 Sep	Deutsche Bank Champ.	$7m	Norton, Mass.	Phil Mickelson
9 Sep	BMW Championship	$7m	Lemont, Illinois	Tiger Woods

World Rankings

	Name	Nationality	Pts Ave	Points	Events
1.	Tiger Woods	American	23.80	952.14	40
2.	Phil Mickelson	American	9.89	425.47	43
3.	Jim Furyk	American	8.22	444.05	54
4.	Ernie Els	South African	7.44	386.65	52
5.	Steve Stricker	American	7.17	300.97	42
6.	Adam Scott	Australian	6.55	334.20	51
7.	Padraig Harrington	Irish	6.07	352.25	58
8.	K.J. Choi	South Korean	5.72	343.17	60
9.	Geoff Ogilvy	Australian	5.64	276.55	49
10.	Rory Sabbatini	South African	5.58	295.76	53
11.	Sergio Garcia	Spanish	5.55	288.85	52
12.	Vijay Singh	Fijian	5.42	346.80	64
13.	Justin Rose	English	4.95	257.65	52
14.	Henrik Stenson	Swedish	4.95	257.20	52
15.	Luke Donald	English	4.89	249.41	51
16.	Zach Johnson	American	4.47	236.87	53
17.	Retief Goosen	South African	4.16	253.85	61
18.	Trevor Immelman	South African	4.06	219.19	54
19.	Angel Cabrera	Agentinian	4.05	198.45	49
20.	Aaron Baddeley	Australian	3.99	219.69	55
21.	Paul Casey	English	3.93	212.02	54
22.	Niclas Fasth	Swedish	3.90	191.33	49
23.	Stewart Cink	American	3.83	202.79	53
24.	Aaron Oberholser	American	3.62	155.81	43
25.	Scott Verplank	American	3.47	173.65	50

World ranking points are accumulated over two years, though events in 2007 carry greater value than those from 2006. Tiger Woods' dominance of the world golf scene is absolute. He has played in fewer events than any other player in the top 25, yet he has more than twice as many points as even his nearest rival, Phil Mickelson.

"If you would have told me 12 years
ago that I would have this many wins
and this many majors I would have
said 'There is no way'."
Tiger Woods

European PGA Tour 2007

The European PGA Tour has grown dramatically over the past two decades, not only in the number of players participating regularly but also in the tournaments played. In fact, the very term European Tour is a misnomer because events are held on every continent – given that the four Majors and the WGC events are included.

The 2007 Tour opened on 9 November 2006 at the HSBC Champions event at Shanghai, China, and didn't actually see European soil until 22 March at the Madeira Islands Open, when all of the world's top players were otherwise engaged at the WGC CA Tournament in Florida. The final event in 2007 is the Omega Mission Hills World Cup at Mission Hills, China, from 22–25 November.

Padraig Harrington, who won The Open at Carnoustie in July (*see* page 167), currently heads the Order of Merit by a wide margin, especially as many of his closest challengers play mainly on the more lucrative US PGA Tour.

European Order of Merit as at 9 September 2007

	Name	Nationality	Events	Money won
1.	Padraig Harrington	Irish	12	€2,138,078
2.	Justin Rose	English	8	€1,811,595
3.	Ernie Els	South African	16	€1,799,378
4.	Henrik Stenson	Swedish	14	€1,770,296
5.	Niclas Fasth	Swedish	17	€1,616,476
6.	Andres Romero	Argentinian	19	€1,543,748
7.	Retief Goosen	South African	18	€1,364,936
8.	Angel Cabrera	Argentinian	11	€1,356,687
9.	Colin Montgomerie	Scottish	20	€1,248,312
10.	Richard Sterne	South African	16	€1,242,496
11.	Paul Casey	English	19	€1,175,739
12.	Sergio Garcia	Spanish	11	€1,168,417
13.	Soren Hansen	Danish	21	€1,115,039
14.	Graeme Storm	English	27	€1,114,084
15.	Gregory Havret	French	27	€1,102,214
16.	Richard Green	Australian	16	€1,028,918
17.	Anders Hansen	Danish	9	€990,625
18.	Raphael Jacquelin	French	23	€944,262
19.	Bradley Dredge	Welsh	19	€873,637
20.	Yong-Eun Yang	South Korean	17	€846,336
21.	Peter Hanson	Swedish	20	€835,364
22.	Trevor Immelman	South African	9	€828,741
23.	Oliver Wilson	English	24	€797,984
24.	Markus Brier	Austrian	22	€795,453
25.	Lee Westwood	English	21	€776,855

European PGA Tour Results 2007

Date	Event	Venue	Winner
12 Nov	HSBC Champions	Shanghai Sheshan, China	Yong-Eun Yang
19 Nov	UBS Hong Kong Open	Fanling, HK	Jose Manuel Lara
26 Nov	Mastercard Masters	Melbourne, Aus	Justin Rose
03 Dec	Blue Chip New Zealand Open	Gulf Harbour, NZ	Nathan Green
10 Dec	Alfred Dunhill Championship	Leopard Creek, RSA	Alvaro Quiros
17 Dec	South African Airways Open	Humewood, RSA	Ernie Els
14 Jan	Joburg Open	Johannesburg, RSA	Ariel Canete
21 Jan	Abu Dhabi Golf Championship	Abu Dhabi	Paul Casey
28 Jan	Commercialbank Qatar Masters	Doha, Qatar	Retief Goosen
4 Feb	Dubai Desert Classic	Emirates, Dubai	Henrik Stenson
11 Feb	Malaysian Open	Saujana, Malaysia	Peter Hedblom
18 Feb	Indonesia Open	Damai Indah, Indonesia	Mikko Ilonen
25 Feb	WGC - Accenture Match Play	Tucson, Arizona	Henrik Stenson
4 Mar	Johnnie Walker Classic	Phuket, Thailand	Anton Haig
11 Mar	Singapore Masters	Laguna, Singapore	Wen-Chong Liang
18 Mar	TCL Classic	Hainan Island, China	Chapchai Nirat
25 Mar	WGC - CA Championship	Doral, Florida	Tiger Woods
25 Mar	Madeira Islands Open	Santo Da Serra, Madeira	Daniel Vancsik
1 Apr	Estoril Open De Portugal	Quinta Da Marinha	Pablo Martin
15 Apr	Volvo China Open	Shanghai Silport, China	Markus Brier
22 Apr	BMW Asian Open	Shanghai Pudong, China	Raphael Jacquelin
29 Apr	Open De Espana	Madrid	Charl Schwartzel
06 May	Telecom Italia Open	Castello Di Tolcinasco	G. Fdez-Castano
13 May	Open De Andalucia	Aloha, Spain	Lee Westwood
20 May	Irish Open	Adare Manor	Padraig Harrington
27 May	BMW PGA Championship	Wentworth, England	Anders Hansen
3 Jun	Wales Open	Celtic Manor	Richard Sterne
10 Jun	BA-CA Golf Open	Fontana, Vienna, Austria	Richard Green
17 Jun	Open De Saint-Omer	Saint Omer, France	Carl Suneson
24 Jun	BMW International Open	Munich Eichenried	Niclas Fasth
1 Jul	Open De France Alstom	Le Golf National, Paris	Graeme Storm
8 Jul	Smurfit Kappa European Open	The K Club, Ireland	Colin Montgomerie
15 Jul	Barclays Scottish Open	Loch Lomond	Gregory Havret
22 Jul	Open Championship	Carnoustie, Scotland	Padraig Harrington
29 Jul	Deutsche Bank Championship	Gut Kaden, Germany	Andres Romero
5 Aug	WGC Bridgestone Invitational	Firestone, Ohio	Tiger Woods
5 Aug	Russian Open Championship	Moscow	Per-Ulrik Johansson
19 Aug	Scandinavian Masters	Arlandastad, Stockholm	Mikko Ilonen
26 Aug	KLM Open	Kennemer, Netherlands	Ross Fisher
2 Sep	Johnnie Walker Championship	Gleneagles, Scotland	Marc Warren
9 Sep	Omega European Masters	Crans-Sur-Sierre, Swi	Brett Rumford

The three Majors played in the USA have been covered in detail earlier in this section.

The Amateur Championship 2007

Date: 18–23 June 2007; *Venue:* Royal Lytham & St Annes/St Annes Old Links

The 2007 Amateur Championship featured 288 golfers out to claim one of the 64 places up for grabs in the match play part of the tournament held at Royal Lytham & St Annes. Drew Weaver, an American golfer from Virginia Tech, beat Australia's Tim Stewart 2&1 in the final, which was played over 36 holes. The young American took a 2 stroke lead over his counterpart, the 2006 Australian amateur champion at the halfway mark of the final. Prior to Weaver's win, the last American to be crowned the amateur champion was Jay Sigel in 1979, while Weaver was also the first American in 24 years to reach the final, following Jim Holtgrieve in 1983. His victory means that he gains automatic qualification for the 2007 Open Championship at Carnoustie and the 2008 US Masters.

Trivia

* The legendary Bobby Jones won the Amateur Championship in 1930 along with the US Open, the Open Championship and the US Amateur Championship to win golf's grand slam, the only man to do so in the same year.

Walker Cup 2007

Date: 8-9 September; *Venue:* Royal County Down, Newcastle, Northern Ireland

The USA beat Great Britain and Ireland 12 ½ to 11 ½ at Royal County Down to retain the Walker Cup. The two teams went into the second and final day all square at 6–6, but when the USA won all four foursomes matches on the Sunday morning they put themselves firmly in the box seat leading 10–6 going into the final afternoon's singles. A spirited fight-back by the GB&I team saw them win the singles 5 ½ to 2 ½ but lose the Cup. The 12 ½ to 11 ½ victory for the USA mirrored the score two years earlier in Chicago, Illinois.

Trivia

* The Walker Cup is named in honour of George Herbert Walker the grandfather and namesake of the former President of the USA, George H.W. Bush and the great-grandfather of the current American President, George W. Bush.

* The 2006 Curtis Cup, the women's version of the Walker Cup, was won by the USA won 11½–6½, their 25th win in 34 meetings.

"I've never seen such naked courage on a golf course.**"**
Peter McEvoy, *former GB&I Captain, about the Britain and Ireland effort*

"I've played Pebble Beach, the Olympic Club, Merion but this one is pretty unbelievable.**"**
Curt Knost, *US Amateur Champion sings the praises of Royal County Down GC*

Women's Golf

McDonald's LPGA Championship 2007

Date: 7–10 June; *Venue:* Bulle Rock Golf Course, Havre de Grace, Maryland, USA

Pos	Name	Score	R1	R2	R3	R4	Total
1.	Suzann Pettersen (Nor)	-14	69	67	71	67	274
2.	Karrie Webb (USA)	-13	68	69	71	67	275
3.	Na On Min (Kor)	-12	71	70	65	70	276
4.	Lindsey Wright (Aus)	-10	71	70	71	66	278
5.	Angela Park (Bra)	-9	67	73	68	71	279

Aa Saint Omer Open 2007

Date: 14–17 June
Venue: Aa Saint Omer Golf Course,
      Lumbres, France

 1 C Suneson (Spa) -8
T2 P Fowler (Aus),
      M Higley (GB),
      F Camels (Fra) -5
 5 M Lundberg (Swe) -4
 6 M Lorenzo-Vera (Fra) -3

Evian Masters 2007

Date: 26–29 July
Venue: Evian Masters Golf Club, Evian-
      les-Bains, France

 1 Natalie Gulbis (USA) −4*,
 2 Jeong Jang (Kor) -4
T3 Lorena Ochoa (Mex),
      Jai Yai Shin (Kor),
      Juli Inkster (USA) -3

* Gulbis won at the first hole of a sudden death play-off.

Women's British Open 2007

Date: 2–5 August; *Venue:* Royal and Ancient Golf Club of St Andrews, Fife, Scotland

 1 Lorena Ochoa (Mex) -5
T2 Jee Young Lee (Kor),
      Maria Hjorth (Swe) -1
 4 Reilly Rankin (USA) Level
T5 Ein-Hee Ji, (Kor),
      Se Ri Pak (Kor) +1

**"I have so many family and friends
here. I wasn't too nervous."**
Lorena Ochoa

Lorena Ochoa from Mexico blew away the field to win the 2007 Ricoh Women's British Open at St Andrews, her 12th LPGA title, but more importantly her maiden Major victory. The world number one led from start to finish, carding a final round 74 for a 5 under par total and a 4-stroke victory. This was her third win of the season. South Korea's Jee Young Lee and Swede Maria Hjorth were tied for second place on -1, while Reilley Rankin took fourth place with level par. "It's hard to describe but it was the most special round I've ever played. It's unbelievable to win my first Major and do it at St Andrews" said Ochoa.

Horse Racing

The Lesters

The Lesters, named in honour of the legendary champion Lester Piggott – who was sadly too ill attend – were presented at the annual awards ceremony at the Grosvenor House Hotel in London on 13 January 2007. Tony McCoy was named Jump Jockey of the Year for the 10th time – he won nine in a row 1996–2004, while Ryan Moore, the champion jockey on the flat, collected that award. Hayley Turner, Apprentice of the Year and Lady Jockey of the Year for 2005, retained the latter trophy, her third in a row. The event, sponsored by *At the Races* TV company and *The Racing Post*, was hosted by Luke Harvey.

FLAT AWARDS	JUMP AWARDS
Jockey of the Year	**Jockey of the Year**
Ryan Moore	Tony McCoy
Apprentice of the Year	**Conditional Jockey of the Year**
Stephen Donohoe	William Kennedy
Ride of the Year	**Ride of the year**
Martin Dwyer, Sir Percy, The Derby,	H. Oliver, Sissinghurst Storm, 32red Online
Epsom, 3 June 2006	Poker Room Chase, Chepstow, 26 April
Lady Jockey of the Year	**Best Ride, Scottish Equitable**
Hayley Turner	Philip Makin, Onyergo, Muss. 17 August
Special Recognition Award	**Special Recognition Award**
Richard Quinn	JP McNamara

Cartier Racing Awards

The Cartier Racing Awards were first held in 1991 and are the most prestigious awards in European horse racing. Sponsored by the world famous Cartier jewellers, there are eight awards, with the Horse of the Year award the most coveted of them all.

Horse of the Year	**Top Sprinter**	**Two-Year-Old Colt**
Ouija Board	Reverence	Teofilo
Top Older Horse	**Three-Year-Old Colt**	**Two-Year-Old Filly**
Ouija Board	George Washington	Finsceal Beo
Top Stayer	**Three-Year-Old Filly**	
Yeats	Mandesha	

Ouija Board, owned by Lord Derby, made history by becoming the first horse to win the prestigious Cartier Horse of the Year award twice, after winning it for the first time in 2004. The five-year-old horse also won the Cartier Older Horse of the Year award following her super performances in the Vodafone Nassau Stakes at Goodwood and a second Breeders' Cup Filly and Mare Turf at Churchill Downs.

Flat Racing

LEADING TRAINERS TURF SEASON 2006 (24 MARCH–11 NOVEMBER)

	Trainer	Wins–Runners (Pct)	2nd	3rd	4th	Prize money	£1 Stake
1.	Sir Michael Stoute	107– 487 (22%)	75	57	45	3,027,295	−64.52
2.	Michael Johnston	158–1005 (16%)	125	110	108	1,868,198	−87.83
3.	Barry Hills	103– 734 (14%)	96	103	68	1,823,744	−135.20
4.	Richard Hannon	127–1067 (12%)	128	133	109	1,753,310	−261.41
5.	Aiden O'Brien (Ire)	11– 74 (15%)	9	7	9	1,741,362	−21.08
6.	Saeed Bin Suroor	70– 247 (28%)	40	21	22	1,610,204	+13.15
7.	Mike Channon	127–1027 (12%)	121	107	118	1,548,626	−107.34
8.	Brian Meehan	74– 532 (14%)	59	61	54	1,472,261	−83.15
9.	Kevin Ryan	95– 827 (11%)	85	93	73	1,314,627	−195.53
10.	Jeremy Noseda	46– 249 (18%)	38	40	30	1,264,719	−44.16

LEADING JOCKEYS TURF SEASON 2006

	Jockey	Wins–Runners (Pct)	2nd	3rd	4th	Prize money	£1 Stake
1.	Ryan Moore	182–1174 (16%)	147	141	127	2,720,806	−152.96
2.	Jamie Spencer	155– 840 (18%)	113	98	88	2,583,778	−72.82
3.	Eddie Ahern	140–1155 (12%)	128	109	129	1,247,622	−264.72
4.	Robert Winston	136– 981 (14%)	121	104	100	1,379,889	−184.32
5.	Frankie Dettori	131– 591 (22%)	81	73	57	3,353,832	−54.06
6.	Neil Callan	129–1028 (13%)	127	128	94	1,521,291	−95.95
7.	Seb Sanders	117– 834 (14%)	105	80	79	1,252,267	−194.08
8.	Richard Hughes	113– 804 (14%)	95	107	76	1,854,639	−73.74
9.	Joe Fanning	108– 938 (12%)	94	99	98	1,054,594	−252.92
10.	Paul Hanagan	107–1040 (10%)	118	101	123	1,132,646	−264.72

LEADING TRAINERS ALL-WEATHER SEASON 2006–07 (6 NOVEMBER–24 MARCH)

	Trainer	Wins–Runners (Pct)	2nd	3rd	4th	Prize money	£1 Stake
1.	Michael Johnston	44–138 (32%)	23	14	14	230,016	+77.79
2.	Kevin Ryan	32–232 (14%)	27	31	27	184,129	−59.55
3.	Richard Hannon	14–128 (11%)	29	22	13	160,613	−39.58
4.	Clive Brittain	16–120 (13%)	14	11	14	144,972	−37.08
5.	Gary Moore	26–150 (17%)	20	12	13	139,017	+57.25

LEADING JOCKEYS ALL-WEATHER SEASON 2006–07

	Jockey	Wins–Runners (Pct)	2nd	3rd	4th	Prize money	£1 Stake
1.	Neil Callan	60–340 (18%)	48	53	33	318,182	+20.22
2.	Joe Fanning	50–247 (20%)	32	31	22	240,255	+9.63
3.	Dane O'Neill	41–303 (14%)	34	45	40	197,532	−16.74
4.	Brett Doyle	38–260 (15%)	28	34	31	205,461	−23.98
5.	Eddie Ahern	36–258 (14%)	36	26	35	270,248	−94.30

The leading trainers are listed by the amount of prize money won; leading jockeys by their wins.

The Vodafone Derby, Epsom Downs, 2 June 2007, 1½m

After 14 attempts to win the Derby, Frankie Dettori, arguably one of the greatest ever jockeys, finally ended his Derby jinx in his 15th Epsom Derby classic by riding the 5-4 favourite Authorized to a 5-length victory over second placed Eagle Mountain (6-1) with the well-backed Aqaleem (9-1) finishing third. All week long in the run-up to the race the spotlight was on Dettori and whether or not he could finally get the monkey off his back and win a Derby. His colt, Authorized, was the red hot favourite going into the race since winning the Dante Stakes at York so impressively. Authorized, trained by Peter Chapple-Hyam, hit the front 2 furlongs out and finished imperiously over his 16 chasing challengers to complete Dettori's sweep of winning all of horse racing's classic races.

Chapple-Hyam celebrated his second Derby victory after Dr Devious triumphed in 1992. It was a well deserved success for Chapple-Hyam who moved to Hong Kong eight years ago, giving away all of his owners to fellow trainers, before returning to England three years ago and starting again from scratch. However, although Authorized's finish over the final 2 furlongs was breathtakingly fast, he was in last place when the horses flew out of the stalls. Amazingly, at one point in the race, Eagle Mountain was also sitting at the rear of the field. Kid Mambo set a furious pace from the outset and when the leaders reached the approach to the descent to Tattenham Corner, Authorized was tenth of the 17 runners. However, when they reached the two-furlong pole, the former champion jockey kicked Authorized into top gear as the son of Montjeu colt surged into the lead a furlong from the finishing post leaving his challengers for dead.

Dettori celebrated in style on the winners' podium as he jumped on top of the trophy table and waved his trophy in the air much to the delight of his fans. He then beckoned his father, himself a former jockey, on to the winners' podium to celebrate his success.

Pos	Horse	Jockey	Trainer	SP	Distance
1.	Authorized	L Dettori	P W Chapple-Hyam	5–4	
2.	Eagle Mountain	J Murtagh	A P O'Brien	6–1	5 lengths
3.	Aqaleem	R Hills	M P Tregoning	9–1	2½ lengths
4.	Lucarno	S Drowne	J H M Gosden	16–1	Head
5.	Soldier Of Fortune	W M Lordan	A P O'Brien	14–1	½ length
6.	Salford Mill	T E Durcan	D R C Elsworth	20–1	½ length
7.	Kid Mambo	J Fanning	T G Mills	50–1	1¾ length
8.	Yellowstone	C O'Donoghue	A P O'Brien	28–1	Neck
9.	Acapulco	F M Berry	A P O'Brien	66–1	3½ lengths
10.	Admiralofthefleet	J A Heffernan	A P O'Brien	14–1	Short head
11.	Mahler	P J Smullen	A P O'Brien	20–1	6 lengths
12.	Anton Chekhov	D P McDonogh	A P O'Brien	50–1	2 lengths
13.	Regime	Martin Dwyer	M L W Bell	20–1	8 lengths
14.	Leander	M Gallagher	B R Johnson	100–1	2½ lengths
15.	Petara Bay	Dane O'Neill	T G Mills	100–1	1 length
16.	Strategic Prince	E Ahern	P F I Cole	20–1	13 lengths
17.	Archipenko	M J Kinane	A P O'Brien	13–2	4 lengths

Non-runners: Arabian Gulf (Sir Michael Stoute), Eastern Anthem (Saeed bin Suroor)

Other Classics

2000 Guineas 1m

Date: 5 May 2007
Venue: Newmarket Racecourse, Suffolk

1. Cockney Rebel *(O Peslier)*		25-1
2. Vital Equine *(C Catlin)*		33-1
3. Dutch Art *(J Fortune)*		14-1
24 ran		

1000 Guineas 1m

Date: 6 May 2007
Venue: Newmarket Racecourse, Suffolk

1. Finsceal Beo *(K Manning)*		5-4 fav
2. Arch Swing *(M Kinane)*		10-1
3. Simply Perfect *(J Murtagh)*		9-1
21 ran		

Vodafone Oaks 1½m

Date: 1 June 2007
Venue: Epsom Downs, Surrey, England

1. Light Shift *(T Durcan)*		13-2
2. Peeping Fawn *(M Dwyer)*		20-1
3. All My Loving *(C Soumillon)*		5-1
14 ran		

Trivia

* Cockney Rebel quickly became one of the most popular horses of 2007. Sadly he broke down in training during August and was immediately retired.

* The Tricast payout, on the first three finishers in the right order, in the 2000 Guineas was £11,518.71 to a £1 bet.

* Peeping Fawn, who was second to Light Shift in the Oaks, avenged that defeat in her next two races – the Irish Oaks at The Curragh in July and the Nassau Stakes at Goodwood in August.

Other Major Races

Vodafone Coronation Cup 1½m

Date: 1 June 2007
Venue: Epsom Downs, Surrey

1. Scorpion *(M Kinane)*		8-1
2. Septimus *(J Murtagh)*		3-1
3. Maraahel *(R Hills)*		7-1
7 ran		

Coral-Eclipse Stakes 1m 2f 7y

Date: 7 July 2007
Venue: Sandown Park, Surrey

1. Notnowcato *(R Moore)*		7-1
2. Authorized *(F Dettori)*		4-7 fav
3. George Washington *(S Heffernan)*		4-1
8 ran		

King George VI and Queen Elizabeth Diamond Stakes 1½m

Date: 28 July 2007
Venue: Ascot Racecourse, Ascot, Berks

1. Dylan Thomas *(J Murtagh)*		5-4 fav
2. Youmzain *(R Hughes)*		12-1
3. Maraahel *(R Hills)*		6-1
7 ran		

Juddmonte International Stakes

Date: 21 August 2007
Venue: York Racecourse, Yorkshire

1. Authorized	*(F Dettori)*	6-4 fav
2. Dylan Thomas	*(J Murtagh)*	2-1
3. Notnowcato	*(R Moore)*	7-2
7 ran		

* Authorized turned the tables on Notnowcato at York. The 2007 Vodafone Derby winner finished second to him in the Eclipse Stakes, but it was Authorized's first race for horses aged four years and older.

Royal Ascot 2007

ASCOT RACECOURSE, BERKSHIRE, 19–23 JUNE

DAY 1

Cockney Rebel, the double classic winner, headed a strong field of eight for the St James's Palace Stakes. Dutch Art, trained by Derby-winner Peter Chapple-Hyam, was also in the field. However, it was Aidan O'Brien's trio of colts who claimed all of the honours with Excellent Art coming through late to win a thrilling race.

The other Group 1 race on the opening day was the Queen Anne Stakes. The field of eight included the highly anticipated return of George Washington and the only filly in the race, Red Eve. In one of the tightest finishes ever seen at the Royal Meeting, the first three horses were separated by a short-head with George Washington a head behind in fourth place. Frankie Dettori won the race on board Ramonti, but at cost. Dettori was found guilty of serious overuse of the whip in this race and was punished with a 14-day suspension.

St James's Palace Stakes (Group 1) 1m

1.	Excellent Art	(J Spencer)	8-1
2.	Duke of Marmalade	(M Kinane)	11-1
3.	Astronomer Royal	(C O'Donoghue)	14-1
	8 ran		

Queen Anne Stakes (Group 1) 1m

1.	Ramonti	(F Dettori)	5-1
2.	Jeremy	(R Moore)	14-1
3.	Turtle Bowl	(O Peslier)	33-1
	8 ran		

DAY 2

Attendance at the course was down 15,000 on day one. Manduro, ridden by Stephane Pasquier, won the feature race of the day – the Prince of Wales's Stakes. Jimmy Fortune certainly lived up to his surname, riding three winners to add to the winner he rode on the opening day.

Prince of Wales's Stakes (Group 1) 1m, 2f

1.	Manduro	(S Pasquier)	15-8 fav
2.	Dylan Thomas	(C Soumillon)	2-1
3.	Notnowcato	(J Murtagh)	13-2
	6 ran, 2 non-runners		

DAY 3

Day three was Ladies' Day, but the most stylish thing on show was unquestionably Yeats, who successfully defended his Ascot Gold Cup in majestic style. Jockey Mick Kinane kicked the red hot six-year old 8-13 favourite into top gear as the field entered the home straight. Yeats became the tenth horse to win the Gold Cup at least twice.

Gold Cup (Group 1) 2m, 4f

1.	Yeats	(M Kinane)	8-13 fav
2.	Geordieland	(J Spencer)	12-1
3.	Le Miracle	(D Boeuf)	50-1
	14 ran		

DAY 4

The feature race on the penultimate day of Royal Ascot was the Group 1 Coronation Stakes. Jim Bolger's Finsceal Beo headed a high-class field of 13 runners. Darjina, who beat Finsceal Beo in the French Guineas at Longchamp, and the unbeaten Mi Emma were also in the field. However, it was the Richard Hannon-trained Indian Ink ridden by Richard Hughes who won in the soft going, with Mi Emma second and Darjina third.

Coronation Stakes (Group 1) 1m

1.	Indian Ink	(R Hughes)	8-1
2.	Mi Emma	(E Pedroza)	100-30jfav
3.	Darjina	(C Soumillon)	7-2
	13 ran		

DAY 5

Soldier's Tale edged out the Australian horse Takeover Target by a head to claim the Golden Jubilee Stakes on the last day of Royal Ascot. Maraahel recorded back-to-back victories by claiming the Hardwicke Stakes after beating the odds-on favourite Scorpion while jockeys Royston French (Maze in the Chesham Stakes) and William Buick (Dark Missile in the Wokingham Stakes) both claimed their first winners at Royal Ascot.

Golden Jubilee Stakes (Group 1) 6f

1.	Soldier's Tale	(J Murtagh)	9-1
2.	Takeover Target	(J Ford)	8-1
3.	Asset	(R Hughes)	14-1
	21 ran		

London Clubs International Trophy 2007

Jimmy Fortune won the London Clubs International Trophy as the leading jockey at Royal Ascot. He rode a 339–1 hat-trick on the second day and entered the Saturday with five winners to his name. Although he didn't increase his total, no one could catch him. Aiden O'Brien collected the trainers' version of the Trophy with four wins in the five days.

LEADING JOCKEYS

5 wins	Jimmy Fortune
3 wins	Michael Kinane
	Johnny Murtagh
	Jamie Spencer

Festival Meetings 2006–07

Ayr Western Meeting 2006

Date: 14–16 September
Venue: Ayr Racecourse, Scotland

DAY ONE
Saga 105.2FM Handicap (Kilkerran Cup)

1.	Krugerrand *(S Donohoe)*	12-1
2.	Best Prospect *(P Makin)*	10-1
3.	Dream Fantasy *(S Sanders)*	10-1
	9 ran	

DAY TWO
totesport.com Ayr Silver Cup

1.	Geojimali *(S Golam)*	20-1
2.	Zomerlust *(J Quinn)*	10–1
3.	Rising Shadow *(P Makin)*	10-1
4.	Ellens Academy *(P Quinn)*	28-1
	26 ran	

Scottish Sun Harry Rosebery Stakes

1.	Aizerra *(A Culhane)*	4–1
2.	Holdin Foldin *(P Cosgrave)*	16-1
3.	Mood Music *(R Mullen)*	9-2
	8 ran	

DAY THREE
totesport Ayr Gold Cup

1.	Fonthill Road *(P Hanagan)*	16-1
2.	Borderlescott *(R French)*	11-2
3.	Advanced *(N Callan)*	40–1
4.	Coleorton Dancer *(A Mullen)*	25-1
	16 ran	

Doonside Cup Stakes

1.	Mashaahed *(R Moore)*	4-1
2.	Ouninpohja *(T Eaves)*	9-2
3.	Profit's Reality *(R Fitzpatrick)*	12-1
	7 ran	

Newmarket July Meeting 2007

Date: 11–13 July
Venue: July Course, Newmarket, Suffolk

Irish Thoroughbred Cherry Hinton Stakes *(Fillies' Group 2)* 6f

1.	You'resothrilling *(M Kinane)*	6-4 fav
2.	Festoso *(P Robinson)*	40-1
3.	Elletelle *(J Murtagh)*	9-2
	14 ran	

UAE Racing Federation Falmouth Stakes *(Fillies' Group 1)* 1m

1.	Simply Perfect *(J Murtagh)*	6-1
2.	Irridescence *(W Marwing)*	11-2
3.	Arch Swing *(M Kinane)*	10-3
	7 ran	

TNT July Stakes *(Group 2)* 6f

1.	Winker Watson *(J Fortune)*	11-4 fav
2.	River Proud *(R Quinn)*	3-1
3.	Swiss Franc *(T Durcan)*	5-1
	13 ran	

Princess of Wales's Wbx.com Stakes *(Group 2)* 1m 4f

1.	Papal Bull *(R Moore)*	11-1
2.	Laverock *(K McEvoy)*	12-1
3.	Shahin *(M Dwyer)*	25-1
	12 ran	

DAY 3
Darley July Cup *(Group 1)* 6f

1.	Sakhee's Secret *(S Drowne)*	9-2
2.	Dutch Art *(J Fortune)*	5-1
3.	Red Clubs *(M Hills)*	16-1
	18 ran	

Trivia

* Horses balloted out of the Ayr Gold Cup can run in the Silver Cup instead.

Glorious Goodwood 2007

Date: 31 July–4 August
Venue: Goodwood, Chichester, W. Sussex

Betfair Cup *(Group 2)* 7f

1. Tariq	*(K McEvoy)*	7-2
2. Asset	*(R Moore)*	5-2 fav
3. Dunelight	*(P Robinson)*	12-1
13 ran		

Gordon Stakes *(Group 3)* 1m 4f

1. Yellowstone	*(J Murtagh)*	5-2 fav
2. Aqaleem	*(R Hills)*	5-2 fav
3. Raincoat	*(R Hughes)*	9-2
9 ran		

Sussex Stakes *(Group 1)* 1m

1. Ramonti	*(L Dettori)*	9-2
2. Excellent Art	*(J Spencer)*	15-8 fav
3. Jeremy	*(R Moore)*	7-2
8 ran		

ABN Amro Goodwood Cup *(Group 2)* 2m

1. Allegretto	*(R Moore)*	8-1
2. Veracity	*(P Robinson)*	10-1
3. Finalmente	*(J Murtagh)*	16-1
15 ran		

Totesport Mile *(Group 2)* 1m

1. Third Set	*(J Quinn)*	5-2 fav
2. Humungous	*(R Moore)*	20-1
3. King of Argos	*(J Murtagh)*	6-1
19 ran		

Stewards' Cup *(Handicap)* 6f

1. Zidane	*(J Spencer)*	6-1 fav
2. Borderlescott	*(R French)*	12-1
3. Knot In Wood	*(P Hanagan)*	7-1
27 ran		

Nassau Stakes *(Group 1)* 1m 2f

1. Peeping Fawn	*(J Murtagh)*	2-1 fav
2. Mandesha	*(C Soumillon)*	7-2
3 Light Shift	*(T Durcan)*	3-1
8 ran		

Richmond Stakes *(Group 2)* 6f

1. Strike The Deal	*(E Ahern)*	7-1
2. Fat Boy	*(R Hughes)*	8-1
3. dd-ht Exhibition	*(J Spencer)*	7-1
3. dd-ht One Great Cat	*(J Murtagh)*	3-1 fav
9 ran		

Ebor Meeting 2007

Date: 21–23 August
Venue: York Racecourse, York

DAY ONE
Great Voltigeur Stakes

1. Lucarno	*(J Fortune)*	7-2
2. Yellowstone	*(J Murtagh)*	9-4 fav
3. Macarthur	*(R Moore)*	12-1
9 ran		

DAY TWO
Darley Yorkshire Oaks

1. Peeping Fawn	*(J Murtagh)*	4-9 fav
2. Allegretto	*(R Moore)*	9-1
3. Trick or Treat	*(T Queally)*	66-1
7 ran		

Totesport Ebor Stakes

1. Purple Moon	*(J Spencer)*	7-2 fav
2. Honolulu	*(J Murtagh)*	7-1
3. Scriptwriter	*(K McEvoy)*	11-2
4. Minkowski	*(S Sanders)*	8-1
19 ran		

DAY THREE
Nunthorpe Stakes

1. Kingsgate Native	*(J Quinn)*	12-1
2. Desert Lord	*(D Holland)*	20-1
3. Dandy Man	*(P Shanahan)*	9-4 fav
16 ran		

Lowther Stakes

1. Nahoodh	*(J Spencer)*	15-2
2. Visit	*(R Moore)*	6-4 fav
3. Fleeting Spirit	*(J Murtagh)*	11-4
10 ran		

Irish Flat Racing 2007

Irish 2000 Guineas 1m

Date: 26 May 2007
Venue: The Curragh, County Kildare

1. Cockney Rebel	*(O Peslier)*	6-4 fav
2. Creachadoir	*(K Manning)*	7-1
3. He's A Decoy	*(M Kinane)*	40-1
12 ran		

Cockney Rebel became the first horse since Rock of Gibraltar in 2002 to complete the double in the English and Irish 2000 Guineas.

Irish 1000 Guineas 1m

Date: 26 May 2007
Venue: The Curragh, County Kildare

1. Finsceal Beo	*(K Manning)*	5-4 fav
2. Arch Swing	*(M Kinane)*	10-1
3. Simply Perfect	*(J Murtagh)*	9-1
21 ran		

Budweiser Irish Derby 1m 4f

Date: 1 July 2007
Venue: The Curragh, County Kildare

1. Soldier Of Fortune	*(JA Heffernan)*	5-1
2. Alexander Of Hales	*(M Kinane)*	33-1
3. Eagle Mountain	*(J Fanning)*	6-4 fav
11 ran		

Darley Irish Oaks 1m 4f

Date: 15 July 2007
Venue: The Curragh, County Kildare

1. Peeping Fawn	*(J Murtagh)*	3-1
2. Light Shift	*(T Durcan)*	9-4 fav
3. All My Loving	*(S Heffernan)*	5-1
12 ran		

Galway Festival

Date: 30 July–5 August 2007
Venue: Galway Racecourse, Galway, County Galway

Tote Galway Mile 1m

1. Incline	*(D Moran)*	25-1
2. Crooked Throw	*(W J Lee)*	20-1
3. Absolute Image	*(P Smullen)*	10-1
18 ran		

William Hill Galway Plate 2m 6f

1. Sir Frederick	*(K Coleman)*	12-1
2. Ballyagran	*(P Carberry)*	20-1
3. Cool Running	*(T McCoy)*	8-1
21 ran		

Guinness Handicap Hurdle 2m

1. Farmer Brown	*(D Russell)*	9-2 fav
2. Freeloader	*(P Whelan)*	16-1
3. Eagle's Pass	*(P Flood)*	20-1
20 ran		

Tattershall Millions Irish Champion Stakes 1½m

Date: 8 September 2007
Venue: Leopardstown Racecourse, Dublin

1. Dylan Thomas	*(K Fallon)*	8–15 fav
2. Duke Of Marmalade	*(JA Heffernan)*	15-2
3. Red Rock Canyon	*(C O'Donoghue)*	100–1
6 ran		

Trivia

* The first three finishers in the Tattershall Millions Irish Champion Stakes were all trained by by AP O'Brien and the first two were owned by Mrs John Magnier, who won more than £525,000 in prize money.

Leading Trainers and Jockeys 2006 Irish Turf Season

LEADING TRAINERS TURF SEASON 2006

	Trainer	Wins–Runners (Pct)	2nd	3rd	4th	Prize money	£1 Stake
1.	Aiden O'Brien	63–306 (21%)	52	36	37	2,734,259	−40.75
2.	Kevin Prendergast	52–322 (16%)	47	42	32	1,867,073	−62.75
3.	Dermot Weld	68–389 (17%)	60	37	43	1,124,374	+5.07
4.	Jim Bolger	38–364 (10%)	26	47	31	1,114,741	−99.44
5.	John Oxx	57–306 (19%)	44	45	29	1,016,697	−17.02
6.	Michael Halford	36–388 (9%)	33	29	32	684,438	−90.88
7.	David Wachman	31–229 (14%)	28	25	25	495,976	−55.27
8.	Ger Lyons	32–307 (10%)	43	29	26	425,587	−117.23
9.	Barry Hills (GB)	2–6 (33%)	1	0	1	388,966	+1.75
10.	Peter Casey	17–130 (13%)	14	13	4	345,647	+10.38

LEADING JOCKEYS TURF SEASON 2006

	Jockey	Wins–Runners (Pct)	2nd	3rd	4th	Prize money	£1 Stake
1.	Declan McDonogh	89–566 (16%)	69	63	67	2,167,118	−92.81
2.	Pat Smullen	76–552 (14%)	78	47	53	1,274,649	−107.23
3.	John Murtagh	71–516 (14%)	66	64	48	1,468,379	−56.65
4.	Fran Berry	57–567 (10%)	55	58	44	1,057,170	−178.29
5.	Keiron Fallon	53–273 (19%)	43	30	33	2,576,888	−70.34
6.	Michael Kinane	48–284 (17%)	34	39	27	1,049,831	−43.37
7.	Wayne Lordan	41–413 (10%)	28	32	33	591,119	−109.17
8.	Kevin Manning	38–396 (10%)	27	49	41	1,096,094	−116.44
9.	Chris Hayes	33–428 (8%)	30	29	32	391,238	−161.92
10.	Seamus Heffernan	33–457 (7%)	38	36	42	622,564	−213.70

As with the sports of rugby union and boxing, there is no differentiation between the North and the Republic. Therefore, if a trainer is based in Belfast, he is considered Irish not British. The leading trainers table is based on the money won for the various owners but the leading jockeys are listed simply on the number of winners they rode.

Trivia

* Aiden O'Brien has won more than £21 million around the world in the last five years. From the start of the 1992 season to the second weekend in September 2007, he sent out around 1,650 runners. A £1 bet on each of them would have resulted in a net loss of almost £300, despite having a 23% winning ratio.

* George Washington, the 2000 Guineas winner in 2006 was retired to stud after finishing sixth in that year's Breeders' Cup Classic. Unfortunately, he proved to be almost infertile, so he was unretired and returned to racing. But he also failed to score on the course in his first three outings of 2007.

United States Racing

Breeders' Cup Classic 1¼m

Date: 4 November 2006
Venue: Churchill Downs, Louisville,
　　　Kentucky

1.	Invasor	(F Jara)
2.	Bernardini	(J Castellano)
3.	Premium Tap	(E Prado)
	13 ran	

Kentucky Derby 1¼m

Date: 5 May 2007
Venue: Churchill Downs, Louisville,
　　　Kentucky

1.	Street Sense	(C Borel)
2.	Hard Spun	(M Pino)
3.	Curlin	(R Albarado)
	20 ran	

Queen Elizabeth II made her first visit to the Kentucky Derby and watched James Tafel's 9-2 favourite Street Sense head home a field of 20 three-year-olds in the $2 million race. Amazingly, Street Sense, ridden by Calvin Borel, came from 19th place early on to win the 133rd running of the race by 2½ lengths from Hard Spun, with Curlin in third place. Street Sense became the first Breeders' Cup Juvenile winner to win the Kentucky Derby. A delighted Borel said: "I knew I had the ability, it's just that I needed to find the horse to get me there."

Preakness Stakes 1¼m

Date: 19 May 2007
Venue: Pimlico Race Track, Baltimore,
　　　Maryland

1.	Curlin	(R Albardo)
2.	Street Sense	(C Borel)
3.	Hard Spun	(M Pino)
	9 ran	

Belmont Stakes 1½m

Date: 9 June 2007
Venue: Belmont Park Race Track,
　　　New York

1.	Rags To Riches	(J Velazquez)
2.	Curlin	(R Albardo)
3.	Tiago	(M Smith)
	7 ran	

Trivia

* Eighteen-year-old Fernando Jara became the youngest jockey to win a Breeders' Cup race.

* Street Sense was the first two-year-old champion to win the Kentucky Derby since Spectacular Bid in 1979.

* Street Sense was in 19th place when he turned into the back stretch but he passed 18 rivals before reaching the winning post at Churchill Down.

* Curlin, winner of the Preakness Stakes, was the only horse to place in all three legs of the 2007 Triple Crown. He was less than 12 lengths from becoming the first Triple Crown winner for a quarter of a century.

* Rags To Riches became the first filly in over a century to win the Belmont Stakes, claiming the final leg of the US Triple Crown.

* Rages to Riches's father, A.P. Indy, won the 1992 Belmont Stakes. While her dam, Better Than Honour, also dropped her half-brother, Jazil, winner of the 2006 Belmont Stakes.

World Racing

Melbourne Cup 3,200 metres

Date: 7 November 2006
Venue: Flemington Racecourse,
　　　　Melbourne, Australia

1.	Delta Blues	*(JAP)*	*(Y Iwata)*
2.	Pop Rock	*(JAP)*	*(D Oliver)*
3.	Maybe Better		*(C Munce)*
	23 ran		

Dubai World Cup 10f

Date: 31 March 2007
Venue: Nad Al Sheba Racecourse, Dubai

1.	Invasor	*(ARG)*	*(F Jara)*
2.	Premium Tap	*(USA)*	*(K Desormeaux)*
3.	Bullish Luck	*(USA)*	*(B Prebble)*
	7 ran		

Prix du Jockey Club

Date: 3 June 2007
Venue: Chantilly, Oise, France

1.	Lawman	*(L Dettori)*
2.	Literato	*(C Lemaire)*
3.	Shamdinan	*(C Soumillon)*
	20 ran	

> "This is just so surreal and
> crazy. People wait all their lives
> to win a Derby and I win two
> in 24 hours."
> *Frankie Dettori*

Prix de Diane Hermes

Date: 10 June 2007
Venue: Chantilly, Oise, France

1.	West Wind	*(L Dettori)*
2.	Mrs. Lindsay	*(J Murtagh)*
3.	Diyakalanie	*(T Thulliez)*
	14 ran	

Trivia

* This is the third time that the Melbourne Cup has been won by a horse from outside of Australia and New Zealand – the first two were Vintage Crop (1993) and Media Puzzle (2002).

* Delta Blues, trained by Katsuhiko Sumii, is the first horse from Asia to win the Melbourne Cup.

* The Melbourne Cup is billed as "the race that stops a nation".

* Known as "the world's richest horse race", the purse for the Dubai World Cup is US$6,000,000.

* Invasor is the third Breeders' Cup winner to win the Dubai World Cup.

* The field of seven for the Dubai World Cup was the smallest to have competed in the race.

* The inaugural Prix du Jockey Club took place in 1936 and is the French equivalent of the English Derby at Epsom. Dettori claimed a unique double with this victory.

* When Frankie Dettori rode West Wind to victory in the Prix de Diane Hermes (French Oaks), he became the first jockey to ride the winners of the Epsom Derby (Authorized), Prix du Jockey Club (French Derby, on Lawman) and Prix de Diane Hermes in the same year.

National Hunt

Leading Trainers and Jockeys 2006–07 Season

LEADING TRAINERS

	Trainer	Wins–Runners (Pct)	2nd	3rd	4th	Prize money	£1 Stake
1.	Dandy Nicholls	124–539 (23%)	101	68	49	2,946,312	−115.74
2.	Johnjo O'Neill	126–821 (15%)	112	95	72	1,692,488	−150.33
3.	David Pipe	134–767 (17%)	90	77	74	1,605,597	−230.26
4.	Alan King	92–417 (22%)	72	53	37	1,569,340	+63.09
5.	Philip Hobbs	111–609 (18%)	93	66	66	1,508,065	−124.48
6.	Nicky Henderson	74–320 (23%)	40	39	28	990,763	−12.94
7.	Venetia Williams	76–417 (18%)	55	41	53	940,602	+24.76
8.	Peter Bowen	74–354 (21%)	44	49	29	928,763	+38.96
9.	Ferdy Murphy	61–439 (14%)	64	38	36	896,148	−56.42
10.	Howard Johnson	54–399 (14%)	48	45	43	783,375	−195.15
11.	Nicky Richards	64–320 (20%)	57	41	30	779,254	−92.85
12.	Evan Williams	66–505 (13%)	50	60	47	623,871	−120.71
13.	N Twiston–Davies	60–432 (14%)	46	35	41	604,251	−114.63
14.	Henry Daly	36–250 (14%)	38	32	25	537,199	−12.10
15.	Gary Moore	45–410 (11%)	51	69	41	529,587	−68.90
16.	Sue Smith	51–437 (12%)	49	54	41	439,240	−94.32
17.	Gordon Elliott (Ire)	4– 22 (18%)	3	6	2	429,375	+20.27
18.	Carl Llewellyn	34–184 (18%)	14	23	21	406,449	+54.02

LEADING JOCKEYS

	Jockey	Wins–Rides (Pct)	2nd	3rd	4th	Prize money	£1 Stake
1.	A P McCoy	184–758 (24%)	117	97	67	2,272,807	−122.15
2.	Richard Johnson	154–847 (18%)	138	108	95	1,997,443	−196.87
3.	Tom O'Brien	107–556 (19%)	82	67	48	962,441	+18.80
4.	Richard Thornton	99–551 (18%)	77	66	49	1,638,282	−68.98
5.	Timmy Murphy	98–542 (18%)	71	53	59	1,452,637	−47.09
6.	Graham Lee	89–675 (13%)	97	65	60	1,030,495	−234.42
7.	Paddy Brennan	80–512 (16%)	59	62	59	945,680	−73.16
8.	Noel Fehily	75–474 (16%)	65	65	40	841,445	+37.54
9.	Ruby Walsh	73–291 (25%)	55	40	22	2,304,412	−90.50
10.	Sam Thomas	73–462 (16%)	68	40	49	765,443	−91.83
11.	Tony Dobbin	69–401 (17%)	59	42	37	859,352	−123.41
12	Mick Fitzgerald	60–369 (16%)	41	47	30	980,243	−95.10
13.	W Hutchinson	59–425 (14%)	39	54	40	524,404	+73.43
14.	Paul Moloney	59–473 (12%)	37	56	50	618,240	−143.79
15.	Tom Scudamore	59–614 (10%)	71	76	71	785,445	−264.84
16.	Leighton Aspell	54–490 (11%)	63	52	56	554,205	−163.71
17.	Phil Kinsella	46–417 (11%)	40	45	31	280,524	+3.20
18.	Mark Bradburne	44–433 (10%)	51	51	43	380,518	−122.22

Cheltenham Festival 2007

Venue: Cheltenham Racecourse, Gloucesershire; **Date:** 13–16 March

Day 1: Philip Carberry rode the 16-1 shot Sublimity to victory in the Smurfit Kappa Champion Hurdle, while his sister, Nina, won the Sporting Index Handicap Chase (Cross Country) on board the 5-2 favourite Heads On The Ground. Gaspara followed up her Imperial Cup triumph with a win in the Fred Winter Juvenile Novices' Handicap Hurdle ridden by Andrew Glassonbury. My Way de Solzen, trained by Alan King and ridden by Robert Thornton, won the Irish Independent Arkle Challenge Trophy Chase. It was a good day for the bookies as big priced winners included 40-1 shot Ebaziyan in the Anglo Irish Bank Supreme Novices' Hurdle and Joes Edge at 50-1 in the William Hill Trophy Handicap Chase.

Cheltenham Hurdle (Grade 1), 2m, 110y

1.	Sublimity	(P Carberry)	16-1
2.	Brave Inca	(R Walsh)	11–2
3.	Afsoun	(M Fitzgerald)	28-1
	Dist: 3l, nk; 8 ran		

Arkle Challenge Trophy Chase (Grade 1), 2m

1.	My Way De Solzen	(R Thornton)	7-2
2.	Fair Along	(R Johnson)	100–30fav
3.	Jack The Giant	(M Fitzgerald)	14-1
	Dist: 5l, 1l; 13 ran		

Day 2: The 6-5 favourite Denman, ridden by Ruby Walsh, won the Royal & Sun Alliance Chase, while Robert Thornton followed up his opening day win by partnering Voy Por Ustedes to success in the Seasons Holidays Queen Mother Champion Chase to complete a double for himself and trainer King. Donald McCain, son of the legendary trainer Ginger McCain, got his first Cheltenham festival winner as a trainer when the 15-2 favourite Cloudy Lane, ridden by Richard Burton, won the Fulke Walwyn Kim Muir Challenge Cup.

Queen Mother Champion Chase (Grade 1), 2m

1.	Voy Por Ustedes	(R Thornton)	5–1
2.	Dempsey	(N Fehily)	20–1
3.	River City	(T Doyle)	33-1
	Dist: 1½l, 5l; 10 ran		

Royal & Sun Alliance Chase (Grade 1), 2m

1.	Denman	(R Walsh)	6–5fav
2.	Snowy Morning	(M Fitzgerald)	10–1fav
3.	According to John	(T Dobbin)	66-1
	Dist: 10l, 3½l; 17 ran		

Cheltenham Festival (continued)

Weatherbys Champion Bumper (Grade 1), 2m 110y

1.	Cork All Star	(B Geraghty)	11-2
2.	Sophocles	(R Johnson)	40–1
3.	Aranleigh	(T McCoy)	8-1
	Dist: 1¼l, 1½l; 24 ran		

Day 3: In the Ladbrokes World Hurdle, Inglis Drever, ridden by Paddy Brennan, regained his crown (he won in 2005) with a narrow victory over Mighty Man. Taranis, ridden by Ruby Walsh and trained by Paul Nicholls, followed in the footsteps of stable-mate Thisthatandtother by claiming victory in the Ryanair Chase. There was drama when the winner of the 4m 1f The National Hunt Chase Challenge Cup, amateur riders' novices chase, Butler's Cabin, collapsed after the race with an oxygen deficiency. Thankfully, the JP McManus-owned horse recovered after a few minutes.

Ladbrokes World (Grade 1), 3my

1.	Inglis Drever	(P Brennan)	5-1
2.	Mighty Man	(R Johnson)	100–30
3.	Blazing Bailey	(R Thornton)	8-1
	Dist: ¾l, 4l; 14 ran		

Day 4: Kauto Star was the hero of the final day of the Festival, winning the Totesport Gold Cup. The 5-4 red hot favourite, ridden by Ruby Walsh and trained by Paul Nicholls, followed up wins in the Betfair Chase at Haydock and the King George VI Chase at Kempton to earn Kauto Star's connections, led by owner Clive Smith, £1 million for completing the sport's "treble". Nicholls then claimed a double as Andreas, ridden by Robert Thornton, won the Johnny Henderson Grand Annual Chase. Thornton had partnered the Alan King-trained Katchit (11-2) to victory in the opening race of the day, the JCB Triumph Hurdle. Tony McCoy finally claimed a win at the 2007 Festival when the 11-8 hot favourite, Wichita Lineman, breezed home in the Brit Insurance Novices' Hurdle.

JCB Triumph Hurdle (Grade 1), 2m 1f

1.	Katchit	(R Thornton)	11-2
2.	Liberate	(R Johnson)	12–1
3.	Mobaaasher	(N Fehily)	33-1
	Dist: 9l, 1¾l; 8 ran		

Totesport Cheltenham Gold Cup Chase (Grade 1), 3m 2½f

1.	Kauto Star	(R Walsh)	5-4fav
2.	Exotic Dancer	(T McCoy)	9–2
3.	Turpin Green	(T Dobbin)	40–1
	Dist: 2½l, 2½l; 18 ran		

Racing Post Leading Rider Award

The 2007 Racing Post Leading Rider award was very close-run thing. Ruby Walsh was within a furlong of snatching the prize with Ouninpohja, in the Vincent O'Brien County Handicap Hurdle, the final race of the Festival. The horse jumped into the lead crossing the final flight, but wandered on th run-in and was passed by Pedrobob, who won by a length. That left Robert "Chocolate" Thornton, who claimed four successes as the winner. If Ouninpohja had prevailed, Walsh would have won because he had ridden more placed horses.

Wins	Jockey
4	Robert Thornton
3	Ruby Walsh
2	Paul Carbery
1	15 jockeys

If two jockeys finish on the same number of wins, the one with the most second-place finishes would win the award. If the jockeys still cannot be separated, then third places are taken into consideration.

The leading trainer was Paul Nicholls, who saddled four winners. Alan King and Jonjo O'Neill both trained three winners and Ferdy Murphy had two successes over the four days.

Trivia

* Clive Smith, owner of Kauto Star, accumulated his personal wealth by designing and building golf courses.

* The 1964 winner of the Supreme Novices' Hurdle, Flyingbolt, a stable-mate of the legendary Arkle, won the 1965 Cotswold Chase, the 1966 Queen Mother Champion Chase and the 1966 Irish Grand National.

"Everyone wants a superstar and we have one. He's a hell of a horse to be associated with."
Ruby Walsh, jockey of Kauto Star

"The money will be spent somehow, but the Gold Cup will be there forever."
Clive Smith, owner of Kauto Star after winning £1 million

"I'm amazed the horse keeps getting knocked – you've got to be positive in this game."
Paul Nicholls, trainer of Kauto Star

"I didn't know if he would win as I have never had a champion hurdle horse, but I wouldn't mind a few more like him."
John Carr, trainer of Sublimity

"Paddy Brennan got it right today didn't he? It's super, I'm over the moon. Days like this make it all worthwhile, hopefully he'll be back next year before he gets too old like me."
Howard Johnson, trainer of Inglis Drever

* Arkle won three successive Cheltenham Gold Cups – in 1964, 1965 and 1966.

* The 2001 Festival was cancelled due to a foot-and-mouth crisis.

* Tony McCoy, with 19 wins, has won at least one race at every Cheltenham Festival since 1996, except in 2005. He rode one winner in 2007.

Grand National 2007

Date: 14 April; *Venue:* Aintree 4½m

1.	Silver Birch	(R Power)	33-1
2.	McKelvey	(T O'Brien)	12-1
3.	Slim Pickings	(B Geraghty)	33-1
4.	Philson Run	(D Jacob)	100-1
	40 ran		

"I haven't had my licence for 12 months yet; we are going to enjoy tonight."

Gordon Elliott
winning trainer

The 2007 Grand National at Aintree sponsored by John Smiths was won by the 33-1 outsider Silver Birch. The race took an eternity to start with numerous resets before proceedings finally got underway. Silver Birch, ridden by Robbie Power and trained by Gordon Elliott, held on as the remaining horses passed the Elbow and headed for the finishing straight to become the sixth Irish-trained winner of the Grand National in the last nine years. "It is an unreal feeling, a dream come true," said Gordon Elliott. Silver Birch overtook Slim Pickings as they both cleared the final fence and then resisted a late charge from McKelvey to claim horse racing's greatest prize. Slim Pickings, a long-time leader, was third, while the 100-1 long shot, Philson Run, was fourth. None of the favourites in the race featured, with the co-favourite Point Barrow falling at the first fence.

Cloudy Bays, who eventually pulled up at the Chair, missed the start by 12 lengths while the grey, The Outlier, took an early lead but by the time the field arrived at the Canal Turn the rank outsider, Naunton Brook, had hit the front with Ballycassidy in second and Bewleys Berry lying third. Slim Pickings led the remaining runners in the race over the penultimate fence, with Silver Birch sitting comfortably a few lengths back. As the last fence came into sight it was Silver Birch that began to command the race as he landed better than his rival. As the horses approached the Elbow, Silver Birch pulled a couple of lengths clear, with the fast-finishing McKelvey starting to nose his way into contention. Although it looked like Silver Birch was beginning to tire, he summoned up the strength to hold on for victory, with McKelvey taking Slim Pickings for second with the post in sight. Monkerhostin set off as the co-favourite with Point Barrow, who was the first to fall, and Joes Edge, who pulled up at the 20th fence. However, Monkerhostin, backed down from 25-1 to 8-1 on the day, refused at the Foinavon Fence first time round.

Trivia

* The Aintree Grand National was first run in 1839.

* Bruce Hobbs, aged 17, was the youngest winning jockey in 1938 on Battleship, which was also the smallest horse ever to win. Meanwhile, Dick Saunders, aged 48, was the oldest successful rider on Grittar in 1982, amazingly his first and only Grand National ride.

* No horse has run in the Grand National more times than Manifesto, who raced times between 1895 and 1904. He won the race twice, in 1897 and 1899, and finished third on three occasions.

* The biggest ever Grand National field was in 1929 when 66 runners faced the starter. Ten runners, in 1883, was the smallest field The safety limit is now 40.

Aintree Festival 2007

The three days of racing at the Aintree Festival have improved immeasuraly in the 40 years since a temperamental two-year-old called Red Rum dead-heated for first place (ridden by Lester Piggott, no less) in the final race of the day during which Foinavon entered the history books. A feature of the Aintree Festival was the number of Cheltenham Festival hard-luck stories who came good on this much flatter and faster track.

Day 1: Mighty Man reversed form from Cheltenham, beating both World Hurdle winner Inglis Drever and that race's favourite Black Jack Ketchum (who fell in the earlier race). In the race over the Aintree fences, the John Smiths Foxhunters Chase, Richard Burton piloted Scots Grey to victory over the 2006 winner Pak Jak.

John Smith's Liverpool Hurdle (Grade 1), 3m ½f

1.	Mighty Man	(R Johnson)	15–8
2.	Black Jack Ketchum	(T McCoy)	7–4fav
3.	Inglis Drever	(P Brennan)	7-2
	Dist: 13l, 9l; 6 ran		

Day 2: Jonjo O'Neill and Tony McCoy collected another second place in a long-distance hurdle when Wichita Lineman was beaten four lengths by Chief Dan George in the Citroen C6 Sefton Novices Hurdle. Monet's Garden, a disappointing fourth in the Ryanair Chase at Cheltenham, bounced back in impressive style to take the John Smith's Melling Chase, beating Festival winners Taranis and Well Chief.

Citroen C6 Sefton Novices Hurdle (Grade 1), 3m ½f

1.	Chief Dan George	(M Fitzgerald)	20-1
2.	Wichita Lineman	(T McCoy)	4–6fav
3.	Imperial Commander	(T Evans)	25–1
	Dist: 4l, 18l; 10 ran		

John Smith's Melling Chase (Grade 1), 3m ½f

1.	Monet's Garden	(T Dobbin)	4–1
2.	Taranis	(R Walsh)	5–1
3.	World Chief	(T Murphy)	4–5fav
	Dist: 3½l, 9l; 6 ran		

Day 3: A baking hot day resulted in a number of runners being withdrawn and, as a result of a Grand National horse collapsing on the course, the penultimate race went off 45 minutes late and the last one was abandoned. Gaspara couldn't repeat his Cheltenham success, finishing second behind Al Eile in the Baltika Beer Aintree Hurdle – who also had won the race in 2005. In the John Smith's Maghull Novices Chase, Twist Magic – faller in the Arkle – beat Fair Along, who had finished second to My Way de Solzan in the same race.

National Hunt Round-up

Hennessy Cognac Gold Cup

Date: 25 November 2006
Venue: Newbury Racecourse, Berkshire
   3m 2½f

1. State of Play	*(P Moloney)*	10-1
2. Juveigneur	*(M Fitzgerald)*	12-1
3. Preacher Boy	*(L Aspell)*	12-1
4. Omni Cosmo Touch	*(D O'Meara)*	28-1

16 ran

Trivia

* The 2006 race was the 50th running of the Hennessy Cognac Gold Cup.

* In 2002 Be My Royal finished first but was subsequently disqualified after testing positive for a banned substance.

Tingle Creek Trophy

Date: 2 December 2006
Venue: Sandown Park, Esher, Surrey
   2m

1. Kauto Star	*(R Walsh)*	4-9 fav
2. Voy Por Ustedes	*(R Thornton)*	4-1
3. Oneway	*(R Johnson)*	66-1

16 ran

Trivia

* It was Kauto Star's second successive win. The race is named after Tingle Creek, a popular National Hunt racehorse during the 1970s who had an excellent record at Sandown meetings.

Stan James King George VI Chase 2006

Date: 26 December
Venue: Kempton Park Racecourse, Sunbury, Middlesex
   3m

1. Kauto Star	*(R Walsh)*	8-13 fav
2. Exotic Dancer	*(A P McCoy)*	9-1
3. Racing Demon	*(T Murphy)*	7-1

9 ran

Trivia

* Punters received a fright at the last fence when Kauto Star, comfortably ahead, ploughed through it. But Ruby Walsh sat tight and kept the partnership intact. Last fence frights became a feature of Kauto Star's races.

Desert Orchid Chase 2006

Date: 27 December
Venue: Kempton Park
   2m

1. Voy Por Ustedes	*(R Thornton)*	4-6 fav
2. Oneway	*(R Johnson)*	10-1
3. Foreman	*(T McCoy)*	5-2

5 ran

Trivia

* This was the first running of the race after the death of Desert Orchid, who won the King George VI Chase a record four times in 1986, 1988, 1989 and 1990.

Welsh Grand National 2006

Date: 27 December
Venue: Chepstow Racecourse, Chepstow
   3m 5½f

1.	Halcon Genelardais	*(W Hutchinson)*	7-1
2.	Mon Mome	*(L Treadwell)*	14-1
3.	Juveigneur	*(M Fitzgerald)*	11-1
4.	Lordofourown	*(P Moloney)*	11-1

   18 ran

Trivia

* The 1994 Welsh Grand National was run in England, at Newbury Racecourse, after the original meeting at Chepstow had been abandoned because of bad weather.

Scottish Grand National 2007

Date: 21 April
Venue: Ayr Racecourse, Ayr, Scotland
   4m 110y

1.	Hot Weld	*(P McDonald)*	14-1
2.	Nine De Sivola	*(G Lee)*	5-1 fav
3.	Parsons Legacy	*(R Johnson)*	8-1
4.	Run For Paddy	*(N Fehily)*	12-1

   23 ran

Trivia

* It is 35 years since a horse has carried as little as Hot Weld's 9st 9lb to victory in the Scottish Grand National. Quick Reply also carried 9–9 to win in 1972, the lightest any winner has borne since the race moved from Bogside in 1966.

Order of Merit 2006–07

Horse racing's new jumping sensation, Kauto Star, won the prestigious 2006–07 Order of Merit after six victories from six races. It was the third time the 65-race Order of Merit competition has been held. Kauto Star's wins included the King George VI Chase and the Cheltenham Gold Cup. Kauto Star, who also won the Betfair Million, earned £200,000 for his Order of Merit win, while Exotic Dancer, runner-up in the Gold Cup, was second (£75,000) and Mighty Man third (£25,000). Meanwhile, Kauto Star's jockey, Ruby Walsh, was the first winner of the jockeys' competition and he picked up a cheque for £20,000. Walsh donated half of his prize money to his chosen charities – DEBRA Ireland (Dystrophic Epidermolysis Bullosa Research) and the Marie Keating Foundation for Breast Cancer. The £320,000 Order of Merit is jointly funded by the British Horseracing Board and the 16 racecourses that stage graded races.

Order of Merit Final Standings

1.	Kauto Star	110pts
2.	Exotic Dancer	82pts
3.	Mighty Man	63pts
4.	Inglis Drever	57pts
5.	Monets Garden	54pts
T6.	Voy Por Ustedes	51pts
T6.	Afsoun	51pts

Irish Jump Racing 2007

Punchestown Festival

Date: 24–27 April 2007
Venue: Punchestown Racecourse, County Kildare

Kerrygold Champion Chase

2m

1. Mansony	*(D Russell)*	13-2
2. Justified	*(T McCoy)*	9-2
3. Steel Band	*(D J Casey)*	40-1
8 ran		

Guinness Gold Cup

3m 1f

1. Neptune Collonges	*(R Walsh)*	8-1
2. Kingscliff	*(R Walford)*	16-1
3. In Compliance	*(B J Geraghty)*	6-4 fav
10 ran		

Dunboyne Castle Hotel and Spa Champion Stayers' Hurdle

3m

1. Refinement	*(T McCoy)*	16-1
2. Powerstation	*(D F O'Regan)*	20-1
3. United	*(L Aspell)*	16-1
9 ran		

Avon Ri Corporate and Leisure Resort Cross Country Steeplechase for the La Touche Cup

4m 2f

1. Spot The Difference	*(J P McNamara)*	16-1
2. Freneys Well	*(N Carberry)*	20-1
3. Star Performance	*(T G M Ryan)*	16-1
18 ran		

ACC Bank Champion Hurdle

2m

1. Silent Oscar	*(R Power)*	20-1
2. Macs Joy	*(B Geraghty)*	7-4 fav
3. Hardy Eustace	*(C O'Dwyer)*	4-1
8 ran		

Galway Races

Date: 30 July–5 August 2007
Venue: Ballybrit Racecourse, Galway, Republic of Ireland

William Hill Galway Plate

2m 6f

1. Sir Frederick	*(K Coleman)*	12-1
2. Ballyagran	*(P Carberry)*	20-1
3. Cool Running	*(T McCoy)*	8-1
22 ran		

Guinness Galway Hurdle Handicap

1. Farmer Brown	*(D Russell)*	9-2 fav
2. Freeloader	*(P Whelan)*	16-1
3. Eagle's Pass	*(P Flood)*	20-1
20 ran		

Lexus Chase

Date: 28 December 2006
Venue: Leopardstown Racecourse, County Dublin

3m

1. The Listener	*(D Jacob)*	7-1
2. Beef Or Salmon	*(A McNamara)*	13-8 fav
3. War Of Attrition	*(Conor O'Dwyer)*	9-4
6 ran		

James Nicholson Wine Merchant Champion Chase

Date: 4 November 2006
Venue: Down Royal Racecourse, County Down, Northern Ireland

3m

1.	Beef or Salmon	*(A McNamara)*	11-4
2.	War Of Attrition	*(C O'Dwyer)*	4-7 fav
3.	Justified	*(P Carberry)*	5-1

7 ran

AIG Europe Champion Hurdle

Date: 28 January 2007
Venue: Leopardstown Racecourse, County Dublin, Republic of Ireland

2m

1.	Hardy Eustace	*(C O'Dwyer)*	9-1
2.	Brave Inca	*(AP McCoy)*	11-8 fav
3.	Macs Joy	*(B Geraghty)*	10-1

7 ran

Leading Trainers and Jockeys 2006–07 Season

LEADING TRAINERS

	Trainer	Wins–Runners (Pct)	2nd	3rd	4th	Prize money	£1 Stake
1.	Noel Meade	17–107 (16%)	17	13	6	196,240	−6.31
2.	Dessie Hughes	18–127 (14%)	10	18	12	168,431	+13.07
3.	Tony Martin	18–89 (20%)	10	10	3	157,781	−22.24
4.	Jessica Harrington	19–142 (13%)	17	9	12	154,152	−30.02
5.	Joseph Crowley	17–88 (19%)	14	7	6	135,207	+15.87
6.	Pat Hughes	7–76 (9%)	3	1	6	133,290	−33.64
7.	Paul John Gilligan	11–48 (23%)	9	5	1	131,496	+24.80
8.	Charlie Swan	13–156 (8%)	18	25	12	129,362	−61.41
9.	Liam Burke	4–63 (6%)	2	4	3	122,590	−30.00
10.	Willie Mullins	16–102 (16%)	15	9	11	119,632	−49.90

LEADING JOCKEYS

	Jockey	Wins–Rides (Pct)	2nd	3rd	4th	Prize money	£1 Stake
1.	Ruby Walsh	125–562 (22%)	89	64	49	1,683,256	−94.50
2.	Davey Russell	79–616 (13%)	65	64	83	1,095,350	−198.69
3.	Barry Geraghty	67–427 (16%)	63	42	36	1,104,428	−94.19
4.	Paul Carberry	64–382 (17%)	50	39	38	950,355	−116.93
5.	Denis O'Regan	56–519 (11%)	42	44	37	570,900	−132.78
6.	A J McNamara	42–512 (8%)	41	47	37	690,045	−223.39
7.	P addy Flood	38–471 (8%)	42	44	31	494,650	−235.44
8.	Niall Madden	36–500 (7%)	45	39	42	588,140	−163.97
9.	David Casey	32–255 (13%)	19	34	21	511,913	−35.64
10.	Nina Carberry	30–163 (18%)	22	22	15	308,256	−23.08

Rugby League

Carnegie Challenge Cup 2007

Quarter-finals

Dates: 9–10 June

Wigan Warriors (12) 25 – (0) 6 Harlequins

Ashton, Richards, Calderwood O'Loughlin	*Tries*	Bannister
Richards 4	*Goals*	Sykes
Barrett	*Drops*	

St Helens (4) 25 – (12) 14 Warrington Wolves

Gilmour 2, Talau, Gardner, Roby	*Tries*	Penny, Fa'afili
Wellens 2	*Goals*	Briers 3
Long	*Drops*	

Bradford Bulls (24) 52 – (10) 20 Huddersfield Giants

B Harris 2, Solomona, Henderson, St Hilaire, Burgess, Tupou (2), Newton	*Tries*	Nero, Lolesi, Paul, Hudson
Deacon 8	*Goals*	Drew 2

Hull FC (8) 23 – (16) 26 **Catalans Dragons**

Briscoe, King, Domic	*Tries*	Mogg 2, Wilson, Greenshields
Tickle 5	*Goals*	Bosc 4
Horne	*Drops*	Guisset, Bosc

Semi-finals

Date: 28 July 2007; *Venue:* Galpham Stadium, Huddersfield

Bradford Bulls (4) 14 – (17) 35 **St Helens**

Evans, Tupou, Vagana	*Tries*	Talau, Gidley, Clough, Pryce, Wellens
Deacon	*Goals*	Long 3, Pryce, Wellens
	Drops	Long

Date: 29 July 2007; *Venue:* Halliwell-Jones Stadium, Warrington

Catalans Dragons (24) 37 – (6) 24 Wigan Warriors

McGuire, Wilson, Mogg, Duport 2	Tries	Leuluai, Higham, Goulding, Calderwood
Croker		
Jones 6	Goals	Richards 4
Jones	Drops	

Final

St Helens won their 11th Challenge Cup final, their third in four years, with a convincing 30–8 victory over the Catalans Dragons at Wembley Stadium. The 2007 World Club Challenge-winning Saints took a narrow 12–4 lead over their French opponents at half-time thanks to tries from James Roby and Ade Gardner. However, in the second-half the English side effortlessly moved through the gears like a Ferrari F1 car, with further tries coming from Paul Wellens, his 23rd of the season, Paul Clough and a second from Gardner, to run out 30–8 winners.

25 AUGUST 2007, WEMBLEY STADIUM, LONDON

Catalans Dragons   8 – 30 St Helens

Catalans Dragons: Greenshields, Murphy, Wilson, Raguin, Khattabi, Mogg, Jones, Guisset, Quigley, Chan, Croker, Gossard, Mounis
Replacements: Casty, Ferriol, Duport, K. Bentley
Tries: Khattabi, Murphy

St Helens: Wellens, Gardner, Gidley, Talau, Meli, Pryce, Long, Fozzard, Cunningham, Cayless, Gilmour, Bennett, Wilkin
Replacements: Roby, Graham, Clough, Fa'asavalu
Tries: Roby, Gardner (2), Wellens, Clough
Goals: Long (5)

Att: 84,241

Trivia

* St Helens won the 2006 BBC Sports Team of the Year award.

* For the first time in 32 years the Lance Todd man of the match trophy was shared – Leon Pryce and Paul Wellens of St Helens.

* The 2002 Challenge Cup final was played at Murrayfield; Wigan beat St Helens 21–12. Twickenham and the Millennium Stadium were also used.

* St Helens lost the inaugural Challenge Cup final 10–3 to Batley at Leeds in 1897.

* St Helens scrum-half Sean Long became the first player in the history of the Challenge Cup to win three Lance Todd trophies following his man of the match performance in the 2006 final against Huddersfield Giants.

* Stacey Jones, the Dragons' scrum-half retired at the end of the 2007 season.

"I can't think of anyone that didn't play well out there. It was a great all-round team performance.**"**
***Daniel Anderson**, St Helens Coach*

engage Super League XI Season 2006

The season commenced on the weekend after the World Club Challenge. The new season witnessed a new team, the Catalans Dragons (Les Catalans), who became the first French side to compete since Paris Saint Germain folded at the end of the Super League II. St Helens wrapped up their fourth Super League title to add to their wins in 1999, 2000 and 2002. On the final day of the season, 16 September 2006, the Castleford Tigers were relegated from Super League after finishing the regular season in 11th place as the Catalans Dragons, who finished bottom of the table of 12 teams, were exempt from relegation. In 2007, Hull Kingston Rovers will be playing in the Super League (Super League XII) for the first time ever after being promoted from LHF Healthplan National League 1.

Final Table

Team	P	W	D	L	F	A	Pts
1. St Helens	**28**	**24**	**0**	**4**	**939**	**430**	**48**
2. Hull	28	20	0	8	720	578	40
3. Leeds	28	19	0	9	869	543	38
4. Bradford	28	16	2	10	802	568	32*
5. Salford	28	13	0	15	600	539	26
6. Warrington	28	13	0	15	743	721	26
7. Harlequins RL	28	11	1	16	556	823	23
8. Wigan	28	12	0	16	644	715	22*
9. Huddersfield	28	11	0	17	609	753	22
10. Wakefield	28	10	0	18	591	717	20
11. Castleford	28	9	1	18	575	968	19
12. Catalans Dragons	28	8	0	20	601	894	16

Bradford and Wigan were deducted 2 points each for breaching the salary cap

Trivia

* St Helens not only finished top of the Super League XI table, they also won the treble by winning the Grand Final and the Challenge Cup.

* In addition to the treble, St Helens also claimed two awards at the 2006 BBC Sports Personality of the Year Awards – Team of the Year and Coach of the Year (Daniel Anderson).

* The 2007 Super League XII season will comprise 27 regular rounds of play as opposed to 28, but for the first time it will also includes a Millennium Magic weekend in Cardiff.

* The newly-formed Catalans Dragons, based in Perpignan, France, were given a three-year exemption from relegation, so Castleford Tigers went down instead.

engage Super League Grand Final 2006

The top two teams from the engage Super League XI season met one another for the honour of being crowned Super League champions. St Helens, the Challenge Cup and League Leaders Shield winners, met Hull FC. The first half proved to be a hard fought tight affair with St Helens going in at half-time with a 10–4 lead. The second 40 minutes was totally dominated by St Helens who added 16 more points to their tally without reply to run out convincing 26–4 winners. Paul Wellens of St Helens collected his fourth individual award of the year in the form of the Harry Sunderland Trophy, awarded to the man of the match, to add to his Rugby League Writers' Association Player of the Year, Super League Players' Player of the Year and the sport's prestigious Man of Steel Award. The final also marked St Helens' veteran prop Paul Anderson's farewell, who decided to hang up his boots after collecting a third Super League ring in a record-equalling sixth Grand Final appearance.

14 OCTOBER 2006 , OLD TRAFFORD, MANCHESTER

St Helens 26 – 4 Hull

St Helens: Wellens, Gardner, Lyon, Talau, Meli, Pryce, Long, P. Anderson, Cunningham, Cayless, Gilmour, Wilkin, Hooper.
Replacements: Roby, Graham, Bennett, Fa'asavalu
Tries: Meli, Pryce, Talau, Gardner, Cunningham
Goals: Lyon (3)

Hull FC: Briscoe, Tony, Domic, Yeaman, Raynor, Cooke, R. Horne, Dowes, Swain, Carvell, McMenemy, Radford, Washbrook.
Replacements: Whiting, G. Horne, Wheeldon, King
Try: Domic

Att: 72,582

Super League Weekend 2007

Billed as the "Millennium Magic" weekend, on Saturday–Sunday, 5–6 May, Cardiff's Millennium Stadium hosted all six round 13 games. For the first time ever, all six Super League games in a single competition round were staged at the same venue. The first three games were played on the Saturday and the other three on the Sunday. The results were:

Harlequins 32 – 28 Catalans Dragons
Hull KR 14 – 10 Hull FC
St Helens 34 – 18 Wigan Warriors
Warrington Wolves 50 – 18 Salford City Reds
Huddersfield Giants 36 – 12 Wakefield Wildcats
Leeds Rhinos 42 – 38 Bradford Bulls

Rugby League Tri-Nations Championship 2006

14 October–25 November 2006; Stadiums in Australia and New Zealand

The fourth edition of the event was co-hosted by Australia and New Zealand. It was contested by the co-hosts and Great Britain. The format had each side facing one another twice, and the top two teams at the end of the group stages contesting the final.

Australia opened the competition by avenging their two defeats at the hands of New Zealand in the 2006 tournament, routinely winning 30–18 in Auckland, then scoring two tries in the last eight minutes to turn a 15–8 deficit into a 20–15 success in Melbourne. Controversy followed the Lions' opening 18–14 defeat by the Kiwis in match three. Nathan Fien, born in Mount Isa, Queensland, Australia, was selected to play for New Zealand against Great Britain under the "grandparent rule", which allows a player to represent a nation if he has a grandparent born there. However, after the game it was discovered that it was Fien's great-grandmother and not his grandmother that had been born in New Zealand. The Tri-Nations subcommittee of the Rugby League International Federation stripped the Kiwis of two points for fielding an ineligible player. Fien, a 27-year-old hooker, was banned from the tournament, while the decision put the Australians in the final. In the aftermath that followed, Selwyn Bennett, Chairman of the New Zealand Rugby League, resigned over the Nathan Fien affair. Bennett said, "There has to be a scapegoat, and I've put my hand up. I was the one who ordered the birth certificate to be sent to the Australians, I was the one who verified it. They've got their scalp."

The competition came alive at Sydney in Game 4 when Great Britain enjoyed their first victory, 23–12, over Australia on Aussie soil for 14 years. However, the Lions' hopes of reaching the final were all but dashed after New Zealand hammered them 34–4 in Wellington. Australia would have had to lose by 33 points to Great Britain for the Lions to have a better points difference than the Kiwis. It never looked like happening in Brisbane as the Kangaroos scored six tries on their way to a 33–10 victory.

Final Championship Standings

Team	P	W	D	L	F	A	Diff.	Pts
1. **Australia**	**4**	**3**	**0**	**1**	**95**	**66**	**29**	**6**
2. New Zealand	4	2	0	2	67	54	13	2*
3. Great Britain	4	1	0	3	37	79	-42	2*

No points given for New Zealand's win over Great Britain because of the Nathan Fien controversy; 18–14 scoreline expunged.

Final

There was little to choose between the two teams during the game and there was no real surprise when it ended 12–12. The golden point extra-time rule then came into play and it was the golden boy himself, Darren Lockyer, who clinched the series for the Kangaroos when he scored a try underneath the posts in the 87th minute of play. It was one of the greatest rugby league matches of all time with either side capable of snatching victory before Lockyer's try, but both missing field goal attempts.

25 NOVEMBER 2006, AUSSIE STADIUM, SYDNEY

Australia 16 – 12 New Zealand

Australia: Hunt, Tate, Gasnier, Hodges, Inglis, Lockyer, Thurston, Kite, Smith, Civoniceva, Ryan, Hindmarsh, O'Donnell
Replacements: Mason, O'Meley, Berrigan, Tupou
Tries: Tate, Lockyer
Goals: Thurston (4)

New Zealand: Webb, Hape, Soliola, Matai, Vatuvei, Vagana, Jones, Wiki, Halatau, Asotasi, Kidwell, Mannering, Fa'alogo
Replacements: Tony, Cayless, Blair, Pritchard
Tries: Pritchard, Soliola
Goals: Jones

Att: 27,325

Trivia

* The inaugural Rugby League Tri-Nations competition was held in Australia and New Zealand in 1999. Australia were the first winners following a narrow 22–20 win over New Zealand.

* The opening game of the 2007 Tri-Nations series was played at the Mt Smart (formerly Ericsson) Stadium. The stadium is situated in Auckland, and was built within the quarried remnants of the Mount Smart volcanic cone.

* In 2005 and 2006, New Zealand's first match on British soil was at Loftus Road, Queens Park Rangers FC, playing Australia in 2005 and GB in 2006.

* Great Britain finished top of the table in the second ever Tri-Nations series held in 2004. The Lions were favourites to beat Australia in the final but ended up being beaten 44–4. The Kangaroos led 38–0 at the interval.

* In the final of the 2005 Rugby League Tri-Nations, the third edition of the event, New Zealand beat Australia 24–0 at Elland Road, Leeds, ending the Kangaroo's 27-year undefeated international tournament record.

> **"**It's a dream come true. I couldn't have written the script any better. It's great to finish with a win. It was a long game, very intense and both teams were hanging in there waiting for the opportunity – but the legs need a good rest now.**"**
> ***Darren Lockyer***
> *who captained Australia, Queensland and the Brisbane Broncos to victory in the Tri-Nations, State of Origin and NRL Premiership, respectively, in 2006*

Other International Rugby League

Championnat de France Elite 2007

Pos	Team	P	W	D	L	PS	PC	PD	Pts
1.	Pia	20	17	0	3	795	355	440	51
2.	Toulouse	20	15	0	4	646	324	322	51
3.	Lezignan	20	13	1	6	585	359	226	47
4.	St Gaudens	20	13	1	6	591	420	171	46
5.	Carcassonne	20	12	1	7	614	333	281	45
6.	UTC	20	10	1	9	516	496	20	41
7.	Limousx	20	10	1	9	490	455	35	38
8.	Villerneuve	20	8	1	11	484	505	–21	34
9.	Villefranche-Cahors	20	4	2	14	461	607	–146	26
10.	Carpentras	20	2	0	18	290	837	–547	21
11.	Lyon-Villeurbane	20	1	1	18	239	1020	–781	18

Grand Final: Pia 20–16 Lezignan

NRL Final Season Table 2007

Pos	Team	P	W	D	L	B	PS	PC	PD	Pts
1.	Melbourne Storm	24	21	0	3	1	627	277	350	44
2.	Manly Sea Eagles	24	18	0	6	1	597	377	220	38
3.	North Queensland Cowboys	24	15	0	9	1	547	618	–71	32
4.	New Zealand Warriors	24	13	1	10	1	593	434	159	29
5.	Parramatta Eels	24	13	0	11	1	573	481	92	28
6.	Sydney Bulldogs	24	12	0	12	1	575	528	47	26
7.	South Sydney Rabbitohs	24	12	0	12	1	408	399	9	26
8.	Brisbane Broncos	24	11	0	13	1	511	476	35	24
9.	Wests Tigers	24	11	0	13	1	541	561	–20	24
10.	Sydney Roosters	24	10	1	13	1	445	610	–165	23
11.	Cronulla Sharks	24	10	0	14	1	463	403	60	22
12.	Gold Coast Titans	24	10	0	14	1	409	559	–150	22
13.	St George–Illawarra Dragons	24	9	0	15	1	431	509	–78	20
14.	Canberra Raiders	24	9	0	15	1	522	652	–130	20
15.	Newcastle Knights	24	9	0	15	1	418	708	–290	20
16.	Penrith Panthers	24	8	0	16	1	539	607	–68	18

The NRL season runs for 24 rounds with each team receiving two weeks off (one of which is officially a bye, for which they receive two points). Although all teams nominally play 12 games at home and away, a number of matches each season are played at other venues. All games are televised, so matches are staggered over each weekend between Friday and Monday. The finals series – involving the top eight – runs for four weeks.

World Club Challenge 2007

St Helens were officially crowned the best rugby league club side in the world after defeating Australia's best, the NRL Championship winning Brisbane Broncos, in a hard fought World Club Challenge match. The Saints welcomed back their inspirational captain Paul Sculthorpe who scored a try and made three superb conversions in what was his first game since September. The Saints went into the game as underdogs to the men from down under, having lost their last two Super League games to Harlequins and Wakefield. Meanwhile, the Broncos had trained hard for two weeks in preparation for the game.

The Broncos started strongly and were the first team to score, taking an 8–0 lead thanks to a Corey Parker try and penalty, and then on 21 minutes Sculthorpe came on for Mike Bennett to give his team the boost they needed. Pressure from the Saints paid off when Long's penalty to touch was ruled to have just made it, despite the TV replay showing that Justin Hodge's leap into the air had managed to keep the ball in play. From the resulting play Ade Gardner body swerved Darius Boyd to score in the corner just before the half-time interval to send the Saints in trailing 8–6 after Sculthorpe's superb conversion.

Just 2 minutes into the second-half, the Broncos scored their second try of the game when Boyd ran on to an inch-perfect kick from Lockyer. However, unluckily for the Saints, the match officials had missed a blatant forward pass in the build-up to the try. Sculthorpe hauled St Helens back into the game before Gidley conceded a second penalty 5 minutes later that Parker slotted between the uprights to edge the Aussies further ahead. However, in a hard fought encounter, particularly in the middle of the pitch, St Helens fought back when Gardner scored his second try of the evening, which along with Sculthorpe's excellent conversion, put the Saints ahead for the first time, 18–14, a lead they held on to for a famous victory.

23 FEBRUARY 2007, REEBOK STADIUM, BOLTON

St Helens 18 – 14 Brisbane Broncos

St Helens: Wellens, Gardner, Gidley, Talau, Meli, Pryce, Long, Fozzard, Roby, Cayless, Gilmour, Bennett, Wilkin
Replacements: Sculthorpe, Graham, Hargreaves, Cunningham
Tries: Gardner 2, Sculthorpe
Cons: Sculthorpe 3

Brisbane Broncos: Hunt, Boyd, Tate, Hodges, Michaels, Lockyer, Perry, Carlaw, Berrigan, Civoniceva, Parker, Thorn, Carroll
Replacements: Thaiday, Eastwood, Hannant, Ennis
Tries: Parker, Boyd
Cons: Parker
Pens: Parker 2

Att: 23,000

Rugby Union Six Nations Championship 2007

France opened their defence of their RBS Six Nations title in sensational form with a crushing 39–3 win over Italy at the Stadio Flaminio, Rome, while England got their campaign off to a flying start with a convincing 42–20 win over Scotland in the Calcutta Cup at Twickenham. Ireland also got off to a winning start, 19–9 against the Welsh in Cardiff. England moved to the top of the table following another home victory, although their 20–7 defeat of Italy was less than inspiring. Scotland won a kicking match (21–9) against Wales at Murrayfield with all 30 points scored by the two captains from kicks. Irish rugby history was made at Croke Park, Dublin, when Ireland played their first ever international at the home of the Gaelic Athletic Association. However, the French spoilt the party when a late try from Vincent Clerc gave the visitors a 20–17 win.

Thanks to a kamikaze opening six minutes by Scotland, Italy claimed their first away win in the Six Nations, 37–17 at Murrayfield, to open round three. Ireland, favourites at the start of the tournament before losing to France a week earlier, got their campaign back on track by thrashing England 43–13 at Croke Park. It was a record win for Ireland over England who played second fiddle to the Irish juggernaut throughout the game. France came from behind to win a thrilling encounter 32–21 against Wales in Paris, their third successive win of the 2007 tournament. Ireland claimed their second successive Triple Crown and their third in four years, with a hard fought 19–18 victory over Scotland at Murrayfield, Ronan O'Gara scoring 19 points, Chris Paterson 18. Italy claimed a historic second Six Nations win of the season after coming from behind to win a thriller in Rome, 23–20 against Wales; the first time in their eight seasons of playing in the competition that they had claimed successive wins. The last of the fourth round matches threw the Six Nations title wide open as England beat France 26–18, ending French dreams of a Grand Slam. It was England's first victory over France since the 2003 World Cup.

On St Patrick's Day, Ireland hammered the Italians 51–24 in Rome and then held their breaths hoping the Scots could win, draw or avoid defeat by more than 23 points to France in Paris, which would be good enough to crown Ireland champions. Scotland ended up with the wooden spoon, but the final French converted try, Elvis Vermeulen touching down, came in the last minute to give them a 27-point win. In the final game of the tournament, England had to win by 57 points to win the title. They were never at the races as Wales avoided five successive defeats with a 27–18 win at the Millennium Stadium.

Six Nations 2007 Results

Date	Match and Result	Date	Match and Result
03 Feb 2007	Italy 3 – 29 France	17 Feb 2007	France 32 – 21 Wales
03 Feb 2007	England 42 – 20 Scotland	10 Mar 2007	Scotland 18 – 19 Ireland
04 Feb 2007	Wales 9 – 19 Ireland	10 Mar 2007	Italy 23 – 20 Wales
10 Feb 2007	England 20 – 7 Italy	11 Mar 2007	England 26 – 18 France
10 Feb 2007	Scotland 21 – 9 Wales	17 Mar 2007	Italy 24 – 51 Ireland
11 Feb 2007	Ireland 17 – 20 France	17 Mar 2007	France 46 – 19 Scotland
17 Feb 2007	Scotland 17 – 37 Italy	17 Mar 2007	Wales 27 – 18 England
17 Feb 2007	Ireland 43 – 13 England		

Six Nations Championship

Country	P	W	D	L	F	A	Pts
1. France	5	4	0	1	155	86	8
2. Ireland	5	4	0	1	149	84	8
3. England	5	3	0	2	119	115	6
4. Italy	5	2	0	3	94	147	4
5. Wales	5	1	0	4	86	113	2
6. Scotland	5	1	0	4	95	153	2

"It is a great feeling. It is well deserved for the team and after a bad game last weekend to England we reacted well against Scotland. We knew from the start of the competition it would be tough between the Irish and us. It was emotional for all of us and we need to use this type of game to progress."

Raphael Ibanez, captain of France

Trivia

* Only three countries have won the Six Nations tournament: France 4, England 3 and Wales 1.

* Anthems:
  England: "God Save The Queen"
  France: "La Marseillaise"
  Ireland: "Ireland's Call"
  ("Amhrán na bhFiann")
  Italy: "Il Canto degli Italiani"
  Scotland: "Flower of Scotland"
  Wales: "Land of our Fathers"
  ("Hen Wlad fy Nhadau")

* Within the Six Nations Championship several other trophies are also contested:
  Calcutta Cup – England v Scotland
  Millennium Trophy –
  England v Ireland
  Centenary Quaich – Scotland v Ireland
  Giuseppe Garibaldi Trophy –
  France v Italy
  Triple Crown – England, Ireland, Scotland and Wales
  Grand Slam – All nations

* England's 2001 Six Nations match against Italy produced three tournament records:
  Most points: 80 England
  Biggest winning margin: 57 points – England 80–23 Italy
  Most tries: 10 England

* Since the inaugural Six Nations in 2000, each of the six countries has played a total of 40 games. The French lead the way with the most wins – 30, followed by Ireland 29, England 27, Wales 15, Scotland 12 and Italy 5.

* England, France and Ireland were all on six points atop of the 2007 Six Nations table with one round to play. If Italy, Scotland and Wales had won, against Ireland, France and England, respectively, then points difference would have been necesssary to separate the top four and Wales would have finished with the wooden spoon. As it was, Ireland, France and Wales won.

"Every Welshman gets up for playing against England and we are so pleased to get the result."
James Hook after scoring 22 points in Wales' 27–18 win over England

"England are so frustrating to watch. One to eight, who showed up? They were appalling. Brian Ashton will be pulling out what little hair he has."
Jeremy Guscott after England lost to Wales

Vodacom Tri-Nations 2007

Two late drop goals from Francois Steyn gave South Africa a late victory over Australia in the tournament opener. New Zealand then travelled to Durban and won 26–21. The Wallabies beat the All Blacks in the third match – their first win in six attempts – a dogged 20–15 success at the MCG. Game four saw Australia overcome an understrength Springboks side in Sydney. The All Blacks' 33–6 win over another weakened South African team in game five was closer than the scoreline suggests. New Zealand's first try came after 68 minutes. It all came down to the final game, at Eden Park, Auckland and New Zealand's 26–12 win over Australia that they retained the Tri-Nations title, their third in a row.

South Africa v Australia – Game 1
16 June; Newlands, Cape Town, SA
South Africa 22 – 19 Australia

South Africa		Australia
Fourie	*Try*	Giteau
Montgomery	*Con*	Mortlock
Montgomery (3)	*Pens*	Mortlock (4)
Steyn (2)	*Drop*	

South Africa v New Zealand – Game 2
23 June; ABSA Stadium, Durban, SA
South Africa 21 – 26 New Zealand

South Africa		New Zealand
Burger, James	*Try*	McCaw, Rokocoko
Montgomery	*Con*	Carter (2)
Montgomery (2),	*Pens*	Carter (3)
Pienaar		
	Drop	Mauger

Australia v New Zealand – Game 3
30 June; Melbourne Cricket Ground, AUS
Australia 20 – 15 New Zealand

Australia		New Zealand
Ashley-Cooper,	*Try*	Woodcock, Gear
Staniforth		
Giteau (2)	*Con*	Carter
Mortlock (2)	*Pens*	Carter

Australia v South Africa – Game 4
7 July; Telstra Stadium, Sydney, AUS
Australia 25 – 17 South Africa

Australia		South Africa
Gerrard,	*Try*	Van Heerden,
Hoiles, Giteau		Paulse
Mortlock (2)	*Con*	Hougaard (2)
Mortlock (2)	*Pens*	Hougaard

New Zealand v South Africa – Game 5
14 July; Jade Stadium, Christchurch, NZ
New Zealand 33 – 6 South Africa

New Zealand		South Africa
Leonard, Evans,	*Try*	
Carter		
Carter (3)	*Con*	
Carter (4)	*Pen*	Hougaard (2)

New Zealand v Australia – Game 6
21 July; Eden Park, Auckland, NZ
New Zealand 26 – 12 Australia

New Zealand		Australia
Woodcock	*Try*	
	Con	
Carter (7)	*Pens*	Mortlock (3)
	Drop	Giteau

VODACOM TRI-NATIONS TABLE

	P	W	D	L	PF	PA	BP	Pts
New Zealand	4	3	0	1	100	59	1	13
Australia	4	2	0	2	76	80	1	9
South Africa	4	1	0	3	66	103	1	5

Other International Rugby Union 2006–07

Autumn Internationals

England's miserable run of form continued and resulted in the dismissale of coach Andy Robinson. Wales drew heart from a draw with Australia, while Ireland and Argentina showed their potential.

4 November 2006

Wales	29 – 29	Australia

5 November 2006

England	20 – 41	New Zealand

11 November 2006

England	18 – 25	Argentina
France	3 – 47	New Zealand
Ireland	32 – 15	South Africa
Italy	18 – 25	Australia
Scotland	48 – 6	Romania
Wales	38 – 20	Pacific Islands

17 November 2006

Wales	61 – 26	Canada

18 November 2006

England	23 – 21	South Africa
France	11 – 23	New Zealand
Italy	16 – 23	Argentina
Scotland	34 – 22	Pacific Islands

19 November 2006

Ireland	21 – 6	Australia

25 November 2006

England	14 – 25	South Africa
France	27 – 26	Argentina
Italy	41 – 6	Canada
Scotland	15 – 44	Australia
Wales	10 – 45	New Zealand

26 November 2006

Ireland	61 – 17	Pacific Islands

Summer Internationals

The futility of summer international tours in a World Cup year was proven in a series of mainly one-sided contests. They were followed by World Cup warm-ups.

26 May 2007

Argentina	22 – 20	Ireland
Australia	29 – 23	Wales
South Africa	58 – 10	England

2 June 2007

USA	10 – 52	Canada
Argentina	16 – 0	Ireland
Australia	31 – 0	Wales
New Zealand	42 – 11	France
South Africa	55 – 22	England

9 June 2007

Argentina	24 – 6	Italy
Australia	49 – 0	Fiji
New Zealand	61 – 10	France
South Africa	35 – 8	Samoa

16 June 2007

New Zealand	64 – 13	Canada

4 August 2007

England	62 – 5	Wales

11 August 2007

England	15 – 21	France
Scotland	31 – 21	Ireland

18 August 2007

France	22 – 9	England
Wales	27 – 20	Argentina

25 August 2007

Wales	7 – 34	France
Scotland	3 – 27	South Africa
Ireland	23 – 20	Italy

Heineken Cup Final 2007

A record crowd for a club game watched the unfancied London Wasps beat the Premiership champions and EDF Cup winners, Leicester Tigers, 25–9 at Twickenham to win their second Heineken Cup final. The Tigers, who only a week before mauled Gloucester in the Premiership final, were completely swarmed by the Wasps who led 13–9 at the interval and then locked the Tigers' cage in the second half scoring 12 points without reply.

20 MAY 2007, TWICKENHAM STADIUM, LONDON

London Wasps 25 – 9 Leicester Tigers

Wasps: Cipriani, Sackey, Waters, Lewsey, Voyce, King, Reddan, French, Ibanez, Vickery, Shaw, Palmer, Worsley, Rees, Dallaglio (c)
Replacements: Ward, Bracken, Leo, Haskell, McMillan, Waldouck, Van Gisbergen
Tries: Reddan, Ibanez
Cons: King 4
Drop Goal: King

Leicester: Murphy, Rabeni, Hipkiss, Gibson, Tuilagi, Goode, Murphy, Ayerza, Chuter, White, Deacon, Kay, Moody, Jennings, Corry (c)
Replacements: Buckland, Moreno, Cullen, Deacon, Humphreys, Vesty, Smith
Pens: Goode 3

Att: 81,076

Trivia

* Wasps used to play their home games at Loftus Road, home to Queens Park Rangers Football Club. They had previously played at Sudbury, near Wembley, Middlesex, but had to move because their spectator facilities were not acceptable for top-flight rugby.

* In 2005–06 the ERC Board allowed Biarritz Olympique (France) to host a semi-final across the Spanish border in Estadio Anoeta, Donostia-San Sebastian, the nearest stadium to Biarritz with the minimum 20,000-seater capacity per ERC rules.

* Toulouse has won the Heineken Cup more times than any other club with three wins – in 1996, 2003 and 2005. Leicester Tigers – the only team to retain the Cup – and Wasps have both won it twice. No team from Scotland, Wales or Italy has won the Cup.

> "Everyone was talking about the Leicester guys – they've had a fantastic season but when you're underdogs it pumps you up"
> *Wasps skipper*
> **Lawrence Dallaglio**

European Challenge Cup Final 2007

ASM Clermont Auvergne ended the domination of English clubs in the European Challenge Cup by taking the trophy back to France for the first time in seven years, since Pau's victory in 2000. The French Championship semi-finalists trailed 6–3 at the interval but then scored 19 points on the bounce and looked on course for a comfortable win until Bath came fighting back with a try and a penalty to set up an exciting finish. However, the French side held on for a victory that also cost Bath a place in next season's Heineken Cup.

19 MAY 2007, TWICKENHAM STOOP, LONDON

Clermont Auvergne 22 – 16 Bath

Clermont Auvergne: Floch, Rougerie (c), Esterhuizen, Marsh, Malzieu, James, Mignoni, Emmanuelli, Ledesma, Scelzo, Cudmore, Privat, Broomhall, Dieude, Vermeulen
Replacements: Miguel, Shvelidze, Jacquet, Longo, Troncon, Bai, Chanal
Tries: Malzieu, Marsh, James
Cons: James 2
Pens: James

Bath: Abendanon, Maddock, Fuimaono-Sapolu, Barkley, Bory, Berne, Walshe, Barnes, Mears, Stevens, Borthwick (c), Grewcock, Beattie, Lipman, Feaunati
Replacements: Dixon, Jarvis, Short, Scaysbrook, Williams, Malone, Cheeseman
Try: Maddock
Con: Barkley
Pens: Barkley (3)

Att: 10,134

Trivia

* Bath won 16 trophies between 1984 and 1996 but have not won a piece of silverware since 1998 when they beat Brive 19–18 in the European Cup final.

* ASM Clermont Auvergne was founded in 1911 as AS Michelin by Marcel Michelin, the son of André Michelin, founder of the Michelin tyre manufacturing company.

* Clermont Auvergne won the Cup in 1999, but they were called Montferrand.

* The European Challenge Cup was known as the Parker Pen Shield from 2001 to 2003 and the Parker Pen Challenge Cup from 2003 to 2005.

* In the European Challenge Cup's 11 seasons, French clubs have won the trophy six times and English clubs five.

"We were probably lucky to come away with a win, to be honest."
Clermont's Kiwi centre
Tony Marsh

English Club Rugby Union 2006–07

GUINNESS PREMIERSHIP

The 12-team Guinness Premiership was the principal tournament followed by National Division One and National Division Two. The competition began on 2 September 2006 and culminated in the final at Twickenham on 12 May 2007. The opening games of the season were played at Twickenham, in the London Double Header; London Irish 20–19 NEC Harlequins and Saracens 19–21 London Wasps. At the end of the league season Gloucester Rugby topped the table, Leicester Tigers were runners-up while Bristol Rugby (third) and Saracens (fourth) claimed the two remaining semi-final places.

Semi-finals
Date: 5 May 2007

Venue: Kingsholm Stadium, Gloucester
Score: Gloucester Rugby 50–9 Saracens

Venue: Welford Road, Leicester
Score: Leicester Tigers 26–14 Bristol Rugby

Final
Date: 12 May 2007

Venue: Twickenham Stadium, London
Score: Gloucester Rugby 16–44 Leicester Tigers

Leicester Tigers won their seventh title to move one ahead of Bath's six wins. Having finished bottom of the 2006–07 Guinness Premiership table the Northampton Saints were relegated to Division One. The Leeds Tykes won Division One and replaced the Saints for the 2007–08 Guinness Premiership season as Leeds Carnegie, while Otley RFU and Waterloo RFC were both relegated from Division One being replaced by Esher RFC, Division Two champions 2006–07), and runners-up Launceston. Blaydon won National Division Three North Championship and Southend won the National Division Three South Championship.

EDF ENERGY ANGLO-WELSH CUP

The EDF Energy Cup, also commonly referred to as the Anglo-Welsh Cup, is contested by all twelve Guinness Premiership sides, plus all four Welsh regions. (Prior to the 2005–06 season the competition was open to all English clubs.) The 2006–07 competition, the 36th edition of the tournament and the first sponsored by EDF, began on 1 September 2006 concluding with the final at Twickenham on 15 April 2007. Leicester Tigers claimed their sixth title trailing Bath's ten wins.

Semi-finals
Date: 24 March 2007

Venue: Millennium Stadium, Cardiff
Score: Leicester Tigers 29–19 Sale Sharks

Venue: Millennium Stadium, Cardiff
Score: Ospreys 27–10 Cardiff Blues

Final

Date: 15 April 2007

Venue: Twickenham Stadium, London
Score: Leicester Tigers 41–35 Ospreys

HEINEKEN CUP

The Heineken Cup is contested by the best teams from England, France, Ireland, Italy, Wales and Scotland and generally regarded as the most prestigious trophy in European rugby. The 2006–07 competition was the 12th edition of the event, with the pool stages commencing on 20 October 2006 and the final played at Twickenham on 20 May 2007.

Quarter-finals Match A
Date: 1 April 2007
Venue: Estadio Anoeta, Donostia-San Sebastian, Spain
Score: Biarritz Olympique *(Fra) (1st seed)* 6–7 Northampton Saints *(Eng) (8th seed)*

Match B
Date: 30 March 2007
Venue: Stradey Park, Llanelli
Score: Llanelli Scarlets *(Wal) (2nd seed)* 24–15 Munster *(Ire) (7th seed)*

Match C
Date: 31 March 2007
Venue: Adams Park, High Wycombe
Score: London Wasps *(Eng) (3rd seed)* 35–13 Leinster *(Ire) (6th seed)*

Match D
Date: 1 April 2007
Venue: Welford Road, Leicester
Score: Leicester Tigers *(Eng) (4th seed)* 21–20 Stade Français *(Fra) (5th seed)*

Semi-finals
Date: 21 April 2007
Venue: Walkers Stadium, Leicester
Score: Leicester Tigers 33–17 Llanelli Scarlets

Date: 22 April 2007
Venue: Ricoh Arena, Coventry
Score: London Wasps 30–13 Northampton Saints

Final
Date: 20 May 2007
Venue: Twickenham Stadium, London
Score: London Wasps 25–9 Leicester Tigers

The Celtic League 2006-07

The Celtic League, known by its sponsors name The Magners League from season 2006–07, is an annual rugby union tournament in which teams from Ireland, Scotland and Wales participate. Along with the Guinness Premiership and the French Top 14, it is one of the three leading club competitions in Europe. The Irish, Scottish and Welsh Rugby Unions use the Celtic League as the sole determinant for European qualification and seeding. The 2006–07 season began on 1 September 2006 and ended on 12 May 2007. Ulster went into the season as the reigning Celtic League champions while Munster had beaten Biarritz 23–19 in the Heineken Cup final at the Millennium Stadium, Cardiff on 20 May 2006. In addition to the 4 points for a win system, a bonus points system is used in the Magners League: 1 extra point is awarded to any side that scores 4 or more tries in a game, while even the losing side can earn a bonus point (or 2 bonus points if it scores 4 tries) if it finishes within 7 points of the match winner. All season long it was a three-way battle to win the title, fought out by the Cardiff Blues, Leinster and the Ospreys and the outcome of the title came down to the last day of the season. The league's record attendance was smashed on 31 December 2006 when Leinster entertained the reigning champions, Ulster, at Lansdowne Road. A huge crowd of 48,000 watched Leinster beat their rivals 20–12 in a game billed as "The Last Stand". This was the last ever game played at Lansdowne Road, home to the Republic of Ireland football team, prior to it being demolished and re-built. Leinster played their remaining home games at Donnybrook. The Cardiff Blues faced Leinster at Cardiff Arms Park while the Ospreys faced Border Reivers at Netherdale. Leinster, the surprise Irish side who had overshadowed their counterparts from the Emerald Isle, knew a win would guarantee them the title, while the Ospreys faced a Borders side that was playing their last ever match, following the Scottish Rugby Union's decision that Scotland would only have two professional teams from season 2007–08 (Edinburgh and Glasgow). Here is how the League table looked prior to the final day's results.

Magners League Table 2006-07 – Prior to Final Game of the Season

Club	Played	Won	Drawn	Lost	Points for	Points against	Bonus points	Points
Leinster	19	12	1	6	461	349	11	61
Ospreys	19	13	0	6	437	358	8	60
Cardiff Blues	19	12	1	6	420	316	8	58

FINAL DAY'S RESULTS
Border Reivers 16 – 24 Ospreys
Cardiff Blues 27 – 11 Leinster

The league was won by the Ospreys by a single point, who had kicked-off their game at 17.30 as opposed to their rivals 19.10 start, their second Championship success in three years. The 2007-08 season kicks off on 31 August 2007 with the defending champions, the Ospreys, facing the 2006-07 runners-up, the Cardiff Blues, at Cardiff Arms Park.

Magners League Table 2006-07

Club	Played	Won	Drawn	Lost	Points for	Points against	Bonus points	Points
Ospreys	20	14	0	6	461	374	8	64
Cardiff Blues	20	13	1	6	447	327	9	63
Leinster	20	12	1	7	472	376	11	61
Llaneli Scarlets	20	12	0	8	490	417	9	57
Ulster	20	11	1	8	423	310	9	55
Munster	20	12	0	8	379	294	6	54
Glasgow Warriors	20	11	0	9	434	419	5	49
Edinburgh Rugby	20	8	1	11	335	423	8	42
Newport Gwent Dragons	20	8	0	12	353	362	7	39
Connacht	20	4	2	14	326	474	6	26
Border Reivers	20	2	0	18	201	545	4	12

Trivia

* In the Republic of Ireland *Magners* is known as *Bulmers Irish Cider* although the *Magners* name is still used in Ireland for the League.

* Felipe Contepomi (Leinster) holds the record for the most number of points scored in a season, with 276 in 2005-06.

Principality Premiership Table 2006–07

Club	Played	Won	Drawn	Lost	PF	PA	Pts
Neath RFC	26	17	2	7	704	473	53
Ebbw Vale	26	16	3	7	557	503	51
Newport RFC	26	16	2	8	619	480	50
Pontypridd RFC	26	16	1	9	543	504	49
Llanelli RFC	26	12	2	12	629	509	38
Glamorgan Wands	26	12	2	12	577	602	38
Aberavon RFC	26	12	2	12	603	615	38
Cardiff RFC	26	12	1	13	601	580	37
Swansea RFC	26	12	0	14	487	611	36
Bedwas RFC	26	11	1	14	446	524	34
Bridgend Ravens	26	11	0	15	461	508	33
Maesteg RFC	26	10	0	16	531	596	30
Cross Keys RFC	26	9	2	15	485	528	29
Llandovery RFC	26	7	0	19	482	692	21

World Club Rugby

French National League 1 Table 2006–07

Pos	Club	P	W	D	L	PF	PA	Bonus	Pts
1.	Stade Français	26	19	1	6	667	433	9	87
2.	Toulouse	26	18	2	6	643	424	10	86
3.	Clermont Auvegrne	26	18	0	8	772	454	12	84
4.	Biarritz	26	16	1	9	549	378	9	76
5.	Perpignan	26	16	1	9	493	398	8	75
6.	Bourgoin	26	11	1	14	543	484	12	58
7.	Montauban	26	10	2	14	475	493	10	54
8.	Bayonne	26	11	1	14	452	647	5	51
9.	Albi	26	11	1	14	333	512	4	50
10.	Brive	26	10	1	15	419	516	8	50
11.	Castres	26	9	1	16	524	576	11	49
12.	Montpellier	26	9	1	16	442	596	10	48
13.	Agen	26	9	1	16	382	520	6	44
14.	Narbonne	26	8	0	18	521	784	7	39

4pts for a win, 2 for a draw; 1 bonus pt for scoring four tries and/or for losing team by 7pts or less. The top six clubs qualified for the 2007–08 Heineken Cup.

PLAYOFFS

Semi-finals

Stade Français	18 – 6	Biarritz
Toulouse	15 – 20	Clermont Auvegrne

Playoff Final

9 June 2007, Stade de France, St Denis

Stade Français	**(0) 23 – (9) 18**	**Clermont Auvergne**
Pichot, Sarno	*Tries*	
Hernandez 2	*Conversions*	
Hernandez 3	*Penalties*	James 5
	Drops	Floch

The stifling defence of Stade Français proved enough for them to claim the French championship in a nervous final at Stade de France. Clermont Auvergne – who didn't score a try – led by 12 points a minute into the second half and were 15–6 up after an hour's play. But Juan Martin Hernandez kicked his third penalty of the game and added the conversion to Argentine scrum half Agustin Pichot's try to give Stade the lead. Brock James restored Clermont's advantage by kicking his fifth penalty after 74 minutes, only for substitute back-row forward Radike Samo to cross for the deciding try after 77 minutes.

Super 14 League Table 2007

Pos	Club	P	W	D	L	PF	PA	Bonus	Pts
1.	Natal Sharks[S]	13	10	0	3	355	214	5	45
2.	Pretoria Bulls[S]	13	9	0	4	388	223	6	42
3.	Canterbury Crusaders[N]	13	8	0	5	382	235	10	42
4.	Auckland Blues[N]	13	9	0	4	355	235	6	42
5.	ACT Brumbies[A]	13	9	0	4	234	173	4	40
6.	Waikato Chiefs[N]	13	7	1	5	373	321	10	40
7.	Western Force[A]	13	6	1	6	276	282	6	32
8.	Wellington Hurricanes[N]	13	6	0	7	247	300	3	27
9.	Otago Highlanders[N]	13	5	0	8	235	301	7	27
10.	W. Province Stormers[S]	13	6	0	7	249	326	3	27
11.	Free State Cheetahs[S]	13	4	1	8	265	342	4	22
12.	Gauteng Lions[S]	13	5	0	8	175	284	2	22
13.	NSW Waratahs[A]	13	3	1	9	266	317	7	21
14.	Queensland Reds[A]	13	2	0	11	201	438	3	11

4pts for a win, 2 for a draw; 1 bonus pt for scoring four tries and/or for losing team by 7pts or less.
[A] = Australia, [N] = New Zealand, [S] = South Africa

The newly revamped Super 14 contained four Australian and five each South African and New Zealand "super" teams, representing regions rather than clubs. Each team plays once against the other 13 teams. At the end of the regular season, the top four go into a playoffs and, in 2007, it was South Africa's team which came out on top. The Bulls and Sharks made it to the final after seeing off New Zealand opposition in the form of the Crusaders and Blues respectively. But there was a slight surprise in the final – a match of outstanding tension and high quality – as the Bulls snatched victory after the final hooter sounded. Trailing 19–13 when the 80 minutes were up, the Bulls kept the ball alive and winger Bryan Habana touched down for a try. It put all the pressure on kicker Derick Hougaard, but he showed no nerves as he sent the ball between the posts to snatch a stunning victory.

Semi-finals

Natal Sharks	36 – 18	Auckland Blues
Pretoria Bulls	27 – 12	Christchurch Crusaders

Final
19 May 2007, ABSA Stadium, Durban, SA

Pretoria Bulls	**(10) 20 – (14) 19**	**Natal Sharks**
Spies, Habana	*Tries*	Pietersen, van den Berg
Hougaard 2	*Conversions*	
Hougaard 2	*Penalties*	Montgomery 3
	Drops	

Rugby World Cup 2007 qualifiers

With the eight sides that made it through to the last eight of the 2003 World Cup gaining automatic entry for France 2007, 86 countries were left to fight it out for the remaining World Cup berths. With over 200 matches played on six continents over the course of two-and-a-half years, the same 12 teams that had come through the qualification process in 2003 came through once again for 2007. The team line-up will be the same for the second tournament in a row.

Qualifying countries

AFRICA	**ASIA**
Namibia	Japan
SOUTH AMERICA	**OCEANIA**
Argentina, Uruguay	Samoa, Fiji, Tonga
NORTH AMERICA	**EUROPE**
Canada, USA	Italy, Romania, Georgia

Final qualifying matches

REPECHAGE ROUND 1

20 January, Casablanca
Morocco 5–10 Portugal

27 January, Lisbon
Portugal 16–15 Morocco
Portugal win 26–20 and will face Uruguay

10 March 2007, Lisbon
Portugal 12 Uruguay 5

24 March 2007, Montevideo
Uruguay 18–12 Portugal
Portugal win 24–23, qualify for the finals.

REPECHAGE ROUND 2

10 February 2007, Auckland
Tonga 85–3 Korea
Tonga qualify for the 2007 World Cup

Trivia

* By defeating Uruguay in the Repechage round, Portugal qualified for the World Cup for the first time. Uruguay thus had the unwanted disctinction of being the only country from the 2003 World Cup not to qualify for the 2007 finals.

* At 22 and 24, respectively, Portugal and Namibia are the lowest-ranked nations to appear in the 2007 World Cup. Russia (19) and Uruguay (20) are the two top-20 nations to miss out.

* There are 95 countries with International Rugby Board (IRB) rankings. Bottom, in September 2007, were Bosnia Herzegovina.

* On 12 November 2005, Germany beat Serbia 108–0 in Heidelberg; it was the most one-side match of the qualifiers.

Rugby World Cup 2007 finals

The 2007 Rugby World Cup is the sixth edition of the competition. An estimated two million fans are expected to watch the 48 games live over the course of the 43 days with a further 3.5 billion watching it on television. Around 400,000 fans will travel to France to watch their nation play, the majority from Britain and Ireland. New Zealand, inaugural Rugby World Cup winners in 1987, are favourites to lift the Webb Ellis Trophy in 2007 after blitzing all before them in the lead-up to the Finals including dispensing with the British Lions in 2005 and two wins over the hosts France on French soil during their successful Tour of Europe in 2006. However, the French, Six Nations Champions in 2007, hope that a wave of fervent home support will see them crowned World Champions in the Stade de France come 20 October. All eyes will also be on the reigning World Champions England, although their hopes of repeating that magical evening four years ago when the boot of Jonny Wilkinson sunk the Wallabies in Sydney seem remote at the least. England are not the same team that performed heroics down under at the 2003 Rugby World Cup, particularly in defence.

Group stage

POOL A	POOL B	POOL C	POOL D
England	Australia	New Zealand	France
South Africa	Wales	Scotland	Ireland
Samoa	Japan	Italy	Argentina
Tonga	Fiji	Romania	Namibia
USA	Canada	Portugal	Georgia

Knock-out stages

QUARTER-FINALS

QF1 (Stade Vélodrome, Marseille)

6 October 2007

B1 v. A2

QF2 (Millennium Stadium, Cardiff)

6 October 2007

C1 v. D2

QF3 (Stade Vélodrome, Marseille)

7 October 2007

A1 v. B2

QF4 (Stade de France, Saint-Denis)

7 October 2007

D1 v. C2

SEMI-FINALS

SF1 (Stade de France, Saint-Denis)

13 October 2007

Winner QF1 v. Winner QF2

SF2 (Stade de France, Saint-Denis)

14 October 2007

Winner QF3 v. Winner QF4

THIRD-PLACE PLAYOFF

19 October (Parc des Princes, Paris)

Loser SF1 v. Loser SF2

FINAL

20 October (Stade de France, St Denis)

Winner SF1 v. Winner SF2

Tennis

Australian Open 2007 15–28 January Flinders Park, Melbourne

Men's Singles Championship

The world number one, Roger Federer of Switzerland, won his third Australian Open with a 7–6 (7–2), 6–4, 6–4 win over Fernando Gonzalez. It was Federer's tenth Grand Slam title and he now joins Bill Tilden (USA) in joint fifth place on the all-time Grand Slam titles list and extended his winning run to 36 matches in the process. On his way to winning the title, Federer became the first man to win a Grand Slam title without dropping a set since Bjorn Borg blew everyone away at the French Open in 1980.

Quarter-finals	(1) Roger Federer *(Swi)*	bt	(7) Tommy Robredo *(Spa)*
	(6) Andy Roddick *(US)*	bt	Mardy Fish *(USA)*
	(12) Tommy Haas *(Ger)*	bt	(3) Nikolay Davydenko *(Rus)*
	(10) Fernando Gonzalez *(Chi)*	bt	(2) Rafael Nadal *(Spa)*
Semi-finals	(1) Roger Federer *(Swi)*	bt	(6) Andy Roddick *(USA)*
	(10) Fernando Gonzalez *(Chi)*	bt	(12) Tommy Haas *(Ger)*
Final	(1) Roger Federer *(Swi)*	bt	(10) Fernando Gonzalez *(Chi)*

Women's Singles Championship

Serena Williams defeated the number one seed Maria Sharapova to win her third Australian Open title. The unseeded American won 6–1, 6–2 to clinch her eighth Grand Slam and complete her return from a knee injury.

Quarter-finals	(1) Maria Sharapova *(Rus)*	bt	(12) Anna Chakvetadze *(Rus)*
	(4) Kim Clijsters *(Bel)*	bt	(6) Martina Hingis *(Swi)*
	Serena Williams *(US)*	bt	(16) Shahar Peer *(Isr)*
	(10) Nicole Vaidisova *(Cze)*	bt	Lucie Safarova *(Cze)*
Semi-finals	(1) Maria Sharapova *(Rus)*	bt	(4) Kim Clijsters *(Bel)*
	Serena Williams *(USA)*	bt	(10) Nicole Vaidisova *(Cze)*
Final	Serena Williams *(USA)*	bt	(1) Maria Sharapova *(Rus)*

Trivia

* After winning the 2007 Australian Open, Roger Federer became the first man to win three of the Grand Slam events on at least three occasions.

* Roger Federer and Serena Williams both claimed their third Australian Open titles in 2007.

* After winning his third Australian Open title in 2007, Roger Federer is now one Grand Slam title away from joining Borg and Rod Laver on 11 Grand Slam tournament wins.

French Open 2007 28 May–10 June, Roland Garros Stadium, Paris

Men's Singles Championship

Roger Federer beat Nikolay Davydenko in straight sets to earn a place in his second French Open final. However, the world number one was slightly off-key and had to fight back after trailing in all three sets. In the second semi-final the defending champion for the past two years, Rafael Nadal, beat Novak Djokovic in straight sets. This set up a Federer/Nadal final, meaning that Federer was just one win away from holding all four Grand Slam titles at once. In the final, Nadal, seeded number two, played some superb tennis to beat the top seed, world number one ranked player and ten-time Major winner, Roger Federer, in four sets, to claim his third successive French Open title. Amazingly, the 21-year-old three-time champion has never lost a match at Roland Garros and he became the first man since Bjorn Borg in 1980 to win the title three years running.

Quarter-finals	(1) Roger Federer *(Swi)*	bt	(9) Tommy Robredo *(Spa)*
	(4) Nikolay Davydenko *(Rus)*	bt	(19) Guillermo Canas *(Arg)*
	(6) Novak Djokovic *(Ser)*	bt	Igor Andreev *(Rus)*
	(2) Rafael Nadal *(Spa)*	bt	(23) Carlos Moya *(Spa)*
Semi-finals	(1) Roger Federer *(Swi)*	bt	Nikolay Davydenko *(Rus)*
	(2) Rafael Nadal *(Spa)*	bt	(6) Novak Djokovic *(Ser)*
Final	(2) Rafael Nadal *(Spa)*	bt	(1) Roger Federer *(Swi)*

Women's Singles Championship

In the women's semi-finals, the defending champion, Justine Henin, easily beat Jelena Jankovic in straight sets to set up a final against Ana Ivanovic, who caused the tournament's biggest shock for years beating Maria Sharapova in straight sets. However, it was Henin who won her third consecutive French Open title and her fourth overall with a powerhouse 6–1, 6–2 demolition of Ana Ivanovic in 65 minutes. It was the Belgian player's sixth career Grand Slam win.

Quarter-finals	(7) Ana Ivanovic *(Ser)*	bt	(3) Svetlana Kuznetsova *(Rus)*
	(4) Jelena Jankovic *(Ser)*	bt	(6) Nicole Vaidisova *(Cze)*
	(1) Justine Henin *(Bel)*	bt	(8) Serena Williams *(USA)*
	(2) Maria Sharapova *(Rus)*	bt	(9) Anna Chakvetadze *(Rus)*
Semi-finals	(7) Ana Ivanovic *(Ser)*	bt	(2) Maria Sharapova *(Rus)*
	(1) Justine Henin *(Bel)*	bt	(4) Jelena Jankovic *(Ser)*
Final	(1) Justine Henin *(Bel)*	bt	(7) Ana Ivanovic *(Ser)*

Trivia

* Roger Federer passed Australian Jack Crawford's record of seven stright Grand Slam finals, which he set in the 1930s.

* In 1928, the French Championships moved to Roland Garros. Garros was a famous French First World War pilot.

Wimbledon 2007

Date: 25 June–8 July
Venue: All England Lawn Tennis and Croquet Club, London, England

MEN'S SINGLES
Roger Federer matched Bjorn Borg's feat of five successive titles (1976–80) after defeating Spain's Rafael Nadal in a classic final. The Swiss world number one won in five sets after a titanic battle lasting 3 hours and 45 minutes on Centre Court. It was the first time he had been taken to five sets in a Grand Slam final. After hitting the winning shot, Federer dropped to his knees as the crowd, including the former Swedish master who was watching from the Royal Box, gave both players a standing ovation after a truly thrilling game of tennis that swayed one way and then the other several times. Amazingly, Federer was playing in his ninth successive Grand Slam final and the 13th of his career, winning 11 of them.

WOMEN'S SINGLES
Venus Williams (USA), seeded 23, clinched her fourth Wimbledon singles title with a straight sets victory over the number 18 seed, France's Marion Bartoli. The 22-year-old French player seemed a little nervous at the start of the final on Centre Court but soon settled down, although she lost the first set. Williams, aged 27 and playing in her sixth Wimbledon singles final, powered her way through the second set, despite needing medical attention to her thigh, to follow up her triumphs in 2000, 2001 and 2005. The pair were the lowest ever seeds to appear in a Wimbledon final, but the number of seeds only increased from 16 to 32 in 2001.

MEN'S DOUBLES
France's number 10 seeds Arnaud Clement and Michael Llodra beat the number 1 seeds, Bob and Mike Bryan, to claim the Wimbledon men's doubles title. The French pair, making their Grand Slam debut, beat the American twins in four sets to become the first French men's doubles champions at Wimbledon for 74 years. Amazingly, the Bryans were playing in their 13th final, searching for their fifth Grand Slam title.

WOMEN'S DOUBLES
Cara Black (Zimbabwe) and Liezel Huber (South Africa), fought back from a set down to beat Slovenia's Katarina Srebotnik and Ai Sugiyama (Japan) to win their second Wimbledon women's doubles title (their first had come in 2005). Srebotnik and Sugiyama, who had seen off the top seeds – Lisa Raymond of the United States and the Australian Samantha Stosur – in the semi-finals, were also beaten finalists in the 2007 French Open.

MIXED DOUBLES
Jamie Murray became the first British player for 20 years to win a senior title at Wimbledon (Jeremy Bates and Jo Durie won the Mixed Doubles in 1987). He and his partner, Jelena Jankovic from Serbia, won the mixed doubles after defeating the number 5 seeds, Sweden's Jonas Bjorkman and Alicia Molik from Australia, over three sets.

Wimbledon Winners

<table>
<tr><td>

MEN'S SINGLES
R Federer *(Swi, 1) bt* R Nadal *(Spa, 2)*
7–6 (9–7), 4–6, 7–6 (7–3), 2–6, 6–2

</td><td>

WOMEN'S SINGLES
V Williams *(US, 23) bt* M Bartoli *(Fr, 18)*
6–4, 6–1

</td></tr>
</table>

MEN'S DOUBLES
A Clement/L Llodra *(Fr, 10) bt* B Bryan/M Bryan *(US, 1)*
6–7 (5–7), 6–3, 6–4, 6–4

WOMEN'S DOUBLES
C Black/L Huber *(Zim/SA, 2) bt* K Srebotnik/A Sigiyama *(Slo/Jap, 4)*
3–6, 6–3, 6–2

MIXED DOUBLES
J Murray/J Jankovic *(GB/Ser) bt* J Bjorkman/A Molik *(Swe/Aus, 5)*
6–4, 3–6, 6–1

MEN'S SINGLES Quarter-finals

(1) Roger Federer *(Swi) bt* (20) Juan Carlos Ferrero *(Spa) 7–6, 3–6, 6–1, 6–3*

(2) Rafael Nadal *(Spa) bt* Tomas Berdych *(Cze) 7–6, 6–4, 6–2*

(12) Richard Gasquet *(Fra) bt* (3) Andy Roddick *(US) 4–6, 4–6, 7–6, 7–6, 8–6*

(4) Novak Djokovic *(Ser) bt* (10) Marcos Baghdatis *(Cyp) 7–6, 7–6, 6–7, 4–6, 7–5*

Semi-finals

Federer *bt* Gasquet *7–6, 6–3, 6–4*   Nadal *bt* Djokovic *Ser) 3–6, 6–1, 4–1 (ret)*

WOMEN'S SINGLES Quarter-finals

(1) Justine Henin *(Bel) bt* (7) Serena Williams *(US) 6–4, 3–6, 6–3*

(18) Marion Bartoli *(Fra) bt* Michaella Krajicek *(Ned) 3–6, 6–3, 6–2*

(6) Ana Ivanovic *(Ser) bt* (14) Nicole Vaidisova *(Cze) 4–6, 6–2, 7–5*

(23) Venus Williams *(US) bt* (5) Svetlana Kuznetsova *(Rus) 6–3, 6–4*

Semi-finals

Bartoli *bt* Henin *1–6, 7–5, 6–1*   V Williams *bt* Ivanovic *6–2, 6–4*

MEN'S DOUBLES Semi-finals

(1) B Bryan *(US)/*M Bryan *(US) bt* (4) F Santoro *(Fra)/*N Zimonjic *(Ser 7–6, 6–4, 7–6*

(10) A Clement *(Fra)/*M Llodra *(Fra) bt* M Melo *(Bra)/*A Sa *(Bra) 7–6, 6–3, 6–3*

WOMEN'S DOUBLES Semi-finals

(4) K Srebotnik *(Slo)/*A Sugiyama *(Jap) bt* (1) L Raymond *(US)/*S Stosur *(Aus) 1–6, 6–3, 6–2*

(2) C Black *(Zim)/*C Black *(SAf) bt* (6) A Molik *(Aus)/*M Santangelo *(Ita) 4–6, 6–4, 6–4*

MIXED DOUBLES Semi-finals

J Murray *(GB)/*J Jankovic *(Ser) bt* (11) D Nestor *(Can)/*E Likhovtseva *(Rus) 6–4, 4–6, 6–4*

(5) J Bjorkman *(Swe)/*A Molik *(Aus) bt* F Santoro *(Fra)/*S Bremond *(Fra) 6–3, 3–6, 6–3*

US Open 2007

Date: 27 August–9 September
Venue: USTA Billie Jean King National Tennis Center, Flushing Meadows-Corona Park,
New York, USA

In the ladies' singles Justine Henin easily disposed of Svetlana Kuznetsova to win her second US Open title and her seventh Grand Slam crown. Roger Federer, the world number one, won his fourth consecutive US Open, the first man to do so in the modern era. Federer's victory meant that he became the first player to win four consecutive Wimbledon singles crowns and US Open titles in the same year. It was the Swiss superstar's 12th Grand Slam title.

Tim Henman's Grand Slam swansong ended in the second round with defeat to Jo-Wilfred Tsonga, but his first round victory over Dmitry Tursenov was a vintage Henman performance and was warmly appreciated by the American crowd.

MEN'S SINGLES	WOMEN'S SINGLES
(1) Roger Federer *(Swi) bt*	*(1)* Justine Henin *(Bel) bt*
(3) Novak Djokovic *(Ser)*	Svetlana Kuznetsova *(Rus)*
7–6 (7–4), 7–6 (7–2), 6–4	6–1, 6–3

MEN'S DOUBLES
(10) Simon Aspelin *(Swe)*/Julian Knowle *(Aut) bt* Lukas Dlouhy/Pavel Vizner *(Cze)*
7–5, 6–4

WOMEN'S DOUBLES
(7) Dinara Safina *(Rus)*/Nathalie Dechy *(Fra) bt* Chan Yung-Jan/Chung Chia-Jung *(Tha)*
6–4, 6–2

MIXED DOUBLES
Victoria Azarenka/Max Mirnyi *(Blr) bt* Meghann Shaughnessy *(USA)*/Leander Paes *(Ind)*
6–4, 7–6

Trivia

* The biggest shock in the ladies' singles was the defeat of defending champion Maria Sharapova in the third round. She was beaten by Polish teenager Agnieszka Radwinska, who is ranked 32nd in the world.

* The 2007 US Open final was Novak Djokovic's first Grand Slam final. He is the first Serbian man to reach any Grand Slam final.

* Roger Federer wore blue for his matches played during the day, but for his evening matches he wore black, which he described as having the look of a tuxedo.

Tim Henman Retrospective

Timothy Henry Henman was born in Weston On The Green, Oxfordshire on 6 September 1974. Tim was once asked during an interview how he fell in love with tennis and he replied: "At five or six years old, I went to Wimbledon and that was the first time I saw Bjorn Borg play, and he was a big influence. There was definitely a moment when I was on Centre Court for the first time – I was watching Borg play his first round match and he'd won the four previous years – when I felt that this is where I wanted to be."

However, Tim first took to tennis long before he saw Borg play, by wielding a racket at his home when he was just three years old. Aged 10 he joined the David Lloyd Slater Squad, where he was coached with other promising young British tennis players. After enjoying a fairly successful junior career that saw him win the 1992 National Junior titles in singles and doubles, he turned professional in 1993. The following year the emerging Henman had squeezed into the top 200 players in the ATP rankings. He broke into the top 100 in 1995 and in 1996 he made the ATP top 30. He also won a silver medal at the Atlanta Olympic Games in 1996 with his partner Neil Broad in the men's doubles (lost to Australia's Todd Woodbridge and Mark Woodforde). In 1997 he won the first of his 11 ATP events (10 ATP Tour and 1 ATP Masters Series) after taking victory in Sydney.

Although he never won a major, Henman always seemed to keep his best form for Wimbledon, where Henmania took over, with his adoring fans taking up residence on Henman Hill during the fortnight of the tournament. In 1998 he reached the Wimbledon semi-finals for the first time and he repeated this achievement in 1999, 2001 and again in 2002. His exploits earned him the nickname Tiger Tim. In July 2002 he reached his highest ever ATP ranking and in 2003 he won his last professional singles title, the Paris Masters. A proud Englishman, Henman played for Great Britain in 52 Davis Cup rubbers with an impressive 38 wins. After struggling with injuries and form, Henman said he would retire after the Davis Cup world group play-off tie with Croatia in September 2007.

Did You Know That?
In 1995, Henman became the first player ever to be disqualified from the Wimbledon tournament. In a moment of anger he smashed a ball that struck a ball girl on the head.

FOR THE RECORD

Major Professional Singles Titles
2003: Paris Masters
2003: Washington ATP
2002: Adelaide ATP
2001: Basel ATP
2001: Copenhagen ATP
2000: Brighton ATP
2000: Vienna ATP
1998: Basel ATP
1998: Tashkent ATP
1997: Tashkent ATP
1997: Sydney ATP

Professional Doubles Titles
2004: Monte Carlo Masters (with Nenad Zimonjic)
1999: Monte Carlo Masters (with Olivier Delaitre)
1999: London International Series (with Greg Rusedski)
1997: Basel International Series (with Marc Rosset)
1995: Seoul Challenger (with Andrew Richardson)
1995: Azores Challenger (with David Saceanu)
1995: Manchester Challenger (with Mark Petchey)
1994: Bramhall Satellite (with Marius Barnard)
1993: Israel Satellite Week 3 (with Miles Maclagan)
1993: Israel Satellite Week 2 (with Miles Maclagan)
1993: Great Britain Satellite (with Wayne Arthurs)
1993: Great Britain Satellite (with Nick Brown)

Other International Tournaments 2006–07

WTA Tour Championships 2006

Venue: Madrid Arena, Madrid, Spain
Date: 7–12 November

Semi-finals	(1) Amelie Mauresmo *(FRA)*	bt	(6) Kim Clijsters *(BEL)*
	(3) Justine Henin-Hardenne *(BEL)*	bt	(2) Maria Sharapova *(RUS)*
Final	(3) Justine Henin-Hardenne *(BEL)*	bt	(1) Amelie Mauresmo *(FRA)*

DOUBLES

Semi-finals	Cara Black/	bt	(2) Zi Yan/Zheng Jie *(CHN)*
	Rennae Stubbs *(ZIM/AUS)*		
	Lisa Raymond/	bt	Kveta Peschke/Francesca
	Samantha Stosur *(USA/AUS)*		Schiavone *(CZE/ITA)*
Final	Raymond/ Stosur *(USA/AUS)*	bt	Black/Stubbs *(ZIM/AUS)*

ATP Tennis Masters Cup 2006

Venue: Qi Zhong Stadium, Shanghai, China
Date: 13–19 November

Semi-finals	(1) R Federer *(SUI)*	bt	(2) R Nadal *(ESP)*
	(8) J Blake *(USA)*	bt	(7) D Nalbandian *(ARG)*
Final	(1) R Federer *(SUI)*	bt	(8) J Blake *(USA)*

DOUBLES

Semi-finals	(3) Knowles/Nestor	bt	(4) Hanley/Ullyett
	(2) Bjorkman/Mirnyi	bt	(6) Damm/Paes
Final	(2) Bjorkman/Mirnyi	bt	(3) Knowles/Nestor

ATP Masters Series 2007

Venue: Rothenbaum Club, Hamburg, Germany
Date: 14–20 May 2007

Semi-finals	(1) Roger Federer *(Sui)*	bt	Carlos Moya *(Spa)*
	(2) Rafael Nadal *(Spa)*	bt	(16) Leyton Hewitt *(Aus)*
Final	(1) Roger Federer *(Sui)*	bt	(2) Rafael Nadal *(Spa)*

DOUBLES

Semi-finals	(1) Bryan/Bryan	bt	(6) Erlich/Ram-
	(5) Hanley/Ullyett	bt	(8) Aspelin/Knowle
Final	(1) Bryan/Bryan	bt	(5) Hanley/Ullyett

The Artois Championships 2007

Date: 11–17 June
Venue: Queen's Club, London

SINGLES
Semi-finals
(2) Andy Roddick *(USA)* 6–4, 7–5 *bt*
(7) Dmitry Tursunov *(Rus)*
Nicolas Mahut *(Fra)* 6–3, 7–6 *bt*
(14) Arnaud Clement *(Fra)*

Final
Roddick 4–6, 7–6 (9–7), 7–6 (7–2) *bt* Mahut

DOUBLES
Final
(4) Knowles/Nestor *(BAH/CAN)* 7–6
(7–4), 7–5 *bt* (1) Bryan/Bryan *(USA)*

WTA DFS Classic 2007

Date: 11–17 June
Venue: Edgbaston Priory Club,
Birmingham

SINGLES
Semi-finals
(1) Maria Sharapova *(Rus)* 7–5, 6–0 *bt*
(5) Marion Bartoli *(Fra)*
(2) Jelena Jankovic *(Ser)* 6–1, 7–5 *bt*
(8) Maria Santangelo *(Ita)*

Final
Jankovic *(Ser)* 4–6, 6–3, 7–5 *bt* Sharapova

DOUBLES
Final
Chan/Chang *(Tpe)* 7–6, 6–3 *bt*
Sun/Tu *(Chi/USA)*

Trivia

* Standing 2.08m (6ft 10in), Ivo Karlovic
is the tallest man in men's tennis history.

ATP Red Letter Days Open

Date: 18–24 June 2007
Venue: City of Nottingham Tennis Centre,
Nottingham

SINGLES
Semi-finals
Ivo Karlovic (Cro) 7–5, 6–4 *bt*
(2) Dmitry Tursunov *(Rus)*
(8) Arnaud Clement *(Fra)* 6–2, 6–4 *bt*
(4) Jonas Bjorkman *(Swe)*

Final
Karlovic 3–6, 6–4, 6–4 (8) Clement

DOUBLES
Semi-finals
(3) Murray/Butorac *(GB/USA)* 6–3, 6–2 *bt*
Del Potro/Pavel *(Arg/Rom)*
(6) Goodall/Hutchins *(GB)* 3–6, 6–3 10–7
bt (1) Erlich/Ram *(Isr)*

Final
Murray/Butorac 4–6, 6–3, 10–5 *bt*
Goodall/Hutchins

WTA Hastings Direct International Championships

Date: 18–24 June 2007
Venue: Devonshire Park, Eastbourne,
England

Semi-finals
(2) Amelie Mauresmo *(Fra)* 6–4* def *bt*
(3) Nadia Petrova *(Rus)*
(1) Justine Henin *(Bel)* 6–1, 6–3 *bt*
(8) Marion Bartoli *(Fra)*
**Petrova pulled out with injury after losing the
first set*

Final
Henin 7–5, 6–7 (4–7), 7–6 (7–2) *bt*
Mauresmo

Davis Cup 2006

This was the 95th time the tournament was played. A total of 16 teams made it to the final World Group stage. The first round matches began over the weekend of 10–12 February 2006, with the final taking place in December. Of the 16 nations, the four teams that made it through to the semi-finals were Argentina, Australia, Russia and the USA. Argentina beat Australia 5–0 and Russia beat the USA 3–2 in a tense encounter.

World Group Teams

Argentina	Chile	The Netherlands	Spain
Australia	Croatia	Romania	Sweden
Austria	France	Russia	Switzerland
Belarus	Germany	Slovakia	United States

Final

In the final, the home nation, Russia, defeated Argentina 3–2 before a delighted partisan crowd of 11,000 in Moscow's Olympic Stadium. "I'm happy to win in front of my home fans. It was really hard to win today as I experienced serious problems with the surface as I failed to adjust my playing to the carpet," said Marat Safin, after his win over Jose Acasuso in the final rubber that clinched the Davis Cup for Russia for only the second time. Russia won their first Davis Cup final in France in 2002, beating the hosts 3–2.

1–3 DECEMBER 2006, OLYMPIC STADIUM, MOSCOW, RUSSIA

Rubber 1	N Davydenko *(Rus)* 6–1, 6–2, 5–7, 6–4 J Chela *(Arg)*
Rubber 2	D Nalbandian *(Arg)* 6–4, 6–4, 6–4 M Safin *(Rus)*
Rubber 3	M Safin/D Tursonov *(Rus)* 6–2, 6–3, 6–4 A Calleri/D Nalbandian *(Arg)*
Rubber 4	D Nalbandian *(Arg)* 6–2, 6–2, 4–6, 6–4 N Davydenko *(Rus)*
Rubber 5	M Safin *(Rus)* 6–3, 3–6, 6–3, 7–6 (5) J Acasuso *(Arg)*

Davis Cup 2007

World Group

FIRST ROUND: 9–11 FEBRUARY 2007

Austria 1–4 Argentina		*(Linz)*
Belarus 2–3 Sweden		*(Minsk)*
Belgium 3–2 Australia		*(Liege)*
Chile 2–3 Russia		*(La Serena)*
Czech Republic 1–4 USA		*(Ostrava)*
France 4–1 Romania	*(Clermont-Ferrand)*
Germany 3–2 Croatia		*(Krefeld)*
Switzerland 2–3 Spain		*(Geneva)*

QUARTER-FINALS: 6–8 APRIL 2007

Belgium 2–3 Germany	*(Ostend)*
Russia 3–2 France	*(Moscow)*
Sweden 4–1 Argentina	*(Gothenburg)*
USA 4–1 Spain	*(Winston–Salem)*

SEMI-FINALS: 21–23 SEPTEMBER 2007

Russia v Germany	*(Moscow)*
Sweden v USA	*(Gothenburg)*

Fed Cup 2006

The quarter-finals saw seven European nations and the USA battle it out for the four semi-final slots. Italy, with no previous Federation Cup wins, beat France, winners in 1997, 2003 and runners-up in the last two competitions; Spain, five-times victors their last in 1998, beat Austria (no wins); USA, champions 17 times, defeated the 1992 winners Germany; and Belgium, winners in 2001, beat Russia the defending champions and winners in 2004.

In the semi-finals played in July, Italy defeated Spain 3–1 and Belgium were convincing winners over the United States, 4–1.

World Group I Teams

Austria	France	Italy	Spain
Belgium	Germany	Russia	USA

Final

Italy beat Belgium 3–2 to win their first ever Federation Cup, but not before a certain amount of drama had unfolded. For the third consecutive year the final of the Federation Cup went to the doubles rubber, and for the second successive year the doubles went to a final set. And so it came down to a final shootout between the host nation's Justine Henin-Hardenne and Kirsten Flipkens against the Italian pair of Francesca Schiavone and Roberta Vinci. The hosts had won the first set 6–3 but lost the second set 2–6. The Italians took a 2–0 lead in the third set before Henin-Hardenne was forced to retire due to a problem with her right knee after aggravating a long-standing injury during her singles victory earlier in the day over Schiavone. It was only the second time in the competition's history that the outcome was decided by injury. "I love this, I hope that Italian tennis can improve and grow up for this so everyone can enjoy it," said a delighted Schiavone. Interestingly Italy relied on all four members of their team, while Belgium only used Henin-Hardenne and Flipkens.

16–17 SEPTEMBER 2006, SPIROUDOME, CHARLEROI, BELGIUM

Rubber 1	F Schiavone *(Ita)*	6–1, 6–3	K Flipkens *(Bel)*
Rubber 2	J Henin-Hardenne *(Bel)*	6–4, 7–5	F Pennetta *(Ita)*
Rubber 3	J Henin-Hardenne *(Bel)*	6–4, 7–5	F Schiavone *(Ita)*
Rubber 4	M Santangelo *(Ita)*	6(3)–7, 6–3, 6–0	K Flipkens *(Bel)*
Rubber 5	K Flipkens/	6–3, 2–6, 0–2	F Schiavone/ R Vinci *(Ita)*
	J Henin-Hardenne *(Bel)*	*(Retired)*	

"I'm very proud of my team and it's an honour for me to be captain of this group.**"**

Corrado Barazzutti

the victorious team captain

Miscellaneous Sports 2006–07

American Football 232
Australian Rules Football 236
Badminton 238
Baseball 240
Basketball 245
Bowls 250
Cycle Racing 252
Darts 258
Equestrian Sports 260
Gaelic Football 264
Gymnastics 266
Handball 269
Hockey 270
Hurling 274

Ice Hockey 276
Motor Racing 282
Motorcycle Racing 294
Rowing 302
Sailing 306
Skating 310
Skiing 312
Winter Sports 315
Snooker 317
Squash 320
Swimming 321
Table Tennis 324
Volleyball 324
Mad Sports World 325

NFL Season 2006

MILESTONES OF THE SEASON

Running the ball, LaDainian Tomlinson of the San Diego Chargers broke the NFL record for most rushing touchdowns in a season with 31. Amazingly he outscored (186) the entire Oakland Raiders team (168). Larry Johnson of the Kansas City Chiefs set a new single-season record for rushing attempts with 416. Michael Vick of the Atlanta Falcons became the first ever NFL quarterback to rush for over 1,000 yards (1,039) during the season and also set an NFL record for highest average yards per carry in a season at 8.4.

On the passing front, on 17 December, playing against the Detroit Lions, Green Bay Packers quarterback Brett Favre set a new career record for the most pass completions. A few days later, he became the first player in NFL history to complete 5,000 passes. He ended 2006 on 414 career touchdown passes, six short of Dan Marino's NFL record of 420.

On 16 December, 46-year-old Danish-born kicker Morten Andersen of Atlanta became the NFL's all-time leading points scorer when he kicked his 2,435th point against the Dallas Cowboys. And Devin Hester of the Chicago Bears tied team-mate Nathan Vasher's record for the longest play in NFL history, returning a missed field goal, by New York Giants' Jay Feely, 108 yards for a touchdown.

Final Divisional Standings

AFC EAST	W	L	T	Pct
New England [2]	12	4	0	.750
N.Y. Jets [1]	10	6	0	.625
Buffalo	7	9	0	.438
Miami	6	10	0	.375

NFC EAST	W	L	T	Pct
Philadelphia [2]	10	6	0	.625
Dallas [1]	9	7	0	.562
N.Y. Giants [1]	8	8	0	.500
Washington	5	11	0	.312

AFC NORTH	W	L	T	Pct
Baltimore [2,3]	13	3	0	.812
Cincinnati	8	8	0	.500
Pittsburgh	8	8	0	.500
Cleveland	4	12	0	.250

NFC NORTH	W	L	T	Pct
Chicago [4,2,3]	13	3	0	.812
Green Bay	8	8	0	.500
Minnesota	6	10	0	.375
Detroit	3	13	0	.188

AFC SOUTH	W	L	T	Pct
Indianapolis [2]	12	4	0	.750
Tennessee	8	8	0	.500
Jacksonville	8	8	0	.500
Houston	6	10	0	.375

NFC SOUTH	W	L	T	Pct
New Orleans [2,3]	10	6	0	.625
Carolina	8	8	0	.500
Atlanta	7	9	0	.438
Tampa Bay	4	12	0	.250

AFC WEST	W	L	T	Pct
San Diego [4,2,3]	14	2	0	.875
Kansas City [1]	9	7	0	.562
Denver	9	7	0	.562
Oakland	2	14	0	.125

NFC WEST	W	L	T	Pct
Seattle [2]	9	7	0	.562
St. Louis	8	8	0	.500
San Francisco	7	9	0	.438
Arizona	5	11	0	.312

[1]clinched play-off berth; [2]clinched division title; [3]clinched first round bye; [4]clinched home field advantage

NFL Play-offs

Play-off Seedings

Seed	AFC	(Record)	Seed	NFC	(Record)
1.	San Diego Chargers	(14–2)	1.	Chicago Bears	(13–3)
2.	Baltimore Ravens	(13–3)	2.	New Orleans Saints	(10–6)
3.	Indianapolis Colts	(12–4)	3.	Philadelphia Eagles	(10–6)
4.	New England Patriots	(12–4)	4.	Seattle Seahawks	(9–7)
5.	New York Jets	(10–6)	5.	Dallas Cowboys	(9–7)
6.	Kansas City Chiefs	(9–7)	6.	New York Giants	(8–8)

American Football Conference National Football Conference

WILD-CARD PLAY-OFFS (6 & 7 JANUARY)

Indianapolis 23–8 Kansas City | Seattle 21–20 Dallas
New England 37–16 NY Jets | Philadelphia 23–20 NY Giants

DIVISIONAL PLAY-OFFS (13 & 14 JANUARY)

Indianapolis 15–6 **Baltimore** | New Orleans 27–24 Philadelphia
New England 24–21 **San Diego** | Chicago 27–24 Seattle (OT)

CHAMPIONSHIP GAMES (21 JANUARY)

Indianapolis 38–34 New England | Chicago 39–14 New Orleans

Neither the Kansas City Chiefs nor the New York Jets could do much from stopping the Indianapolis Colts or New England Patriots on the road in the AFC wild card games. But it was a different story in the NFC. The Philadelphia Eagles held off the New York Giants by a field goal at the Linc, but the real drama had come 24 hours earlier at Qwest Field. Trailing by one point, with seconds left on the clock, the Dallas Cowboys lined up a 22-yard chip-shot field-goal to win the game. However, the goal snap was fumbled by quarterback Tony Romo, who nonetheless had the presence of mind to pick up the ball and run for the end zone, where victory beckoned. He was tackled, however, a yard short of the goal-line and, more agonisingly, a foot short of a first down.

In the Divisional Play-offs, the surprises came in the AFC, as both top seeds fell at home. Indianapolis beat the Baltimore Ravens by five field goals to two, while New England sneaked by the San Diego Padres by three points, continuing coach Marty Schottenheimer's desperate play-off record (5–11). Chicago saw off Seattle at Soldier Field, but the Bears needed Robbie Gould's overtime field goal to win. In New Orleans, the feel-good story of 2006 continued with the Saints downing the Eagles 27–24.

Chicago powered their way to Super Bowl XLI on the back of 196 yards of rushing and three touchdowns in their 39–14 NFC Championship Game victory over the Saints. In the AFC, the Colts, given a surprise second home game of the play-offs, finally made it past the New England Patriots to reach the Super Bowl, coming back from 18 points down to win 38–34, their 32 second-half points being a championship game record.

Super Bowl XLI   4 FEBRUARY 2007, DOLPHIN STADIUM, MIAMI, FLA.

	1	2	3	4	
Indianapolis Colts	6	10	6	7	29
Chicago Bears	14	0	3	0	17

The game got off to a dramatic start when Chicago's Devin Hester returned the Colts' opening kick-off 92 yards for a touchdown, the first opening kick-off return for a TD in Super Bowl history. Robbie Gould kicked the extra point. In treacherous conditions with the rain falling relentlessly, another first for the Super Bowl, the first half was notable for a succession of errors, with four fumbles coming in the first quarter alone, a Super Bowl record, and two more before half-time.

But the Colts' star quarterback Peyton Manning brought them back into the game when he found receiver Reggie Wayne wide open with a lofted 53-yard touchdown pass. However, holder Hunter Smith fumbled the wet ball and was unable to place it for kicker Adam Vinatieri to kick the point after. Two minutes before the end of the first quarter the Bears took an eight-point lead when Rex Grossman threw a four-yard touchdown pass to Muhsin Muhammad. Indianapolis scored all of the next 16 points, through three field goals from Vinatieri and Dominick Rhodes' one-yard touchdown run. After three quarters, the Colts led 22–17, Gould having kicked a field goal for the Bears.

Early in the fourth quarter, Grossman, who had been either very good or really bad throughout the season, threw a pass towards Muhammad which Kelvin Hayden intercepted and returned 56 yards for a touchdown. Vinatieri kicked the extra point to give the Colts a 12-point lead they were never going to relinquish, especially when Chicago's next possession ended with Sanders picking off another Grossman pass. The Colts ran the clock down for their first Super Bowl victory for 36 years and their first since leaving Baltimore in 1984.

Team statistics	Indianapolis	Chicago
Total Net yardage/ave per play:	430 yards, 80 plays, 5.4 ave	265 yards, 47 plays, 5.6 ave
Net Passing:	25 of 38, 239 yards, 1 TD, 1 int	20 of 28, 154 yards, 1 TD, 2 int
Total Receiving:	248 yards, 1 TD	165 yards, 1 TD
Total Rushing:	42 attempts, 191 yards. 1 TD	19 attempts, 119 yards
Fumbles/lost:	2/2	4/3
Punting:	4 for 162 yards, 40.5 ave	5 for 227 yards, 45.2 ave
Kick-off returns:	4 for 89 yards	6 for 138 yards, 1 TD
Punt returns:	3 for 42 yds	1 for 3 yards
Interceptions/returns:	2 for 94 yds, 1 TD	1 for 6 yards
Fumble recoveries:	3	3
First Downs:	24, 12 rush, 11 pass, 1 pen	11, 3 rush 8 pass, 0 pen
Third Down Conversion:	8/18, 44%	3/10, 30%
Fourth Down Conversion:	0/1, 0%	0/1, 0%
Penalties:	6 for 40 yards	4 for 35 yards
Time of possession:	38:04	21:56

SCORING SEQUENCE

First Quarter

CHI – Devin Hester 92 kickoff return *(Robbie Gould kick)*, 14:46 remaining.

IND – Reggie Wayne 53 pass from Peyton Manning *(run failed)*, 6:50. Drive: 9 plays, 80 yards, 4:30.

CHI – Muhsin Muhammad 4 pass from Rex Grossman *(Gould kick)*, 4:34. Drive: 4 plays, 57 yards, 2:00.

Second Quarter

IND – FG Adam Vinatieri 29, 11:17. Drive: Eight plays, 47 yards, 4:52.

IND – Dominick Rhodes 1 run *(Adam Vinatieri kick)*, 6:09. Drive: 7 plays, 58 yards, 3:08.

Third Quarter

IND – FG Vinatieri 24, 7:26. Drive: 13 plays, 56 yards, 7:34.

IND – FG Vinatieri 20, 3:16. Drive: Six plays, 62 yards, 2:07.

CHI – FG Gould 44, 1:14. Drive: Six plays, 14 yards, 2:02.

Fourth Quarter

IND – Kelvin Hayden 56 interception return *(Vinatieri kick)*, 11:44.

"When you turn the ball over as much as we did, it's really hard to win"
Lovie Smith, head coach of the Chicago Bears (the Bears had five turnovers)

Trivia

* Super Bowl XLI was the ninth Super Bowl played in the Miami area and the fourth at Dolphins Stadium; the other five Miami Super Bowls were at the Orange Bowl. New Orleans has also hosted nine Super Bowls.

* The Vince Lombardi Trophy cost $25,000 to make and was made by Tiffany & Co. of New York.

* The NFL pays for up to 150 rings at $5,000 per ring (plus adjustments for increases in gold and diamonds) for the Super Bowl winners. The League also pays for 150 pieces of jewellery for the losing team, but these must not cost more than half of the Super Bowl ring.

* In 2006, Super Bowl XL generated a total economic impact of $261 million for the host city Detroit, according to a study commissioned by Detroit Metro Convention & Visitors Bureau.

* For the 2006 NFL season the official game ball was renamed "The Duke" for the first time since 1969 in honour of the late Wellington Mara, whose family owns the New York Giants. The NFL first used "The Duke" ball in honour of Mara in 1941 after George Halas, owner of the Chicago Bears, and Tim Mara signed a contract with Wilson Sporting Goods to become the NFL's official supplier of game balls, a relationship that continues into its 66th year in 2007.

"How about that? I came down to Miami to play in the soaking rain. You wouldn't expect it. We just kept doing our jobs."
Peyton Manning, Super Bowl MVP

"All season long we have prided ourselves on our defence, but we didn't make plays. We needed to do a better job of tackling."
Brian Urlacher, Chicago Bears LB

Australian Rules Football

Toyota AFL Premiership 2006

The season ran from 30 March to 2 September over 22 rounds, with the top eight teams advancing to play-off (a review of the 2006 play-offs is opposite). The Geelong Cats, predicted to finish as low as 14th by some preseason pundits, dominated the competition and were crowned Minor Premiers as well as easy favourites to end a 44-year wait for the AFL flag. Port Adelaide Power enjoyed a great season, taking second spot on points average ahead of 2006 champions West Coast Eagles. Richmond Tigers collected just three wins to finish with the wooden spoon, two points behind the Carlton Blues. St Kilda had a winning record but missed the play-offs by two points, finishing ninth, behind the Adelaide Crows, with Sydney two points further ahead. Had the Saints beaten the Swans in round 19, they probably would have denied the 2005 champions and 2006 Grand Finalists a play-off berth. Three other Victorian teams were fourth, fifth and sixth, respectively the Kangaroos, Hawks and Magpies.

Team	P	W	D	L	PF	PA	P%	Pts
1. Geelong Cats	22	18	0	4	2542	1664	152.7	72
2. Port Adelaide Power	22	15	0	7	2314	2038	113.5	60
3. West Coast Eagles	22	15	0	7	2162	1935	111.1	60
4. North Melbourne Kangaroos	22	14	0	8	2183	1998	109.2	56
5. Hawthorn Hawks	22	13	0	9	2097	1855	113.0	52
6. Collingwood Magpies	22	13	0	9	2011	1992	100.9	52
7. Sydney Swans	22	12	1	9	2031	1698	119.6	50
8. Adelaide Crows	22	12	0	10	1881	1712	109.8	48
9. St Kilda Saints	22	11	1	10	1874	1941	96.5	46
10. Brisbane Lions	22	9	2	11	1986	1885	105.3	40
11. Fremantle Dockers	22	10	0	12	2254	2198	102.5	40
12. Essendon Bombers	22	10	0	12	2184	2394	91.3	40
13. Western Bulldogs	22	9	1	12	2111	2469	85.5	38
14. Melbourne Demons	22	5	0	17	1890	2418	78.1	20
15. Carlton Blues	22	4	0	18	2167	2911	74.4	16
16. Richmond Tigers	22	3	1	18	1958	2537	77.1	14

Trivia

* Australian rules football was founded in 1857 by Tom Wills, H.C.A. Harrison, W. J. Hammersley and J. B. Thompson, with the sport's first ever game taking place on 7 August 1858 between Scotch College and Melbourne Grammar School.

* An ARL exhibition game between Geelong and Port Adelaide was played at The Brit Oval on 15 October 2006. More than 12,500 fans saw the Cats beat the Storm 13.10 (88) to 10.6 (67). No game is scheduled in 2007 but it is hoped the series will resume in 2008.

Toyota AFL Finals Series 2006

Victorian interest ended at the the semi-final stage as the Melbourne Demons lost to the Fremantle Dockers by 28 points, while the West Coast Eagles crushed Western Suburbs. Suburbs were held to five goals and nine behinds (39 points), while the Eagles amassed 16 goals and 17 behinds (113 points), a winning margin of 74 points. The Eagles saw off the Adelaide Crows in the Preliminary Finals to face defending champions, the Sydney Swans, who had ended the Dockers' season a day earlier, thus setting up a repeat of the 2005 Grand Final. It was a thrilling match. A crowd of 97,431 watched the Eagles take a 26-point lead at half-time, but the Swans had closed to within a point when the final hooter sounded – the fifth Grand Final to be decided by the minimum margin.

ELIMINATION FINALS

Home team	Score	Away team	Score	Venue	Attendance	Date
St Kilda Saints	10.12 (72)	Melbourne Demons	13.12 (90)	MCG	67,528	8/9/07
Adelaide Crows	10.16 (76)	Fremantle Dockers	7.4 (46)	AAMI Stadium	42,208	9/9/07
West Coast Eagles	12.12 (84)	Sydney Swans	13.7 (85)	Subiaco Oval	43,116	9/9/07
Collingwood Magpies	11.14 (80)	Western Bulldogs	18.13 (121)	MCG	84,284	10/9/07

SEMI-FINALS

Home team	Score	Away team	Score	Venue	Attendance	Date
West Coast Eagles	16.17 (113)	Western Bulldogs	5.9 (39)	Subiaco Oval	43,219	16/9/07
Fremantle Dockers	14.18 (102)	Melbourne Demons	11.8 (74)	Subiaco Oval	42,505	15/9/07

PRELIMINARY FINALS

Home team	Score	Away team	Score	Venue	Attendance	Date
Sydney Swans	19.13 (127)	Fremantle Dockers	14.8 (92)	Telstra Stadium	61,373	22/9/07
Adelaide Crows	11.9 (75)	West Coast Eagles	11.19 (85)	AAMI Stadium	50,514	23/9/07

AFL GRAND FINAL

Team 1	Score	Team 2	Score	Venue	Attendance	Date
Sydney Swans	12.12 (84)	West Coast Eagles	12.13 (85)	MCG	97,431	30/9/07

Badminton

Once again China completely dominated the World Badminton Championships winning four of the five gold medals and ten of the 20 medals on offer. The world number one, Lin Dan, defeated compatriot Bao Chunlai to claim the Men's Singles title after losing the 2005 final. Xie Xingfang, Lin Dan's girlfriend, captured the Women's Singles gold defeating Zhang Ning, also from China, in the final. China's Fu Haifeng and Cai Yun defeated the British pair of Robert Blair and Anthony Clark in the Men's Doubles while an all-China Women's Doubles final saw Gao Ling and Huang Sui overcome Zhang Yawen and Wei Yili. The Mixed Doubles final was an all-British affair, with Nathan Robertson and Gail Emms beating Anthony Clark and Donna Kellogg.

IBF World Championships 2006

18–24 SEPTEMBER 2006, PALACIO DE DEPORTES, MADRID, SPAIN

Event	Gold	Silver	Bronze
Men's Singles	Lin Dan *(Chi)*	Bao Chunlai *(Chi)*	Chen Hong *(Chi)* Lee Hyun-il *(Kor)*
Women's Singles	Xie Xingfang *(Chi)*	Zhang Ning *(Chi)*	Xu Huaiwen *(Ger)* Petra Overzier *(Ger)*
Men's Doubles	Fu Haifeng/ Cai Yun *(Chi)*	Anthony Clark/ Robert Blair *(Eng)*	Jens Eriksen/Martin Lundgaard Hansen *(Den)* Lars Paaske/Jonas Rasmussen *(Den)*
Women's Doubles	Gao Ling/ Huang Sui *(Chi)*	Zhang Yawen/ Wei Yili *(Chi)*	Yang Wei/ Zhang Jiewen *(Chi)* Du Jing/Yu Yang *(Chi)*
Mixed Doubles	Nathan Robertson/ Gail Emms *(Eng)*	Anthony Clark/ Donna Kellogg *(Eng)*	Kien Keat Koo/ Pei Tty Wong *(Mly)* Sudket Prapakamol/ Saralee Thoungthongkam *(Th)*

Medal Table

Pos	Country	G	S	B	Total		Pos	Country	G	S	B	Total
1.	**China**	4	3	3	10		5.	South Korea	0	0	1	1
2.	England	1	2	0	3			Malaysia	0	0	1	1
3.	Germany	0	0	2	2			Thailand	0	0	1	1
	Denmark	0	0	2	2							

BWF World Championships 2007

These were the 16th BWF World Championships. Although Thailand did not participate – Bangkok hosted the World Student Games around the same time – 55 nations were represented. Great Britain's Gail Emms and Nathan Robertson, the world mixed doubles champions, lost to Indonesia's Flandy Limpele and Vita Marissa in the quarter-finals, 13–21, 16–21, while Anthony Clark and Donna Kellogg also went out, 13–21, 10–21 to Xie Zhongbo and Zhang Yawen. China's Lin Dan won the men's singles title to become only the second player after Yang Yang to retain his title. Zhu Lin (China) won her first World Championship singles crown.

13–19 AUGUST 2007, NATIONAL SPORTS COMPLEX, KUALA LUMPAR, MALAYSIA

Men's Singles
(1) Lin Dan *(Chn) bt* S. Dwi Kuncoro *(Ina)*
21–11, 22–20

Women's Singles
(5) Zhu Lin *(Chn) bt* Wang Chen *(Hkg)*
21–8, 21–12

Men's Doubles
(3) Markis Kido/Hendra Setiawan *(Ina)*
*bt (13)*Jung Jae Sung/Lee Yong Dae *(Kor)*
21–19, 21–19

Women's Doubles
(3) Yang Wei/Zhang Jiewen *(Chn) bt*
Gao Ling/Huang Sui *(Chn)*
21–16, 21–19

Mixed Doubles
(2) Nova Widianto/Lilyana Natsir *(Ina) bt*
(2) Zheng Bo/Gao Ling *(Chn)*
21–16, 21–14

All England Open Championships 2007

The competition almost witnessed a Chinese whitewash as the 2008 Olympic Game hosts won the men's singles, women's singles, women's doubles and the mixed doubles. Only the pairing of Koo Kien Keat and Tan Boon Heong from Malaysia in the men's doubles final could wrestle one of the titles away from the dominant Chinese players.

6–11 MARCH, NATIONAL INDOOR ARENA, BIRMINGHAM

Men's Singles
Lin Dan *(Chi) bt* Chen Yu *(Chi)*
21–13, 21–12

Women's Singles
Xie Xingfang *(Chi) bt* Pi Hongyan *(Fra)*
21–6, 21–13

Men's Doubles
Koo Kien Keat/Tan Boon Heong *(Mly) bt*
Cai Yun/Fu Haifeng *(Chi)*
21–15, 21–18

Women's Doubles
Wei Yili/Zhang Yawen *(Chi) bt*
Yang Wei/Zhang Jiewen *(Chi)*
21–16, 8–21, 24–22

Mixed Doubles
Zheng Bo/Gao Ling *(Chi) bt*
Anthony Clark/Donna Kellogg *(Eng)*
16–21, 21–18, 21–14

Baseball World Series 2006

The 2006 World Series, the 102nd edition of the Fall Classic, matched the American League champion Detroit Tigers and National League champion St Louis Cardinals. This was the third World Series meeting between these two famous franchises (St Louis had won in 1934, Detroit in 1968), and neither had been expected to go far in the 2006 postseason after poor finishes to the regular season. Here is how this, in truth sloppy, series played out.

Date	Winner		Home field
21 Oct	Cardinals	7–2	Detroit
22 Oct	Tigers	3–1	Detroit
24 Oct	Cardinals	5–0	St Louis
26 Oct	Cardinals	5–4	St Louis
27 Oct	Cardinals	4–2	St Louis

"We've got ourselves a championship."
*St Louis Cardinals 2006 World Series MVP **David Eckstein** talking to the home crowd after game 5*

Game 1

ST LOUIS CARDINALS 7   DETROIT TIGERS 2
21 OCTOBER, COMERICA PARK, DETROIT ATT: 42,479

The Tigers hosted their first World Series game in 22 years and home fans expected rookie pitcher, Justin Verlander, to make short work of St Louis, who were still recovering from a seven-game National League championship series that had ended two days earlier. But it was the Cardinals' rookie pitcher, Anthony Reyes, who stole the show. The most inexperienced pitcher ever to start a World Series opener gave up two runs in eight innings as St Louis won 7–2.

	1	2	3	4	5	6	7	8	9	–	R	H	E
St Louis	0	1	3	0	0	3	0	0	0	–	7	8	2
Detroit	1	0	0	0	0	0	0	0	1	–	2	4	3

W: Anthony Reyes *(1–0)*; L: Justin Verlander *(0–1)*
HR: *St L* – Scott Rolen *(1)*, Albert Pujols *(1)*; *Det* – Craig Monroe *(1)*

Game 2

ST LOUIS CARDINALS 1   DETROIT TIGERS 3
22 OCTOBER, COMERICA PARK, DETROIT ATT: 42,533

The Cards' Jeff Weaver returned to Detroit, where he made his Major League debut in 1999. But he failed to sparkle on a cold night, giving up three runs on nine hits in five innings. Craig Monroe of the Tigers became the fifth player to hit a home run in each of his first two World Series games, while Kenny Rogers threw eight scoreless innings giving up just two hits.

	1	2	3	4	5	6	7	8	9	–	R	H	E
St Louis	0	0	0	0	0	0	0	0	1	–	1	4	1
Detroit	2	0	0	0	1	0	0	0	0	–	3	10	1

W: Kenny Rogers *(1–0)*; L: Jeff Weaver *(0–1)*. S: Doug Jones (1)
HR: *Det* – Craig Monroe *(2)*

Game 3

DETROIT TIGERS 0   ST LOUIS CARDINALS 5

24 OCTOBER, BUSCH STADIUM, ST LOUIS ATT: 46,513

The Detroit Tigers did not resemble the team that sailed into the World Series on the back of superb pitching, solid defence and key runs scored by their entire line-up. Chris Carpenter, in his first World Series start, pitched eight innings, giving up three hits and no walks, while striking out six; he threw only 82 pitches. Jim Edmonds hit a two-run double.

	1	2	3	4	5	6	7	8	9	–	R	H	E
Detroit	0	0	0	0	0	0	0	0	0	–	0	3	1
St Louis	0	0	0	2	0	0	0	2	1	–	5	7	0

W: Chris Carpenter *(1–0)*; L: Nate Robertson *(0–1)*
HR: none

Game 4

DETROIT TIGERS 4   ST LOUIS CARDINALS 5

26 OCTOBER, BUSCH STADIUM, ST LOUIS ATT: 46,470

Leading 3–2 in the seventh inning, Detroit reliever Fernando Rodney picked up a sacrifice bunt in front of the mound, turned and overthrew first base, allowing David Eckstein to score. The Cards then made it 4–3, and although the visitors scored in the top of the eighth inning to level the game at 4–4, the Cardinals scored in the bottom of the eighth to win 5–4.

	1	2	3	4	5	6	7	8	9	–	R	H	E
Detroit	0	1	2	0	0	0	0	1	0	–	4	10	1
St Louis	0	0	1	1	0	0	2	1	X	–	5	9	0

W: Adam Wainwright *(1–0)*; L: Joel Zumaya *(0–1)*.
HR: *Det* – Sean Casey *(1)*

Game 5

DETROIT TIGERS 2   ST LOUIS CARDINALS 4

26 OCTOBER, BUSCH STADIUM, ST LOUIS ATT: 46,638

On a rainy and overcast St Louis day, the Cardinals beat the Tigers 4–2 to clinch the 2006 World Series. In the top of the ninth inning, Detroit's Brandon Inge swung at Adam Wainwright's 0–2 pitch and missed to send the home crowd into a wild frenzy. It was the Cardinals' first World Series victory since 1982, their tenth in all, and the first to end on a strikeout since the Los Angeles Dodgers defeated the Oakland Athletics 4–1 in 1988.

	1	2	3	4	5	6	7	8	9	–	R	H	E
Detroit	0	0	0	2	0	0	0	0	0	–	2	5	2
St Louis	0	1	0	2	0	0	1	0	X	–	4	8	1

W: Jeff Weaver *(1–1)*, L: Justin Verlander *(0–2)*. S: Wainwright (1)
HR: *Det* – Sean Casey *(2)*

Major League Baseball Season 2007

On 31 March 2007, the annual exhibition game, the Civil Rights Game, was played between the reigning world champions, the St Louis Cardinals, and the Cleveland Indians at AutoZone Park, Memphis, Tennessee. Both teams wore uniforms reminiscent of those worn by teams playing in the Negro League, with the Cards winning 5–1. This special game was played to celebrate the history of civil rights in the USA and marked the end of the 2007 pre-season. The 2007 season began the next day, 1 April, and the first game of the season brought up a rematch of the 2006 National League Championship Series game between the New York Mets and the eventual World Series champions, St Louis Cardinals. However, the defending world champions went down 1–6 at home in their Busch Stadium, no April Fool's Day joke for fans of the Cards. The 2007 Major League Baseball (MLB) season is the 104th since the American and National Leagues decided to amalgamate in 1903 to create the MLB.

MLB TABLES *(to 4 August 2007)*

American League

Eastern Division	W	L	PCT	GB
Boston Red Sox	67	43	.609	–
NY Yankees	60	50	.545	7
Toronto Blue Jays	55	54	.505	11.5
Baltimore Orioles	51	58	.468	15.5
Tampa Bay Devil Rays	42	67	.385	24.5

Central Division	W	L	PCT	GB
Cleveland Indians	62	48	.564	–
Detroit Tigers	61	48	.560	.5
Minnesota Twins	56	53	.514	5.5
Chicago White Sox	51	59	.464	11
Kansas City Royals	48	61	.440	13.5

Western Division	W	L	PCT	GB
LA Angels	63	46	.578	–
Seattle Mariners	60	48	.556	2.5
Oakland Athletics	53	58	.477	11
Texas Rangers	48	62	.436	15.5

National League

Eastern Division	W	L	PCT	GB
NY Mets	62	48	.564	–
Atlanta Braves	58	53	.523	4.5
Philadelphia Phillies	57	53	.518	5
Florida Marlins	51	60	.459	11.5
Washington Nationals	50	60	.455	12

Central Division	W	L	PCT	GB
Milwaukee Brewers	60	51	.54	–
Chicago Cubs	58	51.	.532	1
St Louis Cardinals	50	57	.467	8
Houston Astros	48	62	.436	11.5
Cincinatti Reds	47	64	.423	13
Pittsburgh Pirates	44	64	.407	14.5

Western Division	W	L	PCT	GB
Arizona Diamondbacks	62	50	.554	–
San Diego Padres	59	50	.541	1.5
LA Dodgers	58	52	.527	3
Colorado Rockies	56	53	.514	4.5
San Francisco Giants	47	61	.435	13

Major Events

1 April – The 2007 MLB season begins. The Chicago Cubs decided to print players' names on the back of their home jerseys (as did the Los Angeles Dodgers), while a number of teams changed the colour of their jerseys including the Arizona Diamondbacks and Cincinnati Reds.

14 April – The San Francisco Giants' Barry Bonds hit two home runs to move to within 18 of homers all-time leader Hank Aaron as the Giants beat the Pittsburgh Pirates 8–5.

15 April – MLB celebrated the 60th anniversary of Jackie Robinson making his debut for the Brooklyn Dodgers at Ebbets Field, Brooklyn. Robinson was the first player to break the colour barrier in the MLB's 44-year history. The entire rosters of the Los Angeles Dodgers, St. Louis Cardinals and Milwaukee Brewers wore number 42 in Robinson's honour. All jerseys worn during the games were then auctioned, with the entire proceeds donated to the Jackie Robinson Foundation, which awards scholarships to African-American high school graduates to further their academic careers at college.

18 April – Mark Buehrle of the Chicago White Sox shut down the Texas Rangers pitching the entire game without allowing a single legal hit at US Cellular Field, Chicago.

20 April – The Boston Red Sox wore their green St Patrick's Day uniform against the New York Yankees in tribute to the Boston Celtics' former coach and president Red Auerbach who died on 28 October 2006.

22 April – Manny Ramirez, J. D. Drew, Mike Lowell and Jason Varitek smacked four consecutive home runs for the Boston Red Sox against the New York Yankees at Fenway Park, Boston. It was the fifth time in MLB history that this feat had been accomplished.

23 April – The Pittsburgh Pirates and Houston Astros, a game originally scheduled for 15 April but which was cancelled due to heavy rain, honoured Robinson with the players all wearing number 42.

27 April – The Pittsburgh Pirates players all wore the number 42 jersey in honour of Jackie Robinson in their game against the Cincinnati Reds.

28 April – Kirk Radomski, aged 37, a former New York Mets employee, pleaded guilty to distributing banned drugs to dozens of baseball players. He worked for the Mets from 1985–95 as their equipment manager and clubhouse assistant.

29 April – The Colorado Rockies' rookie shortstop Troy Tulowitzki claimed a rare unassisted triple play during the Rockies' 11–7 win over the Atlanta Braves. It was only the 13th time in MLB history that a player managed the feat, first catching a line drive by Chipper Jones, then stepped on to second base to claim Kelly Johnson and tagged Edgar Renteria as he ran between first and second in the seventh inning.

24 May – The Atlanta Braves pitcher John Smoltz won his 200th game against the New York Mets at Turner Field, Atlanta.

31 May – The Toronto Blue Jays' pitcher Roy Halladay won his 100th game against the Chicago White Sox at Rogers Centre, Toronto.

3 June – The Chicago Cubs won their 10,000th game against the Atlanta Braves at Wrigley Field, Chicago, becoming only the second team in MLB history to reach this landmark, after the New York / San Francisco Giants. However, it includes 77 wins in the National Association (1871, 1874 and 1875) that are not regarded as official wins by MLB.

4 June – The seven-time Cy Young Award winner Roger Clemens' return to the New York Yankees line-up was postponed due to injury. The 44-year-old veteran pitcher agreed a $28m deal for the rest of the season at the end of May 2007.

6 June – The San Diego Padres' Trevor Hoffman became the first pitcher to record 500 saves when he finished off a game against the LA Dodgers at Petco Park, San Diego.

10 June – The Chicago White Sox pitcher Mark Buehrle won his 100th game against the Houston Astros at US Cellular Field, Chicago.

12 June – The Detroit Tigers' Justin Verlander, the 2006 Rookie of the Year, pitched the second no-hitter of the season, the first of his career, to help the Tigers to a 4–0 win over the Milwaukee Brewers at Comerica Park, Detroit.

20 June – The Texas Rangers' Sammy Sosa smacked his 600th career home run against the Chicago Cubs at Rangers Ballpark, Arlington, Texas, to become only the fifth player in MLB history to achieve the feat. The 38-year-old claimed the landmark homer in the fifth inning of the 7–3 victory over his former club.

27 June – The Philadelphia Phillies' Ryan Howard smacked his 100th career homer against the Cincinnati Reds at Citizens Bank Park, Philadelphia. He managed the feat in only his 325th game (60 games faster than Ralph Kiner), thereby becoming the fastest player in MLB history to reach the landmark.

28 June – The Toronto Blue Jays' Frank Thomas hit his 500th career homer against the Minnesota Twins at the Hubert H. Humphrey Metrodome, Minneapolis, Minnesota.

28 June – The Houston Astros' Craig Biggio scored his 3,000th career hit against the Colorado Rockies at Minute Maid Park, Houston, to become the 27th member of the 3000 Hit Club. He is one of just nine players to record all 3,000 hits with the same team.

2 July – New York Yankees' pitcher Roger Clemens became the eighth player in MLB history to win 350 career games, beating the Minnesota Twins at Yankee Stadium.

10 July – Ichiro Suzuki, the Seattle Mariners' centre-fielder, hit the first ever inside-the-park home run in All-Star Game history. Ichiro helped the American League to a 5–4 win over the National League at AT&T Park, San Francisco. It was the American League's tenth consecutive win (excluding the 2002 tied game) while their 11 successive All-Star Game unbeaten run equalled the National League's record (1972–1982).

15 July – The Philadelphia Phillies suffered their 10,000th defeat, 10–2 to the St Louis Cardinals at Citizens Bank Park, Philadelphia. The Phillies claimed the unwanted tag of becoming the first team in the four major US sports to lose 10,000 games.

4 August – Alex Rodriguez of the New York Yankees, at 32 years and 8 days, became the youngest player in MLB history to hit 500 home runs (a record achieved in the game against the Kansas City Royals at Yankee Stadium).

4 August – Barry Bonds tied Henry Aaron's Major League baseball record when he hit the 755th home run of his career against the San Diego Padres at Petco Park.

22 August – The Baltimore Orioles allowed the most runs in American League history and second-biggest Major League total ever when being crushed 30–3 by the Texas Rangers at Oriole Park. The largest ever score came on 29 June 1897, when the Chicago Colts scored 36 against the Louisville Colonels.

Trivia

* Barry Bonds hit his 756th homer on 7 August to pass Hank Aaron as the all-time leader for home runs. Bonds hit the landmark bomb before home fans from a pitch from Mike Bacsik of the Washington Nationals. However, his achievement will forever be tainted with claims that he has used steroids despite the fact that the slugger has never tested positive for drug use. Aaron was not there to witness his record being broken but, ever the gentleman, he sent a taped message of congratulations. In 1974 Bacsik's father, also Mike, had pitched to Aaron when he was on 755 homers, but Aaron didn't launch one off him.

Basketball

NBA Regular Season 2006–07

EASTERN CONFERENCE

	W	L	Pct	GB
Atlantic Division				
Toronto Raptors [3]	47	35	0.573	--
New Jersey Nets [6]	41	41	0.500	6
Philadelphia 76ers	35	47	0.427	12
New York Knicks	33	49	0.402	14
Boston Celtics	24	58	0.293	23
Central Division				
Detroit Pistons [1]	53	29	0.646	--
Cleveland Cavaliers [2]	50	32	0.610	3
Chicago Bulls [5]	49	33	0.598	4
Indiana Pacers	35	47	0.427	18
Milwaukee Bucks	28	54	0.341	25
Southeast Division				
Miami Heat [4]	44	38	0.537	0
Washington Wizards [7]	41	41	0.500	3
Orlando Magic [8]	40	42	0.488	4
Charlotte Bobcats	33	49	0.402	11
Atlanta Hawks	30	52	0.366	14

WESTERN CONFERENCE

	W	L	Pct	GB
Northwest Division				
Utah Jazz [4]	51	31	0.622	--
Denver Nuggets [6]	45	37	0.549	6
Minnesota T'Wolves	32	49	0.390	18½
Portland Trail Blazers	32	50	0.390	19
Seattle Super Sonics	31	51	0.378	20
Pacific Division				
Phoenix Suns [2]	61	21	0.744	--
LA Lakers [7]	42	40	0.512	19
Golden St. Warriors [8]	42	40	0.512	19
LA Clippers	40	42	0.488	21
Sacramento Kings	32	49	0.390	28½
Southeast Division				
Dallas Mavericks [1]	67	15	0.817	--
San Antonio Spurs [3]	58	24	0.707	9
Houston Rockets [5]	52	30	0.634	15
New Orleans	39	43	0.476	28
Memphis	22	60	0.268	45

Sacramento vs Minnesota was not played. All other teams played 82-game season.

Team's seeding position in the playoffs. The higher seed always has home court advantage in the last game of a series.

NBA Play-offs

EASTERN CONFERENCE
First Round
Detroit Pistons 4–0 Orlando Magic
Cleveland Cavs 4–0 Washington Wizards
Toronto Raptors 2–4 New Jersey Nets
Miami Heat 4–0 Chicago Bulls

Second Round
Detroit Pistons 4–2 Chicago Bulls
Cleveland Cavaliers 4–2 New Jersey Nets

Conference Final
Detroit Pistons 2–4 Cleveland Cavaliers

WESTERN CONFERENCE
First Round
Dallas Mavericks 2–4 Golden St. Warriors
Phoenix Suns 4–1 Los Angeles Lakers
San Antonio Spurs 4–1 Denver Nuggets
Utah Jazz 4–3 Houston Rockets

Second Round
San Antonio Spurs 4–2 Phoenix Suns
Utah Jazz 4–1 Golden State Warriors

Conference Final
San Antonio Spurs 4–1 Utah Jazz

NBA Play-off review

The 2006–07 season Eastern Conference final was a rematch of last season's second round series between the number one ranked Detroit Pistons and number two Cleveland, and it was the latter who triumphed, coming from two games down to win 4–2. The teams were so evenly matched that the first five games were decided by six points or less, with Game 5 going into double overtime. The Cavaliers closed out the series in Game 6 to clinch the franchise's first ever trip to the NBA finals. The 2006–07 NBA season was the first since 1990 that neither the number one or number two ranked teams in the Western Conference took part in the Conference final. However, the third ranked team, the San Antonio Spurs, faced the fourth ranked team in the shape of the youthful Utah Jazz. And it was experience over youth that clinched the Western Conference final for the seasoned pros at the Spurs with a 4–1 victory, to claim their fourth appearance in the NBA finals.

The San Antonio Spurs won the opening game of the finals series with an 85–76 victory over the Cleveland Cavaliers. Tony Parker led the Spurs with 27 points and 7 assists. The Cavaliers were making their inaugural appearance in the finals in the franchise's 37-year history. In Game 2, the Spurs held off a spirited fight back from the Cavaliers to take a 2–0 lead in the series, although it was much closer than the 11-point margin suggests. The Cavaliers trailed by 27 after three quarters and left themselves with just too much to do.

Despite home court advantage in Game 3, Cleveland slumped to a third consecutive loss to the Spurs, leaving San Antonio one victory away from a fourth championship in nine seasons – they won in 1999, 2003 and 2005. After another low-scoring affair the Spurs were on the verge of the first finals sweep since 2002. And the series ended at its earliest opportunity as San Antonio closed out the championship with a one-point victory over the Cavaliers in Game 4. Manu Ginobili top-scored in the game contributing 27 points for the Spurs, 13 of them coming in the final quarter. Much of the credit must go to Spurs coach Greg Popovich, who has been at the helm for all four victories, while Tim Duncan has been a key cog on the court in all the successes. The Cavaliers combined score of 322 in the series is the lowest in NBA finals history. Parker, who would marry actress Eva Longoria in Paris later in the summer, was named the NBA Play-offs MVP.

FINALS SCOREBOARD

	By Period	1	2	3	4	Tot
Game 1, at AT&T Center, San Antonio, 7/6/07	Cleveland	15	20	14	27	76
San Antonio Spurs 85–76 Cleveland Cavaliers	San Antionio	20	20	24	21	85
Game 2, at AT&T Center, San Antonio, 10/6/07	Cleveland	17	16	29	30	92
San Antonio Spurs 103–92 Cleveland Cavaliers	San Antonio	28	30	31	14	103
Game 3, at Quicken Loans Arena, 12/6/07	San Antonio	16	24	15	20	75
San Antonio Spurs 75–72 Cleveland Cavaliers	Cleveland	18	20	12	22	72
Game 4, at Quicken Loans Arena, 14/6/07	San Antonio	19	20	21	23	83
San Antonio Spurs 83–82 Cleveland Cavaliers	Cleveland	20	14	18	30	82

NBA All-Star Game

In a change with tradition, the NBA's All-Star Weekend was held in Las Vegas, Nevada, rather than the home court of one of the teams. The first of the basketball events was the T-Mobile Rookie Challenge, the game between the Rookies (first year players) and Sophomores (those in their second NBA season). It was the latter who came out on top 155–114, with the New York Knicks's David Lee earning the MVP award. He shot 14 of 14 from the floor, scored 30 points, collected 11 rebounds and handed out four assists. The Sprite Slam Dunk Competition was won by Gerald Green of the Boston Celtics, while the Foot Locker Three-point Shootout went to the Miami Heat's Jason Kapono.

The main event, of course, was the All-Star Game, which was won by the West in another shoot-out, 153–132. MVP was Kobe Bryant of the LA Lakers, his second such award. He scored a game-high 31 points and contributed with five rebounds, six assists and six steals. The attendance at the Thomas & Mack Arena was 15,694.

NBA Stats Leaders 2006–07

Category	Player	Team	Stat
Points per game	Kobe Bryant	Los Angeles Lakers	31.6
Rebounds per game	Kevin Garnett	Minnesota Timberwolves	12.8
Assists per game	Steve Nash	Phoenix Suns	11.6
Steals per game	Baron Davis	Golden State Warriors	2.14
Blocks per game	Marcus Camby	Denver Nuggets	3.3
Field goal percentage	Mikki Moore	New Jersey Nets	60.6%
Free throw percentage	Kyle Korver	Philadelphia 76ers	91.4%
3-point field goal percentage	Jason Kapono	Miami Heat	51.4%

NBA Awards 2006–07

Most valuable player	Dirk Nowitzki	Dallas Mavericks
Rookie of the year	Brandon Roy	Portland Trail Blazers
Defensive player of the year	Marcus Camby	Denver Nuggets
Sixth man of the year	Leandro Barbosa	Phoenix Suns
Most improved player	Monta Ellis	Golden State Warriors
Coach of the year	Sam Mitchell	Toronto Raptors
Executive of the year	Bryan Colangelo	Toronto Raptors
Sportmanship award	Luol Deng	Chicago Bulls

All-NBA First Team 2006–07

F	Dirk Nowitzki	Dallas Mavericks
F	Tim Duncan	San Antonio Spurs
C	Amare Stoudemire	Phoenix Suns
G	Steve Nash	Phoenix Suns
G	Kobe Bryant	Los Angeles Lakers

"I think we had a little Vegas flair in there. I hope the fans enjoyed it a lot."

*West forward, **Shane Marion**, after the All-Star Game was played in the Nevada gambling resort.*

British Basketball

British Basketball League Cup Final 2007

The CH Poujoulat Guildford Heat held off a late rally by the Scottish Phoenix Honda Rocks to run out 81–78 winners in the British Basketball League Cup final. It was the Heat's first trophy, having just been formed 18 months earlier. Brian Dux, the Heat's point guard, scored 21 points in total and was named the game's most valuable player. It was the Rocks' third cup final defeat in the last four seasons.

The Glasgow team started strongly and led 27–16 after the first quarter but the Heat came storming back in the second quarter to lead 42–36 at half-time. At the end of the third quarter the Heat maintained their 14-point advantage and led 57–43. Despite a late fightback the Heat held on to clinch victory. "I certainly couldn't have imagined this a year and a half ago. After everything that went on then this just makes it all worthwhile. I'm just about speechless; I don't know what to say," said a delighted Guildford coach Paul James.

7 JANUARY, NATIONAL INDOOR ARENA, BIRMINGHAM

Guildford Heat 81 – 78 Scottish Rocks

Guildford Heat: Dux 21, McKnight 20, Williams 10, Wardrope 7, Martin 7, Wellington 7, Gilbert 6, Clark 1, May 1, Abu 1.

Scottish Rocks: Davis 21, Hampton 19, Yanders 18, Joseph 9, Wohlers 7, Sterk 4, Murray, Hunter *(dnp)*, Pearson *(dnp)*.

British Basketball League Championship Final Table 2007

Pos	Team	P	W	L	Pts
1.	**Guildford Heat**	**36**	**29**	**7**	**58**
2.	Sheffield Sharks	36	28	8	56
3.	Newcastle Eagles	36	25	11	50
4.	Scottish Rocks	36	22	14	44
5.	Plymouth Raiders	36	20	16	40
6.	MK Lions	36	18	18	36
7.	Leicester Riders	36	13	23	26
8.	London United	36	11	25	22
9.	Chester Jets	36	10	26	20
10.	Worcester Wolves	36	4	32	8

"We have had a rollercoaster ride over the last two years, but hard work by many people has contributed to the club's success – just shows what can be achieved by teamwork both on and off the court."
Mike Davies, chairman of Guildford Heat

BBL Championship 2006–07

Poujoulat Heat Guildford won the BBL Championship after an exciting season-long race that came down to the last day of the regular season, which also saw the two-year-old franchise win British basketball's coveted double. Heat, winners of the BBL Cup back in January, went into the final day needing a win against London United to secure their first ever BBL Championship title.

A packed Guildford Spectrum cheered the Heat on to victory as they saw off United with a resounding 114–85 win, as Mike Martin racked up 22 points and 13 rebounds. However, the Heat had to sweat a little to clinch their first ever Championship as the Sheffield Sharks approached their penultimate game of the season sitting top of the table but with a tricky road game at the home of the defending champions, the Springfield Honda Newcastle Eagles, followed by another away game, at the Marshall Milton Keynes Lions. The Eagles, the 2005–06 champions, were in no mood to lie down and wanted to put on a display to send their fans home happy and they did this with a 94–89 victory over the Sharks in what proved to be a tense affair.

The Eagles' win handed the title to the Heat, while the Sharks had to settle for runners-up spot 2 points adrift. The Sharks won their final game, 66–64 away to the MK Lions for a 28–8 season record, with the Lions finishing sixth. The Heat played 36 league games during the 2006–07 season, winning 29 and losing 7 on their way to a 58 points total.

The top eight teams in the BBL Championship then had to turn their attention to the BBL Championship play-offs, with the Heat hosting London United again in the quarter-finals. Having won that match, the Heat missed out on completing the treble, losing 71–78 to the Scottish Phoenix Honda Rocks in the semi-final, sweet revenge for the Scottish franchise's BBL Cup final defeat to the Heat.

SEMI-FINALS

Scottish Phoenix Honda Rocks	78	–	71	Guildford Heat
Springfield Honda Newcastle Eagles	83	–	73	Sheffield Sharks

FINAL

Springfield Honda Newcastle Eagles 95 – 82 Scottish Phoenix Honda Rocks

Trivia

* The Heat was formed in 2005 by fans of the former BBL franchise Thames Valley Tigers who folded during the same year.

* The Heat played their first BBL game on 1 October 2005 against the Newcastle Eagles at the Metro Radio Arena, losing a nailbiter 89–88 in overtime.

* The Sharks lost two semi-finals during the 2006–07 season, in the BBL Cup and the BBL Trophy, and were just 2 points adrift of winning the BBL title.

* The 2006–07 BBL play-off final was a repeat of last year's final, with the Eagles coming out on top once again.

Bowls

World Indoor Bowls Championships 2007

Date: 8–28 January; *Venue:* Potters Leisure Resort, Hopton on Sea, Great Yarmouth

Scotland's Caroline Brown beat Ellen Falkner, the defending champion and number 1 seed, to win the women's title. Brown, the 26-year-old former world and British Isles junior champion, defeated Falkner in straight sets 9–4, 10–5. In the men's competition Scotland's Alex Marshall made bowls history by winning a record fourth title. Marshall, champion in 1999, 2003 and 2004, defeated the defending champion and number 1 seed Mervyn King 5–7, 13–4, 2–0. The final was the first ever to be decided by a match tie-break. "It's your dream to win it once, but to be the first to do it four times is unbelievable," said a beaming Marshall.

Co-operative Funeralcare World Match Play Championship 2007

Date: 21–22 June; *Venue:* Ponds Forge, Sheffield

Greg Harlow beat fellow Englishman Mervyn King 10–8, 4–10, 2–0 to secure his fourth successive world title. "It's unbelievable, I don't know what it is – I wish we could play all WBT events here. Mervyn played a fantastic game, but all the way through I felt I could win. I really feel at home in Sheffield. Perhaps I should buy a house here," said Harlow.

International Open 2006
Date: 29 October – 5 November
Ponds Forge, Sheffield
Winner: Greg Harlow

Scottish International Open 2006
Date: 25 November–2 December
Dewars, Perth
Winner: Kelvin Kerkow

Women's World Match Play Championships 2007
Date: 19–24 January
Potters Leisure Resort, Norfolk
Winner: Caroline Brown

World Indoor Singles Championships 2007
Date: 8–28 January
Potters Leisure Resort, Norfolk
Winner: Alex Marshall

World Indoor Mixed Pairs Championships 2007
Date: 19–21 January
Potters Leisure Resort, Norfolk
Winners: Greg Harlow & Jo Morris

World Indoor Pairs Championships 2007
Date: 8–14 January
Potters Leisure Resort, Norfolk
Winners: David Gourlay & Billy Jackson

Welsh International Open 2007
Date: 3–9 February
Selwyn Samuel Centre, Llanelli, Wales
Winner: Paul Foster

Canoeing

Flatwater Racing World Championships 2007

Date: 8–12 August 2007
Venue: Regattabahn, Sportpark Duisburg-Wedau, Germany

This was the 36th edition of the International Canoeing Federation tournament. A total of 27 gold medals were up for grabs over five days with the men competing as individuals, in pairs and in quads over 200m, 500m and 1000m in both canoe (Canadian) and kayak, a total of 18 events. The women competed in the kayak only. The results in Duisburg were used to determine how many athletes each federation was allowed to send to the 2008 Olympic Games in Beijing. Tim Brabants (GB) took gold in the 1000m kayak-1 and narrowly missed out on a historic double when he was pipped at the finish line by Canada's Adam Koeverden in the 500m.

FINAL MEDALS TABLE (TOP 10)

Pos	Nation	Gold	Silver	Bronze	Total
1.	Germany	9	6	3	18
2.	Hungary	9	3	6	18
3.	Belarus	1	2	1	4
4.	Russia	1	2	1	4
5.	Slovakia	1	2	1	4
6.	Romania	1	1	1	3
7.	Canada	1	1	0	2
8.	Great Britain	1	1	0	2
9.	France	1	0	1	2
10.	Spain	1	0	1	2

BRITISH MEDALS

Event	Name	Medal
1000m K-1	Tim Brabants	Gold
500m K-1	Tim Brabants	Silver

Trivia

* Hungary's Gyorgy Kolonics won the gold medal in the men's C-2 500m, his 15th World Championship title.

* In the women's events Germany (5) and Hungary (4) won all the gold medals.

> "I always knew it would be difficult out there today, I am really, really pleased."
> **Tim Brabants,** *after winning gold in the Men's K1 (kayak single) 1000m*

Cycle Racing

Tour de France 2007

Date: 7–29 July

This was the most written-about Tour since the 1998 event, which was similarly blemished with a plethora of doping scandals, starting with the arrest of Team Festina's soigneur, Willy Voet. In the 2007 Tour, Patrik Sinkewitz (T-Mobile) failed a drugs test, leading to his withdrawal from the race before Stage 9, which also resulted in German TV pulling the plug on coverage of the race. Alexandre Vinokourov, the pre-race favourite, had a positive test for blood doping leading to the Tour organizers asking his entire Astana team to leave the Tour after Stage 15. Team Cofidis were forced to pull out of the race prior to Stage 17 after their rider Cristian Moreni was found to have tested positive for testosterone, resulting in the police raiding the team hotel and taking all of the team members to a nearby police station for questioning (including Britain's Bradley Wiggins). But the biggest shock of all came when Michael Rasmussen, the race leader, was sacked by his Rabobank team after winning Stage 16, the last mountain stage, for lying about his whereabouts when he missed out-of-competition drugs tests.

The 2007 Tour got underway in London with the Swiss rider, Fabian Cancellera from Team CSC, taking the opening Prologue. Cancellera remained in the *maillot jaune* for the next six Stages before T-Mobile's Lindus Gerdermann took over the race leader's jersey (and the *maillot blanc*) after Stage 7. The young German only spent one day in yellow before Rasmussen took control of the race, a position he held until he was forced to leave the Tour. Prior to the start of Stage 17, riders from eight teams, who formed the Movement for Credible Cycling, made a protest against doping by sitting down at the start line delaying the start by 13 minutes. This too mirrored images of the 1998 Tour when riders protested, with the notable difference being that nine years ago the riders were protesting about having to undergo drugs tests. Alberto Contador from Team Discovery assumed overall lead of the Tour when Rasmussen was sacked but the young Spaniard was not permitted to start Stage 17 in yellow and had to wear his white jersey, awarded to the best young rider in the race. Rasmussen, King of the Mountains winner in both the 2005 and 2006 Tour and who had not failed any 2007 Tour drugs tests, was totally devastated and said to be a "broken man".

Going into the final Stage, only 31 seconds split the top three riders with Contador in yellow followed by Australia's Cadel Evans (Predictor-Lotto) +23 seconds and Contador's Discovery Channel team-mate, Levi Leipheimer, who won the Stage 19 individual time trial at +31 seconds. Contador steered clear of trouble in the final Stage to win the Tour, with Evans second and his team-mate, Leipheimer, third.

Final General Classification

1.	Alberto Contador	*(Spa)*	Discovery Channel 9	1 hours 26 seconds
2.	Cadel Evans	*(Aus)*	Predictor-Lotto	+23 seconds
3.	Levi Leipheimer	*(USA)*	Discovery Channel	+31

4.	Carlos Sastre	*(Spa)*	Team CSC	+7.08
5.	Haimar Zubeldia	*(Spa)*	Euskaltel	+8.17
6.	Alejandro Valverde	*(Spa)*	Caisse d'Epargne	+11.37
7.	Kim Kirchen	*(Lux)*	T-Mobile	+12.18
8.	Yaroslav Popovych	*(Ukr)*	Discovery Channel	+12.25
9.	Mikel Astarloza	*(Spa)*	Euskaltel	+14.14
10.	Oscar Pereiro	*(Spa)*	Caisse d'Epargne	+14.25

GB RIDERS

45.	Charles Wegelius	*(GB)*	Liquigas	+146.25
69.	David Millar	*(GB)*	Saunier Duval-Prodirr	+2:32.07
140.	Geraint Thomas	*(GB)*	Barloworld	+3:46.51

GREEN JERSEY (SPRINTERS) FINAL STANDINGS

1.	Tom Boonen	*(Bel)*	Quick-Step	256 points
2.	Robert Hunter	*(SA)*	Barloworld	234
3.	Erik Zabel	*(Ger)*	Milram	232

POLKA DOT JERSEY (KING OF THE MOUNTAINS) FINAL STANDINGS

1.	Mauricio Soler	*(Col)*	Barloworld	206 points
2.	Alberto Contador	*(Spa)*	Discovery Channel	128
3.	Yaroslav Popovych	*(Ukr)*	Discovery Channel	105

WHITE JERSEY (BEST YOUNG RIDER) FINAL STANDINGS

1.	Alberto Contador	*(Spa)*	Discovery Channel 9	91 hours 26 seconds
2.	Mauricio Soler	*(Col)*	Barloworld	+16.51
3.	Amets Txurruka	*(Spa)*	Euskaltel	+49.34

Trivia

* This was only the second Tour de France for Contador; he finished 31st in 2005.

* Ken Livingstone, the mayor of London, was on the winner's podium when Contador was presented with the yellow jersey. Over one million people lined the streets of London when the 2007 Tour de France began in the capital.

* Contador spent ten days in a coma after suffering swelling to the brain following a crash in the 2002 Tour of Asturias.

* Contador's margin of victory (+23 seconds) was the narrowest since Greg Lemond beat Laurent Fignon by 8 seconds in 1989.

* Geraint Thomas from Wales was the youngest rider in the race and was making his Tour debut.

* Contador, aged 24, is the youngest winner since Jan Ullrich in 1997 and the first Spanish *maillot jaune* winner since Miguel Indurain in 1995.

Tour of Britain 2006

Date: 29 August–3 September

This was the third edition of the Tour of Britain (UCI category 2.1), the UK's largest free viewing sporting event, that saw the 96 riders race 870km over six stages. The overall title was won by Denmark's Martin Pedersen of the CSC Team who won the team title from Unibet.com and the defending champions QuickStep-Innergetic. There was British succes in the shape of 21-year-old Isle of Man cyclist Mark Cavendish of T-Mobile – the Commonwealth Games gold medal winner – who won the green points jersey for the most consistent rider of the week, while Andy Schleck of CSC won the E.ON king of the mountains jersey.

Stage	Date	Route	Distance (km)	Winner
1.	29 August	Glasgow – Castle Douglas	162.6	Martin Pedersen
2.	30 August	Blackpool - Liverpool	163	Roger Hammond
3.	31 August	Bradford - Sheffield	180	Filippo Pozzato
4.	1 September	Wolverhampton - Birmingham	130	Frederik Willems
5.	2 September	Rochester - Canterbury	152	Francesco Chicci
6.	3 September	London: Greenwich – The Mall	82	Tom Boonen

Vuelta a Espana (Tour of Spain) 2006

Date: 26 August–17 September

The 2006 Vuelta was won by the veteran Alexandre Vinokourov of the Astana Team, the Kazakh cyclist's first Grand Tour victory. Only 134 of the 189 riders who began the race took off for the final stage to Madrid and Unipublic director Ignacio Ayuso gave a medal to all 134 men who had endured 21 days of hard racing. Vinokourov, who took the race lead after the 17th stage and ensured victory by winning the penultimate day's time trial, finished the stage in 79th position to claim the maillot oro (gold jersey), the Vuelta's equivalent of the Tour de France's maillot jaune (yellow jersey). The win tasted sweeter for the Kazakhstan rider as he had turned 33-years-old the day before.

FINAL GENERAL CLASSIFICATION

1.	Alexandre Vinokourov *(Kaz)*	Astana Team	81.23.07
2.	Alejandro Valverde *(Spa)*	Caisse d'Epargne-Illes Balears	1.12
3.	Andrey Kashechkin *(Kaz)*	Astana Team	3.12
4.	Carlos Sastre *(Spa)*	Team CSC	3.35
5.	José Angel Gomez Marchante *(Spa)*	Saunier Duval-Prodir	6.51
6.	Thomas Danielson *(USA)*	Discovery Channel Pro Cycling Team	8.09
7.	Samuel Sanchez *(Spa)*	Euskaltel-Euskadi	8.26
8.	Vladimir Karpets *(Rus)*	Caisse d'Epargne-Illes Balears	10.36
9.	Manuel Beltran *(Spa)*	Discovery Channel Pro Cycling Team	10.47

Giro d'Italia 2007

Date: 12 May–3 June

Danilo di Luca, riding for the Liquigas team, sealed a home win in the 2007 Giro d'Italia for the 11th consecutive year, as he crossed the finish line in Milan. Pavel Tonkov of Russia was the last non-Italian winner of the famous cycle race back in 1996. Di Luca finished 1 minute, 55 seconds in front of Luxembourg's Andy Schleck (Team CSC) and 2 minutes, 25 seconds ahead of the third placed rider, Italy's Eddy Mazzoleni from the Astana team. The home riders were so dominant in the race that Schleck was the only non-Italian in the final top six overall standings. It was 31-year-old di Luca's first major Tour success, although he did win the season-long ProTour in 2005. Alessandro Petacchi (Italy/Milram team) won the final stage from Vestone to Milan in a time of 5 hours, 18 minutes, 54 seconds to claim his fifth stage win of the 2007 race. Di Luca won two stages but, more importantly, donned the leader's pink jersey for 13 of the 21 days of racing.

FINAL GENERAL CLASSIFICATION

1.	Danilo Di Luca	*(Ita)*	Liquigas	92.59.39
2.	Andy Schleck	*(Lux)*	Team CSC	1:55
3.	Eddy Mazzoleni	*(Ita)*	Astana Team	2:25
4.	Gilberto Simoni	*(Ita)*	Saunier Duval-Prodir	3:15
5.	Damiano Cunego	*(Ita)*	Lampre-Fondital	3:49
6.	Riccardo Ricco	*(Ita)*	Saunier Duval-Prodir	7:00
7.	Evgeni Petrov	*(Rus)*	Tinkoff Credit Systems	8:34
8.	Marzio Bruseghin	*(Ita)*	Lampre-Fondital	10:14
9.	Franco Pellizotti	*(Ita)*	Liquigas	10:44
10.	David Arroyo Duran	*(Spa)*	Caisse D'Epargne	11:58

> "Before the Giro I thought I could win, but certainly not in this way. Today, I crowned a dream."
> ***Danilo Di Luca***, 2007 Giro winner

Dauphine Libere

Date: 10–17 June 2007

FINAL GENERAL CLASSIFICATION

1.	Christophe Moreau	*(Fra)*	AG2R	29:50:35
2.	Cadel Evans	*(Aus)*	Predictor-Lotto	+14 seconds
3.	Andrey Kashechkin	*(Kaz)*	Astana	+1:27
4.	Denis Menchov	*(Rus)*	Rabobank	+1:52
5.	David Zabriskie	*(USA)*	Team CSC	+2:16

Elite Women's British Road Race Championship

Date: 19 August 2007
Location: Saffon Waldon, Essex

RESULT

1. Nicole Cooke	(Raleigh/Lifeforce/Creation/HB)	3hrs 44mins 39secs
2. Rachel Heal	(Webcor Builders) 3	hrs 45mins 38secs
3. Helen Wyman	(Global)	RT ST
4. Catherine Hare	(Rapha Condor)	RT ST
5. Nikki Harris	(Global)	RT ST
6. Emma Pooley	(Team Specialized Designs for Women)	ST
7. Elizabeth Armistead	(Global)	RT ST
8. Leanne Thompson	(Lune RCC)	3hrs 53mins 16secs
9. Diane Moss	(Team Luciano/Everest)	ST
10. Alice Monger-Godfrey	(Glendene CC/Biketrax)	ST

Paris – Nice 2007

Date: 11–18 March
Location: France

OVERALL CLASSIFICATION

Pos	Nat	Rider	Team	Time
1.	Spa	Alberto Contador	Discover Channel	29.55:22
2.	Ita	Davide Rebellin	Gerolsteiner	+26s
3.	Spa	Luis Leon Sanchez	Caisse d'Epargne	+42s
4.	Svn	Tadej Valjavec	Lampre-Fondital	+49s

Track Cycling World Championships 2007

Date: 29 March–1 April
Location: Palma de Mallorca Spain

Great Britain dominated the championships and topped the medals table after winning seven of the 16 gold medals on offer. In the men's events Chris Hoy and Bradley Wiggins won two gold medals each. Victoria Pendleton won three golds in the women's events.

MEDALS TABLE (TOP 3)

Pos	Country	Gold	Silver	Bronze	Total
1.	Great Britain	7	2	2	11
2.	Australia	2	0	4	6
3.	Netherlands	1	4	1	6

Grand Boucle 2007

Date: 20–24 June

Nicole Cooke from Wales successfully defended her Grande Boucle Feminine title winning the 2007 tour in France. Cooke, aged 24, took over the leader's jersey after Stage 3 and held on to it claiming victory in the five-day spectacle. Cooke and her team-mates won the team classification title.

1.	Nicole Cooke	*(GB)*	Raleigh Lifeforce Creations
2.	Priska Doppmann	*(Swi)*	Raleigh Lifeforce Creations
3.	Emma Pooley	*(GB)*	Team Specialized Dfw

Eneco Tour de Benelux 2007

Date: 21–28 August
Location: Netherlands and Belgium

FINAL GENERAL CLASSIFICATION

Pos	Nat	Rider	Team	Time
1.	Spa	Jose Ivan Gutierrez Palacios	Caisse d'Epargne	26.05'44
2.	GB	David Millar	Saunier Duval-Prodir	11
3.	Swe	Gustav Erik Larsson	Unibet.com	1'05
4.	Bel	Leif Hoste	Predictor-Lotto	1'12
5.	Ned	Thomas Dekker	Rabobank	1'15
6.	Rus	Vladimir Gusev	Discovery Channel	1'17
7.	Ned	Bram Tankink	Quick Step-Innergetic	1'32
8.	Spa	Sebastien Rosseler	Quick Step-Innergetic	1'33
9.	Ger	Paul Martens	Skil Shimano	1'34
10.	Bel	Jurgen Van Den Broeck	Predictor-Lotto	1'34

POINTS CLASSIFICATION

Pos	Nat	Rider	Team	Time
1.	GB	Mark Cavendish	T-Mobile Team	74
2.	Bra	Luciano Andre Pagliarini Mendonca	Saunier Duval-Prodir	60
3.	Spa	Pablo Lastras Garcia	Caisse d'Epargne	51
4.	Ned	Steven De Jongh	Quick Step-Innergetic	51
5.	Bel	Gorik Gardeyn	Unibet.com	49
6.	Nor	Thor Hushovd	Credit Agricole	47
7.	Bel	Steven Caethoven	Chocolade Jacques-Topsport Vlaanderen	43
8.	Spa	Jose Ivan Gutierrez Palacios	Caisse d'Epargne	43
9.	Bel	Wouter Weylandt	Quick Step-Innergetic	40
10.	Ned	Kenny Van Hummel	Skil Shimano	39

Darts

PDC World Championships 2007

Date: 18 December 2006–1 January
Venue: Circus Tavern, Purfleet

Dutchman Raymond van Barneveld won his first PDC World Championship after defeating the 13-time world champion Phil Taylor 7–6 in a pulsating final. A sudden-death leg was required after the score was tied at 6–6 in sets and 5–5 in leg. However, with a double-top checkout, van Barneveld took the title.

QUARTER-FINALS

Andy Jenkins *bt* Colin Osborne 5–4   Raymond van Barneveld *bt* Alan Tabern 5–0

Andy Hamilton *bt* Terry Jenkins 5–4   Phil Taylor *bt* Darren Webster 5–1

SEMI-FINALS

Phil Taylor *bt* Andy Hamilton 5–0   Raymond van Barneveld *bt* Andy Jenkins 6–0

FINAL

Raymond van Barneveld *bt* Phil Taylor 7–6

Trivia

* Dennis Priestley of England won the inaugural PDC World Darts Championship in 1994, defeating Phil Taylor 6–1 in the final.

* Phil Taylor has won the PDC World Championship 11 times and has appeared in all 14 finals (1994–2007).

* Raymond van Barneveld equalled the Canadian, John Part's feat of winning both the BDO and PDC World Championship titles. "Barney's" 2007 PDC title followed BDO successes in 1998, 1999, 2003 and 2005, while Part won the 1994 BDO version and the 2003 PDC edition. The BDO and PDC split in 1994.

* Raymond van Barneveld holds the record for the most 180s scored in a tournament with 51 on his way to winning the 2007 PDC World Championship, beating Phil Taylor's 2006 record of 49 maximums.

* When John Lowe lost in the qualifying rounds for the 2005 PDC finals it brought to an end his record run of 27 consecutive appearances at the World Championships.

* In 2007, Raymond Van Barneveld became the first player to appear in the BDO World Championship and PDC World Championship finals in successive years. In 2006, he lost the BDO final to compatriot Jelle Klaasen.

BDO World Championships 2007

Date: 6–14 January
Venue: Lakeside Country Club, Frimley Green

England's Martin Adams beat Phil Nixon in a thrilling final. Adams led 6–6 in sets before Nixon levelled it at 6–6. However, in the deciding set it was Adams who held his nerve to win, 3–0 in legs. In 1994, following a dispute with the BDO, a rival breakaway group of darts players formed the Professional Darts Corporation (PDC) and every year since the PDC has held its own World Championship at Purfleet's Circus Tavern, Essex.

QUARTER-FINALS

Martin Adams *bt* Ted Hankey 5–3	Mervyn King *bt* Tony Eccles 5–4
Phil Nixon *bt* Paul Hanvidge 5–4	Niels de Ruiter *bt* Gary Robson 5–4

SEMI-FINALS

Martin Adams *bt* Mervyn King 6–5	Phil Nixon *bt* Niels de Ruiter 6–4

FINAL

Martin Adams *bt* Phil Nixon 7–6

WINMAU World Masters 2006

Date: 13–15 October
Venue: Leisure World, Bridlington

Michael van Gerwen from the Netherlands became the youngest winner of a major darts event when he beat England captain Martin Adams by 7–5 in the final of the WINMAU World Masters.

QUARTER-FINALS	SEMI-FINALS
Martin Adams *bt* Co Stompe 3–1	Martin Adams *bt* Steve Farmer 6–0
Steve Farmer *bt* John Walton 3–1	Michael van Gerwen *bt* Mark Webster 6–3
Mark Webster *bt* Brian Woods 3–1	
Michael van Gerwen *bt* Darryl Fitton 3–1	

FINAL

Michael van Gerwen bt Martin Adams 7–5

Equestrian Sports

Blenheim Horse Trials, 1–3 September 2006

FINAL RESULTS – TOP 10

No	Horse		Rider
70.	Springbok 1V	GBR	Daisy Dick
49.	Ensign	GBR	Pippa Funnell
95.	Parkmore Ed	GBR	William Fox-Pitt
9.	Major Sweep	GBR	Rodney Powell
75.	Le Samurai	USA	Amy Tryon
60.	Faere Vision	GBR	Jo May
53.	Sir Percival III	GBR	Francis Whittington
29.	Valdemar	GBR	Hannah Bate
67.	Noble Opposition	AUS	Sam Griffiths
93.	Zinzan II	GBR	Rodney Powell

Horse of the Year Show 4–8 October 2006

The world's most famous horse show, and Britain's biggest indoor equestrian event, the "Show of Champions", returned to the NEC in 2006. Eric Van Der Vleuten, a consistent performer over the five days, claimed the prestigious Penwood Forge Mill Trophy and was named Leading Rider. Britain's leading lady rider, Ellen Whitaker, rode an impressive round on Henri de Here in the Speed Horse of the Year class winning in a time of 49.63 seconds. The finale, and premier show jumping class, the Tack365.com Leading Show Jumper of the Year, was won by the USA's Leading Lady award-winner Laura Kraut on Anthem.

CLASS 51 THE SUPREME PONY OF THE YEAR FOR THE TIMBERWOLF TROPHY

	No.	Horse	Owner	Rider	Prize Money
Champion	1379.	Fairholme Rossetas Rhapsody	Mrs D Moreton	Chloe Willett	£1000.00

CLASS 52 THE PRICEWATERHOUSECOOPERS SUPREME HORSE OF THE YEAR

	No.	Horse	Owner	Rider	Prize Money
Champion	1276.	So Smart	Camilla Neame	Robert Walker	£1000.00

THE PENWOOD FORGE MILL TROPHY – TOP 10

1.	E Van der Vleuten	NED		W Funnell	GBR
2.	B Twomey	IRL	7.	M Whitaker	GBR
3.	G Luckett	GBR		E Whitaker	GBR
4.	L Kraut	USA	9.	N Skelton	GBR
5.	A Said	EGY	10.	L Van Asten	NED

LEADING GENTLEMAN AND LEADING LADY RIDER – TOP 5

1.	E Van der Vleuten	Audi's Paloma	NED
2.	N Skelton	Russel	GBR
3.	B Twomey	Anastasia III	IRL
4.	L Kraut	Anthem	USA
5.	M Whitaker	Insul Tech Portofino 63	GBR

London International Horse Show 15–18 December 2006

Three riders shared the spoils in the Puissance at the London International Horse Show. John Whitaker on Lactic 2, his son Robert on Finbarr V and the Swiss rider Markus Fuchs all cleared 2m 23cm in the knockout high jump event at Olympia. Ben Maher on Onasis won the Accenture Stakes, a speed class. The finale was brought to a stylish ending when the classy French rider Eugenie Angot won The Links of London Grand Prix on Cigale du Taillis in the presence of the Duchess of Cornwall. Tim Stockdale took second place on Fresh Direct Corlato, while John Whitaker's fifth place on Casino made him the show's leading British rider. By finishing sixth on Paparazzi, Alois Pollman-Schweckhorst clinched the Leading Rider of the Show award.

DFS British Jumping Derby

Date: 28 June–1 July 2007
Venue: All England Jumping Course, Hickstead, West Sussex

On the opening day John Whitaker (GB) won the Bunn Leisure Derby Salver on Give Me Remus while David McPherson (GB) claimed victory in the Bunn Leisure Derby Tankard riding Skip Two Ramiro. McPherson claimed a second victory on day two riding Finbarr in the Hickstead Derby Trial while Ellen Whitaker (GB) took the First Round Derby Vase on Cortaflex Kanselier. Day three brought a second win of the meeting for Ellen in the Bunn Leisure Speed Derby, riding Henri de Herne to victory while the Falcon Equine Feeds Derby Trophy went to John Whitaker and Casino, his second win. The flagship event, the DFS Hickstead Derby, was held on the final day and won by Geoff Billington (GB) on Cassabachus.

Festival of British Eventing 2007

Date: 3–5 August
Venue: Gatcombe Park, Gloucestershire

This event, celebrating its 25th anniversary in 2007, took place at Gatcombe Park, home of the Princess Royal. William Fox-Pitt on Cool Mountain took the spoils in a very competitive Dodson & Horrell British Novice Championship. Kristina Gifford won Section 1 of the CIC*** division on Miners Frolic. Meanwhile, Daisy Dick and her 2006 Blenheim winner Springbok IV won Section 2 of the international CIC***.

Badminton Horse Trials 3–6 May 2007

Lucinda Fredericks, aged 41, and her horse, Headley Britannia, completed a unique equestrian double by following up their 2006 Burghley Horse Trials triumph with victory in the 2007 Badminton Horse Trials. The British-born rider, who now represents Australia, knocked down one pole in the show jumping event, but squeezed home by two penalties from Andreas Dibowski from Germany riding FRH Serve Well. Fredericks had led from day one, following a fine display in the dressage discipline. Amazingly, Fredericks had never finished higher than sixth place in six previous appearances at Badminton. The leading rider representing Great Britain was Sarah Cohen, who claimed ninth place on Hide and Seek II.

However, it was the arduous conditions at Badminton which made most of the news. World Champion Zara Phillips, many other top British riders and a number of 2008 Olympic hopefuls decided not to run after taking a look at the course and its condition. Quite simply the ground was rock hard, not surprising really as it had not rained on the course for over a month. Phillips refused to risk Toytown given the horse's history of leg ailments, while even 500 tonnes of topsoil spread across the course failed to improve matters. In fact, by the time the opening dressage stage of the event had been completed, 22 of the 78 original starters had decided to withdraw and a further 18 did not attempt the show jumping stage.

FINAL RESULTS

Rank	Horse	Rider	Nat	Score
1.	Headley Britannia	Lucinda Fredericks	Aus	39.6
2.	FRH Serve Well	Andreas Dibowski	Ger	41.6
3.	Winsome Adante	Kim Severson	USA	43.8
4.	Bonza Katoomba	Matt Ryan	Aus	46.2
5.	Lord Killinghurst	Andrew Nicholson	NZ	46.2
6.	Marius Voigt-Logistik	Hinrich Romeike	Ger	47.7
7.	Snip	Joe Meyer	NZ	48.2
8.	Henry Tankerville	Andrew Nicholson	NZ	39.2
9.	Hide and Seek II	Sarah Cohen	GB	49.4
10.	The Ghost of Hamish	Peter Thomsen	Ger	49.4

Royal Windsor Horse Show 10–13 May 2007

In 1943, Count Robert Orssich and Mr Geoffrey Cross held the inaugural Royal Windsor Horse Show to raise monies for the "Wings for Victory" campaign to aid Britain's war effort against Germany. The inaugural show was called the Windsor Horse and Dog Show and was attended by all the key members of the Royal Family, including King George VI, Queen Elizabeth (the Queen Mother) and the two young princesses, Elizabeth and Margaret. The show is held in Her Majesty The Queen's Home Park adjacent to Windsor Castle and is Britain's largest outdoor equestrian show.

BEWLEY HOMES GRAND PRIX

1.	Fresh Direct Corlato	(T Stockdale)	0,0 in 53.51secs
2.	Murkas Johnny Jumper	(P Charles)	0,4 in 48.92
3.	Lacroix	(R Whitaker)	0,4 in 49.34

LAND ROVER 6 & 7-YEAR-OLDS

1.	To The Point	(G Luckett)	0,0 in 41.56secs
2.	Lara Joy	(G Luckett)	0,0 in 42.04
3.	Ufour Z	(M Sampson)	0,0 in 42.01

WELLS YOUNGS BREWING ST. GEORGE OF ENGLAND PUISSANCE

=1. Finbarr V (R Whitaker) & Lactic II (J Whitaker) both cleared 7.0 ft

3. Eperlan du Fouquet (B Maher)

LAND ROVER INTERNATIONAL DRIVING GRAND PRIX

Horse Teams				*Pony Four-in-Hand Teams*		
1.	Y Chardon	*(Ned)*	133.68pts	*1.* K H Wanstrath	*(Ger)*	143.36pts
2.	B Exell	*(Aus)*	138.75	*2.* J van Dorresteijn	*(Ned)*	154.23
3.	K de Ronde	*(Ned)*	142.47	*3.* L Astegiano	*(USA)*	156.98

Burghley Horse Trials 2007

Date: 30 August – 2 September
Venue: Burghley House, Stamford, Lincolnshire

William Fox-Pitt riding Parkmore Ed won his fourth Burghley Horse Trials title. Going into the final day's show jumping event Andrew Nicholson from New Zealand on Lord Killinghurst led the field. However, the New Zealand pair scuppered their chances of a medal after knocking down two fences compared to Fox-Pitt's one. Great Britain's Polly Stockton took runners-up spot on Tom Quigley while Australia's Andrew Hoy finished third on Master Monarch. It proved to be a successful Burghley Horse Trials for Fox-Pitt who also claimed fifth place on Ballincoola, the horse he won the title with in 2005.

Pos	Rider	Nationality	Horse
1.	William Fox-Pitt	GB	Parkmore Ed
2.	Polly Stockton	GB	Tom Quigley
3.	Andrew Hoy	Aus	Master Monarch

Gaelic Football

All-Ireland Senior Football Final 2006

Kerry, nicknamed the "Kingdom", claimed their 34th GAA senior football crown with a masterful performance against a brave Mayo defeating them 4–15 (27) to 3–5 (14). All six of Kerry's forwards got their names on the score sheet, while manager Jack O'Connor's resolute defence only allowed eight scores during the game. This was the fourth time the two teams had met each other to play for the Sam Maguire trophy and Kerry had come out on top each time: 2–7 to 2–4 in 1932, 0–13 to 1–7 in 1997 and 1–20 to 2–9 in 2004.

Mayo had a mountain to climb early on after Kieran Donaghy had scored two goals, Mike Frank Russell notched 2 points and Sean O'Sullivan and Aidan O'Mahony added points to give Kerry a 2–4 to 0–0 advantage inside 13 minutes. Trailing by 10 points, Mayo manager, Mickey Moran, replaced centre back James Nallen with the towering David Brady to negate Donaghy's dominance of the game. Donaghy lost nearly every challenge to Brady and only managed to score one more point before half-time.

Mayo, with a new found belief, started to show the form that took them to the final, with Alan Dillon hand-passing to Kevin O'Neill to score, cutting Kerry's lead to seven points. But Kerry's response was swift, scoring two points and by a goal from Colm Cooper. Mayo hit back late in the first-half, with Pat Harte sidestepping a challenge on the goal line and tapping home, and O'Neill scoring his second goal. Mayo fans had a new found belief, trailing 3–7 (16) to 3–2 (11), only for Declan O'Sullivan to score another point for Kerry before the break. Mayo's hopes were soon dashed as Kerry added three more points soon after the restart. But the Westerners' dreams really died at the other end because they managed only three scores, all single points from Conor Mortimer frees, in the second-half, while Kerry kept the scoreboard moving. In the last minute Kieran Donaghy drove a thunderous shot over the bar, putting an exclamation point on a dominating afternoon.

17 SEPTEMBER 2006, CROKE PARK, DUBLIN

Kerry 4–15   Mayo 3–5

Kerry: Murphy, M O'Se, McCarthy, T O'Sullivan, T O'Se, Moynihan (0–1), O'Mahony (0–2), D O'Se, Griffin, S O'Sullivan (0–1), Declan O'Sullivan (capt, 1–2), Galvin (0–1), C Cooper (1–2), K Donaghy (1–2), Russell (0–2)
Subs: Brosnan (1–1) for T O'Se (36), Darren O'Sullivan for S O'Sullivan (52), Sheehan (0–1) for Russell (62), Fitzmaurice for Griffin (67), Guiney for O'Mahony (70)

Mayo: Clarke, Geraghty, Heaney, K Higgins, A Higgins, Nallen, Gardiner, McGarrity, Harte (1–0), Padden (0–1), G Brady, Dillon, O'Neill (2–0), C Mortimer (0–3), C MacDonald (0–1)
Subs: D Brady for Nallen (11), T Mortimer for Dillon (47), B Moran for O'Neill (47), Kilcoyne for Padden (52), A Moran for P Gardiner (60)

Att: 82,289

All-Ireland Senior Football Championship 2007

The 2007 Bank of Ireland All-Ireland Senior Football Championship began on 13 May 2007. Kerry, the defending champions, were hotly tipped to claim their 35th crown while Donegal, the unbeaten Allianz National Football League Division 1 champions and runners-up to Tyrone in the Dr McKenna Cup, could not be ignored. On 1 July 2007, Kerry retained their Munster Senior Football Championship title, their 72nd, defeating Cork in the final by 1-15 to 1-13 at FitzGerald Stadium, Killarney. One week later Sligo narrowly edged out Galway (1-10 to 0-12) at Dr Hyde Park, Roscommon to claim their third Connacht Senior Football Championship. Dublin won the Leinster Senior Football Championship title for the third consecutive year, their 47th title, with a 3-14 to 1-14 victory over Laois at Croke Park on 15 July 2007, while on the same day Tyrone took the Ulster title, their 11th, with a 1-15 to 1-13 win over Monaghan at St Tiemach's Park, Clones. In the first semi-final Cork saw off Meath without much difficulty, winning by ten points. The second semi-final was a cracker with Kerry overcoming Dublin by 1-15 to 0-16. It meant that the All-Ireland final was a repeat of the Munster final, something that hadn't been possible until the qualifying competition changed at the start of this century. Sadly, the final was a mismatch from the moment Colm Cooper punched home a goal early in the first half. Cork couldn't find their shooting range and ended up losing by 10 points to give Kerry its 35th All-Ireland title.

Qualifiers Round 1
Fermanagh 1–12 defeated Wexford 1–8
Armagh 0–9 lost to Derry 0–10
Limerick 0–13 lost to Louth 0–14
Mayo 1–19 defeated Cavan 3–7
Down 0–8 lost to Meath 1–10
Roscommon 1–13 lost to Kildare 2–13
Westmeath 0–18 defeated Longford 0–9
Leitrim 1–14 lost to Donegal 1–16 *aet*

Qualifiers Round 2
Derry 2–13 defeated Mayo 1–6
Kildare 1–10 lost to Louth 1–16
Westmeath 1–8 lost to Donegal 1–13
Meath 0–11 defeated Fermanagh 0–9

Qualifiers Round 3
Laois 2–11 lost to Derry 1–18
Monaghan 2–12 lost to Donegal 1–7
Louth 0–14 lost to Cork 0–16
Galway 1–14 lost to Meath 2–14

Ulster Senior Football Final
Tyrone 1–15 defeated Monaghan 1–13

Leinster Senior Football Final
Dublin 3–14 defeated Laois 1–14

Munster Senior Football Final
Kerry 1–15 defeated Cork 1–13

Connacht Senior Football Final
Sligo 1–10 defeated Galway 0–12

Quarter-Finals
Cork 1–11 defeated Sligo 0–8
Meath 1–13 defeated Tyrone 2–8
Dublin 1–23 defeated Derry 0–15
Kerry 1–12 defeated Monaghan 1–11

Semi-Finals
Cork 1–16 defeated Meath 0–9
Kerry 1–15 defeated Dublin 0–16

Final: 16 September, Croke Park, Dublin
Kerry 3–13 defeated Cork 1-9

Gymnastics

World Artistic Gymnastics Championships 2006

Date: 13–21 October *Venue:* NRGi Arena, Aarhus, Denmark

China ended the 2006 World Artistic Gymnastic Championships in Denmark, the 39th edition of the event, top of the medals table with eight goldls (including both team events), more than half of the 14 on offer during the nine days of competition. The hosts of the 2008 Summer Olympic Games now look set to dominate the gymnastics programme in Beijing.

MEN'S TEAM FINAL

1. China
2. Russia
3. Japan
4. Romania
5. Belarus
6. Canada
7. Germany
8. Switzerland

INDIVIDUAL ALL-AROUND (TOP 10)

1.	Wei Yang	(China)
2.	Hiroyuki Tomita	(Japan)
3.	Fabian Hambuechen	(Germany)
4.	Yibing Chen	(China)
5.	Maxim Deviatovski	(Russia)
6.	Takuya Nakase	(Japan)
7.	Tae-Young Yang	(S. Korea)
8.	Dorin Razvan Selariu	(Romania)
9.	Adam Wong	(Canada)
	Rafael Martinez	(Spain)

FLOOR EXERCISE

1.	Marian Dragulescu	(Romania)
2.	Diego Hypolito	(Brazil)
3.	Kyle Shewfelt	(Canada)

POMMEL HORSE

1.	Qin Xiao	(China)
2.	Prashanth Sellathurai	(Australia)
3.	Alexander Artemev	(USA)

RINGS

1.	Yibing Chen	(China)
2.	Jordan Jovtchev	(Bulgaria)
3.	Yuri van Gelder	(Holland)

VAULT

1.	Marian Dragulescu	(Romania)
2.	Dimitri Kaspiarovich	(Belarus)
3.	Fabian Hambuechen	(Germany)

PARALLEL BARS

1.	Wei Yang	(China)
2.	Hiroyuki Tomita	(Japan)
3.	Woo Chul Yoo	(S. Korea)

HORIZONTAL BARS

1.	Philippe Rizzo	(Australia)
2.	Aljaz Pegan	(Slovenia)
3.	Vlasios Maras	(Greece)

Trivia

* None of the exercises in the men's and women's artistic gymnastic events are quite the same. The men complete their floor exercise in silence while the women perform to a musical soundtrack of their choice; in the vault, the women have the advantage of taking off from a springboar, whereas the men leap from the floor.

WOMEN'S TEAM FINAL

1. China
2. United States
3. Russia
4. Romania
5. Ukraine
6. Australia
7. Brazil
8. Spain

INDIVIDUAL ALL-AROUND FINAL (TOP 10)

1.	Vanessa Ferrari	(Italy)
2.	Jana Bieger	(USA)
3.	Sandra Raluca Izbasa	(Romania)
4.	Steliana Nistor	(Romania)
5.	Daria Joura	(Australia)
6.	Panpan Pang	(China)
7.	Hollie Dykes	(Australia)
8.	Beth Tweddle	(Great Britain)
9.	Oksana Chusovitina	(Germany)
10.	Ashley Priess	(USA)

VAULT

1.	Fei Cheng	(China)
2.	Alicia Sacramone	(USA)
3.	Oksana Chusovitina	(Germany)

UNEVEN BARS

1. Beth Tweddle (Great Britain)
2. Anastasia Luikin (USA)
3. Vanessa Ferrari (Italy)

BEAM FINAL

1.	Iryna Krasnianska	(Ukraine)
2.	Sandra Raluca Izbasa	(Romania)
3.	Elyse Hopfner-Hibbs	(Italy)

FLOOR EXERCISE

1.	Fei Cheng	(China)
2.	Jana Bieger	(USA)
3.	Vanessa Ferrari	(Italy)

Artistic Gymnastics World Cup – Glasgow Grand Prix

Date: 10–11 November 2006; *Venue:* Kelvin Hall International Sports Arena, glasgow

MEN'S FINALS

Floor
Matthias Fahrig *(Ger)*

Pommel Horse
Louis Smith *(GB)*

Rings
Alexander Safoshkin *(Rus)*

Vault
Matthias Fahrig *(Ger)*

Parallel Bars
Yann Cucherat *(Fra)*

Horizontal Bar
Yann Cucherat *(Fra)*

WOMEN'S FINALS

Vault
Anna Pavlova *(Rus)*

Uneven Bars
Beth Tweddle *(GBR)*

Beam
Steliana Nistor *(ROM)*

Floor Exercise
Sandra Izbasa *(ROM)*

Trivia

* The Kelvin Hall building dates back to 1927, but the International Sports Arena opened only in 1987.

World Artistic Gymnastics Cup 2006

Date: 16–17 December 2006 *Venue:* Ibirapuera Gymnasium, Sao Paolo, Brazil

Beth Tweddle, aged 21 from Liverpool, crowned an excellent 2006 by winning the uneven bars gold medal at the World Artistic Gymnastics Cup final in Sao Paulo. She also won a silver medal in the floor exercise Two months earlier Tweddle became Great Britain's first ever World Champion in Denmark while she also ended the year as the reigning European Champion on the uneven bars. Tweddle also finished third in the 2006 BBC Sports Personality of the Year Award.

MEN'S FINALS

Floor Exercise
1.	Diego Hypolito	(Brazil)
2.	Kyle Shewfelt	(Canada)
3.	Brandon O'Neill	(Canada)

Pommel Horse
1.	Qin Xiao	(China)
2.	Krisztian Berki	(Hungary)
3.	Haibin Teng	(China)

Rings
1.	Regulo Carmona	(Venezuela)
2.	Olexander Vorobyov	(Ukraine)
3.	Matteo Angioletti	(Italy)

Vault
1.	Marian Dragulescu	(Romania)
2.	Anton Golotsutskov	(Russia)
3.	Diego Hypolito	(Brazil)

Parallel Bars
1.	Xiaopeng Li	(China)
2.	Xu Huang	(China)
3.	Valeriy Goncharov	(Ukraine)

Horizontal Bars
1.	Vlasios Maras	(Greece)
2.	Philippe Rizzo	(Australia)
3.	Aljaz Pegan	(Slovenia)

WOMEN'S FINALS

Vault
1.	Fei Cheng	(China)
2.	Lais Souza	(Brazil)
3.	Elena Zamolodchikova	(Russia)

Uneven Bars
1.	Elizabeth Tweddle	(Great Britain)
2.	Ya Li	(China)
3.	Dariya Zgoba	(Ukraine)

Beam
1.	Ya Li	(China)
2.	Daniele Hypolito	(Brazil)
3.	Lenika De Simone	(Spain)

Floor Exercise
1.	Daiane Dos Santos	(Brazil)
2.	Elizabeth Tweddle	(Great Britain)
3.	Lais Souza	(Brazil)

Trivia

* Brazilian gymnasts enjoyed an exceptional competition on their home floor. It was especially good for the Hypolito family who won medals of all three colours. Diego took gold in the floor exercise and bronze in the vault, while his sister Daniele collected silver on the beam. In addition, Daiane Dos Santos won a gold on the floor and Lais Sousa claimed silver and bronze medals.

Handball

EHF European Women's Handball Championships 2006

Date: 7–17 December *Venue:* Four host cities, Sweden

Norway were crowned European Champions after defeating Russia 27–24 in a closely contested final in Stockholm. As the tournament also serves as a qualifying event for the 2008 Summer Olympic Games, Norway earned a place for the Beijing games. If Norway also win the 2007 World Championships, Russia will qualify for the 2008 Olympics. Furthermore, the first or second (if Europe finishes in the top two continents at the World Championships) best ranked teams in this European Championship, which are outside the top seven at the World Championships, will be eligible to participate in the qualifying tournament for the 2008 Olympic Games.

Semi-finals
Norway 28 France 24
Germany 29 Russia 33

Final
Norway 27 Russia 24

Men's World Handball Championships 2007

Date: 19 January – 4 February *Venue:* Twelve host cities, Germany

A total of 24 national teams participated across 12 German cities, with the final being staged in the magnificent Kolnarena in Cologne. International Handball Federation rules permit each continent (except Oceania) to send three nations, along with the host nation Germany, the holders Spain, while the remaining nine slots are allocated to the continents based on their performance at the previous World Championships. Consequently for the 2007 tournament, Europe was awarded thirteen places, Africa four places, Americas (North and South) three places, Asia three places and Oceania one place.

Hosts Germany beat Poland 29–24 in the Kolnarena to claim their third World Handball Championship. It was Germany's first world title since 1978; they also won the gold medal at the inaugural World Championships in 1938. By taking the silver medal Poland claimed their best result since their 1982 bronze-medal winning performance. In the third place play-off match Denmark thumped European champions France 34–27 to claim the bronze medal in Cologne.

Semi-finals

Germany 32 France 31
Score after full-time was 21–21. After first overtime it was 27–27. Germany won in second period of overtime.

Poland 36 Denmark 33
Score after full-time was 26–26. After first overtime it was 30–30. Poland won in second period of overtime.

Final
Germany 29 Poland 24

Hockey

Men's Hockey World Cup Final

Qualification took place in Changzhou, China from 12–23 April 2006. The 2006 World Cup was the 11th edition of the competition. In the final, the host nation defeated Australia 4–3 to win the cup for the second successive year. Spain beat South Korea 3–2 after extra time in the third place play-off match.

17 SEPTEMBER 2006, MÖNCHENGLADBACH, GERMANY

Australia (2) 3	Germany (1) 4
(Knowles 18, Naylor 25, Elder 38)	*(Zeller 18, Fürste 46,*
	Emmerling 49, Zeller 54)

Women's Hockey World Cup Final

Rome, Italy, was the venue for qualification for the finals from 25 April–6 May 2006. The 2006 World Cup was the 11th edition of the competition. The Netherlands won its sixth world crown after defeating Australia 3–1 in the final. The defending champions, Argentina, defeated Spain 5–0 to claim the bronze medal.

8 OCTOBER 2006, MADRID, SPAIN

Netherlands (0) 3	Australia (0) 1
(Paumen 41, Karres 55, Paumen 66)	*(Sanders 47)*

Indoor World Cup 2007 – Men and Women

This was only the second ever staging of the tournament and followed the inaugural Indoor Hockey World Cup played in Leipzig in 2003 when the host nation, Germany, won both the men's and women's titles. The German men's team made it to their second successive final by defeating Spain 3–2 in the semis, while their opponents in the final, Poland, beat the Czech Republic 4–2. The Spanish women's team caused the biggest upset of the tournament by eliminating the defending champions Germany (4–3) in the semi-finals. In the other women's semi-final the Netherlands easily brushed aside Ukraine with an emphatic 8–0 victory. Germany beat Poland 4–1 in the men's final, while in the ladies' final, the Netherlands beat Spain 4–2 in a thrilling encounter.

RESULTS – MEN'S COMPETITION

Semi-finals		Final	
Germany 3–2 Spain		**Germany 4–1 Poland**	
Poland 4–2 Czech Republic		*Sperling 22. Fuerste 28,*	*Malecki 17*
		Draguhn 36, Deecke 40	

RESULTS – WOMEN'S COMPETITION

Semi-finals	Final
Netherlands 8–0 Ukraine	**Netherlands 4–2 Spain**
Spain 4–3 Germany	*Verhage 5, van Meer 9, Romagosa 34*
	Padalino 28, Verhage 36 Camon 40

BDO Women's Champion Trophy 2007

Six nations participated in the competition – Argentina, Australia, Germany, Japan, Netherlands and Spain. All six nations played each other once in a round robin format to complete five preliminary round games, ending with the top two teams facing each other in the final. The winners receive the gold medal, silver to the runners-up, the third and fourth placed teams play each other for the bronze medal, while the fifth and sixth placed nations meet in the fifth place play-off.

The final day of the competition began with Japan and Spain meeting each other to decide which nation would be relegated from the 2008 Championships. With a 2–0 victory for Japan, making their maiden Champions Trophy appearance, they relegated the Spanish from the top flight. Rika Komazawa scored both goals for Japan. Australia then faced Germany to decide the bronze medal winners after both nations ended the tournament equal on 7 points, although Australia finished higher thanks to their superior goal difference. However, it was Germany that clinched third place and with it the bronze medal after winning the game 2–0, with goals from Janine Beermann and Silja Lorenzen.

In the final The Netherlands defeated the hosts Argentina thanks to a goal after only 3 minutes from Maartje Paumen. Germany claimed the bronze medal following a 2–0 win over Australia.

FINAL ROUND ROBIN STAGE STANDINGS

Pos	Team	Pld	W	D	L	GF	GA	G/D	Pts
1.	**Netherlands**	**5**	**4**	**1**	**0**	**11**	**2**	**9**	**13**
2.	Argentina	5	4	0	1	12	5	7	12
3.	Australia	5	2	1	2	7	7	0	7
4.	Germany	5	2	1	2	5	6	-1	7
5.	Japan	5	1	0	4	2	10	-8	3
6.	Spain	5	0	1	4	5	12	-7	1

RESULTS

5th place play-off	**Final**
Japan 2–0 Spain	Netherlands 1–0 Argentina
	Paumen 2
3rd place play-off	
Australia 0–2 Germany	

British Club Hockey

National Indoor Hockey Championships 2007

Date: 21 January
Venue: National Indoor Arena, Birmingham, England

Men's Competition

Semi-finals
East Grinstead Indoor 8–6
Reading Men's 1s
Loughborough Students Men's 1s 4–4
Canterbury Men's 1s*
Canterbury won 8–7 on penalties

Final
Canterbury Men's 1s 7–6
East Grinstead Indoor

Women's Competition

Semi-finals
Slough Ladies Indoor 8–4
Sutton Coldfield Ladies 1s
Bowden Ladies 1s 6–6
Ipswich Ladies 1s*
Bowden won 2–1 on penalties

Final
Slough Ladies Indoor 7–4
Bowden Ladies 1s

Euro Hockey Nations Championships 2007

Date: 18–26 August
Venue: Belle Vue Leisure Centre, Manchester

This was Britain's biggest single hockey competition since London played host to the men's World Cup in 1986. Eight male teams and eight female teams took part. The top three teams in each championship gained automatic entry to the 2008 Beijing Olympics. England's women knew that nothing short of victory over Spain in the third place play-off would be good enough to secure their place. A goal from Mel Clewlow and two from Crista Cullen were enough to clinch a 3–2 victory for the English girls, who could now book their flights to Beijing. In the women's final, Germany beat the defending champions, the Netherlands, 2–0 to win their first women's title, while both nations had already qualified for the 2008 Olympics. The three most successful hockey nations all made it to the men's semi-finals. Belgium caused an upset by defeating the six-time winners Germany 4–3 in the third place play-off match, while the Netherlands claimed their third Euro Hockey Nations title with a 3–2 win over the two-time winners Spain.

Trivia

* Only three nations have won the women's event – Netherlands six titles, England one and Germany one. The German men have claimed six titles.

* Belle Vue hosted the hockey tournament at the 2002 Commonwealth Games.

GROUP STANDINGS
Men's Competition
Pool A

Team	P	W	D	L	F	A	GD	Pts
Germany	3	2	1	0	10	2	8	7
Belgium	3	1	2	0	10	4	6	5
England	3	1	1	1	9	5	4	4
Czech Rep.	3	0	0	3	0	18	-18	0

Pool B

Team	P	W	D	L	F	A	GD	Pts
Netherlands	3	3	0	0	13	5	8	9
Spain	3	1	1	1	9	5	4	4
France	3	1	0	2	4	14	-10	3
Ireland	3	0	1	2	1	3	-2	1

Relegation Pool

Team	P	W	D	L	F	A	GD	Pts
England	3	2	1	0	15	1	14	7
France	3	2	0	1	4	7	-3	6
Ireland*	3	1	1	1	11	2	9	4
Czech Rep.*	3	0	0	3	0	20	-20	0

*– relegated

Semi-finals
Netherlands 7–2 Belgium
Germany 3–3 Spain (2–4 APS)

Third Place Play-off
Belgium 4–3 Germany

Final
Netherlands 3–2 Spain

GROUP STANDINGS
Women's Competition
Pool A

Team	P	W	D	L	F	A	GD	Pts
Netherlands	3	3	0	0	16	1	15	9
England	3	2	0	1	7	1	6	6
Ireland	3	1	0	2	3	9	-6	3
Italy	3	0	0	3	1	16	-15	0

Pool B

Team	P	W	D	L	F	A	GD	Pts
Germany	3	3	0	0	15	1	14	9
Spain	3	1	1	1	6	4	2	4
Azerbaijan	3	1	1	1	6	10	-4	4
Ukraine	3	0	0	3	2	14	-12	0

Relegation Pool

Team	P	W	D	L	F	A	GD	Pts
Azerbaijan	3	3	0	0	6	2	4	9
Ireland	3	2	0	1	6	3	3	6
Italy*	3	1	0	2	1	4	-3	3
Ukraine*	3	0	0	3	2	6	-4	0

*– relegated

Semi-finals
Netherlands 3–0 Spain
England 1–2 Germany

Third Place Play-off
England 3–2 Spain

Final
Germany 2–0 Netherlands

Trivia

* The men's European Championships began in 1970 in Brussels, with West Germany beating the Netherlands 3–1 in the final. In the women's inaugural final, 1984, the Netherlands beat the Soviet Union 2–0.

* The 2007 Championships were the 11th tournament for men and the 8th for women, but it was only the second time that both the men's and women's tournament had been held at the same venue (the previous instance was the championships held in Barcelona in 2003).

Hurling

All-Ireland Senior Hurling Final 2006

Kilkenny played superbly to beat Cork, a repeat of the 2004 final. The Leinster men beat Cork, record holders with 30 All-Ireland SHC wins, by 1–16 to 1–13. Indeed, it was Kilkenny, nicknamed the Cats, who claimed their own treble by adding the Liam McCarthy Cup to their league and Leinster titles. In a hard fought game, the two teams were level five times before Aidan Fogarty scored for Kilkenny in the 29th minute. The men from Leinster led 1–08 to 0–08 at half-time and increased it to 4 points before points were traded to leave the score at 1–11 to 0–10. Ben O'Connor's goal for the Rebels in the 67th minute made it 1–15 to 1–12 and the Cats' nerves began to surface for the first time. However, in the end it was Brian Cody's men who brilliantly held on for a 3 points win, the county's 29th All-Ireland SHC title since 1904. The victory was even sweeter for Kilkenny, who not only had lost to Cork in the 2004 final and thus were denied a hat-trick of championships, but also they denied the Rebels an All-Ireland hat-trick of their own.

3 SEPTEMBER 2006, CROKE PARK, DUBLIN

Kilkenny 1–16   1–13 Cork

Kilkenny: J McGarry, M Kavanagh, N Hickey, J Tyrell (capt), J Ryall, J Tennyson, T Walsh, J Fitzpatrick (0–01), D Lyng (0–01), R Power (0–01), H Shefflin (0–08 (0–05f)), E Larkin, E Brennan (0–01), M Comerford (0–01), A Fogarty (1–03)
Manager: Brian Cody
Subs used: W O'Dwyer for Larkin (46 mins), R Mulally for Fitzpatrick (69)

Cork: D Og Cusack, B Murphy, D O'Sullivan, P Mulcahy (capt), J Gardiner (0-01), R Curran, S Og O hAilpin, T Kenny, J O'Connor (0-01), T McCarthy, N McCarthy (0–01), B O'Connor (1-04 (0-01f)), N Ronan, B Corcoran, J Deane (0-06 (0-05f))
Manager: John Allen
Subs used: C O'Connor for O hAilpin (blood sub, 35+1–36 mins), K Murphy (Sarsfields) for Ronan (40), W Sherlock for Mulcahy (47), C Naughton for T McCarthy (59), C O'Connor for Murphy (65), C Cusack for Kenny (70)

Yellow cards: Cork – O'Sullivan (23 mins), Mulcahy (44), Gardiner (68), N McCarthy (70+2); Kilkenny – Comerford (23), Hickey (28)

Att: 81,275

"I always say the best team wins the All-Ireland and
we were the best today. Cork were great champions and
I pay tribute to them. But the commitment and workrate our
players showed was outrageous really.**"**
Brian Cody, Kilkenny manager, after winning his fourth Liam McCarthy Cup

All-Ireland Senior Hurling Championship 2007

The 121st All-Ireland Senior Hurling Championships commenced in May 2007 with Kilkenny tipped to retain the Liam McCarthy Cup but Cork, Limerick, Tipperary and Waterford were all expected to test the 29-time All-Ireland Champions. The final will be played at Croke Park, Dublin on 2 September 2007. The same format as 2006 applied to the 2007 Championship with 12 counties participating in Tier 1: Galway the sole representative from Connacht (no Connacht Championship was played); Antrim (2007 Ulster Senior Hurling Champions) the sole representative from Ulster; Dublin, Laois, Kilkenny, Offaly and Wexford representing Leinster; Clare, Cork, Limerick, Tipperary and Waterford representing Munster. The Leinster and Munster Provincial Championships were played as normal with their respective champions and runners-up progressing to the All-Ireland quarter-finals. The six remaining teams from Leinster and Munster then joined Antrim and Galway in the eight-county All-Ireland qualifying series. The eight qualifying teams were sub-divided into two groups of four teams each with each team playing the others in their group only once.

On 1 July, Kilkenny beat Wexford 2–24 to 1-12 at Croke Park to claim their 64th Leinster Senior Hurling title. A week later Waterford beat Limerick 3–14 to 1–14 at Semple Stadium to win their eighth Munster Senior Hurling crown. Waterford also won the 2007 National Hurling League, winning 0-20 to 0-18 over Kerry on 29 April 2007.

Hurling Championship Qualifiers – Group 1A

Team	Pld	W	D	L	F	A	Pts	+/–
Clare	3	3	0	0	7–45	3–40	6	+17
Galway	3	2	0	1	5–65	4–33	4	+35
Antrim	3	1	0	2	4–47	6–65	2	–24
Laois	3	0	0	3	3–38	6–57	0	–28

Hurling Championship Qualifiers – Group 1B

Team	Pld	W	D	L	F	A	Pts	+/–
Tipperary	3	3	0	0	5–53	4–42	6	+14
Cork	3	2	0	1	5–65	2–42	4	+32
Offaly	3	1	0	2	4–49	5–57	2	–11
Dublin	3	0	0	3	3–39	6–65	0	–35

QUARTER-FINALS	SEMI-FINALS
Wexford 3–10 beat Tipperary 1–14	Kilkenny 0–23 beat Wexford 1–10
Limerick 1–23 beat Clare 1–16	Limerick 5–11 beat Waterford 2–15
Kilkenny 3–22 beat Galway 1–18	
Waterford 3–16, 2–17 beat Cork 3–16, 0–20	

FINAL: 2 September at Croke Park, Dublin
Kilkenny 2–19 beat Limerick 1–15

Ice Hockey

NHL Regular Season 2006–07

EASTERN CONFERENCE

Atlantic Division

	W	L	OTL	Pts
New Jersey Devils	49	24	9	107
Pittsburgh Penguins	47	24	11	105
New York Rangers	42	30	10	94
New York Islanders	40	30	12	92
Philadelphia Flyers	22	48	12	56

Northeast Division

	W	L	OTL	Pts
Buffalo Sabres	53	22	7	113
Ottawa Senators	48	25	9	105
Toronto Maple Leafs	40	31	11	91
Montreal Canadiens	42	34	6	90
Boston Bruins	35	41	6	76

Southeast Division

	W	L	OTL	Pts
Atlanta Thrashers	43	28	11	97
Tampa Bay Lightning	44	33	5	93
Carolina Hurricanes	40	34	8	88
Florida Panthers	35	31	16	86
Washington Capitals	28	40	14	70

WESTERN CONFERENCE

Central Division

	W	L	OTL	Pts
Detroit Red Wings	50	19	13	113
Nashville Predators	51	23	8	110
St Louis Blues	34	35	13	81
Columbus Blue Jackets	33	42	7	73
Chicago Blackhawks	31	42	9	71

Northwest Division

	W	L	OTL	Pts
Vancouver Canucks	49	26	7	105
Minnesota Wild	48	26	8	104
Calgary Flames	43	29	10	96
Colorado Avalanche	44	31	7	95
Edmonton Oilers	32	43	7	71

Pacific Division

	W	L	OTL	Pts
Anaheim Ducks	48	20	14	110
San Jose Sharks	51	26	5	107
Dallas Stars	50	25	7	107
Los Angeles Kings	27	41	14	68
Phoenix Coyotes	31	46	5	67

NHL Play-offs

EASTERN CONFERENCE

Quarter-finals
Buffalo Sabres 4–1 NY Islanders
NJ Devils 4–2 Tampa Bay Lightning
Atlanta Thrashers 0–4 NY Rangers
Ottawa Senators 4–2 Pittsburgh Penguins

Semi-finals
Buffalo Sabres 4–2 NY Rangers
NJ Devils 2–4 Ottawa Senators

Final
Buffalo Sabres 1–4 Ottawa Senators

WESTERN CONFERENCE

Quarter-finals
Detroit Red Wings 4–2 Calgary Flames
Anaheim Ducks 4–1 Minnesota Wild
Vancouver Canucks 4–3 Dallas Stars
San Josse Sharks 4–1 Nashville Predators

Semi-finals
Detroit Red Wings 4–2 San Jose Sharks
Anaheim Ducks 4–1 Vancouver Canucks

Final
Anaheim Ducks 4–2 Detroit Red Wings

NHL Stanley Cup Finals 2007

Date: 29 May–6 June 2007
Result: Anaheim Ducks 4–1 Ottawa Senators

Game 1, 28 May, Honda Center, Anaheim
SCORE: Anaheim Ducks 3–2 Ottawa Senators
Ottawa's Mike Fisher opened the scoring after just 98 seconds with a powerplay goal, but then Andy McDonald drew the Ducks level. In the second period a powerplay from Wade Redden put the Senators 2–1 up before Ryan Getzlaf made it 2–2. Travis Moen scored the winner deep in the third period.

Game 2, 30 May, Honda Center, Anaheim
SCORE: Anaheim Ducks 1–0 Ottawa Senators
The game looked to be heading for overtime before Samuel Pahlsson scored with less than 6 minutes remaining to give the Ducks a 2–0 lead in the series.

Game 3, 2 June, Scotiabank Place, Ottawa
SCORE: Ottawa Senators 5–3 Anaheim Ducks
The Ottawa Senators finally made the Stanley Cup final a contest by winning Game 3. Goals from Chris Neil, Mike Fisher, Daniel Alfredsson, Dean McAmmond and Anton Volchenkov reduced their series deficit to 2–1.

Game 4, 4 June, Scotiabank Place, Ottawa
SCORE: Anaheim Ducks 3–2 Ottawa Senators
The Ducks won Game 4 to take a 3–1 lead in the best-of-seven series. There were two goals from Andy McDonald who then set up Dustin Penner's game winner in the third quarter. The signs were not good for the Senators as only one team has come back from 3–1 down to win the Cup since the best-of-seven format was introduced in 1939.

Game 5, 6 June, Honda Center, Anaheim
SCORE: Anaheim Ducks 6–2 Ottawa Senators
The Anaheim Ducks beat the Ottawa Senators on home ice to win the Stanley Cup for the first time in the franchise's history. The Ducks sealed a 4–1 series victory with goals from Andy McDonald, Rob Niedermayer, Ray Emery (og), Francois Beauchemin, Travis Moen and Corey Perry. The Ducks also became the first team from California and the first West Coast team to win the Stanley Cup since the Victoria Cougars in 1925.

Play-offs MVP (Conn Smythe Trophy) – Scott Niedermayer, Anaheim Ducks

"You can't really fathom that we've got it done."
Randy Carlyle
Ducks' coach

"This is one you can only dream of."
Scott Niedermayer
Anaheim Ducks, four-time
Stanley Cup winner

World Ice Hockey Championships 2007

Date: 27 April–13 May
Venue: Mytischi Arena and Khodynka Ice Palace, Moscow, Russia

Twenty-one years had passed since Russia last had the honour of hosting the IHF Ice Hockey World Championships. The 2007 tournament, the 71st edition, brought together the world's top 16 nations, with each one hoping to be crowned world champions. Sweden was out to defend its 2006 world title.

The tournament was won by Canada, the 24th time they have captured the world crown, with their star player, Rick Nash, being named the Most Valuable Player. A total of 56 games were played with 361 goals scored (an average of 6.446 per game), while the attendance figure for the tournament was 330,708 (an average of 5,906 per game). Sweden's Johan Davidsson led the competition in scoring with 14 points, helping his country to fourth place.

Quarter-finals
Russia 4 Czech Republic 0
Sweden 7 Slovakia 4
Canada 5 Switzerland 1
Finland 5 USA 4 (GWS)

Semi-finals
Finland 2 Russia 1 (OT)
Canada 4 Sweden 1

Bronze Medal Game
Russia 3 Sweden 1

Final
May 13
Khodynka Arena, Moscow
Canada 4 Finland 2

"Life is all about making a difference. You guys made a difference in Canada today... We've got the deepest emotional well in the world for the game of hockey. I'll tell you, when Rick Nash was going in on that breakaway in the last minute or so, 31 million Canadians were carrying our emotions with him."
Andy Murray,
Canada's coach talking to the players in the locker room after the final

"Canada was much better than us today. Good for them. We tried to chip away at the lead in the third, but it was too late."
Jukka Hentunen, Team Finland

Trivia

* When Sweden won the 2006 competition they became the first nation in history to win an Olympic gold and the IHF World Championship in the same year.

* All Olympic ice hockey tournaments between 1920 and 1968 also counted as World Ice Hockey Championships.

World Junior Ice Hockey Championships 2007

DATE: 26 December 2006 – 5 January 2007 *VENUE:* Leksand and Mora, Sweden

The 2007 World Junior Ice Hockey Championships were held in the FM Mattsson Arena in Mora and Ejendals Arena in Leksand. Going into the 2007 tournament, Canada and Russia were the clear favourites having won five of the previous six gold medals between them. In the end it was the Canadians who won their third consecutive gold medal, with Russia finishing runners-up for the third year in succession and the USA claiming the bronze medal. Belarus and Germany were relegated to Division 1 for the 2008 tournament while Estonia and Norway moved in the opposite direction.

Trivia

* The inaugural tournament was held in Leningrad, USSR in 1974 and was won by the home nation. Indeed, the Soviet Union dominated the early years of the competition, winning the first seven World Championships.

* At the 1987 WJHC held in Piestany, Czechoslovakia, a huge bench-clearing fight broke-out involving between the Soviet Union, the holders, and Canada, runners-up in 1986, that resulted in both nations being disqualified from the tournament. The overall standings were adjusted making Finland world champions.

Table of Medals (1974–2007)

Nation	Gold	Silver	Bronze	Total
Canada	13	8	5	26
Soviet Union	11	3	2	16
Russia	3	6	3	12
Finland	2	5	6	13
Czechoslovakia	2	0	1	3
Sweden	1	6	5	12
United States	1	1	3	5
CIS	1	0	0	1
Czech Republic	0	5	7	12
Slovakia	0	0	1	1
Switzerland	0	0	1	1

British Ice Hockey 2006–07

The Challenge Cup was the first trophy of the season up for grabs and was won by the Coventry Blaze who beat the Sheffield Steelers 9–4 on aggregate in a two-leg final (4–3 at home and 5 1 away). The Blaze completed a double by winning the Elite League, four points clear of the defending champions, the Belfast Giants, their second league title in three years. The top eight teams in the league went into the play-offs leaving the Hull Stingrays and the bottom placed Edinburgh Capitals out of contention. In the semi-finals the Blaze lost to the league's third best side during the season, the Cardiff Devils, who went on to lose 2–1 in a penalty shoot-out to the Nottingham Panthers (finished fifth in the Elite League) in the play-off championship final. Amazingly the Panthers won all of their play-off matches by means of a penalty shoot-out to claim their first Play-Off Championship success since 1988–89. The Blaze narrowly missed out on completing a treble when they lost the British Knockout Cup to the Devils.

ELITE ICE HOCKEY LEAGUE 2006/07

	Team	GP	W	L(OT)	GF	GA	Pts
1.	**Coventry Blaze**	54	36	15 (3)	186	129	75
2.	Belfast Giants	54	34	17 (3)	192	151	71
3.	Cardiff Devils	54	32	17 (5)	175	152	69
4.	Sheffield Steelers	54	30	16 (8)	163	153	68
5.	Nottingham Panthers	54	29	17 (8)	182	149	66
6.	Manchester Phoenix	54	26	22 (6)	185	184	58
7.	Basingstoke Bison	54	23	25 (6)	160	185	52
8.	Newcastle Vipers	54	24	29 (1)	151	168	49
9.	Hull Stingrays	54	18	33 (3)	113	174	39
10.	Edinburgh Capitals	54	18	33 (3)	160	222	39

ENGLISH PREMIER ICE HOCKEY LEAGUE 2006/07

	Team	GP	W	D	L(OT)	GF	GA	Pts
1.	**Bracknell Bees**	44	33	2	7 (2)	219	114	70
2.	Sheffield Scimitars	44	32	2	10	195	106	66
3.	Slough Jets	44	29	2	11 (2)	203	140	62
4.	Guildford Flames	44	29	3	11 (1)	198	124	62
5.	Milton Keynes Lightning	44	28	2	14	187	132	58
6.	Peterborough Phantoms	44	25	1	13 (5)	228	167	56
7.	Swindon Wildcats	44	22	0	22	192	178	44
8.	Chelmsford Chieftains	44	20	3	21	194	184	43
9.	Romford Raiders	44	14	4	25 (1)	175	234	33
10.	Solihull Barons	43	9	3	31 (1)	141	235	22
11.	Telford Tigers	43	8	1	34	131	229	17
12.	Wightlink Raiders	43	3	0	39 (1)	102	323	7

ENGLISH NATIONAL ICE HOCKEY LEAGUE 2006/07; NORTH

	Team	GP	W	L	D	GF	GA	Pts
1.	**Newcastle ENL**	18	14	3	1	104	52	29
2.	Whittley Warriors	18	13	3	2	128	66	28
3.	Sheffield	18	11	6	1	101	72	23
4.	Flintshire Freeze	18	8	6	4	92	72	20
5.	Blackburn Hawks	18	9	7	2	108	81	20
6.	Nottingham Lions	18	9	7	2	89	70	20
7.	Billingham Bombers	18	8	10	0	85	99	16
8.	Bradford Bulldogs	18	4	12	2	93	125	10
9.	Kingston Jets	18	5	13	0	68	138	10
10.	Grimsby	18	2	16	0	81	168	4

ENGLISH NATIONAL ICE HOCKEY LEAGUE 2006/07; SOUTH

	Team	GP	W	L	D	GF	GA	Pts
1.	**Invicta Dynamos**	22	20	1	1	179	53	41
2.	Streatham Redskins	22	17	4	1	127	62	35
3.	Haringey Greyhounds	22	13	6	3	113	81	29
4.	Oxford City Stars	22	13	8	1	118	98	27
5.	Peterborough Islanders	22	11	6	5	119	91	27
6.	Basingstoke Buffalo	22	11	10	1	138	102	23
7.	Bracknell Hornets	22	10	9	3	86	102	23
8.	Swindon Wildcats	22	9	11	2	92	93	20
9.	Milton Keynes Thunder	22	5	13	4	79	99	14
10.	Lee Valley Lions	22	5	15	2	83	166	12
11.	Solent & Gosport	22	4	18	0	82	198	8
12.	Romford Spitfires	22	2	19	1	50	121	5

"The boys should take a bow for their performances, week in and week out this season.**"**
Paul Thompson, coach of the Coventry Blaze

"This is absolutely fantastic for the team, the fans and the city.**"**
Grant Charman, Coventry Blaze director

Motor Racing

Race of Champions 2006

Date: 16 December 2006
Venue: Stade de France, Paris, France

The Race of Champions is an annual international motorsport tournament featuring national teams comprising of a Formula One driver and a World Rally Championship (WRC) driver. It is traditionally held at the end of the year when the season for both sports has ended. The inaugural competition of 1988 was organized by Michele Mouton and Fredrik Johnson in memory of Henri Toivonen, a rally car driver who along with his co-pilot Sergio Cresto lost their lives in a crash during the 1986 Tour de Corse.

Since the inaugural tournament an individual has been crowned Champion of Champions and awarded the Henri Toivonen Memorial trophy. The Nations Cup was added in 1999 with each competing nation entering one F1 driver and one rally car driver. Finland won the 2006 Nations Cup with Heikki Kovalainen (F1) and the two-time World Rally champion Marcus Gronholm. The Henri Toivonen Memorial trophy was won by Mattias Ekstrom of Sweden.

A1GP 2006–07

The 2006–07 A1 Grand Prix season was the competition's second; A1 Team France won the inaugural World Cup of Motorsport on 12 March 2006. Season two, comprising 24 teams, began at the Circuit Park Zandvoort, Netherlands, on 1 October 2006 and ended after race 11, which was held at Brands Hatch, England, on 29 April 2007. A 12th race was scheduled for Brazil on 17 January 2007, but when the A1GP ruling body ran into a delay in obtaining a terrestrial television licence the race was cancelled. A1 Team Germany won the championship with a total of 128 points, having won three sprint races.

A1GP Race Schedule

Race Date	Circuit	Country	Sprint Winner	Feature Winner
1. 1/10/2006	Zandvoort	Netherlands	South Africa	Germany
2. 8/10/2006	Brno	Czech Republic	Malaysia	Malaysia
3. 12/11/2006	Beijing	China	The Netherlands	Italy
4. 26/11/2006	Sepang	Malaysia	Switzerland	Germany
5. 10/12/2006	Sentul	Indonesia	New Zealand	New Zealand
6. 21/1/2007	Taupo	New Zealand	Germany	Germany
7. 4/2/2007	Eastern Creek	Australia	Germany	Germany
8. 25/2/2007	Durban	South Africa	Germany	Germany
9. 25/3/2007	Mexico City	Mexico	Malaysia	Great Britain
10. 15/4/2007	Shanghai	China	Great Britain	New Zealand

A1GP Season 2006–07 Final Table

Pos	Team	Ned	Cze	Bei	Mys	Idn	Nz	Aus	Zaf	Mex	Sha	Gbr	Ttl Pts
1.	Germany	13	7	2	15	11	17	17	17	2	12	15	128
2.	New Zealand	1	4	2	8	16	12	14	12	5	17	3	93
3.	Great Britain	6	5	9	11	5	–	1	9	15	15	16	92
4.	France	4	4	7	9	8	14	6	5	–	3	7	67
5.	The Netherlands	7	2	6	2	–	9	9	8	–	7	7	57
6.	Malaysia	–	17	–	7	6	–	5	3	12	1	4	55
7.	Italy	5	–	14	–	7	3	–	–	7	4	12	52
8.	Switzerland	3	1	–	13	3	9	7	9	–	5	–	50
9.	USA	9	1	–	5	5	1	3	–	11	2	5	42
10.	Mexico	11	8	5	–	10	–	–	–	1	–	–	35
11.	Canada	–	11	5	6	–	6	–	–	–	5	–	33
12.	Czech Republic	–	11	5	–	4	–	6	–	–	1	–	27
13.	Australia	8	–	8	–	2	–	–	–	7	–	–	25
14.	South Africa	7	–	6	–	–	–	–	–	11	–	–	24
15.	China	2	6	–	–	–	2	9	–	2	–	1	22
16.	Portugal	–	–	–	–	–	–	–	6	4	–	–	10
17.	Brazil	–	–	5	–	–	–	–	4	–	–	–	9
18.	Ireland	–	–	–	1	–	–	–	1	–	6	–	8
19.	India	–	–	–	–	–	4	–	2	–	–	–	6
20.	Singapore*	–	–	3	–	–	–	–	–	–	–	–	3
21.	Indonesia	1	–	–	–	–	–	–	–	–	–	–	1
22.	Pakistan	–	–	–	–	–	–	–	1	–	–	–	1
23.	Lebanon	–	–	–	–	–	–	–	–	–	–	–	0
24.	Greece	–	–	–	–	–	–	–	–	–	–	–	0

*After racing in the South African A1GP, Team Singapore did not show up at any of the remaining races and they did not offer any explanation.

POINTS SYSTEM
Sprint race: 6 points for 1st place down to 1 point for 6th place
Main race: 10 points for 1st place down to 1 point for 10th place
Bonus point: 1 point awarded for the fastest lap of either race
Prize money: main race only

"The performance of both A1 Team Germany and its driver Nico Hulkenberg were excellent this season. Nico possesses everything he needs for the future. There is a long way to go, but he works hard, so why shouldn't he achieve all his goals? I'm proud that my native country won the title. But the personal connections that I have also make this something very special to me."

Michael Schumacher, *after Team Germany won the 2007 A1GP title*

IndyCar

Indianapolis 500

Scotland's Dario Franchitti won the rain-shortened 91st Indianapolis 500-Mile Race and took home a cheque for $1,645,233 from a record race purse of $10,668,815. It was Franchitti's first win at the Brickyard in his fifth attempt to win the Indy 500, while the unfancied racer gave Mario Andretti's Andretti Green Racing its second Indy 500 victory in the past three years following Dan Wheldon's (England) victory in 2005. Franchitti drove the number 27 Canadian Club Dallara/Honda/Firestone in the 166-lap race.

27 MAY 2007, INDIANAPOLIS MOTOR SPEEDWAY, INDIANA, USA

Pos.	Driver/Team	Car No.	Start Pos.	Qual. Speed	Laps	Times Led	Laps Led	Pts
1.	**Dario Franchitti (Sco)/** **Canadian Club**	27	3	225.191	166	3	33	50
2.	Scott Dixon (NZ)/ Target Chip Ganassi Racing	9	4	225.122	166	3	11	40
3.	Helio Castroneves (Bra)/ Team Penske	3	1	225.817	166	3	19	35
4.	Sam Hornish Jr. (USA)/ Team Penske	6	5	225.109	166	1	2	32
5.	Ryan Briscoe (Aus)/ Symantec Luczo Dragon Racing	12	7	224.410	166	0	0	30
6.	Scott Sharp (USA)/ Patron Sharp Rahal Letterman	8	12	223.875	166	0	0	28
7.	Tomas Scheckter (SA)/ Vision Racing	2	10	222.877	166	0	0	26
8.	Danica Patrick (USA)/ Motorola	7	8	224.076	166	0	0	24
9.	Davey Hamilton (USA)/ HP Vision Racing	02	20	222.327	166	0	0	22
10.	Vitor Meira (Bra)/ Delphi Panther	4	19	222.333	166	0	0	20

Due to bad weather conditions, the race was halted after 166 of the 200 scheduled laps had been completed.

Trivia

* Franchitti became only the second Scotsman to win the Indianapolis 500 after Jim Clark's victory in 1965 (Clark also won the 1965 F1 World Championship).

* Danica Patrick became the first woman ever to lead the Indianapolis 500 when she did so before finishing fourth in 2005. She has yet to win a race on the IndyCar Tour.

NASCAR

NASCAR – Nextel Cup Championship 2006

Jimmie Johnson, driving the Hendrick Motorsports' Chevrolet sponsored by Lowe's, won the 2006 NASCAR NEXTEL Cup taking 5 wins from his 36 races, 1 pole position, 13 top 5 finishes, 124 top 10 finishes, with an average finish of 9.7. His first of the season came in the season's opener, the Daytona 500, making it seven wins from the last seven Daytona events for a Chevrolet. The 2006 season was the first for Ford's all-new Fusion, replacing the Tauru both in NASCAR and showrooms across the USA. Chevrolet also debuted a new version of their Monte Carlo, the Monte Carlo Super Sport.

Rank	Driver	No.	Team	Maker	Starts	Wins	Poles	Points
1.	Jimmie Johnson	48	Hendrick	Chevrolet	36	5	1	6470
2.	Matt Kenseth	17	Rousch	Ford	36	4	1	6414
3.	Denny Hamlin	11	Gibbs	Chevrolet	36	2	1	6407
4.	Kevin Harvick	29	Childress	Chevrolet	36	5	3	6397
5.	Dale Earnhardt Jr	8	DEI	Chevrolet	36	1	0	6323
6.	Jeff Gordon	24	Hendrick	Chevrolet	36	2	2	6246
7.	Jeff Burton	31	Childress	Chevrolet	36	1	4	6228
8.	Kasey Kahne	9	Evernham	Dodge	36	6	5	6173
9.	Mark Martin	6	Rousch	Ford	36	0	0	6165
10.	Kyle Busch	5	Hendrick	Chevrolet	36	1	1	6022

NASCAR – Busch Series 2006

The 25th season of the NASCAR Busch Series began on 18 February 2006 at Daytona International Speedway and ended on 18 November 2006 at the Homestead-Miami Speedway. Kevin Harvick from Bakersfield, California, winner of the 2001 Busch Grand National Series Championship, won the 2006 NASCAR Busch Series Championship, claiming victory in 9 of the 35 races he competed in, 23 top 5 finishes and 32 top 10 finishes. Harvick clinched the title on 13 October in the Dollar General 500 (at Lowe's Motor Speedway) with four races of the season remaining, the fastest ever in the Busch Series. Harvick drove three different cars during the 2006 series (#21, #33, #29) for two different teams, Kevin Harvick Incorporated and Richard Childress Racing.

Rank	Driver	Points	Starts	Wins	Poles	Earnings
1.	Kevin Harvick	5648	35	1	9	$1,345,380
2.	Carl Edwards	4824	35	3	4	$1,093,470
3.	Clint Bowyer	4683	35	2	1	$1,008,810
4.	Denny Hamlin	4667	35	6	2	$1,099,010
5.	J.J. Yeley	4487	35	3	0	$954,604

World Rally Championship 2006

The Championship commenced on 20 January in Monte Carlo with Finland's Marcus Gronholm winning the 74th edition of the Monte Carlo Rally in a Ford Focus R5 WRC 06, closely followed home by the two-time world champion, Sebastien Loeb of France in his Citroen Xsara. The Finnish driver won again in Sweden before Loeb and his Kronos Total Citroen team took victory in the Corona Rally Mexico, the first of five successive WRC wins for the reigning world champion. Gronholm then took victory in the 53rd Acropolis Rally before Loeb won his fifth consecutive ADAC Rally of Germany, his sixth win of the season and earning him his 26th career rally victory to tie the record held by the former two-time WRC world champion Carlos Sainz of Spain. Loeb now held a commanding lead in the race for the 2006 title, a lead he never lost. Loeb moved ahead of Sainz on 27 career wins following his success in the Rally of Japan and made it 28 career wins by winning the following race, the Rally of Cyprus. Despite breaking his arm in a mountain-biking accident before the Rally of Turkey that ended his season, Loeb won his third drivers title when his nearest challenger, Gronholm, failed to claim enough points in the third last rally of the year, the Rally of Australia. However, with eight outright wins for the Ford Focus RS WRC (seven by Gronholm and one by Mikko Hirvonen) Ford won the FIA Manufacturers Championship, their first manufacturers title since 1979.

Trivia

* Marcus Gronholm's father, Ulf "Uffe" Gronholm, was also a rally driver and a two-time Finnish champion.

* When he was a teenager, Marcus Gronholm enjoyed motocross in his spare time before a serious knee injury forced him to take up boxing.

* In 2004, Sebastien Loeb and Jean Alesi won the Nations Cup for France in the Tournament of Champions.

* In 2006, Marcus Gronholm and his fellow Finn, the Renault Formula 1 racing driver, Heikki Kovalainen, won the Nations Cup for Finland in the Tournament of Champions.

* In 2004, a special "World Champions Challenge" race was held as part of the Tournament of Champions. Formula 1 world champion, Michael Schumacher, raced 2004 World Rally Championship winner, Sebastien Loeb, with Schumacher ending the victor.

* Sebastien Loeb has won the Champion of Champions title at the Tournament of Champions twice – 2003 and 2005.

WORLD RALLY CHAMPIONSHIP LEADERS *after Rally of New Zealand*

Pos	Driver	Car	Nationality	Points
1.	Marcus Gronholm	Ford	Finland	90
2.	Sebastian Loeb	Citroen	France	80
3.	Marvo Hirvonen	Ford	Finland	69

WRC Events 2006

Rally	Date	Top Driver	Car
Monte-Carlo	20–22 Jan	Marcus Gronholm	Ford Focus RS WRC 06
Swedish	3–5 Feb	Marcus Gronholm	Ford Focus RS WRC 06
Mexican	3–5 Mar	Sebastien Loeb	Citroen Xsara
Spanish	24–26 Mar	Sebastien Loeb	Citroen Xsara
French	7–9 Apr	Sebastien Loeb	Citroen Xsara
Argentinian	28–30 Apr	Sebastien Loeb	Citroen Xsara
Italian	19–21 May	Sebastien Loeb	Citroen Xsara
Greek	2–4 Jun	Marcus Gronholm	Ford Focus RS WRC 06
German	11–13 Aug	Sebastien Loeb	Citroen Xsara
Finnish	18–20 Aug	Marcus Gronholm	Ford Focus RS WRC 06
Japanese	1–3 Sep	Sebastien Loeb	Citroen Xsara
Cypriot	22–24 Sep	Sebastien Loeb	Citroen Xsara
Turkish	13–15 Oct	Marcus Gronholm	Ford Focus RS WRC 06
Australian	27–29 Oct	Mikko Hirvonen	Ford Focus RS WRC 06
New Zealand	17–19 Nov	Marcus Gronholm	Ford Focus RS WRC 06
British	1–3 Dec	Marcus Gronholm	Ford Focus RS WRC 06

Wales Rally GB

The rally was won by Marcus Gronholm from Finland, who gave his BP-Ford team
their first Rally of Great Britain success for 27 years. Of the 111 official starters, 82 were
classified as finishers. The Wales Rally GB was also the sixth and final round of the Tesco
99 Octane British Rally Championship that also incorporated the Mitsubishi Evolution
Challenge. Gwyndaf Evans (Dolgellau) won the six-round Mitsubishi series earning the
Welshman a prize-drive in the 2007 British Rally Championship.

OVERALL TOP 10 DRIVERS AFTER LEG THREE OF THE WALES RALLY GB 2006

Pos	No	Driver	Stage Time	Penalty Time	Total Time
1.	3	Gronholm	03:20:24.8	00:00:00.0	03:20:24.8
2.	7	Stohl	03:22:00.3	00:00:00.0	03:22:00.3
3.	5	Solberg	03:22:20.0	00:00:00.0	03:22:20.0
4.	10	Latvala	03:23:01.9	00:00:00.0	03:23:01.9
5.	1	Pons	03:23:44.7	00:00:00.0	03:23:44.7
6.	6	Atkinson	03:23:52.3	00:00:00.0	03:23:52.3
7.	2	Sordo	03:24:33.1	00:00:00.0	03:24:33.1
8.	15	Duval	03:24:47.4	00:00:00.0	03:24:47.4
9.	11	Rovanpera	03:28:25.1	00:00:00.0	03:28:25.1
10.	18	Kopecky	03:28:52.6	00:00:00.0	03:28:52.6

Lisbon–Dakar Rally 2007

The 2007 Lisbon–Dakar Rally began on 6 January at the Centro Cultural de Belem in Lisbon and ended on 21 January 2007 in Senegal. For the second time in history, and following the 2006 start, the race started off in Portugal and ran through Spain, Morocco, Mauritania, Mali and Senegal. The famous race saw 250 bikers, 187 cars and 88 trucks race against each other in a gruelling 15-day race over thousands of miles. The 2007 race included Giniel De Villiers (runner-up in 2006), Cyril Despres (KTM–Gauloises), Marc Coma (KTM–Repsol), Luc Alphand, Stephane Peterhansel, Carlos Sainz (World Rally Champion in 1990 and 1992), Guerlain Chicherit, Jean-Louis Schlesser, Jutta Kleinschmid and the four-time event winner Ari Vatanen of Finland. The 2007 race was marred by the death of Elmer Symons, a 29-year-old motor racer who died after sustaining injuries in a crash on stage 4. A second fatality occurred on 20 January, the night before the race's finish, when Eric Aubijoux, a 42-year-old motorcyclist, was believed to have died of a heart attack shortly after completing stage 14 of the race.

24-Hours of Le Mans 2007

Date: 16–17 June *Venue:* Le Mans, Sarthe, France

1. Frank Biela, Marco Werner *(Ger)*, Emanuele Pirro *(Ita)*	
	Audi No. 1 – 369 laps
2. Pedro Lamy *(Por)* Stephane Sarrazin, Stephane Bourdais *(Fra)*	
	Peugeot No. 8 – 359 laps
3. Emmanuel Collard, Jean-Christophe Boullion, Romain Dumas *(Fra)*	
	Pescarolo Judd No. 16 – 357 laps
4. Joao Barbosa *(Por)*, Stuart Hall, Martin Short *(GB)*	
	Pescarolo Judd No. 18 – 347 laps
5. David Brabham *(Aus)*, Rickard Rydell *(Swe)*, Darren Turner *(GB)*	
	Aston Martin No. 009 – 342 laps
6. Johnny O'Connell *(USA)*, Jan Magnussen *(Den)*, Ron Fellows *(Can)*	
	Corvette No. 63 – 342 laps
7. Christophe Bouchut *(Fra)*, Fabrizio Gollin *(Ita)*, Casper Elgaard *(Den)*	
	Aston Martin No. 008 – 340 laps
8. Alex Yoong *(Mal)*, Stefan Muck *(Ger)* Jan Charouz *(Cze)*	
	Lola Judd No. 15 – 337 laps
9. Tomas Enge *(Cze)*, Johnny Herbert *(GB)*, Peter Kox *(Ned)*	
	Aston Martin No. 007 – 337 laps
10. Laurent Groppi, Nicolas Prost, Jean-Philippe Belloc *(Fra)*	
	Saleen No. 54 – 336 laps

> "We had nine stressful hours with the Peugeot right behind us, but the more you suffer, the greater the pleasure."
> **Emanuele Pirro,** *Audi driver*

Monte Carlo Rally 2007

The Monte Carlo Rally (Rallye Automobile Monte Carlo) is an annual rallying competition organized by the Automobile Club de Monaco. The drivers race along the beautiful French Riviera in the Principality of Monaco. The inaugural Monte Carlo Rally was the brainchild of Prince Albert I of Monaco and was won by Henri Rougier in a Turcat-Mery. Since 1973, the Monte Carlo Rally has been raced in January and is the first race of the FIA's World Rally Championship calendar. The race used to feature the drivers racing up the famous and dangerous Col de Turini at night on La Bollene to Sospel (or on occasion Sospel to La Bollene) route. However, in 2007 the "Turini" was not featured in the 74th edition of the race that was won by the three-time World Rally Champion Sebastien Loeb on the debut of Citroen's new C4, with his team-mate claiming second place. It was the French driver's 29th rally victory alongside his co-pilot Daniel Elena.

STAGE WINNERS

Stage	Name	Winner
SS1	St Jean En Royans	S Loeb / D Elena
SS2	La Cime Du Mas	S Loeb / D Elena
SS3	St Pierreville 1	D Sordo / M Marti
SS4	Burzet 1	S Loeb / D Elena
SS5	St Martial 1	D Sordo / M Marti
SS6	St Pierreville 2	S Loeb / D Elena
SS7	Burzet 2	D Sordo / M Marti
SS8	St Martial 2	S Loeb / D Elena
SS9	Labatie D'andaure 1	S Loeb / D Elena
SS10	St Bonnet 1	C Atkinson / G Macneall
SS11	Lamastre 1	M Hirvonen / J Lehtinen
SS12	Labatie D'andaure 2	M Hirvonen / J Lehtinen
SS13	St Bonnet 2	C Atkinson / G Macneall
SS14	Lamastre 2	M Hirvonen / J Lehtinen
SS15	Monaco	C Atkinson / G Macneall

Pos	Name	Country	Car Manufacturer	Time
1.	S Loeb	(Fra)	Citroën	3hrs 10mins 27.4secs
2.	D Sordo	(Spa)	Citroën	3:11:05.6
3.	M Grönholm	(Fin)	Ford	3:11:50.2
4.	C Atkinson	(Aus)	Subaru	3:12:55.5
5.	M Hirvonen	(Fin)	Ford	3:12:55.7
6.	P Solberg	(Nor)	Subaru	3:13:39.4
7.	T Gardemeister	(Fin)	M'bishi	3:14:05.5
8.	J Kopecky	(Cze)	Skoda	3:15:06.8
9.	J Cuoq	(Fra)	Peugeot	3:16:27.1
10.	M Stohl	(Nor)	Ford 3	:17:04.7

Speedway Grand Prix 2006

The 2006 Speedway Grand Prix was the 12th edition of the competition to determine the Speedway world champion. The 2006 season began in Krsko, Slovenia and finished in Bydgoszcz, Poland on 23 September. Jason Crump from Australia took the crown.

Championship Results

Race	Date	Grand Prix	Stadium	City	Winner
1.	22 Apr	Slovenia	Matije Gubca Stadium	Krsko	Nicki Pedersen *(Den)*
2.	6 May	Europe *(Pol)*	Olimpic Stadium	Wroclaw	Jason Crump *(Aus)*
3.	20 May	Sweden	Smedstadium	Eskilstuna	Jason Crump *(Aus)*
4.	3 Jun	Great Britain	Millennium Stadium	Cardiff	Jason Crump *(Aus)*
5.	24 Jun	Denmark	Parken Stadium	Copenhagen	Hans Niklas Andersen *(Den)*
6.	29 Jul	Italy	Santa Marina Stadium	Lonigo	Jason Crump *(Aus)*
7.	12 Aug	Scandinavia *(Swe)*	G&B Stadium	Malilla	Andreas Jonsson *(Swe)*
8.	26 Aug	Czech Republic	Marketa Stadium	Prague	Hans Niklas Andersen *(Den)*
9.	9 Sep	Latvia	Spidveja Centrs	Daugavpils	Greg Hancock *(USA)*
10.	23 Sep	Poland	Polonia Stadium	Bydgoszcz	Nicki Pedersen *(Den)*

Final Championship Table

Pos		Rider	Pts	Slo	Euro (Pol)	Swe	GB	Den	Ita	Scan (Swe)	Czb Rep	Lat	Pol
1.	(2)	Jason Crump *(Aus)*	188	20	25	25	25	20	25	16	14	11	7
2.	(5)	Greg Hancock *(USA)*	144	5	20	20	16	13	9	12	4	25	20
3.	(4)	Nicki Pedersen *(Den)*	134	25	14	16	4	6	9	11	6	18	25
4.	(8)	Andreas Jonsson *(Swe)*	119	8	5	10	20	7	9	25	7	16	12
5.	(3)	Leigh Adams *(Aus)*	106	10	7	11	6	12	16	18	12	8	6
6.	(16)	(19) Hans Andersen *(Den)*	101	–	–	–	–	25	18	20	25	4	9
7.	(13)	Matej zagar *(Slo)*	97	9	18	4	9	4	10	4	20	11	8
8.	(7)	Tomasz Gollob *(Pol)*	94	18	9	18	7	3	7	4	6	4	18
9.	(11)	Jarosaw Hampel *(Pol)*	91	4	16	8	18	2	4	10	16	7	6
10.	(10)	Antonio Lindback *(Swe)*	89	9	2	6	8	16	4	3	18	20	3
11.	(9)	Scott Nicholls *(GB)*	83	9	9	5	8	8	20	8	–	9	7
12.	(6)	Bjarne Pedersen *(Den)*	82	5	6	7	12	18	10	8	2	7	7

	Pts										
13. *(15)* Niels Kristian Iversen *(Den)*	51	2	6	4	5	8	5	6	8	4	3
14. *(1)* Tony Rickardsson *(Swe)*	41	16	6	4	10	5	–	–	–	–	–
15. *(12)* Lee Richardson *(GB)*	39	8	4	0	5	9	4	4	3	0	2
16. *(14)* Piotr Protasiewicz *(Pol)*	31	1	3	3	3	1	3	4	5	4	4
17. *(16)* Wiesaw Jagus *(Pol)*	16	–	–	–	–	–	–	–	–	–	16
18. *(20)* Ryan Sullivan *(Aus)*	10	–	–	–	–	–	–	1	9	–	–
19. *(16) (17)* Fredrik Lindgren *(Swe)*	7	–	–	7	–	–	–	ns	–	–	–
20. *(16)* Krzysztof Kasprzak *(Pol)*	6	–	6	–	–	–	–	–	–	–	–
21. *(16)* Kasts Poudzuks *(Lat)*	4	–	–	–	–	–	–	–	–	4	–
22. *(17)* Lubos Tomicek *(Cze)*	4	–	–	–	–	–	–	–	4	–	–
23. *(16)* Matej Ferian *(Slo)*	3	3	–	–	–	–	–	–	–	–	–
24. *(16)* Simon Stead *(GB)*	3	–	–	–	3	–	–	–	–	–	–
25. *(16)* Adrian Rymel *(Cze)*	2	–	–	–	–	–	–	–	2	–	–
26. *(17)* Charlie Gjedde *(Den)*	1	–	–	–	–	1	–	–	–	–	–
27. *(18)* Kenneth Bjerre *(Den)*	1	–	–	–	–	1	–	–	–	–	–
28. *(16)* Mattia Carpanese *(Ita)*	0	–	–	–	–	–	0	–	–	–	–
29. *(17)* Janusz Kolodziej *(Pol)*	0	–	0	–	–	–	–	–	–	–	ns
30. *(17) (18)* Jonas Davidsson *(Swe)*	0	–	–	0	–	–	–	ns	–	–	–
31. *(17)* Daniele Tessari *(Ita)*	0	–	–	–	–	–	0	–	–	–	–
32. *(17)* Grigotijs Laguta *(Lat)*	0	–	–	–	–	–	–	–	–	0	–
33. *(18)* Zdenek Simota *(Cze)*	0	–	–	–	–	–	–	–	0	–	–
34. *(18)* Andrejs Korolovs *(Lat)*	0	–	–	–	–	–	–	–	–	0	–
(17) Izak Santej *(Slo)*	–	ns	–	–	–	–	–	–	–	–	–
(17) Edward Kenneth *(GB)*	–	–	–	–	ns	–	–	–	–	–	–
(18) Jernej Kolenko *(Slo)*	–	ns	–	–	–	–	–	–	–	–	–
(18) Tomasz Gapinski *(Pol)*	–	–	ns	–	–	–	–	–	–	–	–
(18) Eric Andersson *(Swe)*	–	–	–	ns	–	–	–	–	–	–	–
(18) Ben Wilson *(GB)*	–	–	–	–	ns	–	–	–	–	–	–
(18) Simone Terenzani *(Ita)*	–	–	–	–	–	–	ns	–	–	–	–
(18) Karol Zabik *(Pol)*	–	–	–	–	–	–	–	–	–	–	ns

Trivia

* In 1999, Jason Crump won the "Treble" riding for the Peterborough Panthers in Britain, winning the Elite League, the Knockout Cup and the Craven Shield.

* The 1995 Speedway Grand Prix season was the inaugural season in the Speedway Grand Prix era and was won by Hans Nielsen (Denmark).

* Jason Crump made his Speedway Grand Prix debut in 1995 as a wild card in the British Grand Prix and won his first three rides.

* The 2006 Grand Prix of Europe was held in the Olimpic Stadium, Wroclaw, Poland.

* There is also a Speedway World Cup for teams. Since 2001, Australia, Sweden and Poland – champions in 2007 – all have two wins. Denmark have one win, two seconds and three thirds.

World Touring Car Championships 2006

The third World Touring Car Championship season got underway at Monza, Italy on 2 April and finished with the 20th race of the season at the Guia Circuit, Macau on 19 November. Two 50km races took place over each weekend with qualifying laps held to determine the starting grid for race 1, while the grid for race 2 went according to the result of race 1 but with the final positions of the top eight drivers across the line reversed.

Championship Results

Race	Date	Country	Track	Winning Driver
1.	2 April	Italy	Monza	Andy Priaulx *(GB)*
2.				Augusto Farfus Jr. *(Bra)*
3.	30 April	France	Magny-Cours	Dirk Müller *(Ger)*
4.				Andy Priaulx *(GB)*
5.	21 May	Great Britain	Brands Hatch	Yvan Muller *(Fra)*
6.				Alain Menu *(Swi)*
7.	4 June	Germany	Oschersleben	Andy Priaulx *(GB)*
8.				Jörg Müller *(GB)*
9.	2 July	Brazil	Curitiba	Jordi Gené *(Spa)*
10.				Andy Priaulx *(GB)*
11.	30 July	Mexico	Puebla	Salvatore Tavano *(Ita)*
12.				Augusto Farfus Jr *(Bra)*
13.	3 September	Czech Republic	Brno	Jörg Müller *(Ger)*
14.				Robert Huff *(GB)*
15.	24 September	Turkey	Istanbul	Alessandro Zanardi *(Ita)*
16.				Gabriele Tarquini *(Ita)*
17.	8 October	Spain	Valencia	Augusto Farfus Jr *(Bra)*
18.				Jörg Müller *(Ger)*
19.	19 November	Macau	Guia Circuit	Andy Priaulx *(GB)*
20.				Jörg Müller *(Ger)*

Trivia

* The inaugural WTCC was held in 1987 with Roberto Ravaglia claiming the title driving a BMW M3. However, it was unsuccessful and scrapped.

* In 1993, the FIA held the Touring Car World Cup, which was won by Paul Radisich at Monza. Radisich won again in 1994 (Donington Park) and after Frank Biela won in 1995 (Paul Ricard), it was scrapped.

* The WTCC is regarded as the third most important FIA championship after F1 and the Rally Championship.

* Andy Priaulx and Dirk Muller ended the 2004 European Touring Car Championship level on points but Priaulx took the title with five wins compared to Muller's three.

* Andy Priaulx is from Guernsey.

Drivers' Championship Table 2006

Pos	Driver	Team	Car	W	Pts
1.	Andy Priaulx (GB)	BMW Team UK	BMW 320si	5	73
2.	Jörg Müller (Ger)	BMW Team Germany	BMW 320si	4	72
3.	Augusto Farfus (Bra)	N. Technology	Alfa Romeo 156	3	64
4.	Yvan Muller (Fra)	SEAT Sport France	SEAT León	1	62
5.	Gabriele Tarquini (Ita)	SEAT Sport Italia	SEAT León	1	57
6.	Dirk Müller (Ger)	BMW Team Germany	BMW 320si	1	54
7.	Rickard Rydell (Swe)	SEAT Sport Sverige	SEAT León	0	54
8.	James Thompson (GB)	SEAT Sport UK	SEAT León	0	54
9.	Peter Terting (Ger)	SEAT Sport Deutschland	SEAT León	0	49
10.	Jordi Gené (Spa)	SEAT Sport Espana	SEAT León	1	36
11.	Alessandro Zanardi (Ita)	BMW Team Italy-Spain	BMW 320si	1	26
12.	Nicola Larini (Ita)	Chevrolet	Chevrolet Lacetti	0	24
13.	Duncan Huisman (Ned)	BMW Team Italy-Spain	BMW 320si	0	22
14.	Gianni Morbidelli (Ita)	N. Technology	Alfa Romeo 156	0	22
15.	Alain Menu (Swi)	Chevrolet	Chevrolet Lacetti	1	21
16.	Robert Huff (GB)	Chevrolet	Chevrolet Lacetti	1	20
17.	Tom Coronel (Ned)	GR Asia	SEAT León	0	20
18.	Salvatore Tavano (Ita)	N. Technology	Alfa Romeo 156	1	15
19.	Luca Rangoni (Ita)	Proteam Motorsport	BMW 320si	0	14
20.	Fabrizio Giovanardi (Ita)	JAS Motorsport	Honda Accord Euro R	0	8
21.	Ryan Sharp (GB)	JAS Motorsport	Honda Accord Euro R	0	6
22.	Alessandro Balzan (Ita)	DB Motorsport	Alfa Romeo 156	0	5
23.	André Couto (Por)	SEAT Sport España	SEAT León	0	2

Manufacturers' Championship Table

Pos	Manufacturer	Car	Wins	Points
1.	BMW	BMW 320si	8	254
2.	SEAT	SEAT León	2	235
3.	Alfa Romeo	Alfa Romeo 156	3	154
4.	Chevrolet	Chevrolet Lacetti	1	128

"I am nearly numb with emotion. The pressure was massive on me coming here, with the second race the hardest I have ever had, and I didn't know if I had won until I crossed the line. It has been a vintage year. This championship is world class and I'm very glad to be in it and able to drive to win."

Andy Priaulx, *after retaining his World Touring Car Championship in 2006 following the last two races of the season in Macau*

Moto GP Championship 2006

The 2006 MotoGP Championship was the first in 14 years to be decided at the final GP of the season. Going into the final race in Valencia, Valentino Rossi (Yamaha) of Italy enjoyed an 8-point lead over the USA's Nicky Hayden (Honda). However, when Rossi, the five-time MotoGP world champion (1997, 1999, 2001–2005) crashed on lap five, it essentially ended his race resulting in him finishing in 13th place earning 3 points. Meanwhile Hayden finished third to claim 16 points and win his first MotoGP world championship. Over the season no fewer than seven different riders won a MotoGP, including first-time winners Daniel Pedrosa (Spain – Honda), Toni Elias (Spain – Honda) and Troy Bayliss (Australia – Ducati). In the 250cc class, Asprilla's Jorge Lorenzo won his first world championship, taking eight wins over the season, while another Asprilla rider, Alvaro Bautista, won the 125cc crown also claiming eight wins. For a minimum period of five years from 2007, the Federation Internationale de Motocyclisme (FIM) has regulated in MotoGP class that two-stroke bikes will no longer be allowed, and engines will be limited to 800cc four-strokes. Meanwhile, the maximum fuel capacity will be 21 litres.

Grands Prix Results

Date	Grand Prix	Circuit	MotoGP Winner
26 Mar	Spain	Jerez	Loris Capirossi
8 Apr	Qatar	Losail	Valentino Rossi
30 Apr	Turkey	Istanbul	Marco Melandri
14 May	China	Shanghai	Daniel Pedrosa
21 May	France	Le Mans	Marco Melandri
4 June	Italy	Mugello	Valentino Rossi
18 June	Catalonia	Catalunya	Valentino Rossi
24 June	Netherlands	Assen	Nicky Hayden
2 July	England	Donington Park	Daniel Pedrosa
16 July	Germany	Sachsenring	Valentino Rossi
23 July	USA	Laguna Seca	Nicky Hayden
20 Aug	Czech Republic	Brno	Loris Capirossi
10 Sept	Malaysia	Sepang	Valentino Rossi
17 Sept	Australia	Phillip Island	Marco Melandri
24 Sept	Japan	Motegi	Loris Capirossi
15 Oct	Portugal	Estoril	Toni Elias
29 Oct	Valencian Community	Valencia	Troy Bayliss

"I'm just really, really proud. You dream about being world champion and dedicate your whole life to it, so when it comes true it is very special. I may not always have been the fastest but every race I've tried my hardest."

***Nicky Hayden**, after winning the 2006 MotoGP World Championship*

MotoGP World Championship Final Standings 2006

Pos	Rider	Team	Pos	Rider	Team
1.	Nicky Hayden	Honda	12.	Makoto Tamada	Honda
2.	Valentino Rossi	Yamaha	13.	Sete Gibernau	Ducati
3.	Loris Capirossi	Ducati	14.	Shinya Nakano	Kawasaki
4.	Marco Melandri	Honda	15.	Carlos Checa	Yamaha
5.	Daniel Pedrosa	Honda	16.	Randy de Puniet	Kawasaki
6.	Kenny Roberts Jr	Roberts	17.	Alex Hofmann	Ducati
7.	Colin Edwards	Yamaha	18.	James Ellison	Yamaha
8.	Casey Stoner	Honda	19.	Troy Bayliss	Ducati
9.	Toni Elías	Honda	20.	Jose Luis Cardoso	Ducati
10.	John Hopkins	Suzuki	21.	Kousuke Akiyoshi	Suzuki
11.	Chris Vermeulen	Suzuki	22.	Garry McCoy	Ilmor

Points Scoring System – MotoGP Class

Position	1	2	3	4	5	6	7	8	9	10	11	12	13	14	15
Points	25	20	16	13	11	10	9	8	7	6	5	4	3	2	1

Trivia

* A world championship for motorcycle racing was first organized by the Federation Internationale de Motocyclisme (FIM) in 1949, one year before the inaugural Formula 1 motor racing season.

* Britain's Robert Leslie Graham won the inaugural world championship's prestigious 500cc in 1949 class riding an AJS Porcupine.

* In 1989, Eddie Lawson (USA) became the first rider to win consecutive world championships for different manufacturers (1988 – Yamaha and 1989 – Honda). Valentino Rossi won the world championship for Honda from 2001–2003 and for Yamaha in 2004 and 2005.

* Giacomo Agostini has won the most number of MotoGP world championships – eight, while Michael Doohan and Valentino Rossi are both on five wins.

* Giacomo Agostini began an auto racing career in 1978 but never managed to reach Formula 1. He competed in the European Formula 2 series in a Chevron-B42 BMW and British Aurora Formula 1 with his own team and a Williams FW06-1.

* In 17 years of racing, Giacomo Agostini won a record 15 Grand Prix world championship titles and 122 Grand Prix victories. He was world 350cc champion from 1968–1974 and world 500cc champion from 1966–1972 and 1975.

Moto GP Championship 2007

Qatar MotoGP

10 MARCH, QATAR
1. Casey Stoner   *(Aus)* Ducati 43:02.788
2. Valentino Rossi *(Ita)* Yamaha +2.838s
3. Dani Pedrosa   *(Esp)* Honda   +8.530s

Spain MotoGP

25 MARCH, JEREZ
1. Valentino Rossi *(Ita)* Yamaha 45:53.340
2. Dani Pedrosa   *(Spa)* Honda   +1.246s
3. Colin Edwards *(US)* Yamaha +2.701s

Turkey MotoGP

22 APRIL, ISTANBUL
1. Casey Stoner   *(Aus)* Ducati 43:02.788
2. Tomi Elias   *(Spa)* Honda   +6.207s
3. Loris Capirossi *(Ita)* Ducati   +8.102s

China MotoGP

6 MAY 2007, SHANGHAI CIRCUIT
1. Casey Stoner   *(Aus)* Ducati 44:12.891
2. Valentin Rossi *(Ita)* Yamaha +3.036s
3. John Hopkins   *(US)* Suzuki   +6.663s

France MotoGP

19 MAY 2007, LE MANS
1. Chris Vermeulen*(Aus)* Suzuki 50:58.713
2. Marco Melandri*(Ita)* Honda +12.599s
3. Casey Stoner   *(Aus)* Ducati +27.347s

Italy MotoGP

3 JUNE, MUGELLO
1. Valentino Rossi *(Ita)* Yamaha 42:42.385
2. Dani Pedrosa   *(Esp)* Honda   +3.074s
3. Alex Barros   *(Bra)* Ducati   +5.956s

Spain MotoGP

10 JUNE, CATALUNYA
1. Casey Stoner   *(Aus)* Ducati 43:02.788
2. Valentino Rossi *(Ita)* Yamaha +2.838ss
3. Dani Pedrosa   *(Esp)* Honda   +8.530s

Great Britain MotoGP

24 JUNE, DONINGTON PARK
1. Casey Stoner   *(Aus)* Ducati 51:40.739
2. Colin Edwards *(US)* Yamaha +11.768s
3. Chris Vermeulen*(Aus)* Suzuki   +15.678s

Netherlands MotoGP

30 JUNE, ASSEN
1. Valentino Rossi *(Ita)* Yamaha 42:37.149
2. Casey Stoner   *(Aus)* Ducati   +1.809s
3. Nicky Hayden   *(US)* Honda   +6.077s

Germany GP

15 JULY, SACHSENRING
1. Dani Pedrosa   *(Esp)* Honda 41:53.196
2. Loris Capirossi *(Ita)* Ducati   +13.166s
3. Nicky Hayden   *(US)* Honda   +16.780s

USA MotoGP

22 JULY, LAGUNA SECA
1. Casey Stoner   *(Aus)* Ducati 44:20.325
2. Chris Vermeulen*(Aus)* Suzuki   +9.835s
3. Marco Melandri*(Ita)* Honda   +25.341s

Czech Republic MotoGP

17 AUGUST, BRNO
1. Casey Stoner   *(Aus)* Ducati 44:34.720
2. Chris Vermeulen*(Aus)* Suzuki   +4.851s
3. John Hopkins   *(US)* Suzuki   +16.002s

British Superbikes Championship 2006

The British Superbikes Championship is the leading motorsport motorcycle racing championship in Britain. In 2006, racing fans witnessed one of the closest-fought championship fights in the history of the sport. Over the season, 13 Grands Prix were held, with each meeting featuring two races. In a nail-biting finish to the season, the outcome of the title came down to the final Grand Prix at Brands Hatch. The Japanese rider, Ryuichi Kiyonari, runner-up in 2005, claimed the 2006 BSB Championship from British rider Leon Haslam and Spanish star Gregorio Lavilla, the 2005 BSB Champion.

Grands Prix Results

Rnd	Date	Circuit	British Superbike Winner
1.	24–26 March	Brands Hatch	Gregorio Lavilla/Ryuichi Kiyonari
2.	7–9 April	Donington Park	Gregorio Lavilla/Scott Smart
3.	14–17 April	Thruxton	Gregorio Lavilla/Gregorio Lavilla
4.	29–30 April	Oulton Park	Gregorio Lavilla/Gregorio Lavilla
5.	19–21 May	Mondello Park	*All racing cancelled due to torrential rain.*
6.	2–4 June	Mallory Park	Ryuichi Kiyonari/Gregorio Lavilla
7.	16–18 June	Snetterton	Ryuichi Kiyonari/Ryuichi Kiyonari
–	1–2 June	Donington Park	–
8.	14–16 July	Knockhill	Ryuichi Kiyonari/Shane Byrne
9.	21–23 July	Oulton Park	Ryuichi Kiyonari/Ryuichi Kiyonari
10.	11–13 August	Croft	Ryuichi Kiyonari/Leon Haslam
11.	26–28 August	Cadwell Park	Gregorio Lavilla/Leon Haslam
12.	15–17 September	Silverstone	Ryuichi Kiyonari/Ryuichi Kiyonari
13.	29–30 September	Brands Hatch	Ryuichi Kiyonari/Leon Haslam

British Superbike Championship Standings

Pos.	Rider	No	Country	Machine	Points	Wins
1.	**Ryuichi Kiyonari**	**2**	**Japan**	**Honda**	**466**	**11**
2.	Leon Haslam	91	United Kingdom	Ducati	458	3
3.	Gregorio Lavilla	1	Spain	Ducati	377	8
4.	Jonathan Rea	65	United Kingdom	Honda	248	0
5.	Karl Harris	9	United Kingdom	Honda	244	0
6.	Shane Byrne	67	United Kingdom	Suzuki	224	1
7.	Michael Rutter	3	United Kingdom	Honda	206	0
8.	Tommy Hill	8	United Kingdom	Yamaha	187	0
9.	Michael Laverty	33	United Kingdom	Honda	179	0
10.	Glen Richards	75	Australia	Honda	151	0

British Superbikes Championship 2007

	RACE 1			RACE 2		
Brands Hatch	1. G Lavilla	Ducati	28:56.903	Lavilla		31:09.132
9 April	2. L Carrier	Honda	+1.701s	Rea		+1.308s
	3. J Rea	Honda	+4.576s	Camier		+2.103
Thruxton	1. G Lavilla	Ducati	27:58.872	Lavilla		29:01.593
15 April	2. L Carrier	Honda	+0.526s	Kiyonari		+0.113s
	3. R Kiyonari	Honda	+0.833s	S Byrne	Honda	+0.249s
Silverstone	1. R Kiyonari	Honda	28:49.500	Kiyonari		18:37.312
29 April	2. J Rea	Honda	+5.800s	G Lavilla	Ducati	+2.450s
	3. C Walker	Honda	+8.760s	Rea		+11.758s
Oulton Park	1. G Lavilla	Ducati	27:29.245	Kiyonari		27:33.097
7 May	2. L Haslam	Ducati	+0.221s	Haslam		+2.277s
	3. R Kiyonari	Honda	+0.504s	S Byrne	Honda	+4.141s
Snetterton	1. R Kiyonari	Honda	24:00.140	Kiyonari		26:56.071
20 May	2. J Rea	Honda	+0.277s	Rea		+0.125s
	3. L Haslam	Ducati	+8.209s	S Byrne	Honda	+0.920s
Mondello Park	1. L Haslam	Ducati	24:00.140	J Rea	Honda	30:14.164
17 June	2. S Byrne	Honda	+0.158s	Byrne		+2.344s
	3. G Lavilla	Ducati	+3.489s	Lavilla		+2.460s
Knockhill	1. J Rea	Honda	21:28.015	Rea		22:56.710
1 July	2. R Kiyonari	Honda	+6.848s	Haslam		+5.858s
	3. L Haslam	Ducati	+8.851s	Kiyonari		+9.453s
Oulton Park	1. R Kiyonari	Honda	31:03.140	J Rea	Honda	24:33.750
15 July	2. S Byrne	Honda	+20.039s	K Harris	Honda	+12.103s
	3. C Walker	Honda	+20.954s	Byrne		+19.949s
Mallory Park	1. S Byrne	Honda	28:21.458	R Kiyonari	Honda	21:24.315
22 July	2. J Rea	Honda	+2.779s	Haslam		+1.780s
	3. L Haslam	Ducati	+2.938s	Byrne		+4.497s
Croft	1. R Kyonari	Honda	26:51.398	Kiyonari		26:51.188
10 August	2. J Rea	Honda	+1.301s	Rea		+1.763s
	3. T Sykes	Honda	+1.488s	Sykes		+2.157s
Cadwell Park	1. L Haslam	Ducati	26:21.047	J Rea	Honda	27:00.039
27 August	2. R Kyonari	Honda	+2.233s	Kiyonari		+1.085s
	3. T Sykes	Honda	+2.862s	G Lavila	Ducati	+1.208s

World Superbikes Championship 2006

Troy Bayliss followed up his 2001 WSB Championship success (Ducati 998) by claiming his second WSB crown, this time on a Ducati 999. Bayliss was practically uncatchable during the season, winning 12 of the 24 Grands Prix and he wrapped up the title three rounds from the end of the championship.

Grands Prix Results

Rnd	Date	Circuit	World Superbike Winner
1.	25 February	Losail	James Toseland/Troy Corser
2.	5 March	Phillip Island	Troy Corser/Troy Bayliss
3.	23 April	Valencia	Troy Bayliss/Troy Bayliss
4.	7 May	Monza	Troy BaylissTroy Bayliss
5.	28 May	Silverstone	Troy Bayliss/Troy Bayliss
6.	25 June	Misano	Troy Bayliss/Andrew Pitt
7.	23 July	Brno	Yukio Kagayama/Yukio Kagayama
8.	6 August	Brands Hatch	Troy Bayliss/Noriyuki Haga
9.	3 September	Assen	Chris Walker/Troy Bayliss
10.	10 September	EuroSpeedway Lausitz	Yukio Kagayama/James Toseland
11.	1 October	Imola	Alex Barros/Troy Bayliss
12.	8 October	Magny-Cours	James Toseland/Troy Bayliss

Final Championship Table

Rider	Bike	Pts	W	Rider	Bike	Pts	W
1. Troy Bayliss	Ducati	431	12	17. Shinici Nakatomi	Yamaha	48	0
2. James Toseland	Honda	336	3	18. Max Neukirchner	Suzuki	28	0
3. Noriyuki Haga	Yamaha	326	1	19. Sebastien Gimbert	Yamaha	23	0
4. Troy Corser	Suzuki	254	2	20. Fabien Foret	Suzuki	19	0
5. Andrew Pitt	Yamaha	250	1	21. Steve Martin	F Petronas	19	0
6. Alex Barros	Honda	246	1	22. Pierfrancesco Chili	Honda	17	0
7. Yukio Kagayama	Suzuki	211	3	23. Tommy Hill	Yamaha	13	0
8. Lorenzo Lanzi	Ducati	169	0	24. Ivan Clementi	Ducati	10	0
9. Chris Walker	Kawasaki	158	1	25. Marco Borciani	Ducati	9	0
10. Fonsi Nieto	Kawasaki	139	0	26. Vittorio Iannuzzo	Ducati	6	0
11. Michel Fabrizio	Honda	125	0	27. Craig Jones	F Petronas	3	0
12. Karl Muggeridge	Honda	123	0	28. Joshua Brookes	Kawasaki	3	0
13. Norick Abe	Yamaha	112	0	29. Harry Van Beek	Suzuki	2	0
14. Ruben Xaus	Ducati	103	0	30. Lorenzo Alfonsi	Ducati	2	0
15. Régis Laconi	Kawasaki	103	0	31 Jose David De Gea	Honda	2	0
16. Roberto Rolfo	Ducati	69	0	32. Gianluca Nannelli	Honda	1	0

2007 World Superbikes Championship

On 9 September 2007, Japan's Noriyuki Haga (Yamaha) won Race 1 of the German Grand Prix, Round 11 of the 2007 World Superbikes Championships. His victory meant that he now trailed the Championship leader, England's James Toseland (Honda), by 31 points with two races to go. Toseland has eight race wins in the year compared to the Japanese rider's four victories. However, Italy's Max Biaggi (Suzuki) and Australia's Troy Bayliss (Ducati) cannot be ruled out of final contention with just two Grands Prix remaining, the Italian) and French.

Round 1, Qatar, 24 February

Race 1

1. Max Biaggi	*(Ita)*	Suzuki	36:10.115
2. James Toseland	*(GB)*	Honda	+1.483s
3. Lorenzo Lanzi	*(Ita)*	Ducati	+13.994s

Race 2

1. James Toseland	*(GB)*	Honda	36:09.433
2. Max Biaggi	*(Ita)*	Suzuki	+0.738s
3. Troy Corser	*(Aus)*	Yamaha	+6.386s

Round 2, Australia, 24 March

Race 1

1. Troy Bayliss	*(Aus)*	Ducati	34:11.276
2. James Toseland	*(GB)*	Honda	+2.096s
3. Max Biaggi	*(Ita)*	Suzuki	+10.143s

Race 2

1. James Toseland	*(GB)*	Honda	34:16.990
2. Troy Bayliss	*(Aus)*	Ducati	+0.274s
3. Noriyuki Haga	*(Jpn)*	Yamaha	+6.996s

Round 3, Europe, 1 April

Race 1

1. James Toseland	*(GB)*	Honda	35:28.222
2. Troy Corser	*(Aus)*	Yamaha	+1.368s
3. Max Biaggi	*(Ita)*	Suzuki	+2.448s

Race 2

1. Noriyuki Haga	*(Jpn)*	Yamaha	35:26.734
2. Max Biaggi	*(Ita)*	Suzuki	+0.111s
3. Troy Corser	*(Aus)*	Yamaha	+1.100s

Round 4, Spain, 15 April

Race 1

1. Ruben Xaus	*(Spa)*	Ducati	37:14.606
2. Noriyuki Haga	*(Jpn)*	Yamaha	+1.997s
3. Troy Bayliss	*(Aus)*	Ducati	+4.330s

Race 2

1. James Toseland	*(GB)*	Honda	37:02.596
2. Max Biaggi	*(Ita)*	Suzuki	+0.287s
3. Noriyuki Haga	*(Jpn)*	Yamaha	+0.375s

Round 5, Netherlands, 29 April

Race 1

1. James Toseland	*(GB)*	Honda	37:02.097
2. Noriyuki Haga	*(Jpn)*	Yamaha	+0.763s
3. Ruben Xaus	*(Spa)*	Ducati	+3.798s

Race 2

1. Troy Bayliss	*(Aus)*	Ducati	36:54.133
2. James Toseland	*(GB)*	Honda	+0.009s
3. Max Biaggi	*(Ita)*	Suzuki	+7.439

Round 6, Monza, 12 May

Race 1
1. Noriyuki Haga *(Jpn)* Yamaha 32:04.428
2. Troy Bayliss *(Aus)* Ducati +4.403s
3. Max Biaggi *(Ita)* Suzuki +9.703s

Race 2
1. Noriyuki Haga *(Jpn)* Yamaha 32:05.318
2. James Toseland *(GB)* Honda +2.691
3. Troy Bayliss *(Aus)* Ducati +2.841

Round 7, Silverstone, 27 May

Race 1
1. Troy Bayliss *(Aus)* Ducati 46:02.875
2. Noriyuki Haga *(Jpn)* Yamaha +2.035s
3. Troy Corser *(Aus)* Yamaha +4.568

Race 2
Cancelled due to heavy rain

Round 8, San Marino 17 June

Race 1
1. Troy Bayliss *(Aus)* Ducati 38:52.856
2. Troy Corser *(Aus)* Yamaha +2.374s
3. Yuk. Kagayama *(Jap)* Suzuki +8.965s

Race 2
1. Troy Bayliss *(Aus)* Ducati 38:43.506
2. Noriyuki Haga *(Jpn)* Yamaha +2.537s
3. Max Biaggi *(Ita)* Suzuki +6.386s

Round 9, Czech Republic, 22 July

Race 1
1. James Toseland *(GB)* Honda 41:02.730
2. Max Biaggi *(Ita)* Suzuki +0.237s
3. Yuk. Kagayama *(Jap)* Suzuki +1.185s

Race 2
1. Max Biaggi *(Ita)* Suzuki 38:53.022
2. James Toseland *(GB)* Honda +1.510s
3. Michel Fabrizio *(Ita)* Honda +5.419s

Round 10, Great Britain, 6 August

Race 1
1. James Toseland *(GB)* Honda 36:35.120
2. Troy Corser *(Aus)* Yamaha +1.554s
3. Max Biaggi *(Ita)* Suzuki +2.917s

Race 2
1. James Toseland *(GB)* Honda 36:34.177
2. Noriyuki Haga *(Jpn)* Yamaha +1.686s
3. Troy Corser *(Aus)* Yamaha +1.760s

Round 11, Germany, 9 September

Race 1
1. Noriyuki Haga *(Jpn)* Yamaha 40:02.923
2. Max Biaggi *(Ita)* Suzuki +11.007s
3. Troy Corser *(Aus)* Yamaha +11.628s

Race 2
1. Troy Bayliss *(Aus)* Ducati 39:49.291
2. Noriyuki Haga *(Jpn)* Yamaha +1.373s
3. Max Biaggi *(Ita)* Suzuki +13.001s

Scoring System

Position	1	2	3	4	5	6	7	8	9	10	11	12	13	14	15
Points	25	20	16	13	11	10	9	8	7	6	5	4	3	2	1

Rowing World Cup 2007

Great Britain's rowers won the World Cup for the first time, when they dominated the opening and closing regattas. There were three regattas, at Linz Ottensheim in Austria, Amsterdam in the Netherlands and Lucerne Switzerland. Defending champions Germany were second and China – winners of the Amsterdam regatta – took third.

Rowing is a particular strength in Great Britain at present. The coxless four won the first regatta, then by-passed the Amsterdam event to compete as part of the Great Britain 2 boat – winning gold – before returning in Lucerne, where they lost their first races since 2004.

The results section does not have the individual names of the rowers because each entry, including the single sculls, is in the name of the nation they represent. Although there are 22 events in rowing, only 14 are Olympic disciplines and these ones earn World Cup points.

OVERALL STANDINGS

Rank	Nation	Points	Linz	Amsterdam	Lucerne
1.	Great Britain	161	62	40	59
2.	Germany	112	47	32	33
3.	China	101	38	58	5
4.	France	80	20	31	29
5.	New Zealand	78	–	36	42
6.	Czech Republic	68	22	27	19
7.	Netherlands	66	19	22	25
8.	Australia	53	14	18	21
8.	Canada	53	30	–	23
10.	Denmark	51	16	15	20

LINZ REGATTA (17 EVENTS) 1–3/6/07

Event	Gold	Silver	Bronze
Women's Light Single Sculls	Cuba	Austria	Germany
Men's Light Single Sculls	Greece	Netherlands 1	Netherlands 2
Men's Light Pairs	Italy	Netherlands	Great Britain
Women's Single Sculls	Belarus	Czech Republic	United States
Men's Single Sculls	Czech Republic	Great Britain	Germany
Women's Coxless Pairs	Australia	United States 1	United States 2
Men's Coxless Pairs	Great Britain	Croatia	Germany
Women's Double Sculls	China	Germany 1	Germany 2
Men's Double Sculls	Great Britain	Germany	Estonia
Men's Coxless Fours	Great Britain	Netherlands	France
Women's Light Double Sculls	Denmark	China	Canada
Men's Light Double Sculls	Denmark	Great Britain	Canada
Men's Light Fours	China	Italy	Great Britain
Women's Quadruple Sculls	Great Britain	China	Germany
Men's Quadruple Sculls	Poland	Italy	Germany
Women's Eights	Germany	Great Britain	Netherlands
Men's Eights	Canada	Belarus	China

AMSTERDAM (20) 21–24/6/07	Gold	Silver	Bronze
Women's Coxless Fours	Australia 2	Australia 1	China
Men's Light Eights	Germany	Denmark	Netherlands
Men's Light Coxless Pairs	Great Britain	Denmark	Belgium
Women's Light Single Sculls	Netherlands	Austria	Ireland
Men's Light Single Sculls	New Zealand 1	New Zealand 2	Netherlands
Adaptive Rowing Mixed Fours	Great Britain	Netherlands 1	Netherlands 2
Women's Single Sculls	Belarus	China	Sweden
Men's Single Sculls	Czech Republic	Norway	Germany
Women's Coxless Pairs	China	New Zealand	Australia
Men's Coxless Pairs	New Zealand	Croatia	France
Women's Double Sculls	China	New Zealand	Czech Republic
Men's Double Sculls	Estonia	Great Britain	Australia
Men's Coxless Fours	New Zealand	Netherlands	Czech Republic
Women's Light Double Sculls	China 2	China 1	United States
Men's Light Double Sculls	Denmark	Great Britain	Poland
Men's Light Coxless Fours	China	Great Britain	Netherlands
Women's Quadruple Sculls	China	Great Britain	Germany
Men's Quadruple Sculls	Poland	Czech Republic	France
Women's Eights	Netherlands	Germany	China
Men's Eights	Great Britain 2	China	Great Britain 1

LUCERNE (22) 13–15/7/07	Gold	Silver	Bronze
Women's Light Single Sculls	Netherlands	France	Denmark
Men's Light Single Sculls	New Zealand 1	New Zealand 2	Netherlands
Men's Light Coxless Pairs	Italy	Great Britain	Germany
Women's Coxless Fours	Germany	Great Britain	Italy
Men's Fours	Germany	Netherlands	Italy
Women's Light Quad Sculls	Great Britain	Netherlands	Germany
Men's Light Quad Sculls	Italy	Germany	Great Britain
Men's Light Eights	Germany	Italy	Netherlands
Women's Single Sculls	Belarus	Czech Republic	China
Men's Single Sculls	New Zealand	Great Britain	Czech Republic
Women's Coxless Pairs	New Zealand	United States	Romania
Men's Coxless Pairs	Australia	New Zealand	France
Women's Double Sculls	New Zealand	Germany	Italy
Men's Double Sculls	Estonia	Great Britain	Slovenia
Men's Coxless Fours	Netherlands	Great Britain	New Zealand
Women's Light Pairs Sculls	Denmark	Canada	Germany
Men's Light Pairs Sculls	Denmark	Hungary	Great Britain
Men's Light Coxless Fours	Great Britain	France	Netherlands
Women's Quadruple Sculls	Great Britain	Germany	Romania
Men's Quadruple Sculls	Russia	France	Netherlands
Women's Eights	United States	Germany	Czech Republic
Men's Eights	Canada	Germany	Russia

Henley Royal Regatta 2007

The Henley Royal Regatta was staged between Thursday 4 and Sunday 8 July, during one of the wettest summers on record. The events were, as usual, broken down into different categories, those open to all and those limited to clubs, students and juniors.

The main events are the Grand Challenge Cup, for men's eights, and the Stewards Cup, for men's coxless fours. There are three women's events – eights, quadruple sculls and single sculls, while the Thames Challenge Cup is the most sought after of the club events, being the coxed eights competition. Unlike the World Rowing Championships or the World Cup, these are match races, so the margin of victory is not by time but distance so they are estimates. The Grand Challenge Cup was won by Shawnigan Lake of Canada, while boats from Poland, South Africa, Slovenia, Germany, Australia and United States also won classes.

HENLEY RESULTS

Event	Winner	Runner-up	Margin
Open Events – Men			
Grand Challenge	Shawnigan Lake *(Can)*	Australian Inst of Sport	1¼ lengths
Stewards Cup	Leander & Molesey	Brentwood College *(Can)*	2¼ lengths
Queen Mother	Gdansk & Szczecin *(Pol)*	Brentwood College *(Can)*	½ length
Silver Goblets	Di Clementi & Cech *(SA)*	Penkner & Urban *(Ger)*	2¾ lengths
Double Sculls	Spik & Cop *(Slo)*	Sloma & Brzezinski *(Pol)*	5 lengths
Diamond Chall.	AW Campbell *(GB)*	M Drysdale *(NZ)*	1¼ lengths
Open Events – Women			
Remenham	Dortmund RC *(Ger)*	Thames & Leander RC	1½ lengths
Princess Grace	S Australia Inst of Sport B	Hollandia *(NL)*	easily
Princess Royal	M Guerette *(SA)*	JC Goldsack *(GB)*	easily
Intermediate Events – Men			
Ladies Chall Pte	Harvard University *(US)*	Molesey BC & NYAth *(USA)*	1 length
Visitors Challng	Leander Club	Reading Univ & Agecroft	easily
Men's Quad Sc	Leander & London RC	Tideway Scullers School	½ length
Club Events – Men			
Thames Chall	Leander Club	Agecroft RC	5 lengths
Wyfold Chall	1829 Boat Club	London RC A	⅓ length
Britannia Chall	York City RC	Henley RC A	1 length
Student Events – Men			
Temple Chall	Univ of Cal Berkeley *(USA)*	Cornell University *(USA)*	1¼ lengths
Prince Albert	University of London A	Goldie BC	1½ lengths
Junior Events – Men			
Princess Elizbth	Shrewsbury School	Brentwood College *(Can)*	1 foot
Fawley Chall	Henley RC & Maidenhead	Peterborough City & Star	easily

Varsity Boat Race, 7 April 2007, Putney Bridge to Mortlake

The annual Varsity Boat race, sponsored by Xchanging, was won by the heavy favoured Light Blues of Cambridge, although their margin of victory was less than expected, only 11/4 lengths.

Cambridge not only had five returning Blues, but also two members of World Championship-winning boats. However, there was controversy in mid-July when one member of the winning boat was denied his Blue for leaving his course early. German Thorsten Engelmann, who became the heaviest man ever to appear in the Boat Race, returned to Germany to train for the 2008 Beijing Olympic Games two years into his three-year economic degree. The rule Engelmann broke was a relatively recent one, instigated to ensure that only genuine students – i.e. those who intend to complete their studies – compete in the race.

Oxford had the benefit of the Surrey Station in the opening exchanges and used the bend to take a clear lead after the first mile. But the stronger and more powerful Light Blues began to cut into the Oxford lead and, by Hammersmith Bridge, there was little to choose between the boats, though the umpire had occasion to warn the two coxes about getting too close.

Going round the Chiswick Steps, Cambridge finally got their bow in front and they had stretched their advantage over the Dark Blues to a length at Barnes Bridge. Hard as Oxford pressed, it was Cambridge who finished the more composed and they added another quarter of a length to their advantage at the finish. The winning time was 17 minutes, 49 seconds.

After losing two consecutive races Cambridge thus denied Oxford a hat-trick of wins and extended their overall lead in the series – which dates back to 1829 – to 79–73 with one dead-heat.

World Rowing Championships 2007

Date: 26 August–2 September
Venue: Oberschleisheim, Munich, Germany

Great Britain's best hope for gold was the coxless fours who were unbeaten since 2004, but they could only manage a disappointing fourth place behind the gold medal winners New Zealand, Italy (silver) and the Netherlands (bronze). In the double sculls Britain's Anna Bebington and Elise Laverick won bronze while the British men's coxless pair of Matthew Langridge and Colin Smith also won bronze in their event. Gold medals for the British team came by way of success in the women's quadruple sculls (their third consecutive world title) and the men's lightweight four.

Other GB medal winners were Zac Purchase's and Mark Hunter's bronze in the lightweight double sculls and the men's and women's eights both claimed bronze medals.

Team GB Medals Total

Gold – 2   Silver – 0   Bronze – 5

Sailing

America's Cup 07

Team Alinghi from Switzerland won the 32nd America's Cup with a 5–2 win over *Team New Zealand* in their best-of-nine series competition off the coast of Valencia, Spain. *Alinghi* became the first European team to defend sailing's most prestigious prize and joined *Team Dennis Conner* and *Team New Zealand* as the only crews in America's Cup history to win sailing's most prestigious prize as a challenger and defender. When *Alinghi* won the coveted prize in 2003 they brought the Cup to Europe for the first time since its inception in 1851, while their reward for retaining the Cup is the right to organize the 2010 event where, when and how they please.

RACE 1
Team Alinghi beat challengers *Team New Zealand* by 35 seconds in the first race.

RACE 2
Team New Zealand won by 28 seconds to level the series at 1–1.

RACE 3
Team New Zealand won by 25 seconds to nudge ahead in the series, 2–1.

RACE 4
Team Alinghi won by 30 seconds to draw level in the series, 2–2.

RACE 5
Team Alinghi won by 19 seconds to edge 3–2 ahead in the series.

RACE 6
Team Alinghi won by 28 seconds to take a 4–2 lead in the series, needing just one more win in the best of nine series to retain the trophy.

RACE 7
in the closest finish of the 2007 America's Cup, *Team Alinghi* won by just 2 seconds to retain the America's Cup with a 5–2 series victory.

Trivia

* The America's Cup pre-dates the modern Olympic Games by 45 years.

* The trophy was originally named The Royal Yacht Squadron Cup, but was renamed after the first yacht to win the inaugural Cup in 1851, the schooner *America*..

* *Team Alinghi's* success is even more remarkable, given that the team is from Switzerland which is a land-locked country and the America's Cup is an ocean racing event.

* *Team New Zealand* qualified for the America's Cup by winning the Louis Vuitton Cup, the competition to find a challenger.

* Three Italian challengers joined eight other yachts in the Louis Vuitton Cup, and one, *Luna Rossa*, lost 5–0 in the final.

"This is a fantastic day for *Alinghi*, to win the America's Cup again after four years of hard work.**"**
Alinghi *skipper **Brad Butterworth***

Sailing World Championships 2007

Date: 28 June–13 July; *Venue:* Cascais, Portugal

"The Wind Is Calling" was the official motto of the 2007 ISAF Sailing World Championships, which brought together over 1,300 sailors from 76 nations. The championships were the principal qualification regatta for the 2008 Olympic Games, with 75 per cent of all national places to be decided. In the Men's RS.X Ricardo Santos finally claimed gold for Brazil after twice finishing runner-up, while Great Britain took the bronze medal. Over in the Women's RS.X Zofia Klepacka from Poland won the gold medal in a thrilling race from Barbara Kendall (New Zealand) and Australia's Jessica Crisp, her country's only medal at the championships. Rafael Trujillo (Spain) won a thrilling 2007 Finn Gold Cup after some superb sailing, Tom Slingsby from Australia won the Laser Class gold medal, Tatiana Drozdovskaya took the gold for Belarus in the Laser Radial, Robert Scheidt and Prada Bruno took a second gold medal for Brazil in the Star Class with Great Britain's Iain Percy and Simpson Andrew winning the bronze. The Tornado Class was won by Fernando Echavarri and Paz Anton while Great Britain dominated the Yingling Class: Sarah Ayton, Sarah Webb and Pippa Wilson winning gold with Shirley Robertson, Annie Lush and Lucy MacGregor claiming the bronze medal. On the last day of the regatta Great Britain's Stevie Morrison and Ben Rhodes were crowned 49er world champions having led the regatta from the beginning of the tournament, while Holland's Marcelien de Koning and Lobke Berhout won the Women's 470 gold. Great Britain's Christina Bassadone and Clark Saskia claimed the Women's 470 bronze. The curtain was brought down in the final medal race of the day with Australia's Nathan Wilmot and Malcolm Page claiming gold in the Men's 470. Great Britain's tally of six medals, two gold and four bronze, earned them the IOC Cup, which is awarded to the nation that scored the highest medal count.

The Winners

Country	Sail No.	Name
CLASS 470 MEN		
AUS	311	Nathan Wilmot/ Malcolm Page
CLASS 470 WOMEN		
NED	11	Marcelien De Koning/ Lobke Berkhout
49ER		
GBR	3	Stevie Morrison/ Ben Rhodes
FINN		
ESP	100	Rafael Trujillo

Country	Sail No.	Name
LASER		
AUS	191002	Tom Slingsby
LASER RADIAL		
BLR	191176	
RS.X MEN		
BRA	1	Ricardo Santos
RS.X WOMEN		
POL	8	Zofia Klepacka

STAR			YNGLING		
BRA	8127	Robert Scheidt/	GBR	12	Sarah Ayton/
		Bruno Prada			SarahWebb/
					Pippa Wilson
TORNADO					
ESP	1	Fernando Echavarri/			
		Anton Paz			

Velux 5 Oceans Race 2006/07

The Velux 5 Oceans race has been held every four years since 1982, enjoying sponsorship from a variety of organisations. The 2006 race – the longest, 33,000 miles, and toughest event for an individual in any sport – started on 22 October 2006. At the Spanish port of Bilbao, on 4 May 2007, Sir Robin Knox-Johnston CBE completed his second solo circumnavigation of the globe when he took fourth place (159 days) in the appropriately-named yacht *SAGA Insurance*. Aged 68 he was the oldest competitor in the race. Knox-Johnston was the first man to single-handedly circumnavigate the globe non-stop when he won the *Sunday Times* Golden Globe Race on 22 April 1969. The 2006 race was won by Switzerland's Bernard Stamm while only four of the seven yachtsmen who started the race finished it. The three yachtsmen who failed to complete were Britons Mike Golding and Alex Thompson and Graham Dalton from New Zealand.

RESULT

Name	Boat Name	Nat.	Boat Type	Time
Bernard Stamm	*Cheminées Poujoulat*	SWI	Open 60	103 days
Kojiro Shiraishi	*Spirit of Yukoh*	JAP	Open 60	118 days
Unai Basurko	*Pakea*	SPA	Open 60	158 days
Sir Robin Knox-Johnston	*SAGA Insurance*	UK	Open 60	159 days

ISAF World Sailor of the Year Awards 2006

Men – Mike Sanderson (NZL)   Women – Paige Railey (USA)

RS:X European Championships 2007

Date: 5–15 June; *Location:* Limassol, Cyprus

Poland's Przemyslaw Miarczynski and Marina Alabau from Spain were crowned champions after the Medal Races brought the ISAF Grade C1 RS:X European Championships to an end. Miarczynski managed to hold on to take the title from his team-mate Piotr Myszka, while Alabau put her World Championship disappointment behind her with a classy display in the women's fleet.

Qingdao International Regatta 2007

Date: 17–23 August; *Location:* Qingdao, China

Ben Ainslie won the gold medal in the finn class at the Olympic test event in China while the British duo of Stevie Morrison and Ben Rhodes claimed gold in the 49er class and Bryony Shaw took gold in the windsurfing. Sarah Ayton and her crew of Sarah Webb and Pippa Wilson won the yngling class and Britain took a fifth gold medal at the regatta when Paul Goodison won the single-handed laser class.

Fastnet Race 2007

Date: 13 August; *Location:* Queen Anne's Battery in Plymouth via Fastnet rock

The 2007 Fastnet yacht race was postponed for 25 hours after organizers received a severe weather warning. However, less than 24 hours after it got underway many of the 300 boats that set-off were forced to seek shelter due to severe storms off the Dorset and Devon coastlines, while 186 of the 271 yachts withdrew from the race after suffering damage. It was the largest Fastnet field since 1979 when 17 sailors lost their lives during a severe storm off the south coast of Ireland. Chieftain, owned and skippered by Ireland's Ger O'Rourke won the 2007 race. The 2007 delay was the first in the race's 83-year history.

Cowes Week 2007

Date: 4-11 August; *Location:* Off Cowes, Isle of Wight

The first organized yacht race at Cowes, Isle of Wight, was held in 1826 and today it is one of the biggest yachting regattas in the world. Some 8,000 competitors took part in 941 boats from 14 different countries. Skandia announced back in March that the 2007 event would be the last time it would sponsor Cowes.

Ireland's Colm Barrington took his TP62 *Flash Grove* to victory in the Sir Walter Preston Cup while Louise Morton steered her vintage quarter-tonner to a class eight victory. On day 3 Richard and Rachel Donald claimed their second 2007 Cowes win in their class nine *Folkboat* as did Liz Savage in the J80 class. Geoff Carveth, the European and National Champion, won the Laser SB3 class in *Earls Court Boat Show* by 68 seconds from *PWC*, helmed by Cowes three times runner-up Jono Shelley. Glenn Bourke in *Musto* took third place. In Class 1 IRC, Sir Peter Ogden's Swan 601 *Spirit of Jethou* claimed the Queen's Cup by six minutes from Colm Barrington's TP 52 *Flash Glove* with Stephen Ainsworth's Reichel Pugh 60 *Loki* claiming third place. A mere six seconds was all that separated the top three in the Squib class, *Mr Bumble, Kewdeethree* and *Halcyon*.

Meanwhile on land on the Saturday Dame Ellen MacArthur set the fastest time (02:06:06) in the "Star in a Reasonably Priced Dinghy" sailing simulator. The device allows participants to record a time over a short course, simulating how a Laser might sail under those conditions. On the fifth day of racing Barrrington won his third Class 1 trophy in a row and the most coveted prize of the week, the Britannia Cup, in *Flash Grove*.

Figure Skating

European Figure Skating Championships 2007

Date: 22–27 January *Venue:* Torwar Sport Hall, Warsaw, Poland

Italy's Carolina Kostner fought back from a leg injury to win the women's competition and Brian Joubert of France won gold in the men's event. Aliona Savchenko and Robin Szolkowy of Germany skated to gold in the pairs event, while the French duo of Isabelle Delobel and Olivier Schoenfelder won the ice dancing final. It was only the second time in the history of the competition that Poland was chosen to host the competition.

World Figure Skating Championships 2007

Date: 20–24 March *Venue:* Tokyo Metropolitan Gymnasium, Tokyo, Japan

This was the fifth time Japan has played host to the World Figure Skating Championships. The pairs gold medal was won by Xue Shen and Hongbo Zhao of China, while their team-mates Qing Pang and Jian Tong pipped Germany's Aliona Savchenko and Robin Szolkowy for the silver medal. It was the third world title for the Shen–Zhao partnership.

The men's event started with the short programme and the European champion, Brian Joubert of France, took the gold medal with his energetic "James Bond" routine to the sound of "Die Another Day". The two-time and reigning world champion, Stephane Lambiel (Switzerland), finished a disappointing sixth.

The women's title was won by Miki Ando of Japan, while her team-mate, Mao Asada, claimed the silver medal ahead of South Korea's Yu-Na Kim who took the bronze. It was Ando's first medal and both Asada and Kim's first World Championships. It was the first time in the history of the sport that Asian skaters swept the world podium.

Bulgaria's Albena Denkova and Maxim Staviski danced superbly to make certain their crown. Canada's Marie-France Dubreuil and Patrice Lauzon took silver with Tanith Belbin and Benjamin Agosto from the USA winning the bronze medal. Amazingly the one-two-three was an exact repeat of last year's podium at the World Championships.

Results

Pairs
1. Xue Shen/Hongbo Zhao *(Chn)*
2. Qing Pang/Jian Tong *(Chn)*
3. Aliona Savchenko/Robin Szolkowy *(Ger)*

Men's Singles
1. Brian Joubert *(Fra)*
2. Daisuke Takahashi *(Jap)*
3. Stephane Lambiel *(Swi)*

Women's Singles
1. Miki Ando *(Jap)*
2. Mao Asada *(Jap)*
3. Yu-Na Kin *(Kor)*

Ice Dancing
1. Albena Denkova/Maxim Staviski *(Bul)*
2. Marie-France Dubreuil/Patrice Lauzon *(Can)*
3. Tanith Belbin/Benjamin Agosto *(US)*

Speed Skating

World Sprint Speed Skating Championships 2007

Date: 19–21 January 2007 *Venue:* Hamar Olympic Hall, Hamar, Norway

South Korea's Kyou-Hyuk Lee and Germany's Anni Friesinger were crowned the International Skating Union World Sprint Speed Skating Champions of 2007 in Hamar, Norway. Friesinger became the fourth female in history to win the World Sprint title as well as the World All-round title.

Results

Men's Competition

Gold	Kyu-Hyuk Lee (South Korea)
Silver	Pekka Koskela (Finland)
Bronze	Shani Davis (USA)

Women's Competition

Gold	Anni Friesinger (Germany)
Silver	Ireen Wüst (Holland)
Bronze	Cindy Klassen (Canada)

World Short Track Speed Skating Championships 2007

Date: 9–11 March *Venue:* Agora Skating Rink, Milan, Italy

In excess of 160 athletes from 31 nations participated in the championships. The athletes contested the 500m, 1000m, 1500m and 3000m in both the men's and women's events, while the men's relay was a 5000m race and the women's 3000m. In the men's competition, Hyun-Soo Ahn from South Korea won the 1000m on his way to claiming the overall title. In the women's event, South Korea's Sun-Yu Jin only failed to win the 500m on her way to claiming the overall gold medal. Hyun-Soo Ahn and Sun-Yu Jin also helped their country to the gold medal in both relay races.

MEDALS TABLE (TOP 5)

Rank	Nation	Gold	Silver	Bronze	Total
1.	South Korea	9	5	4	18
2.	Canada	2	4	2	8
3.	USA	1	0	4	5
4.	Italy	0	2	0	2
5.	China	0	1	2	3

Skiing

Alpine World Ski Championships 2007

Date: 2–18 February; *Venue:* Are Ski Arena, Are, Sweden

The 2007 FIS Alpine World Ski Championships 2007 took place at the Are Ski Arena in Are, Sweden, the home of the 1954 World Championships, and were officially opened by King Carl XVI Gustaf of Sweden. A total of 350 competitors from 60 nations participated. The races were held on the Gastrappet, Lundsrappet, Stortloppet and VM-Stortloppet slopes. Adverse weather conditions affected the start of many of the events. On the final day of the championships, Austria won the Nations Team event, with Sweden taking silver and the bronze medal going to Switzerland. Austria's winning score was a mere 18 points, while the hosts had to be content with 33 points and third-placed Switzerland ended up scoring 39 points. Half of the available medals went to Scandinavian countries, with Norway collecting two and hosts Sweden threee.

GOLD MEDALISTS

Event	Winner	Nationality	Time
Men			
Downhill	Aksel Lund Svindal	Norway	1:44.68
Giant Slalom	Aksel Lund Svindal	Norway	2:19.64
Slalom	Mario Matt	Austria	1:57.33
Super G	Patrick Staudacher	Austria	1:14.30
Super Combined	Daniel Albrecht	Switzerland	2:28.99
Women			
Downhill	Anja Parsson	Sweden	1:26.89
Giant Slalom	Nicole Hosp	Austria	2:31.72
Slalom	Sarka Zahrobska	Czech Republic	1:43.91
Super G	Anja Parsson	Sweden	1:18.85
Super Combined	Anja Parsson	Sweden	1:57.69

There are no world records per se in the skiing events because each hill and course is different. However, Anja Parson did set a record by becoming the first skier to win gold medals in all five disciplines (the Super G was first contested in 1987), having won the Slalom in St Anton in 2001 and the Giant slalom in both St Moritz – 2003 – and Bormio – 2005.

Aksel Lund Svindal became the first Norwegian to win the Blue Riband event of the championships, the Men's Downhill.

Sarka Zahrobska was the first skier ever to win a World Championship gold medal representing the Czech Republic, when she won the Women's Slalom.

Nations Team Competition

Date: 18 February 2007

Six athletes from each nation, which must include at least two men and two women, compete in a total of four super G and four slalom runs. Each nation enters one skier into each run, alternating between men and women. The placings of all eight competitions are added together and the nation with the lowest number of points wins. If a skier is unable to complete his/her run, that nation receives 9 points.

Medal	*Nation*	*(Team, women in italics)*	*Total*
Gold	Austria	*(Gotschl, Kirchgasser, Schild*, Matt, Strobl, Raich)	18
Silver	Sweden	*(Ottosson, Parson, Byggmark, Jarbyn*, Larsson, Olsson)	33
Bronze	Switzerland	*(Gini, Grand, Styger, Suter*, Albrecht, Berthod)	39

FINAL MEDALS TABLE

Rank	*Nation*	*Gold*	*Silver*	*Bronze*	*Total*
1.	Austria	3	3	3	9
2.	Sweden	3	2	2	7
3.	Norway	2	0	0	2
4.	Switzerland	1	1	4	6
5.	Italy	1	1	1	3
6.	Czech Republic	1	0	0	1
7.	United States	0	3	0	3
8.	Canada	0	1	0	1
9.	France	0	0	1	1

"The moment has come for me to end my career. The major reasons for that are my injuries.**"** *Janica Kostelic, the first woman in Olympic history to win three Alpine gold medals (2002 Salt Lake Games), speaking on 19 April 2007*

Great Britain sent a four-strong team to Are. The best finisher was Noel Baxter, 15th of 25 to complete the two runs of the slalom – there were 74 starters. The other members of the team were Finlay Mickel, Alain Baxter and Chemmy Alcott, who came 27th in the women's giant slalom out of 80 starters.

Trivia

* Emile Allais of France was the first man to win the Triple Crown of alpine skiing with a sweep of all three gold medals (downhill, slalom and combined) at the 1934 World Championships held in Chamonix, France.

* Austria's Anton "Toni" Sailer, nicknamed "Blitz from Kitz", was the first skier at the Olympic Games to win all three alpine skiing events (downhill, slalom and combined). He claimed his triple medal haul at the 1956 Winter Olympics held in Cortina d'Ampezzo, Italy.

* The Nations Team competition is a relatively new concept. Germany was the inaugural winner of the Nations Team competition when they claimed victory at the 2005 FIS World Championships held in Bormio, Italy.

Alpine World Cup Finals 2007

Date: 14–18 March; *Venue:* Lenzerheide, Switzerland

The 2007 Alpine Skiing World Cup began in Levi, Finland on 12 November 2006 after the original opening races scheduled for Solden, Austria on 28 October 2006 had to be cancelled due to adverse weather conditions. The season concluded at the World Cup finals in Lenzerheide, Switzerland.

WORLD CUP FINAL STANDINGS
Men

Event	Winner	Nationality	Points
Combined	Aksel Lund Svindal	Norway	232
Downhill	Didier Cuche	Italy	652
Giant Slalom	Aksel Lund Svindal	Norway	416
Slalom	Benjamin Raich	Austria	605
Super G	Bode Miller	United States	302

Overall

Rank	Skier	Nationality	Points
1.	Aksel Lund Svindal	Norway	1,268
2.	Benjamin Raich	Austria	1,255
3.	Didier Cuche	Switzerland	1,098

Men's Nations Cup

Rank	Nation	Points
1.	Austria	6,610
2.	Switzerland	3,982
3.	Italy	3,080

Women

Event	Winner	Nationality	Points
Combined	Marlies Schild	Austria	220
Downhill	Renate Gotschl	Austria	705
Giant Slalom	Nicole Hosp	Austria	490
Slalom	Marlies Schild	Austria	760
Super G	Renate Gotschl	Austria	540

Overall

Rank	Skier	Nationality	Points
1.	Nicole Hosp	Austria	1,572
2.	Marlies Schild	Austria	1,482
3.	Julia Mancuso	United States	1,356

Women's Nations Cup

Rank	Nation	Points
1.	Austria	8,125
2.	United States	3,143
3.	Sweden	2,340

Overall Nations Cup

Rank	Nation	Points
1.	Austria	14,735
2.	Switzerland	5,861
3.	United States	5,297
4.	Italy	5,136
5.	Sweden	4.177

Winter Sports

European Curling Championships 2006

Date: 9–16 December; *Venue:* St Jakob Arena, Basel, Switzerland

David Murdoch's Scottish rink was defeated 7–6 by the host nation Switzerland in a hard-fought final at Le Gruyère European Curling Championships. Murdoch's team trailed 3–1 and 5–2 to Andreas Schwaller's Swiss outfit before fighting back with a three-ender in the seventh frame to level the scores at 5–5. After the ninth frame the hosts enjoyed a slender 6–5 advantage but once again the defending champions fought back to level the scores at 6–6 after the allotted ten ends. In the extra end the Swiss skip held the hammer and controlled the ice to be left with a straightforward take-out to seal victory and a 7–6 win. Per Carlsen's Swedish foursome claimed the bronze medal.

In the women's final Russia, led by 20-year-old Ludmila Privivkova, won their first ever major championship following a 9–4 victory over Italy, while the hosts finished in third place. The Russian team comprised: Margarita Fomina, Ekaterina Galkina, Nkeirouka Ezekh, Olga Jarkova and skip Ludmila Privivkova.

Winter Universiade 2007

Date: 17–27 January 2007 *Venue:* Palasport Olimpico Stadium, Turin, Italy

The 2007 Winter Universiade featured 18 medal events in 12 sports (Alpine skiing, Biathlon, Cross-country skiing, Curling, Figure skating, Ice hockey, Nordic combined, Short track speed skating, Ski jumping, Snowboarding and Speed skating).

FINAL MEDALS TABLE (TOP 5)

Pos.	Nation	Gold	Silver	Bronze	Total
1.	South Korea	10	12	10	32
2.	Russia	9	13	12	24
3.	Italy	9	13	12	17
4.	Belarus	8	2	4	14
5.	Poland	7	2	3	12

FIBT Bauhaus Bobsleigh/Skeleton World Championships 2007

Date: 25–28 January; *Venue:* St Moritz, Switzerland

Switzerland's Gregor Staehli won his second world skeleton title 13 years after winning his first one. The home crowd favourite totally dominated the event, finishing 1.58 seconds ahead of runner-up Eric Bernotas of the USA and bronze medal winner Zach Lund, also of the USA. Noelle Pikus-Pace of the USA set the four fastest times in all four of her heats to claim victory in the women's skeleton event. Home favourite, Maya Pedersen of

Switzerland, won the silver medal, while Katie Uhlaender of the USA claimed the bronze. Double Olympic gold medal winner and 2003 world champion at Lake Placid, Andre Lange, added to his impressive medal collection by winning the two-man bobsleigh world championship. The silver medal went to Switzerland's Ivo Rueegg and the bronze to Simone Bertazzo of Italy. Lange, aged 33, won the silver medal at the 2006 Calgary World Championships, while his two gold medals came at last year's Turin Winter Olympics.

Did You Know That?
At the 2006 Winter Olympics, Lange became the first driver to take both men's bobsleigh gold medals at the same Winter Olympics since East German Wolfgang Hoppe achieved the double in 1984.

IBU Biathlon World Championships 2007

Date: 2–11 February 2007 *Venue:* Antholz-Anterselva, Germany

Biathlon is the winter sport that combines cross-country skiing and rifle shooting.

FINAL MEDALS TABLE

Pos.	Nation	Gold	Silver	Bronze	Total
1.	Germany	5	3	3	11
2.	Norway	3	2	2	7
3.	France	1	3	2	6
4.	Russia	1	1	1	3
5.	Sweden	1	1	1	3
6.	Czech Republic	0	1	1	2
7.	Ukraine	0	0	1	1

Winter Olympics – Announcement of 2014 Venue

The choice for the host city of the 2014 Winter Olympics came down to a one-in-three decision for the International Olympic Committee (IOC) at a vote in Guatemala City, Guatemala. The choices were Salzburg, Austria, Sochi, Russia or Pyeongchang, South Korea. The IOC had the choice of a traditional alpine setting in the heart of Europe (Salzburg), a splendid and picturesque setting with a backdrop of a coastal and mountain layout on the Black Sea (Sochi) or the opportunity to pioneer winter sports in Asia. "I suppose it will be very close," said Jacques Rogge, the IOC president. Meanwhile, the Russians were getting very tense ahead of the decision with the Sochi chief bidder saying: "This is not a *Muppet Show*. Russia is very serious about this. For President [Vladimir] Putin, it is his personal challenge. He's really passionate about this." And Mr Putin got his wish on 4 July 2007, when Sochi was selected, the Games to run from 7–23 February 2014.

Masters Snooker 2007

The first shock of the tournament came in the first round when the two-time former World Professional Snooker Champion, Mark Williams, was beaten 6–0 by Neil Robertson. In the quarter-finals Stephen Hendry, Stephen Maguire, Ding Junhui and Ronnie O'Sullivan all won their matches. O'Sullivan defeated Maguire 6–4 to set up an encounter against the new kid on the block, Junhui, in the final, after the 19-year-old Chinese star had earlier made a televised 147-maximum break in his 6–3 wildcard round defeat of Anthony Hamilton. It was the sixth time O'Sullivan had reached the Masters final, while Junhui was aiming to win his fourth career title before he turned 20. In the final, O'Sullivan beat Junhui 10–3 to claim his third Masters title (1995 and 2005) in front of a rowdy audience at the Wembley Arena. O'Sullivan lost the first two frames to Junhui but fired home four century breaks to lead 9–3. Junhui, who thought it was a best of 17 final, offered his hand in resignation before leaving the arena believing the contest to be over. However, his return was short-lived as O'Sullivan won frame 13 and the title.

World Snooker Championship Final 2007

JOHN HIGGINS *(SCO)*   **18–13**   **MARK SELBY** *(ENG)*

Frame scores (Higgins first)
73–25; 58–32; 19–95; 25–76; 10–132; 97–0; 98–11; 86–5; 75–0; 85–9; 101–24; 70–61; 59–75; 98–0; 78–55; 116–0; 36–73; 0–110; 35–65; 4–74; 0–66; 48–72; 81–40; 63–70; 75–2; 22–82; 54–77; 71–33; 57–43; 129–1; 78–1

> **"**I thought I might burst into tears
> but I feel calm. I might have one glass of champagne
> just to toast the win.**"**
> ***John Higgins,*** *2007 World Professional Snooker Champion*

Snooker Season 2006–07

The snooker season comprised a series of tournaments played from August 2006 to May 2007. Stephen Hendry began the season as the world's number one ranked player but slipped to number eight for the 2007–08 season. John Higgins, following his second World Professional Snooker Championship victory in May 2007 (his first was in 1998), moved up three places to world number one for the 2007–08 season beginning in August 2007.

The following table highlights the results and dates for all the ranking and major tournaments and invitational events. The season began with a brand new ranking event, the Northern Ireland Trophy, which was an invitation event the previous season but for the 2006–07 season became the first ranking event hosted by Northern Ireland. Meanwhile, prize money on the tour increased by more than £400,000 to £3.26m. The Shanghai Masters was introduced for the 2007–08 season making it the newest world ranking tournament on the snooker circuit. The first edition of the event will be held in August 2007, while the Malta Cup was dropped from the 2007–08 calendar.

NORTHERN IRELAND TROPHY
Date: 13–20 August 2006 *Location:* Belfast
Winner: Ding Junhui *Runner-up :* Ronnie O'Sullivan *Result :* 9–6

POT BLACK CUP
Date: 2 September 2006 *Location:* London
Winner: Mark Williams *Runner-up :* John Higgins *Result :* 1–0 (119–13)

GRAND PRIX*
Date: 21–29 October 2006 *Location:* Aberdeen
Winner: Neil Robertson *Runner-up :* Jamie Cope *Result :* 9–5

BETFRED PREMIER LEAGUE FINAL
Date: 3 December 2006 *Location:* Manchester
Winner: Ronnie O'Sullivan *Runner-up :* Jimmy White *Result :* 7–0

UK CHAMPIONSHIP*
Date: 4–17 December 2006 *Location:* York
Winner: Peter Ebdon *Runner-up :* Stephen Hendry *Result :* 10–6

MASTERS
Date: 14–21 January 2007 *Location:* London
Winner: Ronnie O'Sullivan *Runner-up :* Ding Junhui *Result :* 10–3

MALTA CUP
Date: 29 January–4 February 2007 *Location:* Portomaso
Winner: Shaun Murphy *Runner-up :* Ryan Day *Result :* 9–4

WELSH OPEN
Date: 12–18 February 2007 *Location:* Newport
Winner: Neil Robertson *Runner-up :* Andrew Higginson *Result :* 9–8

CHINA OPEN
Date: 25 March–1 April 2007 *Location:* Beijing
Winner: Graeme Dott *Runner-up :* Jamie Cope *Result :* 9–5

NORTHERN IRELAND TROPHY
Date: 21 April–7 May 2007 *Location:* Sheffield
Winner: John Higgins *Runner-up :* Mark Selby *Result :* 18–13
* *World ranking events during the 2006–07 season*

Trivia

* *Pot Black* was first broadcast by the BBC in the 1960s. At the time, colour television was experimental and bosses felt snooker was the ideal sport to test it.

Top 25 World Rankings for the 2007–08 Season

The professional world rankings for the top 32 snooker players for the 2007–08 season are listed below. The points listed here take into account ranking tournament performances from the previous two seasons (2005–06 and 2006–07).

Rank	2006–07	Player	Points	2005–06	2006–07
1.	4	John Higgins	42250	19150	23100
2.	6	Graeme Dott	37775	19100	18675
3.	5	Shaun Murphy	37700	16350	21350
4.	2	Ken Doherty	35800	20250	15550
5.	3	Ronnie O'Sullivan	33600	12850	20750
6.	7	Peter Ebdon	33550	15550	18000
7.	13	Neil Robertson	33125	12575	20550
8.	1	Stephen Hendry MBE	32475	15100	17375
9.	27	Ding Junhui	30800	14475	16325
10.	9	Stephen Maguire	30550	11000	19550
11.	28	Mark Selby	27400	9125	18275
12.	8	Mark Williams	27125	18300	8825
13.	10	Stephen Lee	26150	13500	12650
14.	15	Ali Carter	25300	9550	15750
15.	11	Steve Davis OBE	24950	13100	11850
16.	17	Ryan Day	24500	10050	14450
17.	30	Joe Swail	24350	12600	11750
18.	18	Joe Perry	23925	11750	12175
19.	12	Barry Hawkins	23750	14600	9150
20.	14	Matthew Stevens	23550	8600	14950
21.	29	Mark King	22425	10100	12325
22.	48	Jamie Cope	22250	10375	11875
23.	24	Stuart Bingham	22150	12300	9850
24.	21	Michael Holt	21613	11275	10338
25.	20	Nigel Bond	20688	10350	10338

Trivia

* Michael White, from Wales, was not permitted to start the 2007–08 World Professional Snooker season in June 2007 as he had not reached the minimum age – 16 – for a player to appear on the tour. White, whose 16th birthday was on 5 July 2007, therefore missed out on the inaugural Shanghai Masters and thus had to wait until the qualifying rounds of the Grand Prix in September 2007 before he could make his tour debut. The young man from Neath earned his Tour card after winning the 2007 European Under-19 Championship. He had actually first won a place on the Pro Tour at the age of 14 when he won the 2006 IBSF World Grand Prix.

Squash

British Open Squash Championships 2006

Date: 18 September 2006 *Venue:* Nottingham University, Nottingham, England

Nicol David retained her title, while Nick Matthew became the first British player to win the competition in 67 years and the first player to hold the British Closed and the British Open in the same year.

MEN'S FINAL
Nick Matthew (ENG) beat Thierry Lincou (FRA) 11-8, 5-11, 11-4, 9-11, 11-6 (91 mins)

WOMEN'S FINAL
Nicol David (MAS) beat Rachael Grinham (AUS) 9-4, 9-1, 9-4 (41 mins)

British National Squash Championships 2007

Date: 10–18 February 2007 *Location:* National Squash Centre, Sportcity, Manchester

MEN'S FINAL
James Willstrop beat John White 12-10, 11-7, 11-5 (44 mins)

WOMEN'S FINAL
Alison Waters beat Jenny Duncalf 5-9, 6-9, 9-3, 9-0, 9-3 (74 mins)

European Team Squash Championships 2007

Date: 2–5 May 2007 *Venue:* FIGS National Centre, Riccione, Italy

The England men's team won their 15th consecutive (32nd overall) European teams title, while the England women's team won their 30th consecutive European teams title. In the men's event England defeated the Netherlands, who were making their first ever appearance in the final, 4–0. Indeed, the Netherlands semi-final victory over France brought to an end a remarkable run that had seen England defeat the French in the previous seven finals. First up in the men's final for England was Adrian Grant whose win was followed by victory for James Willstrop. When Nick Matthew beat Lucas Buit it only left Lee Beachill and Dylan Bennett to contest the dead rubber. In the women's final Alison Waters set England on their way to victory defeating Margriet Huisman, followed up by Tania Bailey's win over Vanessa Atkinson which left Vicky Botwright to beat Annelize Naude in the dead rubber.

MEN'S FINAL   England 4–0 Netherlands

WOMEN'S FINAL   England 3–0 Netherlands

Swimming

FINA 2007 World Swimming Championships 2007

Date: 17 March–1 April; *Venue:* Melbourne, Australia

The 2007 World Aquatics Championships, the 12th FINA World Swimming Championships were held in three different venues across the city of Melbourne: the Melbourne Sports and Acquatic Centre, St Kilda Beach (for the open water events) and the Susie O'Neill Pool (a temporary pool located inside the Rod Laver Arena). More than 200,000 spectators passed through the doors at the various events. The swimming competitions comprised a number of events including: backstroke, breaststroke, butterfly and freestyle ranging in distance from 50m to 1500m. In total, 40 gold medals were available to the winners with Michael Phelps the star of the championships, claiming seven golds to the home favourite, Libby Lenton's, five. Phelps also set five new world records in the 4 x 200m relay, 200m freestyle, 200m butterfly, 200m individual medley and 400m individual medley.

SWIMMING POOL WORLD RECORDS BROKEN

Event	Record breaker	Country	Time
Women's 100m Backstroke	Natalie Coughlin	USA	59.44
Women's 400m Individual Medley	Katie Hoff	USA	4:32.89
Men's 200m Backstroke	Ryan Lochte	USA	1:54.32
Men's 100m Backstroke	Aaron Peirsol	USA	52.98
Women's 200m Freestyle	Federica Pellegrini	ITA	1:56.47
Men's 200m Freestyle	Michael Phelps	USA	1:43.86
Men's 200m Butterfly	Michael Phelps	USA	1:52.09
Men's 200m Individual Medley	Michael Phelps	USA	1:54.98
Men's 400m Individual Medley	Michael Phelps	USA	4:08.26
Women's 200m Freestyle	Laure Manaudou	FRA	1:55.52
Women's 50m Backstroke *(semi-final)*	Leila Vaziri	USA	28.16
Women's 50m Backstroke *(final)*	Leila Vaziri	USA	28.16
Men's 4 x 200m Freestyle Relay		USA	7:03.24
Women's 4 x 200m Freestyle Relay		USA	7:50.09
Women's 4 x 100m Medley Relay		AUS	3:55.74

Trivia

* Two swimming finals ended with dead heats in medal positions. Both swimmers received the higher value medal; no lower value medal was awarded.

* Leila Vaziri of the United States broke the world record in the women's 50m backstroke semi-final. She proved her performance was not a fluke because, in the final, she recorded an identical time in winning the gold medal.

FINAL OVERALL MEDAL TABLE

Country	Gold	Silver	Bronze	Total	Country	Gold	Silver	Bronze	Total
United States	21	14	5	40	Croatia	1	0	0	1
Russia	11	6	7	24	Tunisia	1	0	0	1
Australia	9	7	10	26	Spain	0	4	3	7
China	9	5	2	16	Great Britain	0	2	3	5
France	3	2	2	7	Netherlands	0	2	3	5
Germany	2	5	4	11	Zimbabwe	0	2	0	2
South Africa	2	0	1	3	Hungary	0	1	1	2
Japan	1	4	8	13	Belarus	0	1	0	1
Canada	1	3	1	5	Switzerland	0	1	0	1
Italy	1	2	5	8	Austria	0	0	1	1
Poland	1	2	1	4	Denmark	0	0	1	1
Sweden	1	1	1	3	Egypt	0	0	1	1
Ukraine	1	1	1	3	Greece	0	0	1	1
South Korea	1	0	1	2	Venezuela	0	0	1	1

BRITAIN'S MEDAL WINNERS

Kirsty Balfour	Women's 200m Breaststroke	Silver *(Deadheat)*
Cassandra Patten	Women's 10km Open Water	Silver
Liam Tancock	Men's 100m Backstroke	Bronze
Liam Tancock	Men's 50m Backstroke	Bronze
David Davies	Men's 1,500m Freestyle	Bronze

<u>Championships Trophy</u>

Awarded to the nations whose swimmers recorded the best performances at the World Championships:

	Overall	Pts	Men	Pts	Women	Pts
1.	United States	981	United States	440	United States	541
2.	Australia	769	Australia	316	Australia	543
3.	Japan	415	Italy	238	France	225
4.	Great Britain	357	Japan	195	Japan	220

<u>Trivia</u>

* The United States won gold medals in exactly half of the 40 swimming events in the pool. But they picked up only three bronze medals.

* Russian swimmers were dominant in both the open water and synchronized events, winning four out of six open-water gold medals and six out of seven synchro golds.

ASA British National Swimming Championships

Date: 27 July–1 August 2007 *Venue:* Ponds Forge International Sports Centre, Sheffield

On the first day of the National Championships David Carry, a double Commonwealth Games gold medal winner, broke Paul Palmer's British 400m freestyle record. The 25-year-old Scottish swimmer won the gold medal in 3:47.40 to smash Palmer's record that had stood since 1988.

Trivia

* Liam Tancock became the first British swimmer to go under the 2-minute barrier in the 200m individual medley, swimming the distance in 1:59.91 to claim the title.

* David Carry won the men's open 200m freestyle title in a time of 1:48.02 to add to his 400m gold.

* Fran Hansall claimed two British records at the Championships, a new national record of 54.56 seconds on her way to winning gold in the 100m freestyle. The 17-year-old was then back in the water to claim the 50m butterfly gold with a new British record of 26.74 seconds.

* Mark Foster, aged 37, took gold in the men's 50m butterfly, while Jemma Lowe won the 100m butterfly gold medal in 59.26 seconds having already broke the British record during the heats. The 17-year-old, who became the first Welsh female swimmer to set a new British record in over 30 years, also won a silver medal in the 50m.

* In the men's 200m individual medley James Goddard swam a new personal best time of 2:00.13 to claim the gold medal. Rebecca Adlington won the women's 800m gold medal in a time of 8:25.73, which was within a second of Sarah Hardcastle's British record set in 1986, Britain's oldest swimming record. Simon Burnett took the men's 100m freestyle gold in 49.10 seconds while the men's 800m freestyle title went to Daniel Hogg in a time of 8:16.36.

* Mark Foster claimed his second gold of the championships when he won the 50m freestyle in a time of 22.36 seconds which was, ironically, his fastest time over the distance in four years. "I'm impressed. I've only gone as quick about five times before," said the former six-time world champion.

Table Tennis

World Table Tennis Championships 2007

Date: 21–27 May *Venue:* Zagreb Sports Hall, Zagreb, Croatia

The 2007 Liebherr World Table Tennis Championships were dominated by one country and one country only, China. The outstanding star of the Chinese team was Wang Liqin, who by winning the men's singles crown for a third time (2001, 2005, 2007) has claimed his place in the history of the sport by equalling Zhuang Zedong's triple. For good measure he added the mixed doubles title with Guo Yue (China).

Wang Nan and Zhang Yining (China) retained their women's doubles title beating their Chinese national team colleagues, Guo Yue and Li Xiaoxia. However, Guo Yue made up for the disappointment by claiming the women's singles crown.

Volleyball

FIVB Volleyball World Championships 2006

Date: 17 November–3 December 2006 *Venue:* Japan

In the men's competition Brazil retained their 2002 World Championship title by beating Poland 3–1 in the Final in Tokyo. Bulgaria beat Serbia and Montenegro 3–1 for the Bronze medal. In the women's competition Russia, runners-up in the three previous World Championship Finals, finally got the monkey off their back by winning the gold medal in 2006 with a 3–2 win over Brazil in Osaka. It was Russia's first Women's Volleyball World crown. Serbia beat Italy 3–0 to claim the bronze medal.

Beach Volleyball World Championships 2007

Date: 24–29 July 2007 *Venue:* Gstaad, Switzerland

Todd Rogers and Phil Dalhausser (USA) won the men's final to give the United States a sweep of the gold medals at the 2007 SWATCH-FIVB World Championships powered by 1 to 1 Energy. The American duo defeated Dmitri Barsouk and Igor Kolodinsky of Russia 21–16, 21–14 in 45 minutes. The previous day Misty May-Treanor and Kerri Walsh (USA), the reigning Olympic champions, beat Jia Tian and Jie Wang of China 21–16, 21–10 to win their third consecutive world title.

> **"** I share this award with him as he is becoming one of the great players in the world. I am lucky to have him as a partner.**"**
>
> **Todd Rogers,** *the World Championships' most outstanding player, praising his partner Phil Dalhausser*

It's a Mad, Mad, Mad, Mad Sports World

Adventure Racing World Championship

Date: 26 May–2 June 2007 *Location:* Western Highlands, Scotland

The Adventure Racing World Championship is the culmination of the Adventure Racing World Series, generally regarded as the most extreme series of sporting challenges on earth. Over 50 teams of four from around the world did battle over seven days around the rugged coastline of Fort William and Lochaber. The course was a demanding 500 kilometres, with over 25,000 metres of ascent.

Annual Siku Extreme Arctic Challenge

Date: 20–29 July 2007; *Location:* Greenland

A five-day challenge where teams have to traverse fjords, glaciers and mountain peaks by canoe, mountain bike and on foot.

British and World Marbles Championship

Date: 6 April 2007 *Venue:* The Greyhound, Tinsley Green, Sussex

Twenty-four teams took part and it was an all-German final with one exception. The last remaining British player in the tournament was 10-year-old Zachary McCarthy-Fox from Southwater in Sussex, playing for the runners-up, 1st MC Erzgebirge II, as an honorary German!

British Siberian Husky Dog Racing

The British Siberian Husky Racing Association (BSHRA) was formed in 1996 after the dissolution of the British Sled-dog Racing Association. The objectives of the BSHRA are to provide Siberian Husky owners with a credible British Championship at some of Britain's leading race sites. Various race classes are held during the season including a veterans' competition and a rookie mushers competition.

Imparja Camel Cup

Date: 14 July 2007 *Venue:* Blatherskite Park, Alice Springs, Australia

The quirky Imparja Camel Cup is an annual race dating back to 1979, involving camels and their jockeys, which attracts large crowds, many of whom are tourists. Given the unpredictability of a camel the race is never short of entertainment. The Camel Cup forms part of a nine-race schedule and is organized by the Lions Clubs of Central Australia with all proceeds from the event distributed by the Lions Club to local charities.

International Cherry Pit Spitting Contest

Date: 7 July 2007 *Venue:* Tree-mendus Fruit Farm, Eau Claire, Michigan, USA

The inaugural International Cherry Pit Spitting Contest was held in 1974, when Herb
Teichman, a Michigan cherry farmer, was looking for "something to do" with cherry pits.
Today it is recognized by the *Guinness Book of World Records* as an official competition. The
world record is 100 feet, 4 inches and is held by "Young Gun" Krause.

Ironman World Championships

Date: 21 October 2006; *Location:* Kailua-Kona, Hawaii

The contest comprises three endurance events: a 2.4-mile (3.86-km) ocean swim, a 112-
mile (180.2-km) cycle ride and a 26.2-mile (42.195-km) marathon. The inaugural men's
championship took place in 1978 followed a year later by the women's competition. In the
2006 event, Normann Stadler set a new bike course record of 4:18:23 on his way to the
title, while Michellie Jones became the first female from Australia to claim an Ironman
World Championship title.

 Sister Madonna Buder, a 76-year-old Roman Catholic nun, took part in the 2006
World Championships, making her the oldest woman ever to complete the race. She
finished in last place with a time of 16:59:03 (57 seconds inside the 17 hour cut-off time).

Milk Carton Derby

Date: 7 July 2007 *Venue:* Southwest corner of Green Lake, Seattle, USA

The Milk Carton Derby is an annual tradition where children, adults and companies put
their imaginations to work and build a boat made from milk cartons and race for $10,000
in prize money. Over the course of the year the would-be seafarers stockpile their milk
cartons before moulding them around chicken wire and a plywood frame using nothing
but duct tape. The bizarre race has witnessed some strange and wonderful flotilla over the
years from sleek racing sculls to replicas of Cleopatra's barge, the space shuttle and the
Titanic. The 2007 Grand Showboat award went to a huge duck construction aptly named
Duck Amuck.

Turkish (Kirkpinar) Oil Wrestling Championships

Date: 29 June – 1 July 2007 *Location:* Edirne Stadium, Edirne, Turkey

The Kirkpinar Oil Wrestling Championship is held annually in Edirne and is believed to
date back to the Persian era (1065 BC). The legendary wrestler at that time was a man named
Rostam, who constantly saved his country from evil forces. Traditionally wrestlers *(pehlivans)*
have an apprentice *(cirak)* who they train and teach the art of oil wrestling. When the master
retires from the "Arena of the Brave," his apprentice continues his proud tradition.

The competitors wear very tight short leather trousers called kispet, which are made from water buffalo leather and weigh around 13 kilograms. The wrestlers oil each other with a liquid formed from mixing olive oil and kafur, a substance that was originally used during the Roman Empire as a protection against mosquito bites. There are different weight categories but the most prestigious is the *baspehlivan* (chief wrestler) category and the finals, always held on the third day of Kirkpinar, is attended by the President of Turkey who traditionally awards the baspehlivan's prize. The *aga* (sponsor) and the Mayor of Edirne also attend the awards ceremony.

The 2007 Championship marked the 646th edition of Kirkpinar. The winner of the *baspehlivan* category was Recep Kara from Antalya who defeated Hasan Tuna in the final. Prior to the final an auction is held, with the bids placed on a ram. The highest bidder becomes the *aga* of the following year's Kirkpinar and he welcomes his guests and puts them up at a hotel, holds lavish dinners and organizes the music festivities in the days preceding Kirkpinar. The *aga* also hands out medals to the winners of some of the categories and has the power to stop a match, disqualify wrestlers and even cancel the wrestling events all together. Kirkpinar has produced some legendary wrestlers such as Alico, who holds the unbeaten record of being *baspehlivan* for 27 years and Kara Ahmet who won the 1899 World Wrestling Championship in Paris.

Wife-Carrying World Championships

Date: 7 July 2007 *Location:* Sonkajarvi, Finland

The inaugural championships took place in 1997. The event is recognized by the *Guinness Book of World Records* as an official competition. Dennis Rodman, the former NBA superstar, participated at the 2005 Wife-Carrying World Championships.

Wing Bowl Championships

Date: 2 February 2007 *Location:* Wachovia Centre, Philadelphia, USA

The inaugural Wing Bowl was held in Philadelphia in 1993 and started out as a bit of light-hearted fun when a local radio show host, Al Morganti (WIP Radio), decided to stage the contest rather than wait for the Philadelphia Eagles to reach a Superbowl. Carmen "The Beast from the East" Cordero was the first winner. Codero consumed 100 chicken wings and took home the first prize, a Hibachi! The 2007 Wing Bowl was won by Joey "Jaws" Chestnut who retained his crown after downing a record 182 wings.

World Coal Carrying Championships

Date: 9 April 2007 *Location:* Gawthorpe, Yorkshire

The inaugural competition took place in 1963. In the men's event competitors carry 1cwt of coal (50kg) and run nearly 1 mile (1012.5 metres) with the "sack o' coal" on their shoulders. In the women's race they cover the same distance but are weighed down with a sack of coal weighing 25lb (10kg). The race begins at the Royal Oak public house on Owl Lane and finishes at the maypole on the village green. Since 2003 children's events have been staged, which sees three different age groups battle it out for their own world title. A dirty event, but someone's got to do it!

World Conker Championships

Date: 8 October 2006 *Location:* Ashton, Northamptonshire

Chris Jones took the men's title, Sandy Gardener was the ladies' champion, Celtic Conkerers won the men's team title and France were crowned the ladies' team champions. Competitors need only a conker and a 12-inch piece of string (however, "competition-standard" conkers and laces are supplied to competitors to ensure no sharp practice!). The men's championship began in 1965, the ladies' in 1988 and the team competitions in 1992 (men) and 1995 (women).

World Cow Chip Throwing Championships

Date: 21 April 2007 *Location:* Beaver, Oklahoma, USA

The inaugural World Cow Chip Throwing Championships took place on Labor Day 1970 in Beaver, Oklahoma, and every year since the small town has played host to the event on the third weekend of April. The event is held in conjunction with the Cimarron Territory Celebration and is fully sanctioned by the State of Oklahoma. The winner is the participant who can sling their dried-out piece of bovine dung the furthest. James Pratt won the men's event for the fourth consecutive year (his fifth title in six years), Dana Martin retained the women's title while the Beaver Fire Department successfully defended the team trophy.

World Crazy Golf Championships

Date: 28-29 October 2006 *Location:* Marine Parade, Hastings, East Sussex

The World Crazy Golf Championships is open to any player aged 14 or over and each player must complete six rounds (108 holes), three rounds of mini golf and three rounds of crazy golf. The competition is held annually and is organized by the British Minigolf Association while the 2006 edition, the fourth, witnessed entrants from Czech Republic, Finland, India and Tibet. A total of 87 players entered, 79 played all six rounds and the top 18 players after the sixth round contested the final, their total scores carried over into the final. Tim Davies (GB) won the event for the fourth consecutive year and was proudly crowned World Crazy Golf Champion 2006. In addition to the top prize, the tournament organizers awarded two additional prizes. One was for the Best Dressed Player (Jan Palmer, 13th overall) and the other to the Worst Player (Non Williams, 79th overall) in the competition.

World Custard Pie Throwing Championships

Date: 2 June 2007 *Location:* Maidstone, Kent

The World Custard Pie Championships began in Maidstone in 1967 with the inaugural event held to help raise funds to build a village hall in Coxheath. The idea came from a Charlie Chaplin movie entitled *Behind The Screen* and custard-pie throwing scenes have been a staple of slapstick comedy on the silver screen for almost a century. All the proceeds from this annual slapstick event are donated to charity. Contestants (teams of four) are given five pies each in the heats and ten pies in the final, with five points for a direct hit smack in the face, three points for shoulder-height upwards and one point for a hit on any other part of the body. Each four-person team was required to dress-up, stand behind a table and throw pies with their left hand at their opponents who were standing eight feet away. A total of 2,600 empty pastry cases were filled with 700 pounds of flour and water. The 2007 winners were a team called Ethos. A hugely enjoyable, but very messy, event.

World Egg Throwing Championships

Date: 24 June 2007 *Location:* Thorpe Latimer, near Sleaford, Lincolnshire

The 2007 Persil World Egg Throwing Championships were held at The Swaton Vintage Day. Persil sponsored the event as part of their "Persil Dirt is Good" weekends. The 2007 winners of the throwing and catching competition were Adam Parker, from Martin, Lincolnshire, and Chris Bowett from Walcott, also Lincolnshire, both aged 15. James Bamber from Tiverton in Devon, representing Wacky Nation, became the Persil Russian Egg Roulette champion (this involves five hard-boiled eggs and one raw one). He beat Team Malta's Wendy Howell, a 63-year-old grandmother from Werrington, Peterborough, in the final. The winner of the Egg Throwing with Accuracy competition was a local boy, 9-year-old Darrah Hardy, who claimed the title following an impressive four head-shots at the guest target, Stupid Steve (www.stupidsteve.com). Everyone had a "cracking" time and all profits from the competition were given to local and national charities.

World Gurning Championships

Date: 16 September 2006 *Location:* Egremont, Cumbria

The World Gurning Championships are the climax of the Egremont Crab Fair, which has been held annually since 1267. Participants pull shockingly ugly faces, framed by a horse collar, with the winner decided by the loudest cheer from the spectators. Tommy Mattinson won his sixth title (his ninth in total) in 2006. In 2002, the BBC sent Michaela Strachan to the Crab Fair to record a piece for their popular television show, *Countryfile*. For a laugh and no doubt egged on by her production crew, Michaela entered the ladies' gurning competition and won it!

World Hamburger Eating Championships

Date: 28 October 2006 *Location:* The First Tennessee Pavilion, Chattanooga, Tenn., USA

The Krystal Square Off World Hamburger Eating Championships was first held in 2004. The hungry contestants have to eat as many Krystal hamburgers as possible in the allotted 8 minutes and in 2006 the top 3 all devoured the existing World Record of 69 burgers with the Tsunami winning his third consecutive World title.

World Hen Racing Championships

Date: 4 August 2007 *Venue:* Barley Mow Pub, Bonsall, Derbyshire

The World Hen Racing Championships began at the Barley Mow pub in 1991 when the landlord, Alan Webster, decided to revive the historic tradition in the town. Thousands of hen racing enthusiasts flocked to Bonsall for the 17th annual competition in 2007 to watch 30 of the world's fastest chickens race along a specially made track. Strict rules govern the event – both feet must be on the start line and "fowl" play (pecking) is prohibited – with any offenders shown yellow or red cards. The defending champion, Wendy, owned by Andrew Gregory, failed to progress past heat two, while the lightning quick hen owned by Alan Webster, ironically named Chicken, was plucked out of the final along with Naughty owned by Steve Littlewood. The two hens squared up to each other beak-à-beak and taken off the race menu. Other hens in trouble with the stewards were Lizzie Robinson's Lean Mean Running Machine, who had a peck at Rick Allen's hen Killer. Events came to the boil in the final when the appropriately named hen, Ever Ready, owned by Peter Wright, flapped past Gill Harris's Meredith to be crowned queen of the roost by a short beak. Mr Wright purchased Ever Ready from the animal welfare rescue centre that was the beneficiary of the 2006 event. Needless to say he was cock-a-hoop with his bird's victory. However, Alan Webster, founder of the event and president of world hen racing was not so happy: "I'm pecked off. Seventeen years I've been trying to win my own trophy and when at last I get in the final my chicken goes to pot," said Alan. However, Alan was left with a huge smile on his face after counting the Barley Mow's bar takings. All-in-all everyone agreed that the event had been an egg-cellent success, particularly for the Grantham Lions Children's Hospice.

World Hot Dog Eating Championships

Date: 4 July 2007 *Location:* Coney Island, New York, USA

The inaugural Nathan's Famous Fourth of July International Hot Dog Eating Contest was held in 1916. Joey "Jaws" Chestnut from San Jose, California won the 2007 World Hot Dog Eating Championships after consuming 66 dogs, a new world record. The traditional annual event, sponsored by Nathan's Famous Hot Dogs, takes place on 4 July. Chestnut beat the six-times former world champion from Japan, Takeru "Tsunami" Kobayashi (2001-2006), to bring the coveted (well coveted among hot dog connoisseurs) Mustard

Yellow Belt Back to the USA. Chestnut became Top Dog after sinking the 66 dogs and buns in 12 minutes. The former Top Dog went into the Championships with a damaged jaw but still managed to sink 63 dogs and buns, 8 more than his lifetime best. "Nothing represents summer and the Fourth of July like the Nathan's Famous Hot Dog-Eating Contest. This year our nation has new hope for glory," said Wayne Norbitz, President of Nathan's Famous.

World Lumberjack Championships

Date: 27-29 July 2007 *Location:* Lumberjack Bowl, Hayward, Wisconsin, USA

The inaugural Lumberjack World Championships began in 1960 to commemorate the long and established history of the logging industry across the USA. The World Championships comprise various events ranging from men's and women's logrolling, chopping, the pole climb and Jack & Jill sawing which sees a man and a woman team-up in a race against time to saw their way through a 20-inch piece of white pine wood.

World Mountain Bike Bog Snorkelling Championships

Date: 7 July 2007 *Location:* Llanwrtyd Wells, Powys, Wales

A total of 30 cyclists entered on bikes with tyres filled with lead and water and pedalled across a 41-metre long and 1.8-metre deep underwater trench (that was cut into the peat bog the day before the event). Competitors had to cover two lengths of the trench. Naturally snorkels and wetsuits were essential pieces of kit. Bryan Evans, aged 40 from Bridgend, completed the distance in 1 minute, 1 second to be crowned men's world champion while Emma Wood, from London, was crowned the fastest female in a time of 4 minutes, 27 seconds. After emerging triumphant neither Bryan or Emma anticipated going anywhere near family or friends for a few days as a result of the smell from the bog.

World Nettle Eating Championships

Date: 16 June 2007 *Venue:* The Bottle Inn, near Bridport, Dorset

The 11th Nettle Eating World Championships were won by Paul Collins of Seaton who consumed 56 inches of nettles. Sonia Feukes from Poole won the ladies' competition after consuming 20 inches of nettles.

World Pea-shooting Championship

Date: 20 July 2007 *Location:* Witcham, Cambridgeshire

The participants shoot a pea through a 12-inch tube, 12 feet towards a 12-inch target. The 37th World Pea-shooting Championship was won by George Hollis who used a laser-guided pea-shooter while the runner-up, Alastair Perry, used a traditional pea-shooter.

World Pooh Sticks Championships

Date: 18 March 2007 *Venue:* Days Lock, Little Wittenham, Oxfordshire

Pooh stick racing consists of being given a stick by the race organisers, dropping it into the river and then seeing how long it takes to get to the finish line. And that is it! As the name suggests, this sport was inspired by the game described in A. A. Milne's book *The House at Pooh Corner*, where Pooh Bear and Christopher Robin stand on a bridge in Ashdown Forest and race twigs down the stream. The event was the brainchild of Lynn David, the former lock-keeper at Days Lock, when he decided to organize a fund-raising event for the Royal National Lifeboat Institution (RNLI) in 1983. The World Pooh Sticks Championships are now organised on an annual basis by the Rotary Club of Sinodun.

World Porridge Making Championships

Date: 8 October 2006 *Location:* Carrbridge, Inverness-shire, Scotland

The World Porridge Making Championship title is awarded to the "cook" who makes the best traditional porridge made from oatmeal (untreated without oat flakes). The coveted 2006 title went to an army cook, Sergeant Coleen Hayward MacLeod, whose day job requires her to make porridge for 400 troops from the 1st Royal Irish Regiment stationed at Fort George, near Inverness. "There was some very strong competition and a lot of very good professional chefs taking part in the championship. I just didn't expect to do so well," said the new world champion.

World Snail Racing Championships

Date: 21 July 2007 *Venue:* The Cricket Field, Lynn Road, Congham, Norfolk

The championships were established in the 1960s by Tom Elwes, who sadly died in July 2007. The snails race around their own racetrack, a 13-inch radius circle, which must be kept damp by their trainers. Some trainers jokingly name their snails Schumacher and Speedy, while the 2006 championships were won by a snail named Sidney who covered the course in 3 minutes, 28 seconds. Sidney's owner, 6-year-old Emma Hartley of Castle Acre, was the winning trainer. The world record time is 2 minutes, set in 1995 by Archie. The 2007 event had to be cancelled because the cricket field was waterlogged.

World Stone Skimming Championships

Date: 24 September 2006 *Location:* Easdale Island, Argyll, Scotland

The World Stone Skimming Cup is presented to the over-all winner with Australia's Tony Kynn crowned the 2006 world champion after skimming his stone 63m. The Sea-fari Salver is presented to the leading female skimmer while "The Bertie", presented since

2002 in honour of the competition's founder in 1983 (Albert Baker), is presented to the best Easdale Islander skimmer. Kate Ryan set a new world record in the women's event with a skim measuring 47m.

World Toe Wrestling Championships

Due to the retirement of the organizer, the 2007 World Toe Wrestling Championships were not held. The 2008 championship will take place at The Bentley Brook Inn in Derbyshire and will once again be sponsored by Ben & Jerry's ice-cream. All proceeds from the bizarre event, which sees competitors wear some of the most outrageous costumes, go to the Derbyshire charity When You Wish Upon a Star. The inaugural championships took place in 1976 with the "wrestlers" sitting opposite each other on the "toedium". They then lock their big toes with their foot placed on a small wooden frame dubbed the "toesrack". When the umpire shouts aloud "toedown" they wrestle with both their right and left feet. The winner is the "wrestler" who manages to push his opponent's foot to the bookend on the side of the frame.

World Walking the Plank Championships

Date: 12 August 2007 *Location:* Queenborough Harbour, Isle of Sheppey, Kent

Judges award the "plankers" marks out of 10 in four disciplines:
1. use of piratical language;
2. originality of costume;
3. execution of jump including height of after-splash
4. overall star quality.
The cost of entry was £5, with all the proceeds going to the RNLI – the Royal National Lifeboat Institution charity. The champion was presented with an engraved shield, which he retains for a year and £100 of gold dubloons. "Long" John Lenton, the 2006 world champion, won the 10th edition of the event to retain his crown when he walked the plank of the Salty Sea Pig dressed as a 5-feet tall polystyrene parrot. "Long John" – at most other times a 35-year old lorry driver from Queenborough, Kent – announced to the crowd at the presentation ceremony that he would not be defending his title in 2008: "I am taking a break to get married," he said. "I will have too much organizing to do but I will be available to give advice to other plankers."

World Worm Charming Championships

Date: 30 June 2007 *Location:* Willaston, Cheshire

The inaugural World Worm Charming Championships were held in 1980 and won by Tom Shufflebotham, who collected an astonishing 511 worms in 30 minutes in his allocated 3 x 3-metre plot (for one or two persons). This remains the current world record. Mr M. Gaukroger and Miss C. Gaukroger won the 2007 title, collecting 399 worms in the allotted half an hour.

Sports Obituaries

Alan Ball...................336
Trevor Berbick...................337
Desert Orchid...................338
Derek Dougan...................339
Ferenc Puskas...................340

Clay Regazzoni...................341
Bill Walsh...................342
Bob Woolmer...................343
Other Notable Sports Deaths...................344

Alan Ball MBE (1945–2007)

James Alan Ball was born on 12 May 1945 in Farnworth, Lancashire. At school he signed a youth contract with Wolverhampton Wanderers but Wolves never signed him as a professional when he left school and so the young Ball began training with Bolton Wanderers. However, the Trotters elected not to sign him either, stating that he was too small. Unfazed, the industrious midfield dynamo got a trial with Blackpool in September 1961 and his career finally took off, signing as a professional with the Tangerines in May 1962. He made his league debut on 18 August 1962 in Blackpool's 2–1 win over Liverpool at Anfield.

Ball's stamina and creativity in the Blackpool midfield earned him an England call-up when Alf Ramsey gave him the first of his 72 caps (scoring eight goals) for his country in a 1–1 draw with Yugoslavia in Belgrade on 9 May 1965. Ball was the youngest member of the England squad that won the World Cup in 1966. His outstanding performances for England during the World Cup attracted the attention of Everton who paid a then record £110,000 to sign him in August 1966. During his time at Goodison Park, Ball won his only domestic honour in the game, the 1969–70 First Division Championship. In the summer of 1970 he was a key member of Sir Alf Ramsey's squad that travelled to Mexico to defend the World Cup. However, England lost to West Germany in the quarter-finals.

In December 1971, Arsenal paid a record fee of £220,000 to take Ball to London and in 1973 he became only the second England player to be sent off in a full international, receiving his marching orders away to Poland. When Don Revie took over the job of England manager he made Ball captain but he only held the captaincy for six games, none of which England lost, before being famously omitted from England's squad to play Switzerland which marked the end of his international career.

Ball left Arsenal in December 1976 to join Southampton, helping them back into the First Division in 1978 and then immediately joined the Philadelphia Fury as a player-coach. In 1979 he played for the Vancouver Whitecaps before returning to Blackpool in February 1980 as player-manager but saw his contract terminated by the club a year later. After a second spell at Southampton and a brief period with Eastern Athletic in Hong Kong, he ended his playing career at Bristol Rovers in January 1983, having played 975 competitive games. After his playing days finally ended, Ball went on to manage a number of clubs: Portsmouth (twice), Colchester, Stoke City, Exeter City, Southampton, Manchester City and Portsmouth. He was awarded an MBE in 2000, but sadly he died of a heart attack on 24 April 2007 after tackling a bonfire at his home.

Did You Know That?
Ball signed for Everton, Arsenal and Southampton at the end of the calendar years of 1966, 1971 and 1976 respectively, when each club were the reigning FA Cup holders, a trophy he never won.

> "Alan started life as a road sweeper
> and ended up as the best lead violinist
> Southampton ever had."
> **Lawrie McMenemy**

Trevor Berbick (1955–2006)

Trevor Berbick was born on 1 August 1955 in Norwich, Port Anthonio, Jamaica. Berbick began his boxing career aged 19 and in 1975 took third place at the Panamerican Games in Mexico City after losing his semi-final bout with Michael Dokes (USA). In 1976 he fought in the Montreal Olympic Games despite having just had 11 outings as an amateur, while his inexperience showed in his first round bout with the eventual silver medallist, Romania's Mircea Simon, who easily beat him. However, many commentators at the time agreed that he had a lot of potential and could make it in the professional ranks of the sport. After the Montreal Games Berbick chose to stay in Canada and fight professionally out of Montreal and Halifax, Nova Scotia, winning his first ten professional contests, all by knockout, before losing to Bernando Mercano from Colombia, on 3 April 1979 after being knocked out cold inside 10 seconds.

After winning the vacant Canadian title in 1979, he fought the former world heavyweight champion John Tate in 1980, winning in the ninth round by way of knockout to earn a shot at Larry Holmes's WBC title. His big night came on 11 April 1981 at Caesar's Palace, Las Vegas, where he fought well against a cautious champion, before losing a 15-round unanimous decision. After his loss to Holmes he found himself up against the greatest boxer of all-time, Muhammad Ali, defeating the legend in Nassau to finally bring the curtain down on Ali's illustrious career. Then in 1982, he beat the undefeated Greg Page, a fighter tipped as a future world champion, and two years later he moved to Miramar, Florida, USA and joined Don King's stable of boxers. King got Berbick fights against the undefeated Mitch "Blood" Green and David Bey, both of whom he beat, to earn his second shot at the world title. This time he was up against the WBC champion Pinklon Thomas and he claimed the belt on 22 March 1986 following a unanimous points victory. However, exactly eight months later an up-and-coming 20-year-old boxer brought his reign as world champion crashing to an end in his first defence of the belt, with a devastating display of aggression, power and speed. The boxer was Mike Tyson and referee Mills Lane stopped the fight to save Berbick further punishment.

After losing to Tyson his career went on a downward spiral and in 1992, he was sentenced to five years in prison (he served 15 months) for sexually assaulting his children's babysitter. He fought his last bout in 2000, beating Canada's Shane Sutcliffe in a 12-round unanimous decision. Following the fight a CAT scan revealed a blood clot in his brain and his boxing license was revoked ending his professional career with 50 wins (33 by knockout), 11 losses and 1 draw.

On 28 October 2006, he was murdered at a church in Norwich, Jamaica, by his nephew and another man who hit him with a 2-inch thick steel pipe.

Did You Know That?

Berbick, a deeply religious man, was a preacher in Las Vegas during his professional boxing career.

Desert Orchid (1979–2006)

Sire: Grey Mirage	*Foaled:* 1979	*Owner:* Richard Burridge
Dam: Flower Child	*Country:* England	*Trainer:* David Elsworth
Damsire: Brother	*Colour:* Grey	*Record:* 70 races: 34–11–8
Sex: Gelding	*Breeder:* James Burridge	*Earnings:* £654,066

Born on 11 April 1979, Desert Orchid made an inauspicious start to his racing career. The tall grey, affectionately nicknamed "Dessie", fell heavily in a novice hurdle race at Kempton in 1983, and he took so long in getting back on to his feet that the few in attendance that afternoon feared that his first race might also be his last. Thankfully Dessie was unhurt and began the following racing season, 1983–84, on a winning note when he claimed victory in a novice hurdle race at Ascot. Indeed Dessie won six times from eight starts in his first full season, which included an unplaced finish behind Dawn Run in the 1984 Champion Hurdle at Cheltenham.

In season 1984–85, Dessie's trainer, David Elsworth, had to move the grey up a level, as he was no longer eligible for novice races. Dessie struggled during his first season among the bigger and stronger horses and won just one of his eight starts, in February at Sandown. His season ended badly being pulled up in the Champion Hurdle and the Welsh Champion Hurdle at Chepstow, then in his final race of the season he fell at Ascot. For the 1985–86 season, David Elsworth switched Dessie to steeplechasing and immediately his winning form returned as he notched up four wins in chases at Devon & Exeter, Sandown and Ascot (twice) before unseating his rider at Ascot.

On Boxing Day 1986 he romped home a full 15 lengths ahead of Door Latch in the King George VI Chase. Dessie was among the "big boys" in this race, horses such as Combs Ditch, Forgive 'n' Forget and Wayward Lad, and his starting price of 16/1 indicated the class of company he beat that day. The 1986 King George VI Chase was Dessie's first win with Simon Sherwood in the saddle. Dessie went on to win at Sandown and Wincanton during the 1986–87 season, and the following season he won the Martell Cup at Aintree, his first win on a left-handed track, and the Whitbread Gold Cup at Sandown. Dessie's greatest triumph came at Cheltenham in the 1989 Gold Cup when 58,000 punters watched in the pouring rain as Dessie overhauled Yahoo on a muddy track during the closing stages of the race to win by 1 1/2 lengths. Speaking after the Gold Cup win his rider, Simon Sherwood, said: "I've never known a horse so brave. He hated every step of the way in the ground and dug as deep as he could possibly go." So heroic were Dessie's efforts that the race was voted the best horse race ever by readers of the *Racing Post*. In 1990, Dessie won the Irish Grand National at Fairyhouse. Dessie – a horse racing legend – passed away in his sleep on 13 November 2006.

Did You Know That?

Desert Orchid is the only horse to have won the King George VI Chase four times – 1986, 1988, 1989 and 1990.

Derek Dougan (1938–2007)

Alexander Derek Dougan was born on 20 January 1938 in Belfast. From an early age "The Doog", as he was affectionately known, wanted to be a professional footballer but after leaving school he worked in a toy factory and as an apprentice electrician. When he was 15-years-old he joined the Belfast-based side Distillery and helped the team to their 1956 Irish Cup final win over Glentoran, the team he supported as a boy growing up in east Belfast. In total Dougan made 76 appearances for "The Whites" and scored 17 goals, which attracted the attention of several English league clubs.

He began his professional career with Portsmouth in August 1957, signing for them for £4,000. He made his debut as a 19-year-old just two months later at Old Trafford, where he was their man of the match in a sensational 3–0 victory over the reigning champions Manchester United (the famous "Busby Babes" side). He stayed with Portsmouth until March 1959 (having played 33 league games and scored 9 goals) and then signed for Blackburn Rovers for £11,000. Dougan scored on his debut for Rovers and spent two and a half seasons at Ewood Park, making 59 league appearances and scoring 26 times. He played in the 1960 FA Cup final for Rovers, which they lost 2–0 to Wolverhampton Wanderers.

In July 1961 he packed his bags and signed for Aston Villa for a bargain £15,000. He spent two seasons at Villa Park, making 51 league appearances in which he scored 19 goals, although he was left out of their 1963 League Cup final defeat to rivals Birmingham City. The latter helped him make up his mind to go on his travels again, signing for Peterborough United in 1963 for £21,000. He scored a goal every other game in the league for "The Posh", 38 times from 77 appearances. In 1965 the journeyman striker moved to Leicester City for £25,000 where he kept up his excellent goals per game ratio, finding the net 35 times in 68 league outings for the Foxes. However, it was in March 1967 that The Doog finally found his spiritual home, arriving at Molineux to sign for Wolverhampton Wanderers for £50,000. In 1967 he helped Wolves win promotion to the First Division and in 1974 he was part of the team to win 2–1 in League Cup final against Manchester City. In just over eight seasons with Wolves Dougan had amassed 123 goals from 323 appearances, making him a Wolves' legend and a cult hero among the fans. He was the club's leading goal scorer in 1967–68, 1968–69 and 1971–72.

Dougan made his full international debut for Northern Ireland in a 1–0 win over Czechoslovakia during the 1958 World Cup finals in Sweden. He went on to win 43 caps for his country, scoring 8 times. He had also represented the side at schoolboy, Under-19, amateur and B level. His final international appearance came against Cyprus on 14 February 1973.

Dougan retired from playing in 1976. He died on 24 June 2007 at his home, having suffered a heart attack.

Did You Know That?
Derek Dougan has scored more English league goals – 222 goals in 546 games – than any other Northern Ireland player.

Ferenc Puskás (1927–2006)

Ferenc Puskás Biro was born on 2 April 1927 in Budapest, Hungary. During his early years Puskás was nicknamed "Puskás Öcsi" (öcsi means "little brother"), although he is more famously known as "The Galloping Major" who played for Real Madrid and captained the famous Hungarian team, "The Mighty Magyars".

Puskás left school when he was only 12-years-old and was a professional footballer by the time he was a teenager. He began his professional career with his local side, Budapesti Honved, in 1943 and will always be remembered as being the talismanic and inspirational leader of the Hungarian national football team during the late 1940s and mid-1950s. Between May 1950 and February 1956, he captained his country's Aranycspat (Golden Team) in their golden era which saw them play 51 international matches, winning 43, drawing seven and losing only one. Even this solitary defeat is still questioned by football historians today, while they achieved a consecutive run of 32 unbeaten games in world-class competitions, a record that still stands.

In 1952, Puskás won a gold medal playing for Hungary in the football competition in the Olympic Games hosted by Helsinki, Finland. Between 1945 and 1956, he made 85 appearances for Hungary and scored 84 international goals. This was an all-time record which stood until Iran's Ali Daei broke the record in 2003. In 1954, he captained Hungary in the World Cup finals played in Switzerland, only for them to fall at the last hurdle, losing 3–2 to West Germany in the final despite leading 2–0 at one point in the game. In their final group game Hungary had actually defeated West Germany 8–3 in a match that saw Puskás get injured and miss the final.

As a result of political turmoil in Hungary in 1956, Puskás left his homeland and emigrated to Spain, signing for Real Madrid in 1958. He won three European Cups with Real (in 1959, 1960 and 1966), and in the 1960 European Cup final held in Glasgow, Scotland, he scored four times in Real's 7–3 demolition of Eintracht Frankfurt. His strike partner, Alfredo Di Stéfano scored Real's other three goals. The 1960 Real side is widely regarded as one of the finest club sides ever.

In addition to his appearances for Hungary, Puskás also appeared four times for the Spanish national side in 1961 and 1962, but failed to score. In 1966, he retired from playing and later went into football management. In season 1970–71, he guided Panathinaikos (Greece) to the European Cup final, where they lost to Ajax Amsterdam. In 1981, he returned to Hungary and went on to manage Spain, Australia, the USA, Canada, Paraguay, Chile, Saudi Arabia, Egypt and Hungary.

Ferenc Puskás Biro has deserved his exalted place in football history and is widely considered to be among the top five greatest ever players, a pantheon which also includes Alfredo Di Stéfano, Diego Maradona, Johann Cruyff and Pele. He died on 17 November 2006 after enduring six years with Alzheimer's disease.

Did You Know That?

Hungary's national football stadium was renamed in honour of Ferenc Puskás in 2001.

Clay Regazzoni (1939–2006)

Gianclaudio Giuseppe "Clay" Regazzoni was born on 5 September 1939 in Lugano, Switzerland. He began motor racing in 1963 but was forced to compete across the border in Italy after the Swiss government banned the sport in the country following the death of more than 80 spectators at the 1955 24 Hours of Le Mans race. His first taste of racing came in his own Austin-Healey Sprite and he managed to claim two podium places from his opening three outings. In 1964 he signed for Mini Cooper and the following year he raced in an open wheel car for the first time, participating in Formula Three for Brabham. By 1966 he had moved on to the De Tomaso team before Tecno offered him the use of one of their F3 chassis for the 1967 season. After impressing the Italian constructor he was offered a Formula Two seat in the team for 1968.

Regazzoni and Tecno were a perfect match for Formula Two although his driving for the team was not without controversy after being implicated in the death of the young British driver Chris Lambert at the 1968 F2 Dutch Grand Prix. However, a subsequent enquiry cleared the Swiss driver of all blame and in 1970 he won the F2 Championship for Tecno. Although considered by many drivers at the time to be wreckless behind the wheel, Enzo Ferrari liked what he saw and gave him his F1 debut in 1970. He finished fourth on his debut in the Dutch GP and took the first of his five F1 wins at Monza. Regazzoni's third place in the 1970 world championship was good enough for Ferrari to offer him a place alongside Jacky Ickx in 1971.

At the end of 1972 he moved to BRM and in the 1973 South African GP his car crashed. Mike Hailwood saved his life by pulling him from the blazing wreckage and was awarded the George Medal for his bravery. In 1974 he rejoined the Scuderia as the number two driver to Niki Lauda and that year won the German GP, going on to win the 1975 non-championship Swiss GP at Dijon and the 1975 Italian GP. A few unsettled years followed which saw him move to Ensign in 1977, Shadow in 1978 and then on to Williams in 1979 where he claimed the team's maiden GP win the same year at the British GP. However, in 1980 he returned to Ensign but an accident at the 1980 USA Grand Prix West left him paralyzed from the waist down, ending his career in Formula One.

Regazzoni battled back and competed in the Paris-Dakar Rally and Sebring 12 Hours driving a hand-controlled car during the late 1980s and early 90s and also became well-known for his voluntary work in helping disabled people get equal opportunities in life and society. He died in a car accident in Italy on 15 December 2006.

Did You Know That?
Regazzoni sported the famous bandit moustache.

> "With Clay Regazzoni we lose a courageous driver and man who always lived life that way. I remember him not just as one of my drivers but also as a man with a real passion for Ferrari."
>
> *Ferrari President*
> **Luca di Montezemolo**

Bill Walsh (1931–2007)

William Ernest Walsh was born on 30 November 1931 in Los Angeles, California. Walsh attended San Jose State University where he was a winning collegiate boxer and wide receiver. In 1954 he began his coaching career at Washington High School, Fremont, taking charge of their football and swimming teams. Next he moved on to California University where he served as Marv Levy's assistant and he then did a brief spell of coaching at Stanford University. In 1966 he began his professional coaching career when he was hired as an assistant offensive coach with the AFL's Oakland Raiders. Two years later Walsh packed his bags and joined the Cincinnati Bengals, where he served as an offensive coach under Paul Brown for seven seasons. When Brown resigned in 1975 Walsh hoped to succeeed him. When the job went to Bill "Tiger" Johnson it was time for Walsh to move on, this time as an assistant coach to Tommy Pedro at the San Diego Chargers. Two seasons as head football coach at Stanford University from 1977–1978 were followed by his appointment as the head coach of the San Francisco 49ers in 1979. The 49ers went a dismal 2–14 in 1978 before Walsh's arrival, but things did not get much better for the team as Coach Walsh led them to 2–14 in 1979.

In 1980 Walsh handed the starting quarterback berth to Joe Montana, a player they drafted from Notre Dame in 1979 and they managed a 6–10 season. The Montana-Walsh regime was firing on all cylinders in 1981 as the 49ers won its first ever NFC Championship followed by the franchise's maiden Super Bowl victory, a 26–21 win over the Bengals in Super Bowl XVI. Walsh's new "West coast offense", as it was dubbed by the media, saw a shift in the balance of power in the NFC from the Dallas Cowboys, who the 49ers beat in the 1981 NFC Championship game, to the 49ers. In his ten years in charge at Candlestick Park (1979–1988) Coach Walsh guided the 49ers to six NFC West division titles (1981, 1983, 1984, 1986, 1987 and 1988), three NFC Championships (1981, 1984 and 1988) and three Super Bowl victories – XVI, a 38–16 win over the Miami Dolphins in Superbowl XIX (1984) and a 20–16 win over the Bengals in Superbowl XXIII (1988). When he left the 49ers at the end of the 1988 season Coach Walsh had enshrined his name in the team's history books with an impressive record of 102–63–1 (92–59–1 in the regular season and 10–4 post-season). He served as the 49ers general manager from 1999–2001.

Walsh was named the NFL's coach of the year in 1981 and 1984. A superb motivator and exceptionally gifted tactician, his incisive gameplan strategies earned him the well-deserved nickname of "The Genius". In 1993, he was elected to the Pro Football Hall of Fame. Sadly Walsh died at his Woodside home in Los Angeles on 30 July 2007 after a three-year battle with leukemia.

Did You Know That?

Walsh was responsible for drafting many players who went on not only to become 49ers legends, but NFL greats including Montana, Charles Haley, Ronnie Lott and Jerry Rice.

Bob Woolmer (1948–2007)

Robert "Bob" Andrew Woolmer was born on 14 May 1948 in Kanpur, India. His father, Clarence Woolmer, played Ranji Trophy cricket for the United Provinces. The young Woolmer was educated in Kent and, aged 15, the coach and captain of the Kent Second XI, Colin Page, converted him from an off-spinner to a medium pace bowler. In 1968, aged 20, he signed for Kent and made his championship debut against Essex in 1970. He played in the successful Kent team of the 1970s as a seam-bowling all-rounder. Woolmer made his ODI debut for England on 24 August 1972 against Australia at Old Trafford, but it was not until 1975 that he made his Test debut --against Australia at Lord's, from 31 July–5 August 1975.

Woolmer was dropped after his first Test before re-appearing in the final match of the series at the Oval scoring 149. After scoring two more centuries against the Australians his international career came to a standstill when he decided to sign-up with Kerry Packer's World Series Cricket revolution in 1977. Although he later returned to Test cricket he was not the same player as before, only managing a meagre 139 runs in the last four of his 19 Tests to finish with 1059 runs at an average of 33.09. His Test career came to a permanent end when he went on the rebel tour to South Africa in 1981–82.

After the curtain came down on his career as a top-class player, Woolmer took up coaching and in 1991 he was appointed the coach of Warwickshire. After leading Warwickshire to four trophies in two years, he left Edgbaston to coach South Africa in 1994. Under his coaching the Proteas were transformed into a major force in world cricket following their post-apartheid re-introduction to the sport. Woolmer guided South Africa to 10 Test series wins from 15 played, while the Proteas were equally successful in one-day internationals. However, following South Africa's defeat at the hands of Australia in the 1999 World Cup, ironically played at Edgbaston, he was forced to leave the Proteas. Next came a period as the International Cricket Council's high performance manager – a role he enjoyed – helping emerging cricketing nations develop. In 2004, he was appointed the coach of Pakistan.

However, his time in charge of Pakistan was overshadowed by events in 2007 including the ball-tampering row at The Oval, drugs bans for Shoaib Akhtar and Mohammad Asif, that were subsequently dropped on appeal and a row with Akhtar in South Africa. But his most embarrassing moment in charge of Pakistan came on 17 March 2007 when they lost to Ireland in the 2007 Cricket World Cup, a defeat that resulted in their elimination from the competition. The following day Fletcher was found unconscious in his hotel room and after being taken to hospital, he died. On 22 March 2007, the Jamaican police stated that his death was being treated as a murder. However, they made a subsequent statement on 12 June 2007, saying that they had closed the investigation into his death and confirmed that he had died of natural causes.

Did You Know That?

At the time, his maiden Test century was the slowest ever Test century for England against Australia. He batted for more than 8 hours.

Other Notable Sports Deaths in 2006–07

2006

2 September – Bob Mathias, aged 75; two-time Olympic gold medal winner in the decathlon (1948 London and 1952 Helsinki). His London gold meant at just 17-years-old he became the youngest Olympic gold medallist in a track and field event and in the 1952 Olympics he became the first decathlete to successfully defend his title at an Olympiad.

10 September – Patty Berg, aged 88; won an LPGA Tour record 15 Major titles including the inaugural US Women's Open in 1946 and was one of the 13 founding members of the LPGA Tour in 1950. Patty was the LPGA's leading money winner in 1954, 1955 and 1957.

9 October – Paul Hunter, aged 27; the three-time snooker Masters Champion.

28 October – Red Auerbach, aged 89; the famous basketball coach and NBA Hall of Famer who led the Boston Celtics to nine NBA championships during the 1950s and 60s. Red coached the Celtics to 938 wins, making him the coach with the most wins in NBA history until Lenny Wilkens overtook him on 6 January 1995.

23 November – Guglielmo Papaleo (Willie Pep), aged 84; fought a total of 242 (230–11–1) featherweight bouts during his 26-year career, with 65 knockouts. Pep won 53 consecutive fights and in his 54th bout he out-pointed the defending world champion, Chalky Wright, in 1942.

2 December – Bob Berry, aged 79, an English Test cricketer who played for Lancashire (1948–54), Worcestershire (1955–58) and Derbyshire (1959–62). He was the first cricketer to be capped by three different counties.

13 December – Lamar Hunt, aged 74; owner of the NFL's Kansas City Chiefs who invented the phrase "Super Bowl." He was one of the leading persons behind the merger of the AFL and NFL.

21 December – Sydney Wooderson MBE, aged 92; nicknamed "The Mighty Atom," he was one of Britain's greatest middle-distance runners during the 1930s and 40s. He set the mile world record on 28 August 1938 of 4 minutes, 6.4 seconds at London's Motspur Park.

21 December – Arthur Edward "Scobie" Breasley, aged 92, an Australian jockey who won the Caulfield Cup in Melbourne five times (1942–45 and 1952), the Epsom Derby twice (1964 and 1966) and the Prix de l'Arc de Triomphe in 1958.

2007

1 January – Darrent Williams, aged 24; a cornerback with the Denver Broncos in the NFL who was killed when his white stretch Hummer was sprayed with bullets after a nightclub dispute following a New Year's Eve party in Denver. His death occurred just hours after the Broncos were eliminated from the play-offs.

16 January – Benny Parsons, aged 65; the 1973 NASCAR Winston Cup champion, 1975 Daytona 500 winner and a much respected stock car racing broadcaster.

22 January – Baron Emmanuel "Toulo" de Graffenried, aged 92; the Swiss motor racing driver who competed in 23 Formula One world championship Grands Prix (scored 9 points), debuting in the inaugural F1 Grand Prix, the British, on 13 May 1950.

18 February – Félix Lévitan, aged 95; the cycle race organizer who was the inspiration behind the Tour de France's last stage finishing on the Champs-Élysées in 1975, where it still finishes today.

22 February – Dennis Johnson, aged 52; the star NBA guard who was part of three NBA championship-winning teams (Seattle SuperSonics 1979 and Boston Celtics 1984 and 1986). The legendary Larry Bird once described team-mate Johnson as "The best I've ever played with."

23 February – John Ritchie, aged 65; the former Stoke City legend scored 170 goals for the team between 1962 and 1975 and helped them to a famous 2–1 League Cup final win over Chelsea at Wembley Stadium in 1972.

4 March – Ian Wooldridge OBE, aged 74; the English sports journalist who was best known for his service for the *Daily Mail* that lasted almost 50 years.

8 March – John Vukovich, aged 59; the longest-serving coach in Philadelphia Phillies' history (1988–2004) and a member of their only Baseball World Series championship winning team in 1980.

14 March – Tommy Cavanagh, aged 78; former Huddersfield Town centre forward. He was Tommy Docherty's right-hand man when Manchester United beat Liverpool 2–1 in the 1977 Silver Jubilee FA Cup final and was also assistant to Dave Sexton at United.

7 April – Brian Miller, aged 70; played for Burnley throughout his professional career (1955–66) and was capped once by England (1961).

21 April – Donald Frederick White, aged 81; the rugby union player and coach who made 14 appearances for England from 1947–53 and coached the team from 1969–71.

25 April – Clement Arthur Milton, aged 79; played county cricket for Gloucestershire from 1948–74 and played in six Test matches for England. He also played football for Arsenal (1951–55) and Bristol City (1955) and was capped once for England (1951). He was the last survivor of the 12 men to have played for both England's cricket and football teams at the highest international level.

29 April – Josh Hancock, aged 29, a relief pitcher with the 2006 MLB World Champion St Louis Cardinals.

30 April – Thomas William Cartwright MBE, aged 72; played in five Test matches for England from 1964–65 and played county cricket for Warwickshire (1952–69), Somerset (1970–76) and Glamorgan in 1977.

7 May – Diego "Chico" Corrales, aged 29; a former super featherweight and lightweight world boxing champion who had a professional record of 40–5–0, with 33 wins coming by way of knockout.

9 May – Gino Pariani, aged 79; played football five times for the USA including their famous 1–0 win over England in Bela Horizonte during the 1950 World Cup finals in Brazil.

20 May – Norman Guy Von Nida, aged 93; was the first Australian golfer to win regularly on the British Tour, topping the Order of Merit table in 1947 with seven victories. The PGA Tour of Australia's developmental tour is named the Von Nida Tour in his honour.

4 June – Bill France, Jr., aged 74; transformed NASCAR from a small, southern sport into the billion-dollar sport it is today during his 31 years as its chairman.

24 June – Alexander Derek Dougan, aged 69; scored 222 goals in 546 matches, including 95 goals in 258 games for Wolverhampton Wanderers. He was also capped 43 times for Northern Ireland, scoring eight times, from 1958–73.

24 June – Christopher Michael Benoit, aged 40; a Canadian professional wrestler who won the World Heavyweight Wrestling Championship several times.

2 July – Dilip Narayan Sardesai, aged 66; the only Goan-born cricketer to play Test cricket for India and widely considered to be India's greatest ever batsman against spin bowlers.

17 July – Peter William Denning, aged 57; an English first-class cricketer who played for Somerset from 1969–84. He scored 1,000 runs in a season on six occasions and scored a career 11,559 runs in 269 first-class matches.

22 July – Rolland Mays (Rollie) Stiles, aged 100; was the oldest living MLB player at the time of his death, having played as a baseball pitcher for the St Louis Browns (1930–33). During his three MLB seasons he batted and threw right-handed, and was 9–14 with an ERA of 5.92.

27 July – James Oyebola, aged 47; winner of the super heavyweight boxing bronze medal for England at the 1986 Commonwealth Games in Edinburgh and winner of the WBC international heavyweight title in 1993. He won 18 of his 23 professional fights and retired from boxing in 1996.

25 August – Ray Jones, aged 18; Queens Park Rangers footballer who died in a car accident.

28 August – Antonio Puerta, aged 22; the Sevilla and Spanish international footballer suffered a series of cardiac arrests during a game and he died in hospital three days later.

Sports Awards

BBC Sports Personality of the Year 2006

The BBC Sports Personality of the Year Award is presented annually to one sportsman or sportswoman. The inaugural award was devised by Paul Fox, a BBC producer, in 1954. It is one of the most coveted awards in British sport because the winner is voted for by the general public towards the end of the calendar year.

2006 WINNERS

BBC Sports Personality of the Year: Zara Philipps *(Three-day eventer)*
BBC Sports Personality of the Year Team Award: St Helens *(Rugby league team)*
BBC Sports Personality of the Year Overseas Personality: Roger Federer *(Tennis)*
BBC Sports Personality of the Year Coach Award: Daniel Anderson *(Rugby league)*
BBC Sports Personality of the Year Lifetime Achievement Award: Bjorn Borg *(Tennis)*
BBC Sports Personality of the Year Helen Rollason Award: Paul Hunter *(Snooker – awarded posthumously)*
BBC Sports Personality of the Year Young Personality: Theo Walcott *(Football)*
BBC Sports Personality of the Year Unsung Hero Award: Val Hanover *(From Oswestry in Shropshire, who has spent nearly 30 years organizing events at the North Shropshire Special Olympics Club)*

William Hill Sports Book of the Year 2007

Announced on 21 November 2006

WINNER
My Father and Other Working-Class Football Heroes, by Gary Imlach (Yellow Jersey Press)

Also short-listed
Butcher, by Terry Butcher and Bob Harris (Highdown)
Push Yourself Just a Little Bit Further, by Johnny Green (Orion)
Engineering Archie, by Simon Inglis (English Heritage)
The Great White Hopes, by Graeme Kent (Sutton)
Dragons and All Blacks, by Huw Richards (Mainstream)

Sporting Honours

NEW YEAR'S HONOURS LIST 2007
Commander of the Order of the British Empire (CBE)
Gareth Edwards – *services to sport, particularly rugby*

Officers of the Order of the British Empire (OBE)
Paul Bush – *chef de mission, Scottish Commonwealth Games Team, services to sport*
David Davies – *lately executive director Football Association, services to sport*
Michael Golding – *yachtsman, services to sport*
Roger Knight – *ex-MCC secretary, services to sport*
Ian Mason – *chair Scottish Swimming, services to sport*
Novlette Rennie – *director Sporting Equals, services to diversity in sport*
Susan Wolstenholme – *director British Tennis Foundation, services to disabled sport*
Ian Woosnam – *golfer, services to sport*

Members of the Order of the British Empire (MBE)
John Barrett – *lately tennis commentator, BBC, services to sports broadcasting*
Dr David Davies – *services to Welsh Athletics, in particular Carmarthen Harriers Athletics Club*
Paul John Fletcher – *services to sport and charity, Rawtenstall, Lancs.*
Daphne Geer – *president Southern Counties Amateur Swimming Association, services to sport, Tunbridge Wells, Kent*
Michael Geer – *swimming coach and president Royal Tunbridge Wells Swimming Club, services to sport, Kent*
Steven Gerrard – *footballer, services to sport*
Stephen Grainger – *chief executive Youth Sport Trust, services to school sport, Mansfield, Notts.*
Ivor Gray – *youth football coach, services to sport in Northumberland*
Richard Hatton – *boxer, services to sport*
Roger Ingham – *services to sport in North Yorkshire*
Thomas Lynch – *services to Bicycle Moto Cross (BMX) racing and to ambulance service cycling, London*
Alexander Marshall – *services to bowls, Tranent, East Lothian*
Dr John Lloyd Parry – *services to sports medicine, Maidenhead, Berks.*
Zara Phillips – *individual three-day event world champion, services to equestrianism*
Derek Roberts – *services to the history and sport of cycling*
Anthony Stannard – *head trainer, Malmesbury Amateur Boxing Club, services to sport in Wiltshire*
Jacqueline Stimpson – *water skier, services to disabled sport*
Faye White – *captain Arsenal Ladies' Football Club and England, services to sport*
Mervyn White – *services to motorcycle racing in Northern Ireland, Limavady, Londonderry*
Gary Wolstenholme – *amateur golfer, services to sport*

THE QUEEN'S BIRTHDAY HONOURS LIST 2007

Knighthood

Ian Botham – *services to charity and to cricket*

CBE

Timothy Dewe Phillips, chair All England Lawn Tennis and Croquet Club – *services to sport*
Alison Gail Odell, life vice president British Universities Sports Association – *services to sport*

OBE

Ryan Giggs, footballer – *services to sport*
Terry Griffiths – *services to snooker*
Geoffrey Thompson, former chair Football Association – *services to sport*
Jacqueline Wood, chief executive British Showjumping Association – *services to sport*
John Vernon Ayling, trustee Lord's Taverners Charity – *services to sport*

MBE

Dr Robert Appleyard, founder Yorkshire County Cricket Club Charitable Youth Trust
    services to sport
Margaret Borley, coach Tonbridge Bobcats youth baseball team – *services to sport*
Dee Caffari – *services to sailing*
Carolyn Christophersen – *services to skiing*
Joseph Cohen – *services to Maccabi Youth Sports Trust*
Jane Couch, boxer – *services to sport*
Alan Fennell, coach Glossop Amateur Swimming Club – *services to sport*
Tommy Gilmour – *services to boxing and to the community in Scotland*
Mitsusuke Harada – *services to karate*
Katherine Edith Hardman – *services to school sport*
Eric Hardwick – *services to the Hastings Half Marathon*
Jean Mary Hawes – *services to hockey*
Samuel George Henderson – *services to youth football in Northern Ireland*
James David Hendry – *services to cycling*
Ivan Leslie Jones – *services to charity and to sport in Minehead, Somerset*
Jim Leishman, manager Dunfermline FC – *services to sport*
Lynsey Denise McVicker – *services to hockey in Northern Ireland*
Madge Morgan – *services to lawn bowls for visually impaired people*
Graham Price – *services to rugby union in Wales*
Kristian Radlinski – *services to rugby league*
Teddy Sheringham – *services to football*
Joan Slater, chairman British Ice Teachers Association – *services to ice skating*
Maurice Edward Sly – *services to swimming*
Clasford Stirling, manager Broadwater Farm Football Club – *services to sport*
Michael Uzebu-Asije, coach Eastleigh Amateur Boxing Club – *services to sport*
Michael Wilkins, lately director of sports, University of Kent – *services to higher education
    and to sport*

Sources

Used as resource for a number of sports:

http://en.wikipedia.org
http://news.bbc.co.uk/sport

AI GRAND PRIX
http://www.motoring.co.za

AMERICAN FOOTBALL
http://cbs.sportsline.com
http://www.jazzsports.com
http://www.nfl.com

ATHLETICS
http://www.bostonmarathon.org
http://www.european-athletics.org
http://www.iaaf.org
http://www.sportresult.com
http://www.tilastopaja.org
http://www.tsiklitiria.org/
http://www.ukathletics.net
http://www.visaparalympicworldcup.com

AUSTRALIAN RULES FOOTBALL
http://stats.afl.com.au

BADMINTON
http://www.badmintonengland.co.uk
http://badmintonscotland.org.uk
http://www.horizonsolutions.tv
http://www.nationalbadmintonchamps.co.uk

BASEBALL
www.usatoday.com

BASKETBALL
http://www.bbl.org.uk
http://www.pawprint75.co.uk
http://www.plymouthraiders.com
http://www.serbia2007.fiba.com
http://www.sportserve.co.uk
http://www.usabasketball.com

BEACH VOLLEYBALL
http://www.fivb.org

BOBSLEIGH
http://torino.searchfindread.com/bobsleigh
http://www.bobsleigh.com
http://www.eurosport.com
http://www.sportfocus.com

BOXING
http://www.boxrec.com
http://www.guardian.co.uk
http://www.joecalzaghe.com/

CRICKET
http://content-usa.cricinfo.com
http://cricketworldcup.indya.com
http://wwwcricketarchive.com
http://www.cricinfo.com
http://www.cricket.com.au/
http://www.lgiccrankings.com/
http://www.pcboard.com.pk
http://www.telegraph.optasportsdata.com

CURLING
http://www.winnipegsun.com
http://www.worldcurling.org

CYCLING
http://www.britishcycling.org.uk
http://www.cycling4all.com
http://www.cyclingnews.com
http://www.letour.fr/
http://www.mundipalma2007.com
http://www.recyclingteam.com
http://www.salzburg-2006.com
http://www.tourofbritain.co.uk/

DIVING
http://www.sportcentric.com

EQUESTRIAN
http://events.horses.nl
http://ste-paper.timesonline.co.uk
http://www.badminton-horse.co.uk
http://www.bdwp.co.uk
http://www.blenheim-horse.co.uk/
http://www.gatcombe-horse.co.uk
http://www.hoys.co.uk
http://www.royal-windsor-horse-show.co.uk

F1
http://formula1.about.com
http://www.formula1.com
http://www.gpracing.net192.com
http://www.grandprix.com
http://www.mclaren.com

FIGURE SKATING
http://www.isufs.org
http://www.worlds2007.jp/

FOOTBALL
http://news.independent.co.uk
http://www.canadasoccer.com
http://www.dragonsoccer.co.uk
http://www.fifa.com
http://www.footballconference.co.uk
http://www.football-league.premiumtv.co.uk
http://www.fourfourtwo.premiumtv.co.uk
http://www.irishfa.com

http://www.isporty.com
http://www.scottishfa.co.uk
http://www.telegraph.co.uk
http://www.thefa.com
http://www.wembleystadium.com
http://www.worldcuplatest.com

GAA

http://www.gaa.ie
http://www.rte.ie

GOLF

http://scores.europeantour.com
http://sports.yahoo.com
http://www.alfreddunhilllinks.com
http://www.darrenclarke.com
http://www.evianmasters.com
http://www.golfsurround.com
http://www.hsbcgolf.com
http://www.masters.org
http://www.ncaasports.com
http://www.opengolf.com
http://www.padraigharrington.com
http://www.pgatour.com
http://www.rydercup.sportinglife.com
http://www.thegrove.co.uk
http://www.usopen.com
http://www.volvomasters.com

GYMNASTICS

http://www.bethtweddle.com
http://www.ecgymnastics2007.com
http://www.gymnasticsresults.com
http://www.sportingchampions.org.uk
http://www.womensportreport.com

HANDBALL

http://www.eurosport.co.uk
http://www.handball-wm-2007.de

HOCKEY – FIELD AND INDOOR

http://www.euro-hockey.org
http://www.fieldhockey.com
http://www.fihockey.org
http://www.fixs.co.uk
http://www.tritec.es
http://www.worldhockey.org

HORSE RACING

http://cheltenham-festival.betting-directory.com
http://horses.sportinglife.com
http://leisure.ordnancesurvey.co.uk
http://www.bettinghub.iblog.co.za
http://www.dubaiworldcup.com
http://www.easyodds.com
http://www.frankiedettoriracing.com
http://www.jockeysroom.com
http://www.thesun.co.uk
http://x.horseracingabroad.com

ICE HOCKEY

http://www.britishicehockey.co.uk
http://www.eliteleague.co.uk
http://www.nhl.com
http://www.olympics.org.uk

INDY CARS

http://www.indy500.com

JUDO

http://www.alljudo.net
http://www.pzjudo.pl
http://www.today.az
http://www.twoj.org

KARATE

http://www.wkf.net

KARTING

http://www.cikfia.com

LE MANS 24-HOUR

http://www.lemans.org

MAD SPORTS

http://deadspin.com
http://events.frommers.com
http://llanwrtyd-wells.powys.org.uk/
http://swatonvintageday.sslpowered.com
http://www.2camels.com
http://www.abc.net.au
http://www.americaslibrary.gov
http://www.camelcup.com.au/
http://www.egremontcrabfair.com
http://www.emmawoodphotos.co.uk
http://www.footbag.org
http://www.gbuwh.co.uk
http://www.huskyracing.org.uk/
http://www.kristv.com
http://www.kulicky.com
http://www.natives.co.uk
http://www.rotary-ribi.org
http://www.scase.co.uk
http://www.scotland.org
http://www.seafair.com
http://www.stoneskipping.com/
http://www.thebottleinn.co.uk
http://www.treemendus-fruit.com
http://www.wackynation.com/
http://www.worldconkerchampionships.com/
http://www.wormcharming.com/
http://www.yesbutnobutyes.com

MISCELLANEOUS SPORTS

http://espn.go.com
http://www.baltimoresun.com
http://www.post-gazette.com
http://www.skysports.com

MOTORCYCLING
http://www.answers.com
http://www.britishsuperbike.com
http://www.haynes.co.uk
http://www.iomtt.com
http://www.motogp.com
http://www.motorbike-search-engine.co.uk
http://www.msttiming.com
http://www.reference.com
http://www.superbike-news.co.uk
http://www.webbikeworld.com
http://www.worldsbk.com

NASCAR
http://www.nascar.com

PENTATHLON
http://www.mpagb.org.uk

RALLYING
http://perso.orange.fr
http://www.culturekiosque.com
http://www.fia.com
http://www.walesrallygb.com
http://www.wrc.com

ROWING
http://www.powerhousetiming.com
http://www.row2k.com
http://www.u23-2007.com/
http://www.usrowing.org
http://www.worldrowing.com

RUGBY LEAGUE
http://theinternetforum.info/
http://xtramsn.co.nz
http://www.engagemutual.com
http://www.rleague.com
http://www.rugby.com.au
http://www.superleague.co.uk

RUGBY UNION
http://sport.scotsman.com
http://www.ercrugby.com
http://www.irishrugby.ie
http://www.rbs6nations.com
http://www.tigers.co.uk/
http://www.wru.co.uk

SAILING
http://rolexsydneyhobart.com
http://www.allatsea.net
http://www.americascup.com
http://www.cascaisworlds2007.com/
http://www.cowes.co.uk
http://www.hrr.co.uk
http://www.jog.org.uk
http://www.performingteamsoffshore.com
http://www.sailing.org
www.skandiacowesweek.com
http://www.soling.com
http://www.solingworlds.com
http://www.starclass.org

http://www.timesonline.co.uk

SNOOKER
http://www.worldsnooker.com

SNOWBOARDING
http://burton.motorola.com

SPEED SKATING
http://www.isu.org
http://www.sportcentric.com
http://www.sportresult.com

SPEEDWAY
http://www.speedwayworld.tv/

SQUASH
http://www.etc2007riccione.it
http://www.nationalsquashchamps.co.uk
http://www.squashsite.org.uk

SWIMMING
http://www.beograd2007.org
http://www.britishswimming.org/
http://www.melbourne2007.com.au/

TABLE TENNIS
http://www.bett07.com
http://www.englishtabletennis.org.uk
http://www.ettu.org
http://www.ittf.com
http://www.olympics.org.uk

TENNIS
http://aeltc.wimbledon.org
http://birmingham.lta.org.uk/
http://nottingham.lta.org.uk/
http://tennis.bnpparibas.com
http://www.atptennis.com
http://www.daviscup.com/
http://www.fedcup.com
http://www.itftennis.com/
http://www.lta.org.uk/
http://www.masters-cup.com
http://www.sonyericsson-championships.com

TOURING CARS
http://www.fiawtcc.com/

TRIATHLON
http://www.triathlon.org

WINTER SPORTS
http://www2.biathlon-antholz.it
http://www.are2007.com
http://www.eurosport.com
http://www.post-gazette.com
http://www.universiadetorino2007.org